WILLIAM CLARK'S WORLD

Recent Titles

Forthcoming Titles

WILLIAM CLARK'S WORLD

Describing America in an Age of Unknowns

Peter J. Kastor

Yale UNIVERSITY PRESS

New Haven & London

Yale University Press books may be purchased in quantity for educational, business,
or promotional use. For information, please e-mail sales.press@yale.edu (U.S. office)
or sales@yaleup.co.uk (U.K. office).

Set in Electra type by The Composing Room of Michigan, Inc,
Grand Rapids, Michigan.

Printed in the United States of America by Sheridan Books, Ann Arbor, Michigan.

Library of Congress Cataloging-in-Publication Data

Kastor, Peter J.
William Clark's world : describing America in an age of unknowns / Peter J. Kastor.
p. cm. — (Lamar series in western history)
Includes bibliographical references and index.
ISBN 978-0-300-13901-3 (cloth : alk. paper)   1. Clark, William, 1770–1838.
2. West (U.S.)—Description and travel.   3. Description (Rhetoric)—
History—19th century.   I. Title.
F592.7.C565K37 2010
978'.02—dc22
2010026277

A catalogue record for this book is available from the British Library.

This paper meets the requirements of ANSI/NISO Z39.48-1992
(Permanence of Paper).

10 9 8 7 6 5 4 3 2 1

To Gerald Eades Bentley
1901–1994

CONTENTS

A NOTE ON TERMS

In the same way people struggled to describe the North American West in the early Republic, settling on terms to identify people is no less difficult today. In fact, that task is particularly confusing when it comes to the West, where people of diverse backgrounds and multiple labels were constantly in contact. As a result, the terms I use in this book require some explanation.

I use the term "American" to refer to citizens of the United States. I realize this is an inherently exclusionary choice, since many people claimed the title of American. At the same time, much of this book concerns the way in which citizens of the United States used western description to lay claim to that title. I use the term "Anglo-American" to refer specifically to people and traditions of British ancestry, especially important because they brought with them specific notions of how landscape description figured in the process of landownership. Too often the locution "Anglo-American" is used interchangeably with "white," but many of the white residents of North America came from other European traditions. I use the term "Euro-American" to refer more generally to people in North America of European ancestry.

INTRODUCTION

How do you describe a continent?

That deceptively simple question was a central concern in North America during the late eighteenth and early nineteenth centuries. It was a question that faced William Clark throughout much of his life. Time and again, Clark found himself struggling to describe North America and its residents. He did so in words and in pictures alike, all the while doubting his abilities to describe what he had seen and learned. At issue was the definition of accuracy. At stake was the future of nations. The linkages between the two are the subject of this book.

William Clark's World tells the story of how William Clark and other Americans went about describing the North American West in the decades after the American Revolution. This is the story of how scientific knowledge, public careers, and private fortunes overlapped and often collided. It is also the story of how information moved through North America, as knowledge about the landscape that Indians and European travelers had collected for centuries reached new audiences through the technology of publication.

Most important, this book seeks to answer the following questions. First, how did the United States emerge as a country marked by rapid territorial expansion even as the nation's political leadership and cultural production endlessly warned of the dangers of expansion? Second, how did the nation's politics and culture shift over the early Republic to eventually embrace expansionism? Finally, how did the representation of the West in words and pictures—a fundamentally aesthetic pursuit—intersect with the federal government's efforts to govern the West? The last of these questions provides a preliminary answer to the first, for it was through the intersection of policy-making, writing, and mapping that Americans came to understand the West, initially describing expansion as tremendously dangerous before eventually embracing it as undeniably necessary.

The story of William Clark provides the means to answer these questions. Clark is now known primarily as Meriwether Lewis's sidekick on the Lewis and Clark Expedition, but that venture from 1804 to 1806 was only a brief excursion during a lengthy public career in which Clark helped transform the West. He was among the most important figures in the federal government's effort to manage the migration of whites and the forced relocation of Indians. He also helped to create the written and visual images of the West that defined how Americans understood North America.

No sooner did the United States declare its independence than Americans like Clark set out to map their national domain, a project that seemed so important because so much was at stake. At the most basic level, American settlers, eager to acquire land on the fringes of the Union, desperately sought information that would enable them to travel, find towns, and create farms. But they had broader concerns as well. Americans wanted to portray a unified nation while still acknowledging the political autonomy of states. They wanted to know the legal limits of the country in order to confront the challenges of European empires. They wanted to establish that the United States owned all the territory within its boundaries, refuting American Indians who asserted their own territorial claims. Americans most often sought to realize these desires through travel narratives, maps, atlases, treaties, and scientific reports. All of these objects engaged in the task that I refer to in this book under the general category of western landscape description, and those objects possessed remarkable power in the early American Republic. As they mapped out the West, Americans realized they were explaining the principles of the constitution, developing the nation's foreign policy, describing its racial landscape.

Many believed the most important task in describing the West was to understand the implications of expansion. While some Americans celebrated the possibilities in the West, many worried that the West might be the nation's undoing. Yet in the process of *describing* expansion, Americans shifted their *interpretation* of expansion. Over the course of decades the United States changed from a country in which most forms of print and visual culture expressed a profound ambivalence toward territorial expansion to an aggressively expansionist country which by the 1840s was spewing claims that its survival depended on the acquisition of new land. This journey from one political pole to another was not an easy one.

Explaining expansion was hardly new in the early Republic. After all, Europeans and Indians had been struggling to describe the Americas centuries before the United States came into being, and they would continue to do so long after the early Republic. Meanwhile, travel writing and maps had histories of their own entirely separate from the Americas. But expansion was a particularly pressing matter in the United States during the half century following independence. First, there was the reality that the nation's borders changed on a regular basis. Second, a particular set of conditions granted special cultural power to western landscape description in the early Republic, creating some of the founding motifs of American letters and serving as vital instruments of federal policy.[1]

Western landscape description could also achieve these ends because other forms of cultural production remained in their infancy. Americans produced novels and poetry, but only in small numbers. Besides, this work was of questionable propriety to respectable readers, especially men. Americans produced portraits and genre paintings, but these could not be easily reproduced. Engravers produced thousands of illustrations, but they were often limited to simple images like early political leaders and crude representations of historical events. In stark contrast, travel narratives and maps were respectable, mass-produced objects that circulated throughout the country. They were ideally situated to tackle the task of explaining in both written and visual form what it meant to be American. Perhaps most important, unlike novels and poetry, portraits and landscape paintings, the description of the western landscape of the early Republic exerted a direct impact on the decisions of federal policymakers and settlers alike.

What emerges is a story of the cultural context of policy and the impact of policy upon culture. For the purposes of my book Clark serves as a guide to dramatic changes in western history, an appropriate role given his stint as an explorer leading others through unfamiliar territory. Clark serves as a guide not only to American attitudes about the West, but also to the profound changes that separated the early American Republic from the antebellum era.

Clark could play such a vital role in describing the West because he was on hand to observe the momentous developments of the early Republic. He was born in 1770 and died in 1838. During his lifetime the United States came into being, more than doubled in size, transformed the workings of public life, expanded the meaning of liberty and entrenched the institution of slavery, endured unending and often vicious internal conflict, engaged in various overseas disputes, and inspired the migration of whole peoples even as it caused the wholesale eradication of others.

Meanwhile, the state of Missouri and its jurisdictional predecessors, where Clark spent almost half his life, experienced all of these transformations in demography, politics, and culture in the most intense ways imaginable. Boosters of St. Louis have long described their city as the Gateway to the West, but historians have recently situated the mid–Mississippi Valley not as the western fringe of white settlement, but as the nexus between East and West, North and South. Most recently, Stephen Aron's work has offered a compelling account of how Missouri reflected and propelled both national and continental changes.[2]

These developments established the general context within which Clark operated. On a day-to-day basis, Clark often found himself torn between the most persistent tensions at work in the North American West: the demand by Anglo-American settlers for land, the corresponding demands of Indians that white officials rein in their citizens, and the split within a federal leadership that expressed deep fears about territorial expansion even as it engaged in a process of territorial acquisition and racial conquest.

Throughout his life, Clark thought that describing the West was a first step in crafting a federal policy that could respond to these circumstances. Yet as he learned through experience, describing the West presented enormous representational challenges. Not only did Americans disagree about what media could best describe the West, but many of the people who first engaged in that process were men who, like Clark, struggled against the limitations of their ability to draw and write about western geography and population. Usually possessing limited experience—and often limited interest—in the task of landscape description, these practitioners were hardly great writers or artists. They certainly did not define themselves in such terms, and they had almost no contact with people devoted to aesthetic concerns.

While Clark takes center stage in the story, this is not a biography in the traditional sense of the term. Clark is already the subject of three excellent books. William Foley offers a far-reaching biography that ranges from previously unknown details of Clark's private life to a cohesive overview of his political career. Jay Buckley and Landon Jones have provided more focused studies that explore Clark's life in the context of intercultural contact and conflict between white settlers and Indians.[3]

Likewise, I do not focus on the event for which Clark is now best known: the Lewis and Clark Expedition. First, that expedition is the subject of nu-

merous books that provide detailed and revealing accounts on subjects ranging from travel to science to racial encounter. Second, it is almost impossible
to prevent a narrative of that expedition from overwhelming any competing
narratives of Clark's life and career. As a result, an obvious question—and a
biographical challenge—presents itself: is it possible to tell Clark's story without relying on a detailed recounting of the expedition? I would argue that
the answer is yes, but that a very different vision of Clark in particular and the
West in general emerges as a result. Third, I was long struck by how all the
discussion of the Lewis and Clark Expedition rarely concerned itself with
the way in which information from the expedition actually reached the American public. During the bicentennial commemoration of the Lewis and Clark
Expedition, one of the rare moments when the American public became fascinated with the primary sources of the early Republic, readers immersed
themselves in the various printed editions of the manuscript journals of the
expedition. The definitive edition of the journals, recently completed at the
University of Nebraska under the editorship of Gary Moulton, is a master-
piece of tireless research.[4] Yet those journals were hardly the only written
work either of Lewis or especially of Clark. My goal in this book is to situate
the manuscript journals of the Lewis and Clark Expedition within Clark's
life, a life during which he constantly wrote about and depicted the West.
I emphasize these points because this book departs from many of the standard concerns of books that study Lewis and Clark, western exploration, or
U.S. expansion. Some of the most familiar subjects of the Lewis and Clark
story—the enlisted men on the expedition; Clark's slave, York; the Indian
woman Sacagawea—do not figure prominently in my account specifically
because they are already the subjects of deep and revealing research by other
historians.

The clarity that Clark offers is all the more meaningful because western
landscape description is, by definition, a tale of abstractions. Printed and visual objects often seem to exist outside the lived experience of real people. Interpreting those objects often requires the use of scholarly terminology that is
inaccessible to nonspecialists. Clark's life, on the other hand, offers a way to
keep that story of culture grounded in clear experience and clear language.
With the notion of authorship itself generating no end of discussion among
literary critics, the experience of Clark and other portrayers of the West provides a guided tour to the process of book production.[5] In an age when leading intellectuals were asking weighty questions about science and nature,
Clark's efforts to describe the West became an essential and revealing link in

the process through which information became knowledge. In a turbulent era when the West became the site of increasingly violent racial conflict, Clark's policies as well as his acts of landscape description shaped the federal government's efforts to establish its authority over the West.

Clark also connects the people who populate this book, a diffuse set of Americans who never met as a group but who all went about describing the North American West in ways that had far-reaching implications. These men represented the three constituencies that defined the representation of the expanding United States: public officials and private travelers scattered throughout the West; political leaders in the national capitals of New York, Philadelphia, and Washington; and printers at the center of cartographic publishing in Philadelphia. Regardless of their location or occupation, all of these people attempted to answer a specific question: what would an expanding western domain mean for the United States? The answers varied, depending not only on personal belief, but also on personal interest, professional identity, and representational choices.

In these circumstances western landscape description followed a convulsive trajectory that shifted back and forth between a West that appeared profoundly dangerous and one that was potentially beneficial. Much of that outlook toward expansion turned on two very different Wests that Americans imagined in the years after the Revolution. During the last quarter of the eighteenth century Americans concerned themselves with a *Near West* from the Appalachian Mountains to the Mississippi River. Their comments ranged from guarded optimism to outright boosterism. In sharp contrast, Americans expressed far greater hesitancy about the *Far West* beyond the Mississippi. A very different set of messages emerged for this region that reflected not only diplomatic, demographic, and ecological differences, but also the diverse concerns and aesthetic models that separated the men who described the Near West from those who traveled through the Far West. If describing the Near West was primarily a story of catalyzing benefits, describing the Far West was a story of restraining threats.

Crucial to understanding these tensions between Near and Far West is the fact that the men who fashioned those images were often out of touch with public opinion, especially the public opinion of the very westerners whom they described. American settlers, proslavery advocates, and merchants were all keen to gain access to the opportunities they saw in western regions. Yet even as Americans were celebrating the perceived opportunities in the West, the first published accounts were doubtful. The men who fashioned those accounts had various reasons to describe a dangerous West. In some cases, they had personally witnessed conditions their more enthusiastic countrymen had not. But other factors were no less powerful, ranging from the most crass personal motivations to the most disinterested understandings of the nation's mission and the threats it faced.[6]

This book considers these varied interpretations of the West and is structured accordingly. I open with a prologue that details the technical process of publishing a map, in this case the map that Clark produced from the Lewis and Clark Expedition. Part I introduces Clark as well as the emerging visual techniques and publishing strategies through which Americans described the West. Clark himself was less an actor than an observer during these decades, learning about western policy and the rules of landscape description. Part II follows William Clark across the Mississippi River during the first two decades of the nineteenth century, years in which he went from a struggling young man to one of the most important federal officials governing the territory the United States had acquired through the Louisiana Purchase in 1803. Part III chronicles how Clark's vision of the West faded in the 1820s and 1830s. Even as they drew on Clark's models and learned from his experiences, a new set of Americans began to write and draw the West in very different ways, even as other Americans formulated very different policies for governing the West.

The book concludes at the point where a variety of forces were bringing politics and culture up to speed with popular sentiment in ways that reached full force in the run-up to the Mexican War. These were the conditions for Manifest Destiny, and they reached their ascendancy in the 1830s and 1840s. But during the preceding decades of the early Republic, the West—especially the Far West—was more likely to appear as a dangerous place, and western landscape description warned Americans against most of their greatest ambitions. That image hardly reflected a concerted opposition to expansion, nor did it indicate any widespread sympathy among whites for the Indians who populated the West. Rather, it resulted from the collision of forces that led to a very particular set of representational choices.

Rather than an organized project of cultural nationalism or a concerted argument for territorial expansion, the explaining of the West and its relationship to the nation developed through more ad hoc circumstances that responded to the political culture of federal appointees, the political economy of land speculation, the technologies of early American publishing, and the generic conventions of print and visual culture.

Sorting out the contours of expansionism in American culture is all the more important because Americans have for so long identified expansion as a defining feature of the American experience. The acquisition of new territory, the creation of new states, and the westward population surge provide a unity to the history of the United States. Indeed, some of the earliest claims to a distinctive American cultural tradition pointed to this experience of expansion and conquest. Within the academy, the study of the linkage between expansion and national identity helped define American history, American literature, and American studies.[7]

For all the continuity of expansionism, at the core of this book is my contention that it is too easy to describe a seamless tale of zealous expansionism at the center of the American experience. A vaguely defined Manifest Destiny serves as a shorthand way to explain everything from Puritan theology to the Vietnam War. In academic and popular discussion, either celebrating or condemning American actions, the inexorable expansionist impulse of the United States remains a given.[8] The seductive power of this synthesis leads people to ignore the circumstances in which Americans expressed tremendous ambivalence about the West and about expansion.[9]

Such an outlook makes a certain logical sense. After all, the United States did eventually extend to the Pacific, often subjugating, eradicating, or enslaving western residents. The question is not whether Americans were imperialistic (they certainly were) or whether they engaged in campaigns of conquest (they certainly did). Rather, the question I want to explore is how American culture responded to and engaged conflicting attitudes toward expansion.[10]

For his part William Clark hardly doubted the rising glory of the United States, nor did he show an abiding opposition to Indian subjugation or displacement. But for reasons particular to political, aesthetic, and personal factors, Clark nonetheless contributed to a broader system of western landscape description that questioned the benefits of unchecked expansionism.

Clark and other Americans sought to explain the challenges of the West through maps and travel narratives, among the most abundantly produced and actively consumed forms of cultural production in the early American Republic. The notion of written and visual culture usually brings to mind novels, poetry, and fine arts. This remains the case in large part because, for all the talk of canon busting, much of the scholarship on print and visual culture has concerned itself with a largely traditional set of objects and concerns when it comes to the West and the early American Republic. The result is that western landscape description is shoehorned into a set of contemporary aesthetic concerns that did not fully appear on the American scene until the antebellum era. Describing the West becomes a study in Romantic individualism, all roads leading to the American Renaissance or to Jack Kerouac. Not surprisingly, the occasional flashes of self-revelation in early exploration literature have always proven more attractive than the functionalist rhetoric that dominates both manuscript journals and published narratives. In this tautology, landscape description becomes a way to understand the rise of pastoralism, the tension between man and nature, or the way nature provides a means of reflection on the self.[11]

Historians have offered little help because they tend to read western landscape description as sources rather than as texts. Historians have long situated the quest for geographic information within a broader discussion of the Enlightenment. For a generation now, work in the social and cultural history of intercultural contact has used the artifacts of western description to transform our understanding of North America. Indeed, it has helped create the notion of a continental history. In an effort to reinterpret western sources, scholars have emphasized the severe distortions of those written records. They have usually attributed those problems to the cultural baggage of white observers, not to generic conventions of print and visual culture. While I study many of the same places, this book is not a study of intercultural contact. Rather, I want to consider how people who observed contact in the West attempted to describe it. This is primarily the story of Anglo-American observers, but it takes place within a multiracial and multiethnic setting where describing the West usually entailed appropriating the knowledge of western residents from numerous backgrounds.[12]

I am concerned less with the specific state of geographic knowledge (what did Americans know about the West and when did they know it?) than with the way people sought to package that knowledge and the way that knowledge informed federal policy. Mapping the land—whether by individual settlers or competing European empires—was inextricably linked to claiming ownership of the West.[13] At the same time, western landscape description provided written and visual means for Americans to understand themselves and the continent they inhabited.[14]

Immersed in this world of intercultural contact, Clark was almost entirely removed from the concerns of an American artistic community located predominately in the Northeast. It was in the West, surrounded by the complex realities of contact on various frontiers, that Clark developed his approach to writing and drawing the West. As a result, my own work draws both substantively and stylistically on recent studies of the political culture of the frontiers of North America, but also on a separate scholarly tradition of analyzing the West's place in American culture and identity that stretches back over decades and suggests ways to work across traditional disciplinary boundaries.

Over a half century ago, Henry Nash Smith explored the tensions between popular sentiment, popular literature, and political action. Connecting those works of society, literature, and politics was possible only through an inter-disciplinary approach, and in the process of crafting *Virgin Land*, Smith helped define American studies. Meanwhile, a small community of histori-ans and historical geographers has long grasped the revealing complexities of western landscape description.[15] John Logan Allen later sought to test Smith's conclusions by considering how maps described the same western spaces.[16] A superb documentary editor, Donald Jackson devoted a lifetime to publish-ing documents of Anglo-American expansion in the North American West.[17] Most recently, in monographs, edited volumes, museum exhibit guides, and document collections, James Ronda and Carolyn Gilman have used the Lewis and Clark Expedition to engage in an extensive and thoughtful con-sideration of western exploration and landscape description.[18]

If William Clark provides the means to understand these developments, his close friend Meriwether Lewis suggests the analytical pitfalls. The remark-able popularity of Stephen Ambrose's *Undaunted Courage*, which focused on Lewis, and the nationwide commemoration of the bicentennial of the Lewis and Clark Expedition helped solidify Lewis's status as the quintessen-tial western describer. Lewis's interest in science, his flashes of emotional self-expression, even the personal crises that came at the end of his life have all made him immensely attractive. Even as academic observers have raised crit-icisms about that popular treatment of Lewis—its triumphalism, its detach-ment from historical context, its refusal to tackle the realities of Indian removal—they have nonetheless shown a similar fondness for him. His oc-casional flights of literary fancy have captivated literary critics. Meanwhile, his blindness to the realities of Indian culture has offered historians revealing ev-idence of the roots of racial conquest.

Yet the men who produced the first accounts of the West were rarely ar-tistically minded writers or Enlightenment thinkers, nor were they connected to the networks of art and learning in the northeastern United States. Instead, they were usually southern and western. These men were pragmatic more than anything else, and they concluded that western landscape description was a means to advance both their individual careers and public policy. Put simply, they were less likely to be men like Lewis, an emotionally revealing writer with intellectual aspirations, than like Clark, an emotionally restrained writer with limited scientific ambitions.

These were usually men of talent rather than genius, and the materials they produced were hardly testaments to either Enlightenment rationalism or romantic sentimentalism. In most cases, western landscape description was a means to an end. In some circumstances, the ends were wholly commercial. That was certainly the case for various travelers but especially for publishers hoping to reap profits from books, maps, and atlases. In other circumstances, the ends were professional. That was overwhelmingly the case with government officials, whether explorers, surveyors, or negotiators. Throughout the early Republic, the publishing of books and maps served a vital purpose for these men: they often were the calling card, the resume, the credentials that were supposed to connect men on the frontiers of the Union to their patrons in the East. Published accounts could advance a career, stave off criticism, help elevate a low-status tradesman to a more stable life and more reputable social station. In Clark's case, describing the West transformed him from an anonymous man with declining prospects into a trusted federal official and the leading citizen of Missouri.

Along the way, the men who described the West occasionally imported the languages of science, art, or literature, but usually with the awkwardness of all second languages. Their first language was primarily the rough terminology of the frontier, where intercultural contact, surveying and governing, violent conflict, and the scramble for opportunity in the federal system permeated daily life. As a result, they did indeed reveal themselves through their work, but rarely in terms that contemporary readers have come to expect.

Accordingly, explaining what the United States had become as it expanded into the West was the work of men with jarringly small ambitions. But that, too, is an important part of the story, suggesting how a national culture hardly required cultural nationalism. Individual maps, multipage atlases, school geographies, travel narratives, scientific reports, newspaper and magazine accounts, and lengthy books all attempted to make sense of the North American West. Their authors claimed they had presented Americans with ways to see places they would never visit and to understand how western landscapes related to continental developments. But how to go about doing so was no small question.

Clark's efforts to describe the United States in words and in pictures were part of a larger effort to convert the nation from paper into reality. Convinced that the federal hold on the West was more fragile in reality than it appeared in legislation, treaties, and newspapers, Clark joined other Americans who believed that describing the western landscape could contribute to a federal policy that would enable the United States to overcome the challenges of expansion. In the process, Americans like Clark claimed ownership of their country, inventing the means to describe that country for themselves and for a larger world.

PROLOGUE

In his office William Clark kept a history of his own devising. That history could not be missed, and it was unmistakable to anybody who came to visit. It was a prominent object in a prominent building. As a public official, Clark occupied various offices in the public buildings of St. Louis. But the history that Clark kept on public display was in the office he maintained at home. Completed in 1818, the Clark house was not the largest in St. Louis, but it was an imposing presence made of brick, this in a frontier outpost better known for its small wood structures.[1]

The history that stood in Clark's office was a recent history, focusing primarily on the first decades of the nineteenth century. In it Clark told the story of a complicated world, with nations scattered across the landscape, their boundaries ill-defined and their relationships as varied as their cultures. The story was as much environmental as it was social, dominated by a landscape where mountains, rivers, and resources shaped the lives of its occupants. In this history Clark also told the story of a world transformed, as old political relationships collapsed and whole populations ceased to exist. Most of all, however, Clark's history told the story of a world understood. Focusing on the western half of North America, the history attempted to combine knowledge from numerous sources into a single, cohesive, clear representation of a continent that Clark believed he had rescued from ignorance and misrepresentation.

Clark tried to do all this with scarcely any words. For Clark's history was no book. Instead, it was a map he had drawn in his own hand, a large object, just over two by four feet. He initially considered the map finished in 1810, but in 1812 he drew additional details based on American commercial efforts in the Pacific Northwest. By the time Clark moved into his new house in 1818, the map recorded a demographic and political landscape that no longer existed, since Indian populations had undergone dramatic upheavals that Clark himself had often caused. Eventually called William Clark's Master Map of the North American West by historians and geographers, it was an appropriate name (Fig. 1). Clark himself reveled in the title of master, whether that meant his status as a master over his slaves, the vaguer notion that he was master of his house, or the reputation Clark helped cultivate that he was the master interpreter of conditions in the West.[2]

In addition to the recent history of the West, Clark's master map offered two other abstract but very similar histories. The first was a history of Clark's life, an autobiography of sorts and the only kind Clark could write. The map recorded his efforts to explore the landscape, govern the people, and manage development in the West. The second was a history of national development in the West.

Clark's Master Map of the North American West of 1810 was published in 1814 under the title "A Map of Lewis and Clark's track, across the western portion of North America from the Mississippi to the Pacific Ocean: by order of the executive of the United States in 1804, 5 & 6." It accompanied every copy of the two-volume book entitled *History of the Expedition under the Command of Captains Lewis and Clark, to the sources of the Missouri, thence across the Rocky Mountains and down the river Columbia to the Pacific Ocean: Performed during the years 1804–5-6 by order of the government of the United States.* Clark's map, the book that contained it, the expedition that produced both, and his subsequent public career were part of a concerted national effort through which the United States sought to manage territorial expansion. They were also part of a concerted personal effort by Clark to become a leading figure in the West.[3]

William Clark's World explores that struggle to write, draw, and govern the West during the early American Republic. Yet if this study considers the broad processes and implications of American expansionism, it does so through one man—William Clark—and the people who surrounded him. Understanding why Clark drew his map and published the book requires some background on how people produced maps and books in the early Republic. Fortunately, "A Map of Lewis and Clark's Track" and *History of the Expedition* provide the means to do so.

So the brief story that follows—the creation and publication of Clark's map—needs to be understood in various ways. First and foremost, it serves as an orientation to my book, providing an overview of the technical process for

Figure 1. William Clark, *A Map of Part of the Continent of North America . . .* (1810). Yale Collection of Western Americana, Beinecke Rare Book and Manuscript Library, Yale University.

producing maps and books in the early American Republic. Second, the creation of both "A Map of Lewis and Clark's Track" and *History of the Expedition* is a necessary primer on the mechanics of publishing western landscape description.

That story begins with the Lewis and Clark Expedition, for *History of the Expedition* and "A Map of Lewis and Clark's Track" were the products of that venture through the North American West from 1804 to 1806. Under the official leadership of Meriwether Lewis, Clark enjoyed the unofficial title of cocaptain. Throughout that journey, the two men struggled to record what they saw, as did other members of the expedition who kept journals of their own. Once the expedition returned, they sought the means to describe the West to a public audience. While Lewis took charge of producing a book, Clark focused on creating a map.

Lewis and Clark now entered the rough and tumble world of American publishing. Printing was an occupation marked by limited profit margins as well as large overhead charges for expensive printing equipment, and American printers were a notoriously difficult bunch that showed little patience for risky projects.[4] Lewis negotiated a contract but committed suicide in 1809 before making any substantive progress on the manuscript. Clark inherited the project and struggled to find an editor and publisher who would see the project through to completion.

As editorial work on the book continued in Philadelphia, Clark followed the time-honored process of producing large-scale maps, a combination of originality and collaboration, honesty and theft, mathematics and aesthetics, art and craft. These principles were clear from the start. This was never entirely Clark's map, but rather the product of information from numerous sources. Clark began with his own extensive field notes. These numerous hand-drawn sketches ran in an almost continuous series, one section of territory leading to the next. With their birds-eye view of a focused geographic space, they approximated the composites of aerial and satellite photographs common today.[5] In addition to these hand-drawn representations of the landscape, Lewis and Clark had repeatedly attempted to locate their longitude and latitude, providing fixed points of reference that would complement Clark's visual observations. Navigational sightings would enable Clark to align his work to the other maps he would consult.[6]

Raised in a family that regularly bought and sold land, Clark was an experienced surveyor. Still, his knowledge was limited primarily to local surveys covering a small area. Converting a group of surveys into a publishable map would (appropriately enough) take him into uncharted territory. By taking each local sketch, reducing its scale, fixing its location through the results of celestial observation, and overlaying points of longitude and latitude, Clark would have everything he needed to produce a map of the territory through which he traveled: the Missouri and Columbia rivers as well as a portion of the Rocky Mountains.

But Clark's map needed to be of a different sort. He intended to create a vast regional map, and at this point his project ceased to be a work of individual surveying and became instead an act of collation from numerous sources. Clark had plenty of models in the numerous maps that attempted to describe countries, continents, or the entire globe. What he lacked in technical training he made up for in firsthand experience. Most published maps of North America were the work of cartographers who rarely visited the places they described, but rather acquired information from numerous sources. In contrast to surveyors, who spent most of their careers traipsing through countryside, mapmakers were usually located in the major cities that were the centers of cartography in Europe and the Americas. They spent their careers indoors, perched over paper or metal printing plates.[7]

Lewis and Clark had consulted a series of maps for the very practical purpose of learning what they could about the land through which they were about to travel. These maps also provided instructive models in the ways cartographers produced large-scale maps and the ways that information later appeared in published maps.[8]

When the Lewis and Clark Expedition traversed the North American West, Clark made several attempts at drawing large-scale maps. He incorporated the materials he had consulted before the expedition, but he increasingly drew on the geographic knowledge that the expedition acquired from the Indians of the North American West. In conversations, on handwritten maps drawn by Indians, and through Indian commentary on Euro-American maps, Lewis and Clark slowly acquired details that would fill the gaps between what they had seen and what other white cartographers had drawn. Indeed, it was that information which provided Clark with the means to offer a revolutionary map of the West. All published maps claimed to be new in some way. Their cartouches, the densely written and often highly decorative illustrations in the corners of the maps, often made a virtue of the fact that they were little more than reproductions of existing maps combined with fragments of new information (Fig. 2). For Clark, it was Indian knowledge that would enable him to sketch a world beyond what he personally observed.[9]

18   *Prologue*

Figure 2. Cartouche from John Mitchell, *A Map of the British and French Dominions in North America . . .* (London, 1755). Geography and Map Division, Library of Congress.

It was this combination of firsthand observation, detailed measurements of distance, repeated celestial observation, extensive Indian information, and consultation with existing maps that Clark had to combine in order to produce an object that would reach the standards for accuracy in the highly competitive world of published maps.

As he finished work on the map in 1810, Clark included his own cartouche. He entitled his work "A Map of Part of the Continent of North America" and explained that it was "compiled from the information of the best informed

travellers through that quarter of the globe . . . corrected by celestial observation." Those "informed travellers" included not only Lewis and Clark but
a host of other Europeans and Americans who had produced their own written and visual accounts of the West. If the map made conspicuous reference
to Clark's breadth of white sources, it made no mention of the Indian knowledge that Clark repeatedly detailed in his manuscript journals. Never one to
challenge the conventions of writing or mapmaking, Clark simply participated in a broader project that denied Indian knowledge of the land and, in
the end, Indian ownership of the land. It was a project that had shaped intercultural contact from the moment Europeans arrived in the Americas, and
it was a project that would be at the center of Clark's career.[10] In the same way
that local surveys established property ownership for individuals and land
companies, regional and continental maps became the way that white governments asserted ownership against the counterclaims of Indians or competing white governments. Europeans had often mapped land they had not
even surveyed in the interest of these claims. Now Clark hoped to combine
the techniques of local surveys and continental cartography in pursuit of the
national interest.[11]

Clark also physically inscribed himself onto the landscape. Text larger than
almost any other showed "Clarks River" northwest of the Rocky Mountains,
and the cartouche again referred to "the Missouri Jefferson Lewis and the
Upper Part of Clarks river." Jefferson, Lewis, and Clark were only a few of the
Anglo-American names that the Lewis and Clark Expedition substituted for
Indian names either that they did not know or which they sought to eliminate.
The cartouche likewise explained that the map showed "Lewis & Clarks rout
over the Rocky Mountains in 1805 on their route to the pacific from the
United States." Finally, the cartouche included the signature "By William
Clark." He was only the latest to sign his work, for maps were only part of a
larger effort by Euro-Americans to announce their imprint on the landscape.[12]

Manuscripts like Clark's master map have a certain immediacy to them,
capturing the physical process of representing the land in Clark's occasionally cramped handwriting, the inkblots on the paper, and the occasional
crossed-out error or superimposed correction. Clark sent his hand-drawn
map to Philadelphia, where it was copied and engraved onto metal printing
plates.[13] When Clark received the published version in 1814, it was clearly the
reflection of his own efforts, but it also bore the marks of an extensive collaboration (Figs. 3–6).

The map and the book were part of a flood of published attempts to de-

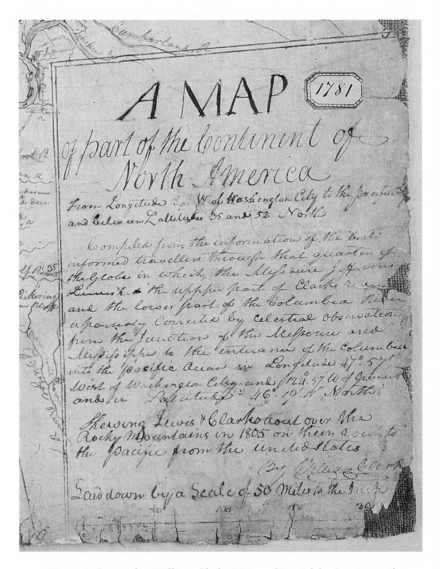

Figure 3. Cartouche, William Clark, *A Map of Part of the Continent of North America* . . .

scribe western North America. They came at a time when white residents of the United States were acquiring unprecedented knowledge about the continent. They also came at the high point of cultural power for maps, atlases, travel narratives, and other similar published accounts of the West. Nothing could have been better for Clark. He produced his greatest work as a cartographer at the very moment when maps and travel narratives reached their

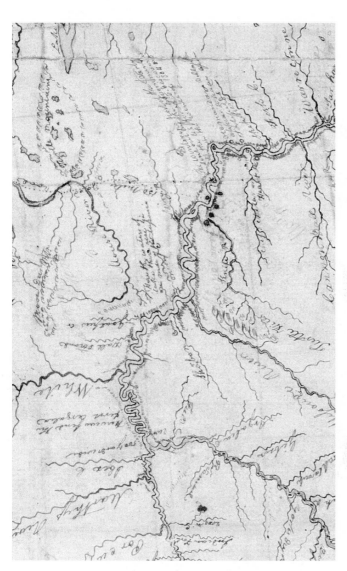

Figure 4. William Clark, *A Map of Part of the Continent of North America . . .* (detail)

Figure 5. *A Map of Lewis and Clark's Track, Across the Western Portion of North America from the Mississippi to the Pacific Ocean . . . .* (Philadelphia: Bradford and Inskeep, 1814). Geography and Map Division, Library of Congress.

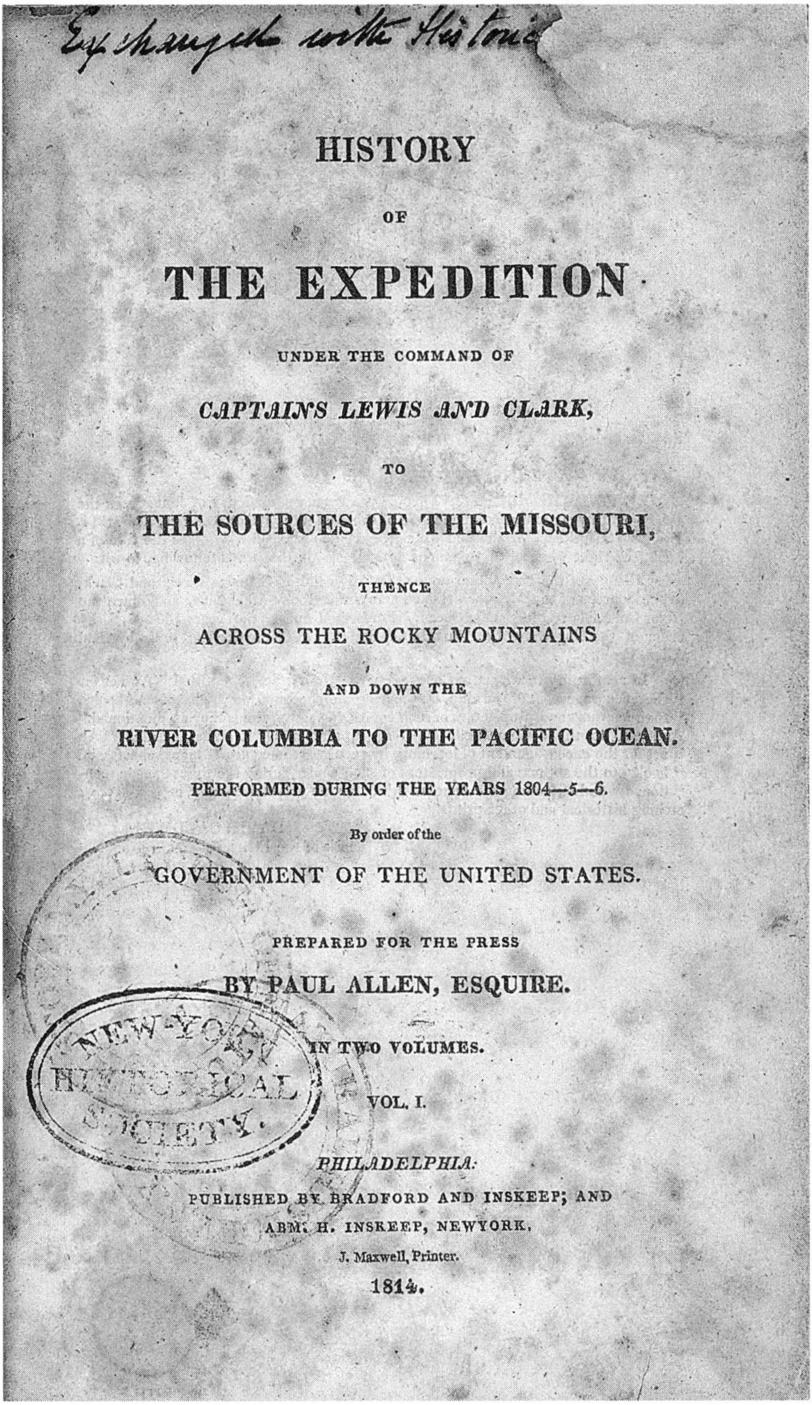

Exchanged with Historic

HISTORY

OF

THE EXPEDITION

UNDER THE COMMAND OF

CAPTAINS LEWIS AND CLARK,

TO

THE SOURCES OF THE MISSOURI,

THENCE

ACROSS THE ROCKY MOUNTAINS

AND DOWN THE

RIVER COLUMBIA TO THE PACIFIC OCEAN.

PERFORMED DURING THE YEARS 1804—5—6.

By order of the

GOVERNMENT OF THE UNITED STATES.

PREPARED FOR THE PRESS

BY PAUL ALLEN, ESQUIRE.

IN TWO VOLUMES.

VOL. I.

PHILADELPHIA:

PUBLISHED BY BRADFORD AND INSKEEP; AND

ABM. H. INSKEEP, NEWYORK.

J. Maxwell, Printer.

1814.

Figure 6. Frontispiece of *History of the Expedition under the Command of Captains Lewis and Clark* . . . (Philadelphia: Bradford and Inskeep, 1814). David Rumsey Map Collection, http://www.davidrumsey.com.

own zenith in American culture. Likewise, Clark died at the very moment that cultural power began to decline. Throughout his life, domestic politics and international relations, economics and law, art and taste all seemed to depend on how Americans represented the physical spaces they occupied or claimed to own. Of course, in rendering those representations, Americans were doing more than describing North America. Americans were trying to describe themselves, to visualize their nation, its occupants, and its institutions.

History of the Expedition and "A Map of Lewis and Clark's Track" were only the most ambitious efforts in a lifetime spent describing the North American West. How Clark physically created this map is a story of technique. Surveying methods, printing technology, and editorial practice had combined to establish a process in the United States for producing the published accounts of the western landscape and its occupants. Why Clark described the West as he did, and why that depiction could be so important, is a story of culture, politics, and negotiation across national and racial lines. How Americans eventually described their country in ways different from the world of Clark is a story that reaches back to the birth of both William Clark and the country he served. Likewise, it is a story that ends not only with the death of William Clark, but with the emergence of a country that seemed so different from the one he had known and had worked so hard to describe.

Part I

A World Encountered

A Western Future

Twenty years before William Clark created his master map, he made some of his first attempts to describe his place in the North American West. He did so in the brief, often unrevealing sentences typical of men of his background and experience. In 1789 the nineteen-year-old Clark marched through some "first-rate land" and plenty of "second-rate land." He used these phrases repeatedly in the journal that chronicled his first venture across the Ohio River. Two years later, he kept a similar journal on another western trip. In both cases, Clark traveled with men bent on vengeance, and in both cases he struggled against his limited ability to describe what he saw.[1]

In 1789 and again in 1791 Clark volunteered for paramilitary forces that gathered in the midst of a bloody contest to determine both international and interracial supremacy in the Near West, extending from the trans-Appalachian backcountry to the Mississippi River. He joined other volunteers from Kentucky only a few years after his family moved west at the vanguard of Anglo-Americans settlers who hoped to convert the Near West from the eastern fringe of a multinational, multiracial frontier into the western fringe of an independent United States. Clark first learned how to represent the West in these circumstances.[2]

Clark was hardly alone in this struggle to describe the West. As three very different men set about the task of describing the Near West of Clark's childhood, they exemplified the options as well as the goals that were available to Americans hoping to understand the West. In 1784 Thomas Jefferson, John Filson, and Jedidiah Morse completed three of the first projects that sought to situate Kentucky within the broader nation created by the American Revolution. Clark came of age in the midst of the overlapping and occasionally conflicting efforts of these men, who situated the Ohio River Valley of the

Clark family—the Near West—into forms of geographic representation that were always thinly veiled manifestos on American cultural development. All three men were struggling to answer the most immediate questions of American politics in the 1780s. What were the United States? How did the states relate to one another and what (if anything) connected them as a whole? What were the appropriate powers of state and central governments? Finally, what would become of the nation's western frontiers, where the normal rules and conclusions often did not apply? In 1784, three years before the Constitution sought to answer those questions, Jefferson, Filson, and Morse hoped to visualize American federalism through their description of the land and its occupants.

CLARK'S FAMILY

Clark was born into a world where understanding the land was a matter of the utmost importance. Knowing the difference between first rate and second rate was not a matter of aesthetics, but one of survival for a family that made its living from the land. He grew up in an agricultural society in which families depended on the productivity of the land for their income. Meanwhile, owning that land rested on an Anglo-American tradition of describing the land in ways that fit very specific legal and cultural rules. This was not an abstract process. To the contrary, Clark came from a family engaged in a frenzied campaign to own the land that would secure their status and provide for their future.

His parents, John and Ann Clark, were products of the lesser gentry of Tidewater Virginia, and as members of the gentry they possessed greater wealth than most other Virginians. They owned land and slaves, which enabled them to live in relative leisure. Nonetheless, the fact that they moved to Kentucky was not a good sign, and they joined a growing number of Virginians who, throughout the late eighteenth and early nineteenth centuries, concluded that the Old Dominion could not deliver on its promise.

Possession of fertile land that could sustain a family's financial independence propelled Americans in general and Virginians in particular away from the eastern seaboard and toward the trans-Appalachian backcountry in staggering numbers. In 1749 John and Ann Clark joined the westward movement when they bought a 410-acre plantation in Albemarle County, Virginia, exchanging the center of Virginia's plantation society for the fringe of white settlement. The following year Ann gave birth to the first of ten children. While the Albemarle plantation sustained the family's pretensions to gentry status, the Clarks did not possess the means to provide for ten adults. The solution for the four girls was obvious: to make certain they found husbands of sufficient finances. But the six boys were a problem. Tradition and law dictated that the oldest of them, named Jonathan for his father but not to be confused with a younger brother named John, would inherit the bulk of the land. Besides, even if John and Ann Clark did want to divide their holdings, they lacked the wealth to establish all of the boys with sufficient land to sustain themselves as farmers, let alone planters.[3]

The answer came in the form of the American Revolution. Not only did the struggle for independence provide an immediate solution by occupying the older boys through years in which they might otherwise have scrambled for land, but the particular way in which the Clark boys fought the Revolution linked the larger struggle with Great Britain to the very personal struggle to build a future on the Virginia frontier. The Revolution also introduced the terms the Clarks would use to tell their story in words and pictures.

Over the eight-year military conflict from 1775 to 1783, five of the six Clark boys served in the military. The youngest, William, was born on August 1, 1770. He was too young to serve. William's earliest memories were of the Revolution and of the stories about his brothers.

Of the five brothers, it was George Rogers Clark who loomed largest in William's life. It was an appropriate relationship, for George was a larger-than-life figure. Yet he pursued a path very common to younger sons of the gentry, men of ambition who knew they were unlikely to inherit the bulk of the family wealth. George arrived in the West at the vanguard of white newcomers—many of them young men like himself—for whom western settlement and Indian warfare combined to guarantee both the promise of wealth and the possibility of social advancement.

Even before the Revolution began George became a speculator in western Virginia. He fought in Lord Dunmore's War, the last major conflict between British settlers and Indians before the Revolution. By the time the British colonies declared their independence in 1776, George Rogers Clark and other men like him were ready to launch a wholesale race war in the trans-Appalachian backcountry. In 1777 he proposed a military venture to the Illinois Country, a vaguely defined region encompassing much of what is now Indiana and Illinois as well as portions of eastern Missouri, Michigan, Ohio, and Indiana. Over the next two years Clark led a campaign of destruction throughout the Illinois Country. He eradicated whole Indian villages, destroyed

British forts, and joined a coalition of American, Indian, and Spanish forces that helped defend St. Louis against an attack by Britain's Indian allies.[4]

The Revolution came at a fortuitous moment to western settlers of the type who joined the army of George Rogers Clark. For many western settlers, the Revolution was indeed a struggle for independence, not just for the colonies but for themselves. The one precondition for personal and economic independence, political participation and liberty, and rough equality alongside other settlers was the acquisition of land. Indians who defended their territorial claims and British officials who sought to restrain white settlers in the interest of preventing frontier conflict were the greatest impediments to this goal. For settlers like George Rogers Clark, the Revolution finally provided the chance to remove Indians, nicely packaged within the high-minded principle of liberty. For public officials at the state and national levels, tapping those energies produced an effective military force.[5]

George Rogers Clark and his men were volunteers who served the government of Virginia, and Jefferson, the governor of Virginia, struggled to coordinate that army with the strategic vision of George Washington, the commander of the Continental Army. In 1780 Jefferson informed Washington that "such being the popularity of Colo. [Colonel] Clarke and the confidence of the western people in him that he could raise the requisite number at any time." To attract and reward volunteers, Jefferson recommended that Clark's enlisted men each receive three hundred acres, their officers even more. When Jefferson later had no currency to pay Clark's volunteers, he simply sent Clark a stack of additional promissory notes for western land grants. Not only was it all Jefferson could offer, but for Clark and so many of his men it truly did seem better than gold.[6]

Jefferson understood these sentiments because they were his own. Like George Rogers Clark, Thomas Jefferson was one of ten children born to gentry parents who had traded Tidewater Virginia for Albemarle County. Likewise, he knew how much landownership mattered to liberty and independence because the debts that mounted throughout his adult life threatened to rob him of both land and independence. Jefferson often hoped to rescue his finances through speculation in western lands, one of the most popular forms of investment for the Virginia gentry.[7]

As George Rogers Clark and his volunteers set about claiming the Near West for the United States and for themselves, other Americans were engaged in a similar act of representation, only on a grander scale. In 1784 Jefferson, along with Filson and Morse, produced works that exemplified the ways in

which Americans understood the Near West as well as the disputes that en-
sued as Americans argued about the West's role in the new nation. Convinced
of their right to shape the region as they saw fit, Americans made plans.

JEFFERSON'S WEST

Few Americans struggled harder to describe the West than Jefferson. If it
was not necessarily a task he was born to do, it was certainly one for which he
was raised. Jefferson looked on western landscape description as a way to resolve the most challenging problems of domestic governance. He specifically
worried about the West of George Rogers Clark. For all the benefits that came
from unleashing the energies of frontier settlers like Clark, Jefferson joined a
growing chorus of American officials who feared that those same energies
could lead to regional chaos in the West, a situation which could consume
the fragile Republic. Yet even as he sought to map out Virginia and the West
during the 1770s and 1780s Jefferson revealed an ambivalence toward the
mapmaker's craft.[8]

At first glance Jefferson seemed ideally poised to think in spatial terms and
to embrace maps as a way to understand the world around him. When his father, Peter Jefferson, died in 1757, the twenty-four-year-old Thomas learned
that among the property left to him were surveying instruments. Like so many
members of the Virginia gentry, including the Clarks, Peter Jefferson was a
trained surveyor, always an important skill for anybody attempting to purchase land.[9] But for Peter Jefferson surveying brought other important benefits. In the 1740s he collaborated with Joshua Fry, an English-born scientist
and former instructor at the College of William and Mary, to survey the Virginia–North Carolina boundary. The two men later produced a landmark
map of Virginia. Their collaboration is more than an amusing story of unlikely friendship on the frontiers of the British Empire. Creating the map was
the first in a series of efforts by Peter Jefferson to move from planter to public official with a reputation beyond Albemarle County. Creating the map
was a lesson in the close relationship between science, cartography, and patronage (Fig. 7).[10]

The Fry-Jefferson map reflected the state of geographic knowledge throughout the British colonies. Surveyors and mapmakers had created maps of the
eastern seaboard with all the telltale signs of accuracy. Highly detailed, they
presented topography, county boundaries, major land grants, large cities, and
small towns. Equally important, they agreed with each other, a consensus

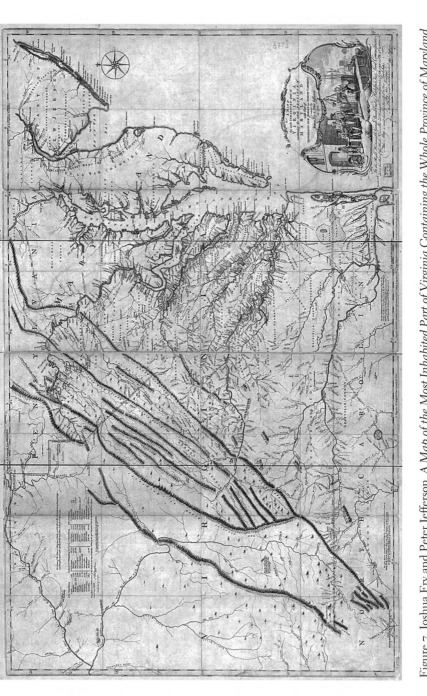

Figure 7. Joshua Fry and Peter Jefferson, *A Map of the Most Inhabited Part of Virginia Containing the Whole Province of Maryland with part of Pensilvania, New Jersey and North Carolina* (London: Thos. Jefferys, 1755). Geography and Map Division, Library of Congress. This edition from 1755 is almost identical to the original version of 1751. The same publisher, Thomas Jefferys, produced

that suggested an unshakable understanding of the landscape. The West was
another matter. European maps conflicted radically in their measurements of
the landscape. They left enormous areas blank, lacking the details that might
have suggested an accurate knowledge of topography.[11]

As a senior official at the state and national levels in the 1770s and 1780s,
Thomas Jefferson eschewed maps altogether. It was a surprising decision, for
not only was his father a skilled surveyor, but he himself was an avid map collector. But Jefferson knew as well as anybody the limitations of cartographic
knowledge in the West as well as the reality that the Near West remained a
highly contested zone where Indians and white settlers were struggling to establish the rules.[12] Consider two of Jefferson's most famous documents: his
draft of Virginia's first state constitution in 1776 and *Notes on the State of Virginia*. Both claimed to define what constituted Virginia, yet both acknowledged the absence of an acceptable survey, let alone an acceptable map, of
its boundaries.[13]

Compounding the shortage of geographic knowledge were Jefferson's
doubts about Virginia's ability to manage the West, and his experience with
George Rogers Clark had shown why. Unleashing angry settlers in a race
war was an acceptable expediency in wartime, but it hardly made for effective long-term management. Meanwhile, numerous states had overlapping
claims in the West that threatened to destroy the fragile national Union. Jefferson soon became one of the most vocal advocates of a general cession in
the Northwest, with all states surrendering their claims to the Continental
Congress.[14]

As states ceded their claims to territory northwest of the Ohio, Jefferson eagerly joined a committee assigned to construct plans for governing the cession
that he had helped orchestrate. Jefferson in turn was the driving force in crafting the committee's report. Submitted to Congress on March 1, 1784, the report
presented Jefferson's vision of a grand master plan for the trans-Appalachian
West that extended well beyond the cessions in the Northwest.[15]

The report came without a map. It was only after Jefferson traveled to Paris
as the American minister to France later in 1784 that he attempted to illustrate
this vision of western policy. Whether Jefferson himself actually drew a map
or not remains a matter of conjecture. The man who eventually produced a
final, hand-drawn version was David Hartley, an English scientist and trusted
correspondent of Jefferson. Hartley crafted a simple map that dissected the territory between the Appalachian mountains and the Mississippi River into
fourteen new jurisdictions (Fig. 8).[16]

Figure 8. David Hartley, "Jefferson-Hartley Map of the United States East
of the Mississippi River" (manuscript map, 1784). Clements Library,
University of Michigan.

This map seems deceptively detailed. Later celebrated for the apparent
power of its simplicity, in 1784 this map was an admission of ignorance. The
standard convention in European territorial planning was to use whatever details were available or to fabricate them in an effort to convince people of a
map's accuracy. Even if those details were suspect, maps of this sort assumed
the authority of knowledge. Throughout 1783 Jefferson had consulted a variety of maps and travel accounts in an effort to ascertain reliable descriptions
of the natural landscape as well as credible European boundaries. In the end,
Jefferson doubted many of his sources, acknowledging the numerous conflicts between the various maps he actually used to establish the final boundaries of the Northwest.[17] Nor could he commission a map in the United
States, which lacked both trained cartographers and cartographic publishers.

The Jefferson-Hartley map of the Northwest was a remarkably crude de-
vice, especially in comparison to the published maps that filled Jefferson's library.[18] But that very crudeness was essential, for it denied the realities at work
in the West. Now Jefferson had written and drawn a vision of the West in
which Indians quite literally disappeared. He had done the same thing in

Notes on the State of Virginia, discussing Indians in generally sentimental terms that situated them in Virginia's history, not its present. Jefferson never entirely denied Indian landownership, throughout his life periodically maintaining a vigorous defense of Indian territorial claims.[19] While he might defend those claims as a matter of principle, however, as a policymaker at the state and federal levels Jefferson consistently endorsed a system of law, philosophy, and hard-nosed policy that repeatedly justified the forced removal of Indians by denying that Indians owned the land on which they lived.

The Plan for Government of the Western Territory of 1784 became the foundation of the Northwest Ordinance of 1787, which codified a system for creating new states that the United States applied with few changes through the creation of the last new state, Hawaii, in 1959. At the core of Jefferson's plan was the radical notion that new states enter the Union on equal terms rather than as subordinate colonies on a European model. At the same time, Congress limited itself to the northwestern territory that the states had actually ceded. The Jefferson-Hartley map, with its plan for new polities running the length of the Mississippi River, remained a fanciful plan for a long-term future. The Northwest Ordinance, like Jefferson's plan of 1784, remained a practical tool of policy, one that acknowledged the limits of American geographic knowledge.

In the years between Jefferson's plan in 1784 and the Northwest Ordinance of 1787, Congress had already taken one other vital step to map out the West. In 1785, Congress passed "An Ordinance for ascertaining the mode of disposing of land in the Western Territory." It was a bland title for a momentous document. The Land Ordinance of 1785 mandated an elaborate survey of the land that became the Northwest Territory. The survey was supposed to subdivide the land into a series of townships, the primary administrative unit and ideally the basis for a town. Each township, in turn, was subdivided into thirty-six sections, which could be further subdivided for sale to the public. In the same way that the Northwest Ordinance of 1787 established a model of government that the United States applied throughout North America, the Land Ordinance established a model of surveying and ownership that the federal government eventually applied to three-quarters of the land in the continental United States.[20]

The Land Ordinance of 1785 was supposed to promote the rapid, stable, and equitable transformation of the public domain into private property. Combined with the Northwest Ordinance, it also demonstrated the similarities in mapping at the national level and the individual level. Just as the

Hartley-Jefferson map was supposed to establish future states, so the Land Ordinance was supposed to map out a foundation for individual farmers. The Land Ordinance also suggested just how important individual landowner- ship would be in western politics and western policy. Landownership soon be- came a divisive matter, as speculators and individual settlers immediately engaged in fierce battles over who could claim, purchase, and eventually own the land in the Northwest.[21]

Jefferson himself had promoted the Land Ordinance. As a policymaker, he believed it would prevent chaos in the West. As an advocate of individual independence, he believed it would enable settlers to own landed property, which to Jefferson was the foundation of independence and freedom. As a Virginian and as an attorney, Jefferson welcomed the systematic creation of private property through deeds and surveys.

Jefferson had used the instruments of policy and of law to describe the Northwest, just as he had used the instruments of the Enlightenment to de- scribe Virginia. Located in between was Kentucky, the place the Clarks even- tually called home. As Jefferson completed his plan for the Northwest in 1784, a man very much like Clark, John Filson, was engaged in his own project to describe Kentucky. And just as Jefferson hoped that landscape description would create a political order in the Northwest where none existed, Filson be- lieved that landscape description would give Kentucky its own identity.

FILSON'S KENTUCKY

Jefferson's vision of the West was one of a fundamentally peaceful and or- derly world that achieved civilization through a combination of careful plan- ning and prudent settlement. A few enlightened Indians provided a noble history to a territory which they had magically vacated. This was not the world of John Filson. The differences were as much in the storytelling as they were in the story. Whereas Jefferson's writings in the 1770s and 1780s reflected the way in which policymakers and intellectuals set about describing the land- scape, Filson represented another tradition in landscape description. In his celebration of the people and the land of Kentucky, Filson exemplified the numerous travel narratives written for the specific purpose of advancing set- tlement and increasing real estate values. If Jefferson described Virginia through the language of scientific rationalism, Filson described Kentucky in the language of western adventure. And if Jefferson eschewed maps in the *Notes* and created a map for the Plan that denied both landscape and population, Filson situated a map inextricably within his narrative of Kentucky. There was no room for a free agent like George Rogers Clark in Jefferson's plan for a neatly organized Northwest. In sharp contrast, Filson quite literally wrote Clark into the history of Kentucky. And if Jefferson the policymaker helped propel the career of George Rogers Clark, Filson better expressed the outlook of Clark and settlers like him.

Filson came from Pennsylvania, the state which, along with Virginia, became one of the chief wellsprings for white settlement in the Ohio River Valley. Just as the details of Filson's early life have almost disappeared from the documentary record, so too has the production history of his one major literary work. But a few things are clear. By the 1780s, he had invested his future in the development of the Ohio River Valley. Not only had he moved there, but like so many other aspiring white settlers, George Rogers Clark among them, Filson dabbled in western land speculation.[22] And by 1784 he had written a book. As was true of so many books of its time, *The Discovery, Settlement and Present State of Kentucke* was merely the beginning of a longer title that was as much an advertisement as a description of the book's contents.[23]

Eventually, people referred to the book as *History of Kentucke*. It was an odd title, for, according to Filson, Kentucky had only the most recent of histories, dating to the arrival of white settlers. But even proclaiming that history was a big statement. After all, in 1784 there was no recognized political entity called Kentucke. Although formally known as the Kentucky District of Virginia, the region was somehow distinct in Filson's view. He began the process of distinguishing it, just as Jefferson had done in *Notes on the State of Virginia*, by imposing geographical boundaries: the border with North Carolina in the South, the Ohio River in the North, the Cumberland Mountains in the East, and the Mississippi in the West.[24] What Filson described was less a political entity than a cultural one, a region that was somehow different from Virginia, if not separated from it. Like a variety of western writers, Filson claimed that western experiences gave the place a clear identity. How to describe such a place raised obvious representational challenges: "The generality of those geographers, who have attempted a map, or description of America, seem either to have had no knowledge of Kentucke, or to have neglected it, although a place of infinite importance. And the rest have proceeded so erroneously, that they have left the world as much in darkness as before."[25] But if that was the case, what would constitute an accurate—what Filson called a proper—description? The answer rested less in geography than in history.

Filson's work exemplified the promotional literature of white settlers and landholders celebrating the possibilities in the Near West. Every landscape was fertile; every river was calm but nonetheless sufficiently speedy to promote trade; everything was abundant. And in referring to abundance, Filson introduced a term which, more than any other, became the barometer for the goals and opinions of the men who attempted to describe western North America. "Abundance" was a term both vague and specific. To Filson, it was a catchall that suggested the opportunities for commercial development in Kentucky: "This country is generally level, and abounding with limestone"; "on some parts of this river, we find abundance of cane, some salt licks, and sulpherous and bituminous springs"; "we may suppose that barley and oats will increase abundantly."[26]

Like most chroniclers, Filson believed that a place did not exist until his own people claimed it. Therefore, there was no Kentucky until James McBride explored the region west of the Appalachians and south of the Ohio River in 1754. Filson acknowledged that "this region was formerly claimed by various tribes of Indians," but, again like Jefferson, he explained that the Indians' "title, if they had any, originated in such a manner as to render it doubtful which ought to possess it."[27] But Filson outdid Jefferson in the celebratory quality of his description.

Whereas *Notes on the State of Virginia* emphasized the emerging institutions of culture and refinement in eastern Virginia, Filson discussed a culture of civility in the West. The rapid settlement of Kentucky had produced a population "upwards of thirty thousand souls." Although "the inhabitants, at present, have not extraordinarily good houses, as usual in a newly settled country," Filson claimed, "they are, in general, polite, humane, hospitable, and very complaisant." He described a population that was diverse yet unified, obeying a code of conduct informed by the "wholesome laws" originating in Virginia.[28]

Jefferson had not been shy in celebrating Virginia, but he did so for a different reason. *Notes on the State of Virginia* countered the specific claims of European detractors who charged that the North American Continent was incapable of natural or cultural productivity. Filson had more pragmatic goals in mind. A return on his financial investment in Kentucky's future depended on the influx of additional settlers who would build towns and raise property values. In crafting a book to attract those settlers with promises of fertile lands and civil neighbors, Filson was only the latest in a series of entrepreneurs who, from the moment Europeans started permanent settlements in the

Americas, published accounts to promote their speculative schemes. Writ-ing in a scientific manner about rivers, fields, and resources offered a guise of credibility for authors who, like so many early American mapmakers, were describing land they often had never fully investigated.

In forty-eight pages Filson offered a treatise on Kentucky with a clear mes-sage of civilization achieved. How Kentucky reached that stage consumed an extended appendix which not only increased the length of the book but trans-formed its story. In the process, Filson created one of the first mythic heroes of the United States. He also began the process of inscribing the Clark fam-ily into the history of western settlement.

Filson began with "The ADVENTURES of COL. DANIEL BOON; containing a NARRATIVE of the WARS of Kentucke." In thirty-five pages, this first-person narrative of Boone's life chronicled the transition from the world of early ex-ploration and Indians with ambiguous claims to the world of civilization and civility. Boone described how a "howling wilderness, the habitation of sav-ages and wild beasts, becomes a fruitful field . . . the habitation of civiliza-tion."[29] It was a heroic story of privation, conquest, and masculine leadership which transformed the West during the turbulent years of the mid-eighteenth century. The Seven Years' War and the American Revolution were merely the backdrop for a local conflict between aspiring white settlers and the Indians or European colonial officials who hoped to restrain them.

Filson then wrote of repeated attacks by Indians and British volunteers dur-ing the Revolutionary War. The assaults were "shocking to humanity, and too barbarous to relate."[30] The response was quick, and it came from George Rogers Clark: "As soon as General Clark, then at the Falls of the Ohio, who was ever our ready friend, and merits the love and gratitude of all his coun-try-men, understood the circumstances of this unfortunate action, he ordered an expedition."[31]

Filson concluded with victory, as the Kentucky settlers triumphed over their Indian adversaries. Indeed, Indians were essential to the way he defined Kentucky. To Filson, Kentucky was not simply a bounded geographic space but also the site of a particular American experience rooted in conquest and improvement. Settlers had replaced Indian savagery with a rough-hewn equality rooted in the opportunities that came from landownership and the absence of unnatural class distinctions. Defining the American experience in terms of Indians resonated not simply on frontiers but throughout the United States.[32] Yet in Kentucky during the 1780s such a reading was particularly po-tent. Filson's account of Boone's life was, in fact, a far cry from Boone's own initial opinion that Indians and white settlers could reach a state of peaceful accommodation.[33]

Unlike Jefferson, who used maps in an indifferent manner during the 1780s, Filson was willing to invest in cartographic representation. He commissioned Henry Pursell to produce a large, highly detailed map designed to coincide with publication of *History of Kentucke* but to be sold separately.[34] This map was quite literally a road map for the kind of settlers Filson hoped to attract with his book. It showed routes that connected the emerging settlements of Kentucky to the population centers of the neighboring states, especially Virginia. It also attempted to combine the celebratory language of Filson's description with the heroic history of Boone's biography. The linkage was especially clear in a horseshoe-shaped curve on the main branch of the Licking River. The river ran through a region with an "Abundance of Cane" and "a fine salt spring," but these were located near the site where "a bloody battle [was] fought." Meanwhile, Filson's account of emerging civil communities took visual form in the towns of Lexington and Louisville, which appear as diversified settlements connected to the larger world by roads heading in all directions (Figs. 9 and 10).

Pursell's map had more in common with the geographic work of Peter Jefferson than with that of Thomas Jefferson. Whereas Filson and Peter Jefferson charted the overlap of white settlement, preexisting boundaries, and the natural landscape, Thomas Jefferson specifically avoided the social and geographic realities that might interfere with his own efforts to imagine an orderly, organized West. Pursell's map provided a western counterpart to the Fry-Jefferson map, much as *History of Kentucke* provided a western counterpart to *Notes on the State of Virginia*.

Filson's map also quite literally inscribed George Rogers Clark onto the landscape in ways distinct from the written narrative of the *History of Kentucke*. Whereas the book described Clark as a heroic warrior in the racial struggle for control of Kentucky, the map situated him within the subsequent process of developing Kentucky for white settlement. In the top left of Filson's map are references to Clarkville, Clark Creek, and "Genl. Clark's Grant 150,000 acres."[35]

If Filson believed his book could promote his fortunes in the West, he apparently also hoped it would establish connections in the East. In November 1784, Filson wrote to George Washington "to express that perfect respect which I with my fellow citizens of the United States owe to your excellency." Soon afterward, he wrote again to inform Washington of the publication of

Figure 9. John Filson, *This Map of Kentucke . . .* (Philadelphia: H. D. Pursell, 1784). Geography and Map Division, Library of Congress.

his book and his map, copies of which Washington would soon receive.[36] Washington expressed his own notions about landownership and landscape representation in his replies to Filson. By January 1785, Washington had received Filson's letter but not the book or the map. He thanked Filson for the gift even as he expressed preliminary concerns: "It has long been my wish to see an extensive & accurate map of the Western Territory set on foot, & and amply encouraged:—but I would have this work founded upon actual surveys and careful observations—any thing short of these is, in my opinion, not only defective and of little use, but serve as often to mislead as to direct the

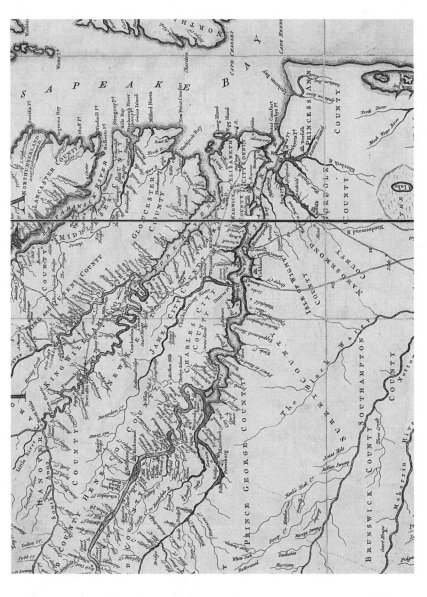

Figure 10. Comparative closeup of Fry–Jefferson map of Virginia (top) and Filson map of Kentucky (bottom).

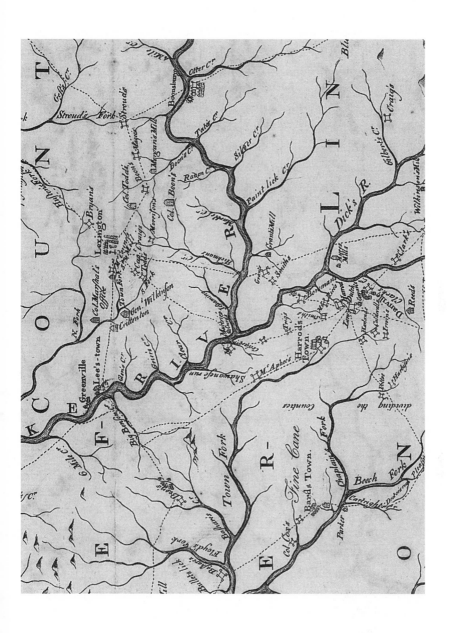

examiner." Washington never indicated whether he considered Filson's work defective in these ways, sending only a brief thank you letter when Filson's work actually reached him in March 1785.[37]

Filson's reasons for contacting Washington in the first place go a long way toward explaining Washington's reaction. If Washington's fame made him a logical choice to create positive publicity about the book, Filson had reasons to believe Washington himself might offer a friendly reading. Washington was an avid western speculator as well as a talented surveyor. Like Filson— or for that matter the Clarks—Washington embraced the notion that describing the West was a necessary first step toward owning the West. He drew meticulous maps of his own landholdings and despised the often slipshod western surveys that undermined profits in speculation.[38]

Like Jefferson, Filson hoped to create a vision of the nation's future in the West. In his Plan for Western Government, Jefferson imagined an ideal political landscape, with a well-organized West that avoided the problems that had plagued eastern states as well as European empires. Like Filson, Jefferson saw tremendous potential in the West and eventually imagined western settlers as idealized Americans. Nonetheless, Jefferson believed the West required a far stronger government than Filson ever acknowledged, in no small part because Jefferson worried about the very impulses that Filson celebrated. Jefferson and Filson both situated George Rogers Clark differently when they considered the past and the future. To Jefferson, the very independence that made Clark so valuable in war made him dangerous in peace. To Filson, veterans of the Revolutionary struggle like Clark seemed the best candidates to build Kentucky.

MORSE'S GLOBE

While Filson crafted a national character through a frontier experience and Jefferson was attempting to resolve federal relationships through the creation of the Northwest Territory, Jedidiah Morse was situating the East as the solution to the West's problems.

Although he was eventually best known as the father of the man who invented Morse code, Jedidiah Morse has also been called the Father of American Geography.[39] Born in Woodstock, Connecticut, in 1761, Morse had all the proper credentials to enter New England's cultural aristocracy, if not its economic elite. Like his father before him, Morse studied for the ministry at Yale and became an ordained Congregational clergyman. For a man

who eventually attempted to describe the entire world, Morse remained remarkably untraveled, even in his own country. He settled into a congrega-
tion in Charlestown, Massachusetts. He moved about New England and
made occasional trips to New York, Pennsylvania, and (after 1800) Washington, D.C. A single visit to Georgia seems to have been his only excursion
in the South. Although none of these trips took him west of the Atlantic
seaboard, Morse nonetheless considered himself qualified to describe his
nation.[40]

An inward-looking New Englander, Morse was the stereotypical latter-day
Puritan. He was also a stereotypical New Englander in his obsessive correspondence, not only writing a prodigious number of letters but preserving
much of his ingoing and outgoing correspondence. This fact alone makes
him crucial to understanding the production of landscape description. Unlike so many other mapmakers and publishers, Morse left a detailed paper
trail of the process through which he produced his materials.

Like Jefferson and Filson, Morse saw the United States—and the ideal
American—in his own image. Morse was hardly the first New Englander to
do so, and hardly the last either. Indeed, he wrote in the midst of a heated argument among Americans during the 1780s about what region would serve
as the wellspring for population and culture. This was very much a battle
between Jefferson, Filson, and Morse, as Americans debated the relative influence of the East (a general term for the Northeast), the South, or the West
in defining the nation's future. That battle played out in constitutional debates and in arguments that appeared in newspaper articles, pamphlets, and
speeches.[41] Those arguments also defined the struggle to represent the United
States during the 1780s.

Morse was a quick study and a fast writer. Barely a year after graduating
from Yale in 1783, he had completed a geography book he entitled *Geography Made Easy*. Traditionally containing only a few maps, geographies resembled almanacs, reproducing vital statistics on regions of the world. Often
designed as teaching tools, in the classroom they doubled as spelling and
grammar textbooks. After the American Revolution, a growing number of geographies also attempted to teach Americans what it meant to be American,
using the description of the United States as a spatial entity to explain how its
people and polities related to one another.[42]

Morse imagined his project as one that would celebrate the American ex-
periment and unify American citizens. Operating in a community of like-
minded New England nationalists, he hoped to create tools that would teach

Figure 11. Map of the United States from *Geography Made Easy* (New Haven:
Meigs, Bowen, and Dana, 1784). Beinecke Rare Book and Manuscript
Library, Yale University.

children to think of themselves as Americans even as they taught them literacy and geography.[43] Unconcerned about copyright, Morse simply copied
data from British geographies while adding an American emphasis. Criticizing European geographies for their meager details on the United States,
Morse presented information culled from various published sources as
well as the firsthand comments of the few people he knew outside of New
England.[44]

Geography Made Easy described the United States in words rather than
pictures, reflecting the same realities of American cartography that shaped
both Jefferson's and Filson's work. The book began with two maps, one a standard global view divided into two hemispheres, the other a map of the United

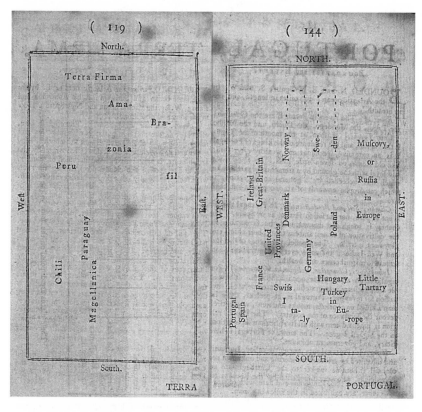

Figure 12. General representations of South America and Europe from the 1784
edition of *Geography Made Easy*. Beinecke Rare Book and Manuscript
Library, Yale University.

States. Morse also opted for more abstract representations of the world in the
belief that figurative maps helped students learn the names and relative geographic positions of individual counties (Figs. 11 and 12).

Yet there were practical matters at work in shaping how Morse represented
the United States in visual form. Whereas the Jefferson-Hartley map reflected
the absence of geographic knowledge, Morse's similarly crude map of the
United States reflected the limited capacity of the cartographic industry in the
United States. Amos Doolittle, who produced the two maps that accompanied *Geography Made Easy*, was a talented engraver but not an experienced
mapmaker. His work could offer none of the details of its European competitors. In fact, what Doolittle offered instead was a watered-down version of
European maps, one that clearly copied details from a series of standard

British maps of North America. The small physical size of the map combined with the limited printing technologies of Morse's publisher to provide only the most basic visual outline of the United States.[45]

When it came to the United States, Morse shared Jefferson's conviction that landscape description could visualize a harmonious nation. Nonetheless, Morse and Jefferson could not have been more different in their conclusions about the people of that nation and its future in the West. If Morse had removed Europe as the traditional center for printed geographies, he had simply replaced it with New England. It was in the New England states that Morse found virtue, sophistication, and a model for national development. Within the region, Connecticut "was the root from whence spring the four flourishing New-England states, the inhabitants of which are noted for the simplicity of their manners, the purity of their morals, their noble independence, the equal distribution of their property, the industrious cultivation of their lands, and for enjoyment of all the necessaries and conveniences of life."[46]

When it came to the Virginia of Jefferson and the Clarks, Morse was more critical. He described an early period of racial amity between Indians and white settlers of Maryland that would have continued "had it not been for the malicious insinuations of some Virginian planters, who, envious of their property, inflamed the Indians." The rising wealth of those planters created a Virginia in which "you no longer find that simplicity and uniformity of manners, and hospitable and friendly intercourse among the inhabitants, which is peculiar to that people, where property is equally distributed, and a happy mediocrity is uniformly preserved."[47]

In his discussion of Virginia, Morse also introduced a concern that ran throughout *Geography Made Easy*. Morse repeatedly expressed his fears that wealth led to luxury, luxury led to corruption, and corruption led to decline. He saw this corruption in forms typical to men of his faith: indifferent religious attendance regardless of denomination, the petty tyranny of slaveholders, the indolence of luxury. Such concerns resonated in New England, but plenty of Americans who did not share Morse's Puritan (or puritanical) roots were likewise worried that wealth could be the undoing of the republican experience in the United States. These fears appeared throughout the early Republic and found expression in everything from political pamphlets to fine art. Yet if culture in its various forms—political culture, visual culture, print culture—expressed these fears, most living Americans did not. In general terms, Americans countered that prosperity would create not only individual happiness, but also the means for equality between citizens and unity among states. And in individual terms, few Americans rejected opportunities for wealth or comfort.[48]

Like others who shared his fears of corruption, Morse implicitly criticized the expansionism of white settlers crossing into the trans-Appalachian backcountry and the trans-Mississippi West. Unlike Jefferson and Filson, who considered the West so essential to the nation's development, Morse treated it as an afterthought. Only after he had discussed all of the British and Spanish colonies in North America did Morse allow himself "some general observations concerning the country west of the Allegany mountains." Morse actually shared the conclusions of Jefferson and Filson when it came to the productive capacity of the West. But why would he believe otherwise? Having never actually traveled west of the Appalachian Mountains, Morse relied on the overwhelmingly promotional literature by boosters of the West like Filson. Morse considered the western reserve of the United States "not only the most extensive, but by far the richest, and most valuable part of our country." It had "the finest land in the world . . . [and] there is nothing in other parts of the globe, which resembles the prodigious chain of lakes in this part of the world." But that very potential, which Jefferson and Morse celebrated without hesitation, carried the seeds of obvious problems for Morse. For now the West "remains in it original state, and lies buried in the midst of its own spontaneous luxuriousness." For Morse, luxury was never a good thing, nor was land in its initial stage of development. The great question for Morse — as indeed it was for Jefferson and Filson — was whether the West could develop an appropriate culture.[49]

While Morse's fears about the West might be rooted in the particular culture of the Northeast, the concern about how frontiers could decivilize even the most virtuous soul was common currency in western landscape description during the eighteenth century. At the same time that boosters like Filson were celebrating the West as a place where hearty and ambitious men could realize their potential while redeeming the promise of the Revolution, there was a similar tradition of lamenting the way western settlers could succumb to a host of temptations. Maps rarely announced this fear, but books often did. The usual culprit was the general condition of frontier life. Weak institutions of civil society could not check the natural, baser human instincts. Meanwhile, Indians presented a seductive alternative that promised a carefree existence. A common complaint about Indians themselves was the way in which the very fertility of the West enabled Indians to live without having to work. White commentators concluded that the same impulse might over-come white settlers. The West would quite literally take civilized Americans and transform them into uncivilized savages.[50]

Families like the Clarks were exactly what worried Jedidiah Morse. A gen-erally unreligious family, they were products of the slaveholding society that sought its own luxury through the suffering of others. George Rogers Clark had gone west, and while he had fought for the same cause of indepen-dence that Morse himself endorsed, he had done so by descending into the uncivilized violence and chaos that the New Englander associated with the West.

AMERICA'S FUTURE

If Jefferson, Filson, and Morse created different histories for the West, they nonetheless saw the place in the same terms, especially when situated along-side the East. Their published work celebrated the possibilities awaiting white settlers in the Near West, so long as those settlers did not descend into the dangers of disorder and racial conflict. They responded to a similar set of po-litical concerns about the nation's future in the West. In their discussions of the landscape, all three men sought to establish the qualities of an ideal Amer-ican. Likewise, their struggle to represent that future reflected the state of American geographic knowledge and cartographic capabilities.

First was the notion of emptiness. All three men sought to describe the West as an empty landscape. They did so in maps even more so than in text. Simple geographic ignorance led Morse to produce a map that pictured the Near West without detail. The effort to impose a new racial and political order onto the West likewise led Jefferson and Filson to remove both Indians and European empires. The absence of detail also served a policymaking goal, for removing Indians from the picture enabled the government of Thomas Jefferson and the settlers of John Filson to claim the West as their own.

Jefferson, Filson, and Morse believed their books and their maps would contribute to the institutions that would civilize the West. Morse celebrated the civilized culture already in place in New England; Jefferson saw himself as the vanguard of a civilizing process in Virginia; and Filson described the emergence of towns and commerce that would replace the savage Indians of an ill-defined West with the emerging civilization of a place called Kentucky.

In the end, all three men imagined a battle between civilization and savagery. The question was simply whether that battle could be won. Morse had few hopes for the West, but Filson and Jefferson were more optimistic. Filson described Kentucky as a place where frontiersmen had already successfully wrested control from Indians and were on their way to creating a land of economic prosperity populated by agreeable neighbors. Jefferson believed that a careful, enlightened policy could establish the political foundations for regional stability and integration. For all three men, visualizing federalism always began by quite literally removing Indians from the picture. Doolittle's map for *Geography Made Easy* almost entirely ignored Indians. After writing a book that focused on the conflict between white settlers and Indians, Filson included a map that showed Kentucky cleansed of those Indians. Hartley's map of Jefferson's plan for western government did the same, superimposing new states, and consequently denying that the Indians in the region were both numerous and powerful.

In all these geographic debates in 1784, Jefferson, Filson, and Morse engaged the broader political debates raging throughout the 1780s. In their vision of a unified nation struggling to preserve civilization in the West, they predicted much of the language codified in the federal Constitution three years later. The connections to Jefferson's Plan for the Northwest are the most obvious, for the administration of the Northwest and the eventual addition of new states required exactly the sort of centralized government created by the Constitution. But Filson welcomed the Constitution as well, for it provided the means to transform Kentucky from a fringe of Virginia into a state of its own. Meanwhile, Morse's simplistic maps of the United States and his written description of them provided a geographic expression of the legal architecture of federalism.[51]

As these men used the representation of the West to address national concerns, they also found their lives tied to the West and to landscape description. Filson moved to Kentucky, became a land speculator, and opened a school to earn additional income.[52] He continued to see the value of writing about the West. *History of Kentucke* brought him both revenue and reputation as various editions appeared overseas, including French and German translations.[53] It was perhaps the first description of the West by a self-proclaimed American to have such a wide readership. Indeed, it was the beginning of a new genre, at least for Americans. For centuries Europeans had published accounts of their journeys to the United States, and in the second half of the eighteenth century a surge in these travel accounts had appeared, first as Englishmen explored their American empire and later as they sought to understand what the Americans had wrought after independence. Among the most famous of these was Michel Guillaume Jean de Crèvecoeur's *Letters of an American Farmer,* published in 1782, two years before *History of Kentucke.* This was only one in a series of books by Europeans expressing a combination of amazement, delight, and disgust at the emerging culture of the new Republic. Crèvecoeur soon published the biography of Boone as a separate book.[54]

Then John Filson disappeared. In 1788 he headed west from Cincinnati to examine the territory near the Great Miami River. His book may have described a land where whites had successfully crushed Indian power, but Filson most likely died at the hands of Indians in the Ohio Country, Indians who had learned during the Revolution to be wary of eager Anglo-American travelers. In death Filson sustained his own narrative of the West as a place where settlers keen on bringing civilization through landscape description faced off against bloodthirsty Indians. Filson's investment in a western future proved wise. The land he owned surged in value as white settlers continued to descend on the Ohio River Valley. Filson also left behind three unfinished manuscripts, all of them journals of his travels through the West.[55]

Filson died just as Thomas Jefferson prepared to take charge of western policy. In 1790, Jefferson joined the administration of George Washington as the nation's first secretary of state. In addition to supervising foreign affairs, Jefferson's extensive mandate included responsibility for the civil administration of the Northwest Territory. That task returned Jefferson to the same challenges of western government—and to much the same western geography—he had faced as governor of Virginia. What had once been Virginia's claims northwest of the Ohio were now part of a larger Northwest Territory, its extensive civil and military government reporting to Jefferson and his colleague in the administration, Secretary of War Henry Knox. When he took office in 1790, Jefferson still believed that one of the prerequisites for governing the Northwest was to describe it. That meant an elaborate system of regional surveys by federal officials, which in turn could lead to local surveys by private landholders. Speculators and settlers alike clamored for the federal government to expedite the process of selling public lands, but those demands only heightened the fears of territorial officials, who believed that an inaccurate map of the Northwest would have grave social and political consequences.[56]

Finally, Jedidiah Morse concluded that landscape description could be a good way to supplement his meager salary as a minister. He followed the sales of his geography with keen interest and no small amount of pride. In the years after 1784 he scarcely missed an opportunity to inform friends and family in terms similar to a letter he wrote his father in 1785 announcing that "my Geographies sell beyond my most sanguine Expectations." That same letter to his father also revealed what an amateur publisher like Morse considered good sales: "I have sold between 3 & 400 within 3 Weeks—The reason why I have not sent you more was because I could not send them so fast as they were wanted here."[57]

Although he often celebrated the standard Congregational values of thrift, modesty, and restraint, Morse was hardly averse to becoming an ardent promoter of his own work. Like Filson, he saw a particular value in circulating his work among the nation's political leadership. Just as Filson sent a copy of his book to Washington, so in 1785 Morse contacted Rev. Daniel Jones, the chaplain of Congress: "I have lately published a compendious System of Geography from the best information I could procure on the subject & such has been its reception by the public that I am encouraged to make preparation for a second Edition." He would gladly send a copy for free. The benefits of providing what would become the de facto official geography of Congress were obvious to him.[58]

In addition to multiple editions of *Geography Made Easy*, in 1789 Morse produced *The American Geography*. More than 500 pages long, the book dwarfed the 214-page *Geography Made Easy*. Yet the two books had much in common. They were organized similarly, Morse having simply included more details in the second book. Likewise, Morse once again limited himself primarily to text. Doolittle produced another map of the United States, this time divided into two sheets, one for the North and one for the South. It was an appropriate distinction considering Morse's criticism of southern culture.[59]

As Morse's vision of North America circulated throughout the 1780s, so too did Filson's and Jefferson's visions of the West. Less than a year after the Jefferson-Hartley map began life as a simple drawing designed to explain Jefferson's plan for western development, Francis Bailey's *Pocket Almanack* appeared with a map of the United States that included Jefferson's eight new jurisdictions. The man who produced the map was none other than Henry Pursell, who earlier that year had created the far more detailed map for Filson's *History of Kentucke*. As in his map for Filson, Pursell removed most references to Indians as he imposed the new American jurisdictions onto the Northwest. In the Southwest he listed the Chickasaw, Creek, and Choctaw

Indians in a small, cursive font overshadowed by the large, bold typeface that announced North Carolina, South Carolina, and Georgia.[60]

Meanwhile, Pursell's map of Kentucky acquired a life of its own. One of Filson's unfinished projects was a collaborative effort with Gilbert Imlay, a veteran of the Continental Army who, like Filson, settled in Kentucky. Better known as the ne'er-do-well lover of Mary Wollstonecraft who abandoned the British writer and radical along with their illegitimate child, in 1792, Imlay published *A Topographical Description of the Western Territory of North America.* . . . Eschewing the celebratory adventure that marked Filson's accounts of Daniel Boone (not surprising since Imlay defaulted on payments to Boone in a land deal), this book followed the structure of Morse's geographies and Jefferson's *Notes on the State of Virginia.*[61] In overblown language that would have made Filson proud, Imlay explained that "Nature in her pride has given to the regions of this fair river a fertility so astonishing, that to believe it, occular demonstration becomes necessary. During these times of barbarous war and massacre, the people of Kentucky and Cumberland, secured by their numbers and strength, except in their outermost plantations, enjoyed perfect security." Imlay also reproduced Pursell's map. In the same way that the Fry-Jefferson map became the foundation for most representations of eastern Virginia, Pursell's map provided a model that other cartographers later appropriated for their representations of the West.[62]

These maps were among the first visual representations of the United States created by American citizens. Together with the written work of Jefferson, Filson, and Morse, they sought to describe a neatly organized United States populated and controlled by its white citizens. Yet the maps were more the product of geographic ignorance than of geographic knowledge. The states themselves were engaged in the more time-consuming process of conducting formal surveys that would enable them to settle nasty, long-standing boundary disputes.

Jefferson, Filson, and Morse all used maps in different ways, and all three men considered their maps accurate. Perhaps so, but these maps more accurately reflected the structure the men imagined for the future than the lived reality in North America. Jefferson, Filson, and Morse exemplified the means by which Americans described the West, respectively: policy documents, travel narratives and regional history, and published geographies. The limitations of those documents were equally telling. All three men considered geographic knowledge vital to the nation's future. Not only were they forced to acknowledge their own ignorance, but the maps they produced likewise revealed the nation's limited ability to represent itself.

CLARK'S EDUCATION

Morse's relatively quiet world of publishing, education, and religious pursuit in the quiet towns of New England seems a far cry from the activity of Virginia, Kentucky, and the Northwest. So, too, do the refined comforts of plantation life at Monticello. Yet the work of men like Jefferson, Morse, and Filson created principles for understanding the West that shaped the life of the young William Clark. Clark himself probably never identified those linkages, but Jefferson's concern for governing the Northwest, Filson's desire to promote Kentucky, and Morse's efforts to write about the United States all informed Clark's upbringing and education. They also came together to determine how Clark would describe the West when he kept those journals during the military campaigns of 1789 and 1791.

The fact that Clark even joined those ventures was a testament to the work of Filson and Jefferson, not to mention of George Rogers Clark. In 1782, George Rogers Clark resigned his military commission in disgust, frustrated by Virginia officials whom he considered unable to adequately support western operations and unwilling to grant Clark the command autonomy he considered his right. Nonetheless, Clark never lost his enthusiasm for Kentucky, throughout the Revolution beckoning his family to join him in the West. Two of their sons had died in the Revolution, but in the fall of 1784 John and Ann Clark gathered their remaining children, their slaves, and their personal possessions and left for Kentucky. Their departure coincided with Jefferson's Plan for Western Government, Filson's *History*, and Morse's *Geography*. Meanwhile, in that same year residents of the Kentucky district of Virginia began efforts to write a constitution for a separate state.[63]

The Clarks were not alone. Thousands of migrants, many of them from Virginia, descended on Kentucky in the 1780s. Together they helped build a world very much as Jefferson, Filson, and Morse had imagined it. In keeping with Filson's predictions, settlers in Kentucky squeezed out most of the remaining Indians and set to work building towns, farms, and plantations. In keeping with Jefferson's predictions, other settlers stayed north of the Ohio River, making immediate demands on the Continental Congress for a system of government that would establish order and security. To many observers, the big question remained whether these newcomers would build a new civilization or, as Morse feared, degenerate into lawlessness.

Whatever George Rogers Clark's promises, his family continued to struggle to preserve its old standard of living and its leadership in local politics. Although the Clarks remained a leading family in western Kentucky, they never entered Kentucky's emerging elite. It was in the Kentucky of his adolescence rather than the Virginia of his childhood that William Clark's future took shape. It was also in Kentucky that Clark learned to describe the world around him. Educated primarily at home, he learned to read and write but apparently never settled on a consistent manner of spelling. Yet if Clark had scant practice as a writer, he certainly acquired an intense training in landscape description. He learned the rudiments of surveying, a skill necessary for any planter family keen on protecting the land it claimed and acquiring more land in the future. For example, George Rogers Clark claimed thousands of acres in the West, either purchased directly or received as grants for his military service during the Revolution. Yet title alone was not sufficient. In the time-honored fashion of Anglo-European law, the next step for Clark was to commission a local survey that confirmed the extent of the claim. This survey was supposed to prevent the most obvious sort of conflicts between neighbors who might otherwise claim they owned the same land. But a survey also constituted the first act of improving the land, itself a necessary part of any claim.[64]

William Clark acquired his skills as a surveyor at the moment when representing the landscape in more general terms was emerging as an essential component of American education in particular and American culture more generally. At a time when men established their republican credentials by what they read, newspapers assumed primacy as proof of a man's engagement with the world around him. But maps, western regional histories, and travel narratives consumed the space of libraries for literate Americans. They were among the most respectable forms of book-length reading for respectable white men in the early Republic.[65]

Equally important, young boys in eighteenth-century America often learned to read and write through geography textbooks that doubled as primers in literacy. Morse had been a keen advocate of this approach to education, and while there is no evidence that Clark owned a copy of *Geography Made Easy*, his education took form in geographical terms. For example, Clark learned mathematics through geography. Exercises in an early mathematical notebook consisted of figuring distances between major cities on both sides of the Atlantic.[66]

It was in these circumstances that young William Clark joined the expeditions of 1789 and 1791 that marked the beginning of his military career as well as of his literary journey. Both were brief expeditions that followed the general patterns of revenge in the Ohio Valley. Just as Indian raids sought violent justice for the transgressions of white settlers, so Kentucky militiamen usually abandoned their military activities after killing a few Indians. Clark recorded these activities in his journals, for his own sense of Kentucky's history was rooted in the story of racial conflict that he had learned from his brother and that Filson had memorialized in print. Clark also paid close attention to the land. His constant references to "first-rate land" and "second-rate land" reflected the concerns of a young man raised in a family that staked its fortune as well as its future on the productivity of western lands.[67]

In these first extensive journals, Clark regularly recorded where he traveled, occasionally described the men with whom he served, and almost never recorded his feelings. Doing so would have been inappropriate given the rules of recording military movements, describing travel, or surveying the region. But one thing Clark did describe was the land: its features, its shifting elevations, its potential productivity.

Clark participated in these military campaigns at the moment of Kentucky's transformation. Throughout the 1780s, Kentucky remained the western district of Virginia. Although Clark clearly identified himself with the frontier concerns that Filson described, he and his family were still legally Virginians. It was not until the 1790s that delegates from Kentucky and leaders from Virginia concluded an amicable plan for a permanent separation, by which point there was a federal government in place to orchestrate the creation of new states. In 1792, Kentucky entered the Union as the first new state carved from the West. It was not part of the Northwest Territory, but other general provisions for statehood—particularly equality alongside existing states and the need for effective surveying and rules of landed property—were the same.

Federal leaders like Thomas Jefferson saw the creation of Kentucky as an effective way to reduce the tensions of expansion. Its white citizens were secure in their equality within the federal system and in their superiority over slaves and the remaining Indians. Filson and Morse had described westward expansion as a fundamentally dangerous, violent process. Yet Filson had also celebrated the families that succeeded in civilizing Kentucky. Equally important, Filson embraced the notion that Americans could realize the promise of the Revolution through the acquisition of western lands. In the 1780s the Clark family seized that promise as well. The task facing William Clark was to find his own way in the West in the years after the Revolution.

2

THREE TREATIES, ONE NATION

The Clark family may have staked its future on Kentucky, but William Clark did not remain there. He soon found himself drawing on his experiences in the campaigns of 1789 and 1791 as he led an expedition on an unfamiliar river, its banks populated by unfamiliar people governed by officials who proved suspicious of the American newcomer. At first glance, this event in Clark's life seems obvious: his journey west with the Lewis and Clark Expedition. But rather than the distant West of the Missouri and the Columbia rivers that Clark eventually explored with Meriwether Lewis, Clark descended the Mississippi River in 1795. Rather than serving as Lewis's cocaptain, Clark was leading his first major independent command. And rather than marking the start of his career as an explorer in the Far West, Clark's venture down the Mississippi came at the end of the American effort to gain control of the Near West.

As he neared the Chickasaw Bluffs in Tennessee, Clark faced off against Manuel Gayoso de Lemos, a Spanish official almost twenty years his senior. Clark recorded their encounter in a detailed report to his commander, General Anthony Wayne. "In the course of conversation during my stay," Clark explained, "I endeavored to gain some intelligence relative to the claims of which the Spaniards founded their pretext to build Forts where they were now proceeding to do—The Governor gave me some account of the former boundaries of the two Floridas—and of an attempt to draw a line between them and the Indian Lands." Clark responded to Gayoso de Lemos by announcing American claims to all the land east of the Mississippi. He acknowledged that he "was treated with every politeness by the Governor." Perhaps so, but the Spanish were unwilling to make any concessions to the twenty-five-year-old emissary from the United States.[1]

In addition to his written report to Wayne, Clark included his drawings illustrating the layout of Fort St. Ferdinand, the Spanish outpost overlooking Chickasaw Bluffs, and Gayoso de Lemos's personal galley.[2] Clark's hand was unsteady in more ways than one. The lines were rarely straight. More important, Clark was a novice on the diplomatic landscape he now entered (Fig. 13).

This type of drawing was typical of men in Clark's profession. Army officers had to draw military emplacements, and some of the first maps they created were for military purposes. Through impersonal reports and hand-drawn images, Clark situated himself in a dangerous world of intersecting rivers, colliding populations, and overlapping territorial claims. In making this journey down the Mississippi Clark negotiated, wrote, and drew without ever once calling himself a diplomat, a writer, or an artist.

Clark's official report formed part of a growing discussion of the southwestern frontier in the 1790s that involved policymakers and mapmakers, surveyors and scientists. The development of this southwestern discussion coincided with the creation of a domestic mapmaking industry that slowly began to create a more detailed visual representation of North America. Yet even as the United States produced a growing number of maps in the 1790s, federal officials continued to ignore them as instruments of policy. Instead, they looked to treaties as a way to remap North America.

And during the 1790s the United States secured three major agreements that sought to define the United States once and for all: the Treaty of Amity, Commerce and Navigation with Great Britain in 1794 (soon called Jay's Treaty and eventually the Jay Treaty); the Treaty of Greenville in 1795; and the Treaty of Friendship, Limits, and Navigation Between Spain and the United States in 1795 (also called Pinckney's Treaty and eventually known as the Treaty of San Lorenzo). These treaties remapped the international boundaries of North America even as they mapped the extent of American expansionism. They revealed a federal leadership that clearly sought to acquire new territory but always within specific limits that reflected equally powerful fears about unchecked expansionism.

In the midst of this renegotiation of landownership, Clark began a career in the federal government that repeatedly situated him at the center of these international disputes. Throughout the 1790s he found himself in an international struggle which forced Americans to acknowledge that the greatest challenges of foreign and domestic policy resided in the West. Americans

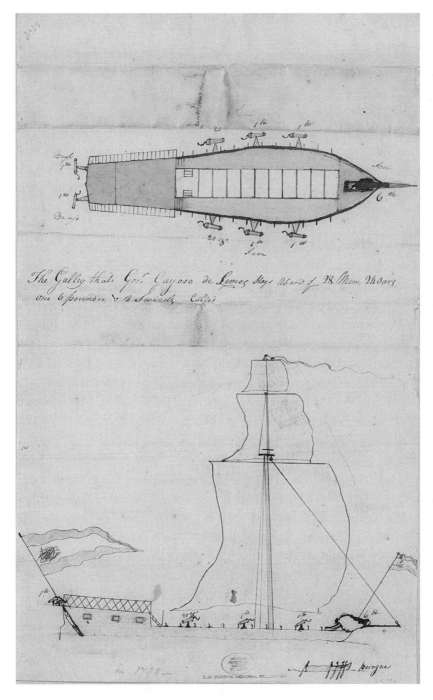

Figure 13. William Clark, pen-and-ink sketch of Governor Gayoso de Lemos's galley. *Clark Family Collection*, Missouri History Museum, St. Louis.

concluded that mapping the western landscape was the necessary first step in resolving those problems.

"CLEAR AND INDISPUTABLE BOUNDARIES"

In the 1780s, Jefferson, Filson, and Morse had all tried to answer the great constitutional questions unleashed by the American Revolution. In the 1790s, Americans asked a similar question: what are the United States? Only now the question concerned international boundaries rather than domestic relationships.

The Continental Congress did not even suggest what the national domain should be for the first two years after the Declaration of Independence. Congress developed periodic guidelines in the 1770s, but only when a peace treaty with Britain appeared likely in 1781 did Congress consider the issue in depth, repeatedly insisting on "clear and indisputable Boundaries" separating the United States from Spanish Louisiana and British Canada.[3] The notion of clear and indisputable boundaries had a potent meaning to elite Americans in 1781, who continued to understand national territorial claims in the same way they understood personal property. Wedded to a notion of individual landownership premised on written deeds that carried the legitimacy of law, they saw treaties in similar terms, as legal documents that bound parties together.[4]

When American and British negotiators finally agreed to the terms of peace in 1783, they defined the United States with boundaries almost identical to those which Congress sought in 1781. They also selected *A Map of the British and French Dominions in North America* (1755), a work by John Mitchell, as an acceptable visual representation of the United States.[5] The treaty proclaimed its accuracy, explaining that specific references to well-mapped points of reference guaranteed "that all disputes which might arise in future on the subject of the boundaries of the said United States may be prevented." For all the certainty of this statement, disagreements on the boundaries of the United States soon exploded, and Mitchell's map was partly to blame.

In 1789 the federal government inherited from the Continental Congress the task of resolving boundary disputes between states and with foreign powers. Meanwhile, William Clark inherited George Rogers Clark's engagement with the West. If the struggle to conquer and describe the emerging settlements of the trans-Appalachian West had defined William Clark's childhood in the 1770s and 1780s, he became an adult in the dispute over the international boundaries of the trans-Mississippi West in the 1790s.

On March 6, 1792, George Washington wrote to the Senate proposing a list of thirty-six men from Pennsylvania and Virginia he was nominating for the junior ranks of the U.S. Army. Two of these men came from the Kentucky District, still part of Virginia but then only three months from statehood. The twenty-two-year-old William Clark was one of them, and the Senate quietly approved his commission as a second lieutenant in the U.S. Army. Clark was ideally poised for the commission. Like a large number of other junior officers, he came from respectable, if not elite, origins, and he enjoyed sufficient political connections to secure the patronage of federal leaders. His brothers' service during the Revolution not only suggested a certain military talent within the family, but also helped make his case in a more sentimental way, since many of the people seeking federal patronage claimed it was a just reward for sacrifices they or their families had made during the Revolution.[6]

Clark joined an army whose identity took shape in the West. In the Northwest, the memory of George Rogers Clark left bitter resentments among Indians. Meanwhile, in the Southwest settlers as well as white planters were keen on expanding into western North Carolina (later Tennessee) and Georgia, where they immediately came into contact and conflict with Indians.[7] As Indians resisted white expansionism, settlers responded violently, either individually or through volunteer militias like the ones William Clark joined in the 1789 and 1791 raids. The federal government's inability to impose its will on either group also made a mockery of Jefferson's vision of a Northwest in which all occupants acknowledged government authority.

These borderland tensions posed dire transatlantic circumstances. Indians had a long tradition of alliances with European powers. Convinced that Britain intended to restore control over its former colonies, American officials reacted angrily when British troops refused to abandon outposts within U.S. territory and when British merchants exploited long-standing relationships with Indians that excluded Americans from trade in their own country. American fears mounted not only because they believed Britain was part of a constellation of threats in the West, but also as a result of troubling news on the Atlantic. American merchants found themselves excluded from lucrative trade routes in the British Caribbean. These diplomatic, strategic, and commercial policies appeared to be a concerted British effort to undermine the United States.

While Britain challenged the United States in the North and on the At-

lantic, Spain resisted American efforts in the South and in the Gulf of Mexico. Unwilling to relinquish sovereign authority over the Mississippi River,
Spanish officials continued to impose a western border for the United States
at the eastern bank of the Mississippi River, not "a line to be drawn along the
middle of the River Mississippi," as dictated by the Treaty of Paris. Spain also
claimed a vast stretch of territory east of the Mississippi, its boundaries uncertain but certainly including territory claimed by Georgia. Some Spanish
officials also conceived of the disputed land as a nominally independent Indian territory. A logical extension of Spanish imperial policy, this approach
created a protective buffer without any substantive cost, in large part because
the Spanish could assume that U.S. policy itself would guarantee that Indians saw Spain as a more reliable ally.[8]

As the federal government sought a response to these challenges, American
policymakers had already constructed a tight link between landscape description and national property. They had struggled to use maps, treaties, and
other documents to justify their territorial claims. But throughout the 1780s,
they often concluded that those documents were inadequate, failing to provide either the specific details or the overall vision that fit with American
goals. That same problem remained in place in the 1790s, as western description portrayed the borderlands in ways that undermined American
claims.

John Mitchell's map not only had been one of the few pieces of common
ground for British and American negotiators in the run-up to the Treaty of
Paris, but also remained the foundation for much of the cartography of North
America, especially the eastern third of the continent. It was, in fact, a text-
book example of how North American mapmaking had developed in the
eighteenth century. Numerous maps published in western Europe had
copied Mitchell's information, adding either details or different interpretations. Some referred directly to Mitchell, less to give credit where it was due
than to invoke his map's reputation for accuracy. Regardless of provenance or
style, however, these maps directly refuted the image of the United States as
Americans tried to describe it. The United States was hardly a cohesive set of
states with distinct boundaries under the control of white settlers. In these
maps the United States was instead an amorphous geography where whites
and Indians jostled for power.[9]

Mitchell's map hardly denied white authority, specifically British authority, which publishers reinforced through the costly addition of color. For
example, the red, green, and yellow strips that constituted Virginia, the Caro-

linas, and Georgia extended west of the Mississippi, further than even the most ambitious British or American officials claimed. But the West was also a place filled with Indians. Indian villages filled the landscape of the Northwest Territory and the land immediately beyond the Mississippi. The Gulf Coast west of the Mississippi was dominated by "Wandering Savage Indians." Nor were things much different in the British colonies to the east. While Mitchell claimed the "English have Factories & Settlements in all the Towns of the Creek Indians," the villagers of southwest Georgia were hardly under British control. Rather, Mitchell was more likely to describe alliances, a word which suggested freedom more than dependence for the Indians of the southwestern frontier.[10]

The notion of Indian power in the West was a common theme in late eighteenth-century European maps. A French map from 1777 based on Mitchell's work carried these principles even further. European and Indian polities were almost completely indistinguishable. Using color to indicate major rivers rather than impose European colonial boundaries, the map began by almost eliminating the European polities that dominated most maps (Fig. 14). The text labeling did little to change this state of affairs: major European colonies commanded the largest print, but they were often little different from the Indian names that quite literally existed alongside them.[11] European maps and travel accounts had good reasons to chart Indian power just as Americans had reason to deny it. Europeans might pursue different Indian policies, but they all recognized the importance of Indian alliances, just as European mapmakers recognized the value of charting those relationships.

Americans rejected this European notion of accuracy. After all, Jefferson had avoided all visual references to Indians in his plans for the Northwest. The cartographers who produced maps for Filson and Morse provided almost no indication of an Indian presence in American territory. Their textual discussion was more varied, but always in ways that quite literally removed Indians from the story. Indians remained an alien concept to Morse in the 1780s and 1790s. Jefferson described Indians as part of Virginia's history, but their declining numbers left them very much a historical entity. Filson did the same, creating a narrative that concluded with white settlers achieving victory over the Indians of the West.

The problem was that Americans in general—and American policymakers in particular—continued to rely on British maps. British maps filled the private libraries of public officials and stocked the shelves of government offices. When Jefferson commissioned a map for the 1786 edition of *Notes on the*

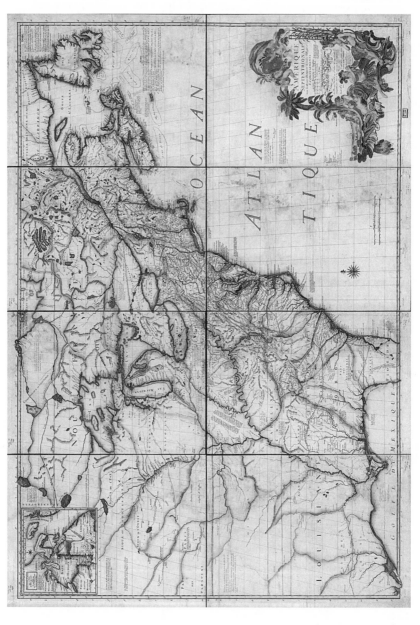

Figure 14. *Amérique Septentrionale avec les Routes, Distances en Miles, Villages et Etablissements François et Anglois* (Paris: 1777), Geography and Map Division, Library of Congress.

State of Virginia, seemingly a manifesto on American independence from Britain, he actually chose an Englishman, John Faden, to produce a map for the book.[12] When he became secretary of state, Jefferson was still forced to rely on European maps, many of which told a story he did not want to hear. President Washington shared Jefferson's concerns, both about foreign policy and about western mapping. While never a book collector like Jefferson, Washington compiled his own vast collection of maps. Equally important, Washington understood the process and implications of mapmaking far better than his secretary of state. A trained surveyor, Washington as a young man reveled in the opportunities he had to measure the western frontiers. As an avid land speculator, Washington knew that his personal wealth depended on geographic knowledge. He drafted numerous surveys to indicate the land he owned. During the Revolutionary War, he also learned the strategic value of geographic information.[13]

By 1790 Mitchell's map had become entirely unacceptable to Americans. Not only did it proclaim Indian sovereignty in a way that American cartographers rejected, but even its topographical information had come into question.[14] As Americans sought to impose their own boundaries onto the western landscape, the American cartographic industry offered little help. By the mid-1790s, Philadelphia, with its combination of scientific institutions and printers, had established itself as the center of cartographic publishing. Despite their technical skill, however, the mapmakers in Philadelphia usually limited themselves to duplicating the work of state surveyors. When it came to the West or the nation's borderlands, they had little to offer.[15]

THREE TREATIES

It was in these circumstances that William Clark received his commission as a lieutenant. He traded the Kentucky militia for the U.S. Army, crossed the Ohio River, and entered the battle for control of the Northwest Territory. Stationed on the distant frontiers of the United States, Clark was nonetheless perfectly located to observe firsthand a complete reversal of American diplomatic fortunes. Three interconnected treaties signed within less than a year confirmed an American vision of landownership in the Near West. They also constituted the first moment of territorial expansion since the conclusion of the Revolutionary War. For white settlers like the Clarks, the treaties of 1794–95 suggested a federal government committed to territorial acquisition. Within the administration, however, the very absence of reliable geographic information continued to generate ambivalence about further moves into the West.

The United States sent its army to the West and its diplomats to the East. The first efforts were disastrous. Saber rattling by the United States hardly intimidated Spain or Britain to the point of ceding territory, abandoning Indian alliances, or removing their fortifications. Indian affairs went even worse. The army in which Clark served continued to experience military defeat at the hands of Indians in the Northwest. Clark's journal was filled with scorn for men at all levels. Writing as a proud member of the officer corps, he was deeply critical of volunteers, whom he considered disorganized and undisciplined. He referred to his commanding officer, General Anthony Wayne, as "his excellency," a title that hardly seemed one of respect. In a rare attempt at writing humor, Clark recorded how a tree nearly fell on Wayne and how "fortune in one of her uncountable pranks . . . had nearly deprived the legion of its *Leader,* had nearly deprived certain individuals of theire A.W."[16]

In 1793, tensions between Britain and France erupted into open warfare that eventually consumed most of Europe for the next twenty-two years. Although unleashed by the French Revolution, the conflict was seen by many Americans as merely the latest example of the violent imperial contests that had gripped Europe for centuries.

The Washington administration, in a mood of desperation, dispatched John Jay, the nation's first chief justice but also an experienced diplomat, to Britain. Jay took with him a broad and imposing mandate designed to normalize relations with Great Britain. First and foremost, Americans demanded that Britain remove restrictions on American overseas trade. But there were western concerns as well, primarily that the British renounce alliances with Indians at war with the United States and redraw the U.S.–Canadian boundary.

The power of geographic knowledge immediately informed the boundary negotiations. Whatever problems Americans might have with British maps and British surveys, they had nothing to offer in return. Indeed, it soon became clear that officials in England understood the geography of North America better than the Americans. The point of departure for their negotiations was a map of the United States of 1793 by none other than William Faden, the British mapmaker who had provided maps for Jefferson's *Notes on the State of Virginia.* Jay proved unwilling to challenge his British counterpart, Baron Grenville, Britain's secretary of state for foreign affairs, on the details of North American geography.[17]

If the negotiations responded to the authority of British geographic knowledge, they concluded with a reminder of just how little Europeans and Euro-Americans actually knew about the geography of the borderlands. The treaty that Jay and Grenville completed in November 1794 acknowledged that "it is uncertain whether the river Mississippi extends so far to the northward as to be intersected by a line to be drawn due west from the Lake of the Woods, in the manner mentioned in the treaty of peace between His Majesty and the United States." The treaty offered only the vague hope that "measures shall be taken in concert" by the United States and Great Britain to conduct a survey of the Upper Mississippi.[18] Such a joint venture would impose a boundary where none existed, in the process establishing government controls on a region which, like so many frontiers, was characterized by the give-and-take among residents who persistently rejected the authority of distant, centralized governments.

Entitled the Treaty of Amity, Commerce and Navigation, the document appropriately pointed to the general amity of the discussions between Jay and Grenville. What Jay did not know was that the details of the treaty, soon labeled Mr. Jay's Treaty or simply the Jay Treaty, generated tremendous controversy back home.[19] The Senate eventually ratified the treaty in 1795, but the factional lines that formed around it crystallized into the formal party structures of the Federalists and the Democratic-Republicans.

Much of this animosity stemmed from arguments over the Atlantic commercial provisions of the treaty. Critics charged that the treaty made too many concessions and forced the United States into a de facto alliance with Great Britain. For all those disputes, Americans found little disagreement in the provisions of the Jay Treaty that dealt with the West, in large part because the agreement delivered what the Americans wanted: clear borders and domestic authority. The treaty redefined the U.S.-Canadian border and even created a commission to resolve any remaining disputes, removing Mitchell's map as the final arbiter of international boundaries. Perhaps more important, the British pledged not to assist Indians at war with the United States. In fact, in the months preceding the negotiations British officials in North America had received orders to avoid actions that antagonized the Americans.[20]

This sudden shift in British policy could not have come at a more opportune moment, for the United States seemed poised for a breakthrough in the Northwest. The army in which William Clark served had been both reinforced and reorganized, and by 1794 the United States had created a force that could finally match that of the Indians of the Ohio Valley. On August 20,

American and Indian forces collided near the banks of the Maumee River, where the Indians had established a defensive line among recently uprooted trees. Those trees gave the battle its name — Fallen Timbers — and at that site the U.S. Army won its first significant victory over the Indians of the North-west. When the Indians sought refuge with the British at Fort Miami, the troops there quite literally locked the doors, leaving the Indians with few op-tions.[21]

Clark's journal of the campaign included "a fiew observations or reflec-tions on the Business of this day." First and foremost, he believed that the scattered, disorganized, and undisciplined U.S. forces could easily have been defeated "had the Enemy for once forsaken theire long established mode of fighting (Viz.)." The passage betrayed the telltale spelling eccentricities that marked Clark's writing throughout his life, but the tone of his journal was a clear break from most of his writing, both before and after. Throughout the journal, Clark criticized both enlisted men and high-ranking officers, reserv-ing praise primarily for junior officers. While not offering direct praise of him-self, he went out of his way to recognize men very much like himself. Rarely would Clark again express such explicit criticism in his journals. As a result, Clark's campaign journal of 1794 is an attractive document but hardly a rep-resentative one. In its direct language and even in its humor it seems to open a window onto Clark's personality that other documents do not. Nonethe-less, the persona that Clark was otherwise crafting through his written work was one of dispassionate observation rather than passionate commentary.[22]

When Indian negotiators met with the Americans the following year they signed an agreement, the Treaty of Greenville, which, like the Jay Treaty, es-tablished the boundaries of the United States and the extent of its powers. Also like the Jay Treaty, the Treaty of Greenville defined the landscape, des-ignating a "general boundary line between the lands of the United States" running through the rivers of the Northwest Territory. That boundary also established major land cessions by the Indians. And while the treaty did ac-knowledge certain areas of Indian sovereignty, it also mandated that Ameri-can citizens be allowed to pass through Indian land. Meanwhile, the Indians were forced to acknowledge certain land claims by whites within their terri-tory, including the tract of 150,000 acres that Congress had awarded to George Rogers Clark and his soldiers.[23]

Clark remained with the army as it enforced the Treaty of Greenville. He eventually secured promotion to captain at the very moment the federal gov-ernment was succeeding in its policy of racial conquest in the Northwest. As

Indians surrendered their claims to most of what now constitutes the state of Ohio, the U.S. Army of William Clark achieved what the volunteer army of George Rogers Clark had not. It was a crucial moment in Clark's life, marking his first experience with diplomacy and treaty making. In the Northwest Territory, he learned how the United States could redefine the landscape through warfare and through treaties.

While the Jay Treaty and the victory at Fallen Timbers enabled the United States to secure seemingly clear international boundaries and appropriate internal divisions, the situation on the southwestern frontier still appeared grave. Relations between the United States and Spain remained tense well into 1795. Borderland officials eyed each other with suspicion: Americans were convinced that the Spanish were hatching separatist schemes in western states, and the Spaniards were convinced that Americans coveted Spanish territory.

Clark experienced those tensions firsthand when he descended the Mississippi in 1795 and confronted Gayoso de Lemos. When Clark reported to General Wayne on the encounter, his comments on geography were revealing. Although Clark began his report with the salutation "Sir," he occasionally referred to Wayne as "your Excellency," albeit without the sarcasm evident in his private journal of the 1794 campaign. He explained how Gayoso de Lemos "gave me some account of the former boundaries of the two Floridas," a term commonly used to discuss West Florida (the region from Baton Rouge to Pensacola) and East Florida (the region from Pensacola to the Atlantic, including the Florida Peninsula). Gayoso de Lemos detailed "an attempt to draw a line between them and the Indian lands. . . . I enquired wheather that was his pretext for building the Fort at this place—He answered evasively and with a shrug 'it is a Ministerial business for which I cannot account.'" Clark and the Spaniard both recognized the ongoing challenge of borderland claims, and both hoped to capitalize on the situation.[24]

What men like Clark and Gayoso de Lemos could not know was that the United States and Spain had reached a diplomatic breakthrough. In October 1795 American and Spanish negotiators concluded the Treaty of San Lorenzo. In stark contrast to the Jay Treaty, in February 1796 the Senate eagerly ratified the agreement because the terms seemed so favorable to the United States. Spain not only guaranteed the right of Americans to trade down the Mississippi River, but also ceded most of the contested territory east of the Mississippi, reserving to Spain only the Gulf Coast and the Florida Peninsula, a region known as East and West Florida. In the process, the treaty provided the sort of definite boundaries the United States had sought for over a decade. "To prevent all disputes on the subject of the boundaries," the treaty designated "the thirty first degree of latitude North of the Equator" as the line between the Floridas and the United States.[25]

The Jay Treaty and the Treaty of San Lorenzo helped resolve long-standing border disputes. Meanwhile, guarantees in both treaties that neither Spain nor Britain would ally itself with Indians at war with the United States enabled the federal government to pursue its policy of conquest in the Near West more aggressively. Yet for all the benefits they contained, the three treaties of 1795–96 hardly indicated any excessive diplomatic muscle on the part of the United States. To the contrary, forces outside the United States, mostly in Europe, dictated North American affairs. Once Spain formed an alliance with France and declared war on Great Britain, both Spain and Britain were eager to resolve disputes that might propel the United States into a military alliance with either opposing empire. Indians bore the brunt of these decisions. As old European alliances disappeared, Indians suddenly found themselves forced to make concessions to the United States.[26]

Indians had the most to lose from the remapping of North American borders while the men who made their livelihood describing North America had plenty to gain. Included among these men were authors like Jedidiah Morse, who released new editions of his various geographies, each time claiming to report on the latest changes in national borders; the growing cadre of mapmakers and cartographic publishers in Philadelphia; and the first cohort of federal surveyors, men commissioned first to establish the extent of the national domain and, subsequently, to subdivide the land for settlement.

Among the first Americans to show how surveying could establish public careers were Thomas Hutchins and Andrew Ellicott. Hutchins was the nation's first geographer general, a civilian counterpart to the rank of surveyor general Hutchins had attained in the Continental Army. Hutchins had also supervised the implementation of the Land Ordinance of 1785, conducting the first major survey of the Northwest Territory. One of his subordinates in the Northwest, Ellicott had led several federal surveying expeditions in the Southwest before securing a more permanent appointment as public surveyor in Pennsylvania. Men like Hutchins and Ellicott understood the connections between publishing and public careers. They published travel narratives, maps, and guides to surveying. They also wrote to government officials, just as Morse had, either to create public careers and elite connections for themselves or to increase sales of their book projects. These projects in turn not only brought them direct income, but also served the equally important task of establishing their expertise with the government officials who controlled public patronage.[27]

TRAVERSING THE WESTERN MAP

In 1798, Ellicott surveyed the boundaries of the newly created Mississippi Territory, the land ceded by Spain in the Treaty of San Lorenzo. He eventually published a book of his adventures in which he heaped criticism upon his Spanish counterpart, Gayoso de Lemos, the man who had intercepted Clark only three years before. As they passed through the same territory—both geographic and diplomatic—Clark and Ellicott never actually met one another, but both kept journals written in very similar terms. There were few references to feelings, sentiments, or personal relationships. Nonetheless, these men wrote autobiographically, situating themselves as heroic figures on dangerous frontiers.[28]

Clark continued to write journals in the years that followed, and he retained the same style even as his career prospects took a dramatic turn. In July 1796, he resigned his commission in the army. With the immediate western crises that had fueled the army's growth in the early 1790s apparently resolved by the treaties of 1794–95, junior officers like Clark doubted their chances for distinction and promotion. In the years that followed, Clark traversed the Mississippi Valley in an often elusive quest to make himself into a successful entrepreneur.[29]

After a brief return to Mulberry Hill, the Clark family plantation in Kentucky, Clark traveled west in circumstances that exemplified the diplomatic and ethnic complexities of the Far West. In 1797 he arrived in St. Louis to contest a lawsuit filed against his family. The following year Clark transported tobacco down the Mississippi River. He visited New Orleans, where he deposited the shipment before boarding an American vessel bound for the East Coast. To authorize his departure from the Spanish town, Clark received a passport from none other than Gayoso de Lemos, by then promoted to governor-general of Louisiana and West Florida. En route home via the Atlantic seaboard, he briefly passed through the new federal capital under construction on the banks of the Potomac.[30]

On all of these journeys, Clark kept a journal, never questioning the need for a written record of his travels.[31] He wrote in the same sparse language that characterized the Kentucky campaigns of 1789 and 1791 and the encounter with Gayoso de Lemos in 1795. In the process, he chronicled the very real consequences of political, diplomatic, and cartographic change in North America. In St. Louis, he attempted to resolve the sort of disputes in landownership that proliferated throughout the West as European legal systems collided. His Mississippi trip of 1798 would have been unimaginable only a few years earlier. Three years after encountering Spanish control over the Mississippi during his meeting with Gayoso de Lemos in 1795, Clark participated in exactly the sort of venture that had guided American diplomacy in the West. Transporting goods like tobacco from the Near West to the commercial entrepot at New Orleans before final transshipment to the eastern United States or to Europe had been at the core of the nation's political economy. Finally, in Washington, D.C., Clark saw a town under construction, much like the federal government that soon moved there. If Washington itself remained an unpleasant location that visitors long described as an unimpressive capital foolishly located on swampland, the federal system was heading in a more positive direction. Throughout the 1790s, the federal government had successfully remapped the national domain. Yet for all these changes, Clark himself faced innumerable frustrations. He eventually came to regret his decision to leave the army as he struggled through a series of unsuccessful and unsatisfying business ventures.

Clark's second chance for a public career came unexpectedly. Only a few years later all the careful remapping of North America exploded in a series of changes entirely beyond the control of the United States. Like Morse and Ellicott before him, Clark exploited the sudden demands of landscape description to find his own place in the United States.

3

EXPANSION

Whether he was campaigning in Kentucky in 1789 or descending the Mississippi in 1795, William Clark had described the West in a way that placed him at the center of the action even as his personality seemed banished to the periphery. Clark described events rather than feelings. He described the land in the technical language of a surveyor rather than in the romantic imagery of the poet or novelist.

Clark had developed the means of describing the West and himself during an eighteenth-century childhood, and he carried those techniques with him into the nineteenth century. How Clark understood himself and the nation's western future is apparent in one of the few letters that displayed the sort of emotional content that we now demand of personal correspondence. In July 1803, Clark composed a letter that he hoped would change his life. The recipient, an occasional associate who shared Clark's background and his outlook, had invited Clark to join him in a strange task of questionable value. Yet Clark was at a loose end in the summer of 1803, so he eagerly accepted the offer, explaining that "the enterprise &c. is Such as I have long anticipated and am much pleased with." Making a passing (and misleading) allusion to the state of affairs in Kentucky, Clark added, "My situation in life will admit of my absence the length of time necessary to accomplish such an undertaking."[1]

Clark wrote the letter to Meriwether Lewis, and the venture he joined was the Lewis and Clark Expedition. Yet the expedition Clark joined in July 1803 was hardly the expedition that Lewis and Clark led the following year. Lewis had written to Clark on June 19, 1803, describing a venture of scientific and commercial inquiry on foreign territory. In May 1804, Lewis and Clark together led an expedition of territorial mastery on land that somehow had to become American. In the year separating the two, the United States was transformed in ways that placed landscape description at the center of federal policymaking.

Only two weeks before Clark wrote to Lewis, news had arrived in Washington that the United States had acquired a vast new western domain. Reports circulated rapidly throughout the country, but none of the Kentucky newspapers had carried the news by July 18, and Clark's letter shows no sign that he was aware of a change in national circumstances.[2] It was not until August 1803, one month after receiving Lewis's letter, that Clark began discussing a treaty through which France ceded its territory on the North American continent to the United States. Clark knew as well as anybody the benefits of this treaty, for the Jefferson administration first sought to acquire territory from France specifically to satisfy western settlers like the Clark family. But Clark soon learned the dangers that many Americans associated with the treaty that became known as the Louisiana Purchase.

In the year separating Clark's letter to Lewis in July 1803 and the departure of the Lewis and Clark Expedition in May 1804, Americans argued about those benefits and dangers. Chief among American concerns were the threats they associated with governing foreign territory. Exacerbating those fears was the simple fact that Americans did not know what they had bought. Indeed, the Louisiana Purchase reversed the relationship between treaties and other forms of geographic representation that American policymakers had sought throughout the 1790s. It would take mapmaking to resolve problems within the treaty, not the other way around. Worse still, creating those maps would require surveying distant and difficult landscapes. Faced with the reality of governing the Far West, the federal government abandoned both the vague information from European sources and the occasionally overenthusiastic proclamations that had rationalized the purchase.

Four months after writing to Lewis in July 1803, Clark began to chart out the Far West for the Jefferson administration. In November he drew a map of the area surrounding the Grand Tower. Located on the western banks of the Mississippi River about halfway between St. Louis and the confluence with the Ohio River, the Grand Tower, Clark knew, was a familiar navigational landmark. It also was not far from the site of Clark's encounter with the Spanish eight years earlier, and he drew the Grand Tower in a manner reminiscent of those earlier drawings (Fig. 15).[3]

Clark's letter of July 1803 to Lewis expressed unrestrained enthusiasm, but

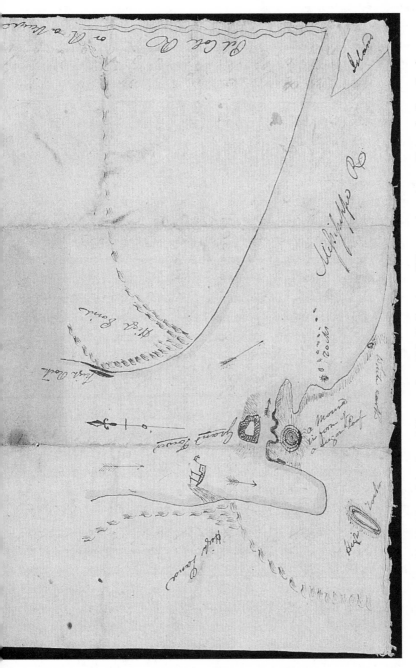

Figure 15. Clark's Map of the Grand Tower, 1803. Yale Collection of Western Americana, Beinecke Rare Book and Manuscript Library, Yale University.

his notes on the western landscape were more circumspect. This state of affairs was hardly so contradictory as it may seem. Clark saw enormous opportunities in joining an expedition that would bring nothing less than a rebirth
of his flagging prospects. But Clark's preliminary maps of the West, including places like the Grand Tower, reflected a broader set of fears about what
was known as well as what was unknown.

"I AM HAPPY TO HERE OF THE SESSION OF LOUISIANA TO THE UNITED STATES"

Few people understood the circumstances surrounding the Louisiana Purchase better than William Clark. Distant though he might be from the politicians who approved the agreement, his experiences in the West during the
1790s exemplified the conditions that put the United States on a diplomatic
course ending with the Louisiana Purchase. In 1803, Clark worried that the
West would never deliver on its promise. In superficial terms, he was thriving, having inherited the family's estate in Kentucky and thrown himself into
life as a planter. But that inheritance had come at a cost, both emotional and
financial.

Clark received the plantation in 1799 on the death of his father, John Clark,
who died less than a year after Clark's mother, Ann. Youngest sons rarely received a family's primary estate, but two of Clark's brothers were dead, while
the other two had abandoned Kentucky and returned to Virginia. Called
Mulberry Hill, the Clark plantation was hardly so grand as that name might
imply. As the planter and merchant elite built fortunes in Kentucky, William
Clark struggled against mounting debts.

For proof that all those visions of the West—advancement through the military at the personal level, preservation of its gentry status at the family level,
and opportunity for white settlers at the national level—were slipping away,
William Clark needed to look no further than the man who had symbolized
those visions, George Rogers Clark. George Rogers Clark remained embit-
tered by his experiences during the Revolution and was struggling to manage
his own investments in western lands. He was barely fifty years old in 1803, yet
his physical condition was deteriorating through a combination of ill health
and heavy drinking. William Clark took charge of Mulberry Hill because his
oldest brother was in no condition to do so himself.[4]

Clark shared the outlook of many Americans who situated the Louisiana
Purchase within a set of concerns about the territory east of the Mississippi.

Clark understood those distinctions better than most. In 1797, the travels of William Clark reflected the aspirations that Americans associated with the Treaty of San Lorenzo. Normalizing relations with Spain enabled Americans to travel down the Mississippi and do business in trading centers like St. Louis and New Orleans. Clark had visited both places in the 1790s. He recognized, as did thousands of other Americans in the Near West, that prosperity depended on trade down the Mississippi.[5]

As Clark pursued commercial opportunities in the 1790s, he knew of Jefferson's plans to explore the Far West. In 1783, Jefferson had written to George Rogers Clark proposing he lead an expedition "exploring the country from the Mississippi to California." Clark responded that Jefferson's proposal "would be Extreamly agreable to me could I afford it." Although Clark was keen on preserving a good relationship with Jefferson, the letter resonated with Clark's long-simmering anger that government officials like Jefferson had failed to support him—either logistically or financially—during the Revolution.[6]

In the years afterward, Jefferson pursued two very different approaches in the West. He never abandoned his goal of conducting a major expedition to explore the Far West. After George Rogers Clark declined, Jefferson approached a variety of men with an eclectic set of interests and skills. Although Jefferson discussed different goals with these would-be explorers, his own objectives remained consistent throughout the 1780s and 1790s. Jefferson combined a personal interest in science with a strong desire to see the United States engage in the booming commercial opportunities of the Far West. He knew that French and British traders were reaping tremendous profits from the fur trade in the continental interior. Much of that trade moved east through St. Louis, but it also continued further west to the Pacific Coast, where it was only one piece of a truly global system of trade. Merchant ships traveling across the Pacific from North America to Asia also transported goods that reached the Atlantic en route to the United States or to Europe. Jefferson imagined an American entree to that system that would mean wealth for American citizens, revenue for federal coffers, and, perhaps most important to Jefferson, proof that the United States was finally a global economic power on a par with other countries that so often dismissed it as a provincial backwater.[7]

Exactly when Jefferson began planning the Lewis and Clark Expedition is a subject of some conjecture. After all, the expedition that Lewis and Clark began in 1804 was the logical extension of ideas Jefferson had been developing since the 1770s. When Jefferson became president in 1801, he believed he finally had the resources and the political muscle to bring the expedition to reality. In addition, the man he chose to lead that expedition was close at hand. Lewis came to Washington with Jefferson to serve as his personal secretary. Meanwhile, throughout 1802 and early 1803 Jefferson corresponded with the nation's leading scientists, many of them located in Philadelphia, prepared to seek funding from Congress, and petitioned the Spanish government for a passport that would permit an American expedition to ascend the Missouri River.

Jefferson hoped to combine political economy with scientific inquiry. Once again, individual and national self-interest would overlap. Jefferson personally sought information about the West, a quest he shared with the small community of scientists and intellectuals scattered throughout the United States. But Jefferson also recognized that mounting a major scientific expedition would mark the United States as a civilized nation, a matter of international competition no less important to Jefferson than his desire for the United States to challenge European commercial supremacy.[8]

Lewis was apparently thrilled by the opportunity. He left Washington in March 1803 to assemble materials, recruit men, and begin a rushed education in the natural sciences. By June 1803 he was back in Washington for final consultations with Jefferson. It was from Washington that Lewis wrote to Clark. He wrote with excitement about a grand expedition of national importance, and in the final paragraph added, "If therefore there is anything under those circumstances, in this enterprise, which would induce you to participate with me in it's fatiegues, it's dangers and it's honors, believe me there is no man on earth with whom I should feel equal pleasure in sharing them as with yourself."[9]

The sentiments of that passage reverberated through the letter. "Thus, my friend," Lewis wrote before making his formal offer. Likewise, Lewis began the letter by explaining that he wrote to Clark "from the long and interrupted friendship and confidence which has subsisted between us." It is those passages that have entered the Lewis and Clark lore, evidence of a friendship that gives an added human dimension to the grand study of the Lewis and Clark Expedition. Yet Lewis's references to such a friendship are questionable at best. Meanwhile, his plans for the expedition were either deceptive or self-deluding.

Clark in fact had had only the most passing relationship with Lewis. The two men had served together briefly in the army during the 1790s and preserved only an occasional acquaintance in the years that followed. They also demonstrated distinctly different personalities. When Clark served as Lewis's commander in 1795, the measured and deferential Clark knew Lewis as an impulsive junior officer whose penchant for disputes with other officers made him a troublesome subordinate. This does not mean the men disliked each other, but it does call into question Lewis's words.[10] But Lewis had also spent two years learning about politics and leadership from Jefferson, who conspicuously deployed friendship in his letters to secure relationships with friend and foe alike.[11] Besides, Lewis had reasons to assume that he and Clark would naturally be friends. Both came from Virginia's lesser gentry, both had joined the army in the 1790s when their gentry status had appeared to be in peril, and both had pledged themselves to Jefferson and the leadership of the Democratic-Republicans. Throughout his adult life, Clark made only a few comments about the dominant political struggle between the Democratic-Republicans and the Federalists. Yet if he did not engage in party combat, he was quick to proclaim his loyalty to the Democratic-Republican leadership.

If Lewis described a friendship that seemed more hopeful than real, the same dubious enthusiasm applied to the expedition he planned to lead, for in the summer of 1803 that expedition seemed to be going nowhere. Lewis informed Clark that he had "liberal passports from the Ministers both of France and England." France owned the vaguely defined colony of Louisiana that contained the Missouri River while Britain owned the Oregon Country, which included the Columbia River, which Lewis planned to descend en route to the Pacific Coast. At the same time, Lewis ignored the enormous diplomatic impediment blocking the expedition. France had acquired Louisiana from Spain in 1800 and had agreed to let Spain continue the daily administration of the colony. Spanish officials were convinced this was hardly the peaceful scientific venture Jefferson described. Instead, all of the evidence before them suggested the United States was an aggressively expansionistic country that was keen on acquiring territory in the Far West. Likewise, whereas Jefferson claimed the expedition would engage in peaceful commerce with Indians, the Spanish saw a blatant effort by the United States to build alliances that could only erode Spain's limited influence in the villages of the upper Missouri.

Most important, relations between the United States and Spain were on the verge of collapse in 1803. It was in those circumstances that Near West and Far West collided, linking Clark's history in Kentucky to his future in Louisiana.

Federal leaders had long expressed concerns that foreign control over the Mississippi River threatened the long-term security of the United States and the prosperity of settlers in western states and territories. When the Spanish imposed new restrictions on American trade in 1802 (a move that Americans soon referred to as the Mississippi Crisis), the Jefferson administration committed itself to acquiring New Orleans and the Gulf Coast while rejecting plans to expand further west. The Mississippi Crisis generated such attention in Washington specifically because Kentuckians mobilized so loudly. The state legislators, congressional representatives, newspaper editors, and pamphleteers from Kentucky all spoke on behalf of William Clark and other Kentuckians who demanded an aggressive federal response. Convinced that restrictions down the Mississippi River would choke the western economy, Kentuckians issued provocative statements suggesting that failure to resolve the situation to their satisfaction could lead them to leave the federal Union in favor of an independent alliance or formal annexation by Spain.[12]

In the end, expansion would come not through the planning of American policymakers but through the mandate of Europeans. In 1803 France sold Louisiana to the United States for reasons of its own. France had acquired Louisiana from Spain through the retrocession of 1800 primarily as a source of raw materials and strategic defense for the lucrative sugar plantations on the island colony of Saint Domingue. By 1803 Napoleon had decided to abandon Saint Domingue in the face of the revolt by slaves and free people of color who soon declared the independent republic of Haiti. Without Saint Domingue, he had little need for Louisiana. The purchase came as an immense surprise to American policymakers at home and abroad. American negotiators, in keeping with the American plan to consolidate control of the Near West rather than expand into the Far West, had sought the purchase of New Orleans and the Gulf Coast. Although they eagerly agreed to a Louisiana Purchase that clearly extended into the Far West, they remained focused on the benefits of securing control of the Mississippi.[13]

On August 21, Clark was in Louisville recruiting men for the expedition. He informed Lewis that "I am happy to here of the Session of Louisiana to the United States, this is an inestimable treasure to the Western People, who appear to feel its value."[14] Happy indeed, and for multiple reasons. The "Western People" whom Clark discussed were in Kentucky and Ohio, residents of the Near West who read or heard reports that the Louisiana Purchase had ended the Mississippi Crisis in a way that guaranteed American control of the Mississippi River. Meanwhile, those same reports indicated that the

United States would acquire territory in the Far West, specifically the territory surrounding the lower Missouri. With Spain removed from the picture, the Lewis and Clark Expedition could proceed.

"THE LATEST DISCOVERIES"

Despite Clark's personal eagerness to explore the Far West, the print culture of the United States was hard-pressed to justify expansion. The public reaction to the Louisiana Purchase emerged from the concerns of Clark's Kentucky. American newspapers explained the Louisiana Purchase as a solution to the Mississippi Crisis.[15] Meanwhile, a series of pamphlets from 1803 and 1804 provided the most thorough explication of these principles. Before 1803, there were few calls for acquiring the borderlands of Canada, the farmlands fronting the mid-Mississippi Valley, or the plains and forests beyond the Great Lakes. Suddenly, Americans who had always emphasized the need to protect the Near West faced the challenge of responding to decades of cultural production that argued against acquiring the Far West.[16]

The written response to the Louisiana Purchase was revealing. Pamphleteers and editorialists eager to help secure approval of the treaty and extend federal rule west of the Mississippi claimed that the greatest benefit of the purchase was the peaceful resolution of the Mississippi Crisis. Samuel Brazer crystallized that argument in a pamphlet in 1804, writing, "The acquisition of the vast territory of *Louisiana*, in itself was a great, a wonderful achievement of wisdom and policy. The means by which it was obtained, afford an honorable, an unprecedented example of magnanimity and justice."[17] Only a few Americans described any great benefit to territorial acquisition in the Far West. Equally important, most of the benefits they described were continental trade, land on which to relocate Indians, or potentially a new home for emancipated slaves. These predictions outnumbered those few commentators who described white settlement in the Far West.[18]

Nor did these predictions reflect concrete plans. The pragmatic goals of the pamphlets soon became clear. Once the immediate legislative needs of 1803–04 were secure, the Louisiana Purchase ceased to be a subject in the highly politicized world of newspaper and pamphlet publishing. Far from unleashing a wellspring of print culture that celebrated territorial acquisition, the Louisiana Purchase had demanded an intense but short-lived effort to build public support for the treaty and its domestic implementation. The Democratic-Republicans would soon list the purchase among the great accomplishments of the Jefferson administration, but exactly why it was so great had more to do with preserving the peace and promoting commerce in the Mississippi and Ohio valleys than with acquiring land further west.

Meanwhile, the Jefferson administration showed little interest in these published statements on Louisiana outside their immediate political benefit. They certainly did not figure in the administration's planning. Instead, the two key players in formulating a Louisiana policy—Jefferson and his secretary of state, James Madison—consulted other sources. And what they found did not please them. The existing modes of landscape description—maps, travel narratives, and history texts—undermined the administration's efforts in the Near West and warned of new dangers in the Far West.

While Congress debated the Louisiana Purchase and then sought to develop a plan for governing the Far West, Jefferson and Madison struggled to determine exactly what constituted Louisiana. Most crucially, they hoped to find evidence that the Louisiana Purchase included a legitimate claim to the Floridas. After all, the administration had pursued negotiations with France only in order to secure a cession of New Orleans and the Floridas. Their research would test the possibilities of books and maps as policymaking tools.

Unlike the three treaties of the 1790s, which had tried to define boundaries through specific geographic references, the text of the Louisiana Purchase indicated only that France sold to the United States what it had acquired from Spain in the retrocession of 1800. Jefferson and Madison both expressed their frustration over the absence of geographic specificity, and their irritation mounted as they faced the reality that their own libraries had little to offer.[19] Apparently lost on them was the fact that those very circumstances explained the treaty in the first place. Unlike the situation in London in 1794, when John Jay and Lord Grenville concluded that Faden's map had provided the means to resolve the problems left over from Mitchell's map, there was no single map that negotiators could use in Paris in 1803.

Europeans had long argued about the boundaries of Louisiana. Treaties, travel narratives, and maps had all contributed to this state of affairs. As tools of imperial policy, British, French, and Spanish maps made expansive and inevitably conflicting claims to the boundaries of Louisiana. Louisiana lacked a unifying visual descriptive text which, like Mitchell's map of 1755, could provide the consensus that would serve as the basis for American policymaking or international diplomacy. Instead, an abundance of maps produced in the eighteenth century represented profoundly different boundaries.[20]

Only a few months before news of the Louisiana Purchase reached the

United States, Jefferson had developed a course of study on western geography for Lewis. Jefferson specifically encouraged him to study the books and maps of the British explorers James Cook, Alexander Mackenzie, and George Vancouver. Jefferson also told Lewis to consult Aaron Arrowsmith's *Map Exhibiting all the New Discoveries in the Interior Parts of North America*. These materials now assume a certain primacy of place for understanding Jefferson's vision of the West, in large part because their role in planning the Lewis and Clark Expedition brought them greater attention in the midst of the bicentennial observations for the expedition (Fig. 16).[21]

Yet for all their appeal, the works of Arrowsmith, Cook, Mackenzie, and Vancouver were of little help in 1803–04, when Jefferson and Madison faced the more immediate task of establishing American claims with foreign powers and constructing a domestic policy for governing Louisiana. Arrowsmith's map offers a revealing case in point. Much as Jefferson depended on that map in planning the Lewis and Clark Expedition, it failed to assist Jefferson and Madison in their pursuit of specific boundaries for Louisiana. What international boundaries Arrowsmith did show seem intended almost more to please the eye than to satisfy diplomats. Broad stripes of green and pink provided a general indication of those places where the United States, British Canada, and Spanish North America came together. Fading at their fringes rather than presenting clear lines, these boundaries were also limited almost exclusively to waterways. As a result, a green line marks the Mississippi River as the clear western terminus of the United States, while the collision of pink and green lines on the Pacific Coast near San Francisco shows where Spanish California gave way to British Oregon.[22]

Other maps tried to show the western boundaries of Louisiana, but their estimates were so radically different that, rather than come together to constitute accuracy, their very abundance undermined any confidence that American policymakers knew the extent of their own possessions. The two maps that Americans had actively consulted in negotiations with Britain— Mitchell's 1755 map and Faden's 1793 map—were of little help, Mitchell refusing to indicate any boundary line for Louisiana, and Faden artfully avoiding the matter by including a southwestern boundary line that quite literally disappeared off the edge of the map.[23]

Equally important, the models Jefferson proposed to Lewis actually said very little about Louisiana. Cook, Mackenzie, and Vancouver all focused on northwestern territory that members of the administration specifically concluded was outside Louisiana. American maps were no better because they

Figure 16. Aaron Arrowsmith, *A Map Exhibiting all the New Discoveries in the Interior Parts of North America* . . . (London: A. Arrowsmith, 1802). Geography and Map Division,

so often followed the European, especially the British, lead. They did so because they had to: European maps remained the standard of accuracy. Duplicating them and invoking references to them were essential for Americans
hoping to establish their own claims to accuracy in a context in which the
United States had no great tradition of producing reliable maps. Jefferson
and Madison specifically avoided the emerging American trade in geographies and atlases. Much as they might have preferred American sources,
Americans had yet to provide the information that served the administration's
goals.

Bereft of a detailed description of North America that satisfied their needs,
Jefferson and Madison next turned to history. Drawing primarily on an edition of Antoine-Simon le Page du Pratz's *History of Louisiana* of 1763, they attempted to chronicle the geographic construction of western North America,
primarily through a chronology of international agreements between Britain,
France, and Spain. To this they added details from Mackenzie's narratives
and *Narrative and Topographical Description of Louisiana and West-Florida*,
a book by Thomas Hutchins, the nation's first geographer general and the
man responsible for surveying the Northwest Territory.[24] Hutchins was the
closest thing to an American source that Jefferson and Madison would use.
Yet Hutchins proved inadequate to the administration's needs. Barely a
decade after Hutchins had enjoyed a strong reputation for geographic accuracy and commitment to his adopted country, Jefferson concluded that
"Hutchins's incorrectness appears by his erroneous statemt. [statement] of
Louis XIV's grant to Crozat. his ideas & language are so loose that it would
be idle to found arguments on his *very words*." He added, "Hutchins very ig-
norant in sayg. that before 1762 Louisiana in the French maps went only to
45°. I have a map of 1720. copied from theirs & going to 60°. Mitchell's map
carries it beyond 47°."[25] Jefferson also believed "if it be our interest to give
the English a passage to the navigable water of the Missippi we shall do it as
a favor, but it is better to keep the right in our power & not to treat it away."[26]

Jefferson's and Madison's initial solution to this problem drew directly on
the experience of the 1790s. They wanted a treaty that would impose boundaries onto the landscape. Unlike the situation only a few years earlier, however, when the United States had resolved so many boundary disputes
through the three major treaties of 1794–95, none of the Europeans were willing to negotiate North American boundaries with the United States. Whatever possibility there might be for determining the western boundary of
Louisiana, the American demand for West Florida and the Spanish com-

mitment to preserving its Gulf Coast possessions soured diplomatic relations. Meanwhile, Great Britain showed no interest in beginning extensive negotiations to establish a line separating Louisiana from Canada.

By the end of 1803, the United States lacked either a treaty that would rewrite maps or a map that would inform treaties. By March 1804, Jefferson was ready to propose a broad western mapping project to help remedy this situation. His tentative plans included "the mission of Capt. Lewis" already under way as well as new expeditions to the Mississippi Valley, the central Plains, and the western fringe of the lower Mississippi Valley. All of these ventures would chart the vital waterways of the continental interior. In addition, Jefferson believed "these several surveys will enable us to prepare a map of Louisiana, which in it's contour and main waters will be perfectly correct, & will give us a skeleton to be filled up with details hereafter."[27]

Jefferson's scientific interests and his relationship to Lewis have always made the project of western exploration appear uniquely Jeffersonian. By 1804, however, this was hardly the case. After years in which Congress had balked at funding even a single major expedition, it now supported a set of major expeditions. The reason was simple: describing the West had become a crucial facet of foreign and domestic policy. The United States could not settle its boundaries with the Europeans or establish a government for its expanded territory until the federal government knew just what the United States had acquired from France. The United States was now in the business of landscape description.

INSTRUCTIONS

In 1804, Clark devised a set of "inquiries relitive to the *Indians* of Louisiania."[28] It marked the beginning of a concerted interest in Indian culture, in many ways an early form of ethnography, that remained with Clark throughout his life. It was also a far cry from the terms he used to write about Indians in the 1790s. Of the ten general categories in his list of "inquiries," Clark listed "War" seventh, a remarkable shift from a written record which, to that point, had always associated Indians first and foremost with violence and warfare. This was less the result of a change of heart than of a change of writing. Clark wrote that list in response to instructions, whether by that he meant the orders he received from his superiors or the education he was receiving from the people who helped plan the Lewis and Clark Expedition. Nor was he alone. In 1803 and 1804, the small group of men who came to constitute

Jefferson's cadre of explorers received a similar set of instructions for a grand mapping project in the Far West.

The most famous of those instructions can also be the most misleading. On June 20, 1803, only one day after Lewis had written to Clark inviting him to join the expedition, Jefferson presented Lewis with a lengthy set of instructions. Although Jefferson's general goals remained intact, both Lewis and Jefferson's planning for the expedition underwent important changes in the nine months between news of the Louisiana Purchase in July 1803 and the Lewis and Clark Expedition's departure from St. Louis in May 1804.

Jefferson's instructions to Lewis of June 20, 1803, are a treasure trove. Focused yet thorough, they provide invaluable details about the president's goals for the expedition and his approach to science. They framed Lewis's thinking throughout the expedition, especially when it came to how best to describe the land through which he traveled. But they do not capture how Jefferson came to conceive of western exploration in the years after 1803, nor were they the only guide that informed the actions of Lewis, Clark, and the rest of Jefferson's western explorers.

Jefferson's instructions were an eighteenth-century document, reflecting not only principles of science and political economy rooted in the Enlightenment, but also the geopolitical conditions of eighteenth-century North America. For example, on July 13, 1803, Caspar Wistar raised an obvious question in a letter to Jefferson when he wondered "if the expedition should go on without any change in the original plan, in Consequence of the late happy events respecting Louisiana."[29] Wistar was a Philadelphia physician and a member of the cohort of intellectuals who Jefferson trusted in his planning for western exploration. Yet Jefferson never answered Wistar's question, even when Wistar's subsequent letters included reminders that ranged from subtle to obvious. Jefferson and Lewis made passing reference to the purchase but never corresponded about its implications for the expedition.[30]

Only in November 1803, less than a month after Congress approved the Louisiana Purchase, did Jefferson send Lewis an additional set of instructions reflecting the nineteenth-century reality of a United States transformed by territorial expansion. "As the boundaries of interior Louisiana are the *high lands inclosing all the waters which run into the Missisipi or Missouri directly or indirectly,* with a greater breadth on the Gulf of Mexico," Jefferson explained, "it becomes interesting to fix with precision by celestial observation the longitude & latitude of the sources of these rivers, and furnishing points in the contour of our new limits." Jefferson considered this geographic information "as of major importance, & therefore not to be delayed or hazarded by any episodes whatever."[31] This was fundamentally a set of mapmaking instructions, in sharp contrast to the diverse objectives of his earlier instructions. It also continued the task of establishing "Clear and Indisputable Boundaries" that the Continental Congress had sought in the 1770s.

Jefferson's letter of November 1803 had done what his instructions of June 1803 could not: directly connect the Lewis and Clark Expedition to matters of imminent national concern. The need for cartographic knowledge of the new national domain, demographic knowledge of the residents over whom the United States now claimed sovereignty, and environmental knowledge about the land where Americans might someday live combined with no less important suggestions about how best to gather, compile, and present that information.

The topics Jefferson introduced in his June 1803 instructions provided a template that the federal government would apply to other western expeditions in the years ahead. In the summer of 1803, Jefferson dispatched a series of queries to a few trusted contacts in the West. Written after news of the Louisiana Purchase had reached the United States, these queries were primarily concerned with demography, trade, borders, and military affairs in Louisiana. In other words, Jefferson was asking pragmatic questions about a place the United States needed to govern, not abstract scientific questions to satisfy his personal interests. In his own "inquiries relitive to the *Indians* of Louisiania" Clark framed his questions in a similar manner.[32]

Not only did Jefferson pursue information from a broad range of sources, but he was also planning a course of western exploration that extended far beyond Lewis and Clark. In the summer of 1804 William Dunbar planned a brief excursion up the Red River to the hot springs at the upper Ouachita River. Jefferson proposed a more ambitious project to further ascend the Red River under the leadership of Thomas Freeman. In the summer of 1805, General James Wilkinson, the senior military official in the West, planned two expeditions, one to the "Head of the Mississippi and the other for the Osage Towns."[33] Both would establish contacts with Indians and identify potential military forts for the United States. He quickly selected one of his junior officers, Zebulon Pike, to begin planning the expedition up the Mississippi.

All of these projects proceeded with similar instructions. Although informed to varying degrees by Jefferson's personal interest in science, all of the expeditions were, first and foremost, supposed to gather the geographic information that would enable the United States to determine the boundaries of Louisiana and to establish vital commercial and diplomatic ties with the Indians of the Far West. Jefferson's instructions to Freeman began in blunt terms. "The government of the US. being desirous of informing itself of the content of the country lately ceded to them under the name of Louisiana," he explained, "to wit the same, with it's principal rivers, geographically delineated to learn the character of it's soil, climate, productions, & inhabitants."[34]

Wilkinson wrote his own set of instructions for Pike's mission up the Mississippi River. In the process of establishing outposts and negotiating with Indians, Pike would "be pleased to take the course of the River and calculate distances by time, noting rivers, creeks, Highlands, Prairies, Islands, rapids, shoals, mines, Quarries, Timer, water Soil, Indian Villages and Settlements, in a Diary to comprehend reflections on the wind and weather."[35] Pike's primary task was one of negotiation, perhaps with Europeans but certainly with Indians. That broader vision of Indian negotiation serves as an important context for understanding the Lewis and Clark Expedition in particular and federal Indian policy in general. Among the most oft-cited and actively debated passages in Jefferson's instructions of June 1803 to Lewis was his injunction that Lewis "in all your intercourse with the natives, treat them in the most friendly & conciliatory manner which their own conduct will admit." This has always been an appealing passage for those wishing to claim that Jefferson sought interracial peace in the West. Likewise, it has seemed disingenuous at best and manipulative at worst to those explaining a broader Anglo-American project of Indian abuse in which Jefferson actively participated. After all, only four months earlier Jefferson had instructed William Henry Harrison, the governor of the Indiana Territory, to take a hard line with Indians, explaining that "our strength and their weakness is now so visible that they must see we have only to shut our hand to crush them, and that all our liberalities to them proceed from motives of pure humanity only."[36]

Wilkinson's instructions addressed the pragmatic objectives of borderland diplomacy that were of primary concern to officials in the West as well as to the federal leadership in Washington. Located in St. Louis, Wilkinson may have been a thousand miles from Jefferson and he may not have shared Jefferson's scientific inclinations, but both men believed that western landscape description could solve the same problems of domestic governance and international relations.

LEADERS

Clark did not meet all of Jefferson's explorers, but he would have understood them. The men who led the Jefferson administration's expeditions into
the Far West all sought membership in a broader national community that
would bring immediate benefits to them. For some, that meant appointment
in the western bureaucracy, civil or military. For others, it meant membership
in the nation's community of scientists and intellectuals. But regardless of
their specific occupations, they all sought the connections that would prevent them from being relegated to static anonymity.

Dunbar and Freeman, whom Jefferson tapped to lead expeditions up the
Red River, offer similar cases in point. Both came from the fringes of the
British Isles, Freeman from Ireland and Dunbar from Scotland, before pursuing very divergent routes that would end in their collaboration in western
exploration. Dunbar was born into a wealthy family, while the limited docu-
mentation on Freeman's early life suggests he came from more modest
means. Dunbar completed a university degree, studying science and mathematics, before moving first to Philadelphia in 1771 and later to West Florida,
where he became a successful planter and merchant. Freeman immigrated
to the United States and struggled to find work as a surveyor until finally becoming employed as a land agent for George Washington in the years immediately after the Revolution.[37] During the 1790s, it was surveying that
enabled Dunbar and Freeman to refashion their identities. Dunbar became
increasingly prominent and well connected with the Spanish administration
and eventually became surveyor general for West Florida. Freeman earned
Washington's favor and was eventually employed on the survey for the new
federal capital on the banks of the Potomac.

While both men participated in the technical process of surveying, they
did so from very different intellectual and institutional traditions. When the
Treaty of San Lorenzo transformed much of Spanish West Florida into the
Mississippi Territory in the United States, science provided the means for
Dunbar to reinvent himself once again, this time as an American citizen. A
shared commitment to science immediately made Dunbar one of the few
men whom Jefferson trusted in the Southwest. Occasionally at odds with
other Mississippi planters and with the territorial government, Dunbar always
enjoyed a close relationship with the president.[38] Along the way, he had managed to build inroads with the American Philosophical Society through correspondence on subjects ranging from southwestern ecology to the remains

of wooly mammoths. As a result, by 1803 he was one of the few people Jefferson trusted to supply reliable information on the landscape of the lower Mississippi Valley.[39]

In 1804 Jefferson selected George Hunter to join Dunbar for the Ouachita River Expedition. He hoped Hunter would serve with Freeman for the Red River Expedition of 1806, but Hunter lost interest in the project and was replaced by Peter Custis. Like Dunbar, Hunter and Custis had impeccable scientific credentials. Like Dunbar, Hunter was a Scot who had migrated to the United States through Philadelphia, where (unlike Dunbar) he chose to stay. Trained as a chemist, he had made brief trips through the Ohio River Valley. Custis came from prominent American stock. Born in Virginia into a family that boasted kinship with members of the state and national elite, including Washington and Jefferson, Custis was completing medical studies in Philadelphia in 1806 when Jefferson selected him to replace Hunter for the Red River Expedition.[40]

In stark contrast, during the twenty years between his private service for Washington and his public service to Jefferson, Freeman's models for describing the West were not the enlightened thinkers who influenced Jefferson's views on how to plan western expeditions and record their results or Dunbar on his road to social connection. Rather, Freeman looked to other surveyors, men who had found ways to combine the process of writing books and creating maps with the equally challenging task of establishing their reputations and advancing their careers.

Dunbar, Hunter, and Custis all sought membership in a broader community of scientists. Freeman, Lewis, Clark, and Pike all sought membership in the federal bureaucracy. Whereas the foreign-born Freeman used federal patronage to advance his entree to American society, Lewis, Clark, and Pike saw the expeditions as a sure way to move out of the shadows. All three men struggled with the considerable legacies of heroes from the Revolution who nonetheless had never realized the promise of independence. Lewis's father was a lieutenant in the Continental Army who died from illness in 1779 when his son was only five years old. George Rogers Clark may have survived the Revolution, but he never tired of telling his younger brother William of how federal leaders had betrayed him, even after Clark had delivered the Illinois Country to the United States. Like George Rogers Clark, Pike's father and namesake had served in the Revolution, and, although still in uniform in 1806, he was an aging major whose promotion was stalled by illness and injury.

As the explorers received their instructions from 1803 to 1805, they all believed that describing the Far West would create very specific opportunities. Nobody knew this better than Andrew Ellicott, the one man who connected most of these explorers. Ellicott was a skilled surveyor who enjoyed public employment most of his life. Patronage from both Benjamin Franklin and Thomas Jefferson helped Ellicott secure the coveted post of chief surveyor for the federal capital, where one of his subordinates was Thomas Freeman. Ellicott was so impressed that he selected Freeman as his immediate subordinate on the Southwest survey in 1798 designed to determine the new boundary established by the Treaty of San Lorenzo. Among Ellicott's antagonists was none other than William Dunbar, who served as one of the Spanish commissioners and was keen to ingratiate himself with Ellicott's nemesis, the Spanish official Manuel Gayoso de Lemos. Gayoso de Lemos later wrote fawning letters to Dunbar, admiring his scientific acumen and thanking him for his assistance with the Americans. Only three years earlier, Gayoso de Lemos had confronted Clark as he descended the Mississippi near the Chickasaw Bluffs.[41]

By 1803 Ellicott was in Lancaster, Pennsylvania and held the post of secretary for the Public Land Office in Pennsylvania. When Jefferson asked Ellicott to train Lewis in celestial observation and land navigation, Ellicott immediately informed the president that "I shall be very happy to see Captn. Lewis, and will with pleasure give him all the information, and instruction in my power."[42] He was keen to ingratiate himself with the new administration, and certainly had no affection for Jefferson's predecessor. Ellicott had recently completed a book, *The Journal of Andrew Ellicott*, which recounted his adventures on the southwestern boundary survey. This was only the latest travel narrative to describe a fundamentally dangerous West. Likewise, it announced Ellicott's personal talents in overcoming the threats of an unfamiliar landscape and a contested diplomatic terrain.[43] The book was released only after delays occasioned by the Adams administration, which, fearful that Ellicott would divulge confidential government correspondence, had sought to restrict its publication. Always ambitious and possessing a keen understanding of how landscape description could build political connections, Ellicott knew better than to refuse Jefferson's request to train Lewis.

DEPARTURES

Clark apparently never met Ellicott, in part because he needed no specialized training as a surveyor. Clark already possessed those skills. Instead, he proceeded straight to Louisville, crossing the Ohio River to Clarksville, a town in the Indiana Territory named for George Rogers Clark and located on some of the land that Virginia had awarded to his men during the Revolution. When Lewis arrived in October, Clark could lay claim to being the expert on the West and on landscape description.

Clark displayed his knowledge and his skills when he drew the Grand Tower as the expedition reached the confluence of the Mississippi and the Ohio rivers. It was the first in a series of drawings Clark made. The keelboat that was the largest of the vessels in which the expedition traveled was the subject of another drawing. One of the most abundantly reproduced visual images of the expedition, it bore considerable similarity to Clark's sketch of Gayoso de Lemos's galley in 1795 (Fig. 17).

In November, the men who had joined Captain Lewis's Expedition (as it had become known in the national press) built a winter camp on the eastern banks of the Mississippi River, waiting not only for warmer weather but also for the formal transfer of Louisiana to the United States. That process began in December 1803, when the United States took charge in lower Louisiana, an area corresponding roughly to what is now the state of Louisiana. Everything else the United States had acquired, a vast swath of the Far West, was the subject of a formal transfer ceremony in March 1804. Clark was on hand in St. Louis to participate in the ceremonies.

Throughout these months, Clark harbored a lingering resentment at the way he was treated by the federal government. In August 1803, Jefferson captured Clark's sentiments when he wrote to Secretary of War Henry Dearborn that "William Clarke accepts with great glee the office of going with Capt. Lewis up the Missouri."[44] Perhaps so, but Dearborn, rejecting the captain's commission that Clark had achieved in the 1790s and that would have put him on a par with Lewis, soon concluded that Clark could reenter the ranks of government appointees only as a first lieutenant in the army. Jefferson was not prepared to overturn this decision. After all, he always imagined this as Lewis's expedition, with Clark serving as a fellow officer but clearly a subordinate. Besides, Jefferson knew better than to upset the status-conscious members of the army officer corps, who were quick to complain when elected officials interfered with the army's internal procedures for promotion and advancement. Although Lewis immediately referred to Clark as cocaptain, a gesture for which Clark was instantly and eternally grateful, this sign of respect came only after a rough lesson in the workings of federal patronage and political influence.[45]

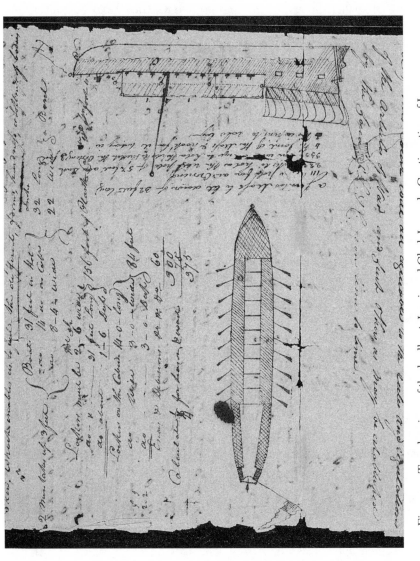

Figure 17. Two drawings of the keelboat, Lewis and Clark Journals, Continuation of January 17–January 20, 1804. Yale Collection of Western Americana, Beinecke Rare Book and Manuscript

Meanwhile, Clark began keeping a journal, following Jefferson's orders but drawing on the experience of writing he had developed throughout his adult life. There were no references to Dearborn's decision or to Clark's feelings in general. Instead, this was a technical journal, one in which the land, rather than Clark, was the principal subject. On May 14, 1804, the date historians now consider the official beginning of the Lewis and Clark Expedition, Clark simply recorded, "Set out from Camp River a Dubois at 4 oClock P. M. and proceded up the Missouris under Sail to the first Island in the Missouri and Camped on the upper point opposit a Creek on the South Side below a ledge of limestone rock Called Colewater, made 4½ miles." When it came to the membership of the expedition, he listed the total number of men and added, "men in high Spirits."[46]

And then Clark disappeared. He was not the only one. From 1804 to 1806, four federal expeditions disappeared into the West. Hunter and Dunbar, Lewis and Clark, Zebulon Pike, and Freeman and Custis began their journeys. Bits of information drifted back to Washington in both private and official correspondence. Stories from various sources (some more dubious than others) appeared in newspapers. But Americans concluded that a full reckoning of the explorers' experiences—or even knowledge of their survival— would have to await their return.

Part II

A World Explored

4

EXPLORERS

When the explorers returned, they had a story to tell. William Clark certainly did, although telling it pushed him to the limits of his abilities.

As he traveled through the Far West, Clark carried with him the bits and pieces of a story. In a series of small notebooks, he scribbled records of the daily activities of the expedition, coordinates of longitude and latitude, descriptions of flora and fauna, and observations on the residents of the Far West. So, too, did Meriwether Lewis and five other members of the expedition: Sergeants Charles Floyd, Patrick Gass, and John Ordway and Privates Joseph Whitehouse and Robert Frazer. Meanwhile, Jefferson's other explorers—Hunter and Dunbar, Freeman and Custis, and Zebulon Pike—had their own journals and their own stories to tell.

In the end, it was Clark's journals that shaped the ways Americans understood western exploration. That seems odd today, since Lewis is often treated as the official voice of the expedition or, for that matter, of all western exploration. But Clark was a more voluminous writer than Lewis, who apparently did not keep a journal during extended periods of the expedition. Drawing on an experience of journal writing he had first demonstrated in the raids of 1789 and 1791, Clark found it easy to follow Jefferson's instructions and kept a meticulous account of daily events. Over the course of the expedition, on only ten days did Clark fail to leave a written record. It was a remarkable achievement for a man who, throughout this period, never considered himself a writer.

The same could be said of all of the journal writers, who were hardly members of the nation's literary class. And yet this sort of material would have made perfect sense to many people engaged in the task of settling and mapping the North American West. These notes were the logical extension of the sorts of materials surveyors had always kept.

Interspersed among Clark's notes were numerous area maps and local surveys, many of them similar to the sketch of the Grand Tower he had drawn in 1803. One of the illustrations included the approaches to the Great Falls of the Missouri River, including Clark's sketches of the Missouri, his list of where the expedition camped, and various navigation sightings (Fig. 18).

When Clark reached the Great Falls on June 17, he described "a Sucession of rapids & Cascades to the Falls, which we had herd for Several miles makeing a dedly Sound, I beheld those Cateracts with astonishment." Whatever his astonishment, however, he estimated distances across the river and recorded in technical detail his effort to approach the falls. This was a far cry from the journal of Lewis, who had reached the same place four days earlier. Lewis wrote one of his most eloquent and expressive journal entries, describing his struggle to give "the enlightened world some just idea of this truly magnifficent and sublimely grand object, which has from the commencement of time been concealed from the view of civilized man; but this was fruitless and vain."[1]

Lewis's passage remains one of the most oft-cited selections from the journals of the Lewis and Clark Expedition. Clark limited his written and visual account to the technical matters of surveying. Whatever their differences of expression, both men sought to answer the same, deceptively simple question: what made for an accurate representation of the landscape? Clark never engaged the metaphysical implications of that question. He simply relied on the style of landscape representation he had used throughout his life, using surveying and mapmaking to describe what he had seen.

Lewis's and Clark's competing descriptions of the Great Falls form part of the larger written record that now goes under various names, most commonly "the journals of Lewis and Clark." Those manuscript journals primarily serve to let contemporary readers relive the events of the Lewis and Clark Expedition. Now available in various edited editions, the journals are a treasure trove of information on everything from science to American Indian life to the preconceptions of white observers like Lewis and Clark. The definitive edition, created by a team at the University of Nebraska under the direction of Gary Moulton, provides a model of deep research and careful editing. Yet the very capacity of those journals to tell such a remarkable story creates an enormous problem. Looking backward, informed by the work of editors and historians, the journals create a narrative of a single Lewis and Clark Expedition. Indeed, one of the primary tasks of editors has been to impose coherence and remove ambiguity from the manuscript journals. The actions and meanings

Figure 18. Route about May 29–June 11, 1805. Yale Collection of Western Americana, Beinecke Rare Book and Manuscript Library, Yale University.

of the expedition seem clear to Americans today, and by implication they appeared clear to Americans two centuries ago.

Clark certainly did not see things that way, nor for that matter did the other explorers who traveled west at Jefferson's behest. Understanding how Americans conceived of the Far West—and how American explorers like Clark conceived of themselves—begins with encountering Jefferson's western expeditions the way most Americans did: through the slow process of publication. That process started before many of the expeditions were completed, and it was often outside the explorers' control. The explorers, the correspondents with whom they exchanged letters, the editors who publicized accounts of the expeditions, and the disparate observers who read those accounts all struggled to make sense of the West. Before anybody read the manuscript journals of Lewis or Clark, published accounts had given the Lewis and Clark Expedition its name and its meaning. Those accounts had also described the Far West in familiar terms. The United States might claim the West, but it did not control it. The West might create opportunities, but it remained a place of danger.

Throughout these years, the meaning of those expeditions and of the West took form within changing global circumstances. Jefferson's explorers helped propel the United States to the brink of war. They also failed in their task of asserting clear federal sovereignty in Louisiana. Clark worried about threats he himself had helped to create. Yet he was among the great beneficiaries, finding not only employment but his own identity as somebody the United States could trust to face those challenges.

NEWS FROM THE WEST

Clark began telling his story of the expedition even before he returned. In this project he was hardly alone, because all of Jefferson's explorers attempted to interpret what they had seen in the West. But their ability to do so responded to the particulars of print culture and the circulation of knowledge in the early Republic. Those first reports told a story of high adventure for the explorers themselves but had little to say about the potential for white settlement in the Far West.

In the last week of March and the first week of April 1805, Lewis and Clark dispatched nine letters, three by Lewis and six by Clark.[2] They wrote from Fort Mandan, a rudimentary outpost where Lewis, Clark, and the men under their command had spent the winter of 1804–05. The fort took its name from the nearby Mandan villages, which commanded the Missouri River in what is now North Dakota.

Both men wrote to Jefferson, but they also wrote to friends and family. And the nine letters were almost identical. Not only did Clark often repeat material from one letter to the next, but he and Lewis had clearly prepared the letters together.[3] To this package Clark added a map that he had worked on for months. On January 5, 1805, what Clark called "a cold day . . . [with] Some Snow," he stated that "I imploy my Self drawing a Connection of the Countrey from what information I have recved."[4] In his first attempt to describe the territory west of the Mississippi, Clark relied on many of the tried-and-true cartographic methods that Europeans and Euro-Americans had applied to North America. Clark combined his own surveys of the Missouri with other European maps and with information he had acquired from Indians to create a single portrait of the North American West. The nine letters from Lewis and Clark have survived to this day. But Clark's map is gone.

Lewis and Clark bundled their written reports together with numerous scientific samples and sent them down the Missouri River. Selecting the men who would deliver those materials to St. Louis also gave Lewis and Clark an easy means to prune out the men who seemed unreliable, preserving a hand-picked cadre to continue west. The scientific materials went to Jefferson, but the written reports soon entered the public domain.

These letters provide a revealing indication of the collaborative working relationship between Lewis and Clark, but their circulation offers an equally telling story about the distribution of knowledge. In the late summer of 1805, Americans slowly began learning of "Captain Lewis's" expedition up the Missouri River through these reports. In November 1805, at least half a dozen newspapers reprinted a letter "from a gentleman in the Indiana Territory."[5] The gentleman was most likely William Henry Harrison, the recipient of one of Clark's letters. Better known now as the aging president who died in 1841 a month after delivering the longest inaugural in U.S. presidential history, in 1805 Harrison was the youthful governor of the Indiana Territory. Harrison began his career in the U.S. Army, serving alongside Lewis and Clark in the brutal military campaign to assert control of the Northwest Territory during the 1790s. Like Lewis and Clark, he came from the Virginia gentry, and like both of them he hoped to make his name through federal appointment in the West. Harrison and Clark struck up an early friendship in the 1790s that remained in place in the years that followed.

Still other letters, usually from Clark rather than Lewis, found their way into print. A letter to Clark's brother Jonathan attracted as much press as his letter to Harrison.[6] When the editors of the *Political Observatory* sought to explain how news of the West reached the isolated corner of Walpole, New Hampshire, they detailed a tortuous path through which "letters were received from Capt. Clark to his correspondents in Kentucky. A gentleman from Jefferson county, has obligingly favored the edition of the Kentucky Gazette with the following account," which in turn was reprinted by the *Political Observatory.*[7]

Many of these newspaper accounts did exactly what Lewis and Clark wanted. The two had worked carefully to make certain their reports to public officials and personal associates created a uniform story of the West. Lewis and Clark also sought uniformity because they had a keen awareness of how news traveled in the United States. In an era before newspapers hired their own reporters, they printed and reprinted the reports of public officials and private citizens. Lewis and Clark knew that private letters often became public. They also knew that any one of their letters might not reach its intended recipient, who in turn would need to depend on one of the other letters for information. As a result, the Lewis and Clark Expedition first took shape in the American imagination through newspapers that reported on the expedition's activities and later celebrated its leaders when they returned.[8]

This does not mean that Lewis and Clark conspired in some sophisticated project of relating a self-serving story. They certainly wanted to provide Jefferson with detailed answers to his questions. And they were eager to inform their friends and family that they were safe. The reason they collaborated in all their writing was to prevent errors and to share information. That said, their correspondence is nonetheless striking for its unwavering message of success. Repeating each other almost verbatim, these preliminary accounts told a consistent story of the West in 1805.

The accounts also began the process of elevating Clark's notoriety and social standing. It was Clark's letter to Kentucky rather than Lewis's report to Washington that received the widest distribution in 1805. Better yet, these accounts always referred to him as Captain Clark. Whether they were referring to the title Lewis used in discussing his cocaptain or to the highest rank Clark had received in the 1790s did not matter. The newspapers were ignoring the snub Clark perceived in the decision by Secretary of War Henry Dearborn to grant Clark only a lieutenant's commission. These reports also celebrated the leadership of Lewis and Clark: "The greatest friendship has existed with the party; and the men who have returned speak in the highest terms of the humanity, and uncommon pains and attention of both the captains, Lewis and Clark, towards the whole of them."[9]

The accounts of 1805 began the process of introducing what eventually became the most prominent features of the American story of Lewis and Clark, features that have remained in place for two centuries. For example, those accounts highlighted the friendly collaboration between Lewis and Clark, the easy camaraderie within the expedition, the defiance of the Sioux villagers of the mid-Missouri Valley followed by the welcoming embrace of the Mandan and Hidatsa. Some of these stories have withstood close scrutiny. Every shred of evidence indicates that Lewis and Clark did indeed become each other's best friend. That friendship in turn contributed to an effective leadership collaboration. Likewise, the expedition as a whole cohered over the course of 1804 and 1805. After initial disputes by enlisted men that Lewis and Clark believed was best handled by strict discipline—including corporal punishment—the expedition became a cohesive team. Meanwhile, it seems clear that Lewis and Clark shrewdly negotiated their way through the complex Indian diplomatic landscape.

In other areas, however, the reports contained gross errors. Some of these were scientific errors that reflected the beliefs and knowledge of the early American Republic. More striking are the erroneous conclusions about American Indians. Although they recorded events in remarkable detail, the explorers always interpreted those events through a specific cultural lens that reinforced their own beliefs in the cultural supremacy of Anglo-Americans and the uncivilized life of Indians. While the explorers became increasingly sympathetic toward Indians, they nonetheless returned from the journey still convinced of their own superiority. Likewise, the journals described Indians who challenged federal claims to the West as duplicitous, dangerous, and treacherous. The journals touted those who welcomed the explorers as industrious and rational.[10]

The experience of Clark—or, rather, the news of Clark—also captured the ways in which Americans first learned details of the West acquired through the Louisiana Purchase. Lewis's and Clark's expedition may have disappeared, but news of its activities was just beginning to make an impact. Meanwhile, that news was surrounded by other stories of western exploration.

In the spring of 1805, newspapers throughout the United States reported that the Hunter-Dunbar expedition had "completed the object of their mission, and have procured materials for an accurate chart of the river, and the immediate country it passes through. The doctor [Dunbar] gives a flattering account of the country . . . He found a great variety of soil and situation."[11]

And in one of the rare examples of unqualified celebration for the western landscape, a newspaper article of 1805 recounted Hunter's belief that the soil was "generally fertile and capable of the highest cultivation." This article ran in the *Orleans Gazette*, published in nearby New Orleans, a place where local boosters were keen to celebrate the productive capacity of the lower Mississippi Valley.[12]

Accounts of Pike's Mississippi Expedition told a similar story of success, in no small part through Pike's efforts. On April 18, 1806, as Pike was still descending the Mississippi, he drafted a lengthy report to his commander, General James Wilkinson, that emphasized Pike's leadership, his fortitude in trying physical circumstances, and his commitment to national objectives. Indians played a crucial role in announcing Pike's bravery and linking his own honor to that of the nation: "Indeed, Sir, the insolence of the savages in this quarter is unbounded; and unless an immediate example is made, we shall certainly be obliged to enter in a general war with them."[13] Pike arrived in St. Louis on April 30, 1806, and newspapers soon reported on the expedition in the terms Pike first introduced.[14]

In June 1806, less than two months after returning from the Mississippi Expedition, Pike was hard at work on what would become the fifth western expedition during the Jefferson administration. He had a new set of instructions, signed by Wilkinson but written by Pike himself. Although Pike and Wilkinson developed the specific wording of the instructions, the Jefferson administration approved of the venture. Pike was to ascend the Arkansas River. Like Lewis and Clark, he was supposed to make federal sovereignty a reality in the Far West by securing cartographic knowledge and pledges of fealty from Indian villages.[15]

In February 1806, before many of these reports even arrived, Jefferson had already announced western exploration a success. He was writing to his associates in the scientific community, distributing selected morsels of information from Lewis and Clark.[16] He also submitted a lengthy report to the House of Representatives that combined Lewis's and Clark's report from Fort Mandan, Hunter's and Dunbar's report, and a report from John Sibley (an Indian agent and trained physician stationed in Natchitoches, an old settlement located just east of the contested Red River borderland). As Jefferson obviously intended, the document was immediately released to the public. In his

covering letter, he continued to characterize western exploration as fundamentally commercial, diplomatic, and cartographic.[17]

As far as Jefferson was concerned at this time the best was yet to come. He
eagerly awaited additional news from Lewis and Clark. Dunbar and Hunter
and Pike had established a model for the successful survey of the western waterways. Freeman and Custis were also ready to begin their expedition up the
Red River, and Pike was soon preparing to ascend the Arkansas. While all of
these expeditions reflected the scientific interests of Jefferson and his intellectual cohort, they also presented the chance for a policymaking breakthrough. A broad topographical survey of the Far West would provide the
cartographic details that Americans so desperately needed in their efforts to
negotiate the boundaries of Louisiana. A broad demographic survey would
further help the federal government secure its authority in the Far West. A
broad set of preliminary negotiations with Indians would enable the United
States to begin the process of securing sovereignty over the people who controlled the Far West.

THE END OF EXPLORATION

It was in these circumstances that news began circulating from St. Louis
in late September 1806 that Lewis and Clark had returned. Americans celebrated not only Lewis and Clark, but also the Jefferson administration's grand
plan to survey the Far West and to make federal sovereignty a reality. Within
months, all those ambitions were suddenly, dramatically gone. Jefferson's visions of mapping the Far West had collapsed. Clark—along with Jefferson's
other explorers—had contributed to that danger, although they did not know
they had done so. More important, Jefferson never could admit it, either to
himself or to others. Yet from 1804 to 1806, the effort to map the West helped
propel the United States to the brink of war.

Clark had staked his future on the expedition he had joined alongside
Lewis. Unknown to Clark, the Spanish contemplated the mission with considerable anxiety, in large part because they did not see it in isolation. The
Spanish were convinced that Americans were an expansionistic lot bound
and determined to extend their control into the Far West. This perspective
first led the Spanish to reject the American request for a passport for Lewis to
lead an expedition while Spain still governed Louisiana. The Spanish interpreted the Louisiana Purchase and western explorations as Americans them-

selves later did: as the expansionist policy of an expansionist culture. Completely unaware of the administration's concerns about expansion, the Spanish nonetheless drew a reasonable conclusion. They responded accordingly, dispatching troops to stop not only Lewis and Clark but also the expeditions under Freeman and Custis and Pike.[18]

If the Spanish were unable to locate Lewis and Clark as they passed through the North, they were far more successful in the South. Spanish troops intercepted Freeman and Custis, who wisely ordered their men to reverse course and return to New Orleans. In February 1807, the Spanish found Pike and his men, who had mistaken the Rio Grande for the Arkansas River, traveling into Spanish Mexico rather than back toward the United States. Unlike Freeman and Custis, who were allowed to return home without delay, Pike and his men were imprisoned in Mexico City before American protests finally secured their release and a return to the United States in August 1807.

The Spanish considered themselves confirmed in their suspicions of American adventurism. Meanwhile, American newspapers circulated news of these developments in dire terms that contradicted the reports of success that greeted Lewis and Clark. Jefferson himself had considered western exploration to be a reasonable exercise in surveying and science. He failed to perceive how the Spanish could perceive these expeditions as the provocative acts of a hostile nation.[19]

Throughout 1806 and 1807, American, Spanish, and Indian leaders struggled to broker an uneasy peace. In Washington, the Jefferson administration abandoned its belligerence toward Spain. In Madrid, Spanish officials sent orders to their subordinates in North America to remain vigilant but concluded that military conflict was unlikely. On the borderlands, Indian leaders effectively manipulated these circumstances to preserve their own autonomy while avoiding the open warfare that would inevitably consume their villages.[20]

The most important decision Jefferson made was to abandon western exploration altogether, for it was western exploration which had done so much to spike tensions. Jefferson also had other concerns that consumed his attention. Convinced that Aaron Burr, Jefferson's vice president from 1801 to 1805, had launched a separatist scheme in the Southwest, Jefferson sought to crush any threats to the Union in the West.[21] In June 1807, the British warship *Leopard* fired on the American *Chesapeake*, killing three men and wounding eighteen others, before British marines forcibly removed four men they suspected of being deserters from the Royal Navy. In preparation for the war with Great Britain that seemed imminent, Congress authorized an embargo of all foreign trade that would keep American ships safely at home before the fighting erupted. As federal policymakers realized the futility of launching any military operations against Great Britain, the Jefferson administration opted to preserve the embargo as a form of commercial coercion it hoped would force the British to capitulate. The embargo proved to be a disaster, nearly ruining the American economy while failing to cause any real hardship in Great Britain. But it did reorient federal concerns from the West to the East and forced the United States to abandon its aggressive posture toward Spain.[22]

As a result, by the end of 1807 the federal government was out of the business of exploring the West, and not a moment too soon for most of the explorers. They already had their sights set on other objectives, not the least of which was to tell the story of their experiences in the West. Freeman and Custis had already delivered their report to Jefferson. Pike soon began work on a book that would chronicle both of his expeditions as well as his imprisonment in Mexico. When Clark finally returned from his travels to the Far West, he found that his efforts to write and draw the landscape were inseparable from his role in responding to the domestic and international threats facing the United States. Clark also concluded that describing the West could serve the United States, just as the threats in the West could serve his own future.

"THE INCLUDED COMMISSION HAVEING ANSWERED THE PURPOSE FOR WHICH IT WAS INTENDED, I TAKE THE LIBERTY OF RETURNING IT TO YOU"

Writing to Jefferson from Fort Mandan in 1805, Clark had explained, "It being the wish of Capt. Lewis, I take the liberty to send you for your own perusal, the notes which I have taken in the form of a journal in their original state." Lewis's wishes indeed. Clark kept a draft of his letter, which included extensive alterations by Lewis. Clark acknowledged that "many parts are incorrect, owing to the variety of information received at different times," but he was eager to send news nonetheless.[23]

This seems the typically cautious language of Clark. Yet it was also a common statement reaching Jefferson from the West in 1805 and 1806. Clark used what would become the standard formula that American explorers deployed in their initial attempts to interpret what they had seen.[24] None of Jefferson's explorers wrote in ignorance of the public circumstances that surrounded them. First and foremost, they were writing to their superiors in Washington in the hope of establishing themselves as reliable public servants. Second, they correctly assumed that their reports would soon appear in print.

These preliminary reports all described the Far West as a place of remarkable danger. The premature end to the Freeman and Custis Expedition and to Pike's Arkansas Expedition, the numerous reports of interception by Europeans and Indians, the accounts of great mountain ranges, all of these details combined to cast the Far West in remarkably unpleasant terms. Lewis's and Clark's reports from Fort Mandan listed a generally fertile landscape and a booming Indian trade in the lower Missouri Valley, yet these were the exceptions that proved the rule. Most of the reports—especially the newspaper accounts—had little to say about the prospects for settlement. Instead, they described hostile Indians as well as the competition from European merchants and the imperial governments that supported them.

The rushed preliminary reports established the explorers as men of action. Subsequent reports established them as men of science or diplomacy. Whether they traveled through frigid mountains or fetid bayous, whether they encountered peaceful Indians or belligerent Spaniards, the explorers all told a story of triumphs. Their victories were varied: victory over diplomatic adversity; victory over the landscape; victory in the acquisition of knowledge; and victory over ignorance itself. The result was an inherently contradictory story of the West. At one moment, the Far West remained dangerous and uninviting, its landscape almost insurmountable to even the most resolute adventurers. At another, the Far West had created a new cadre of heroic Americans, servants of the federal government who could overcome the greatest challenges.

It was Pike who announced those victories in the most unequivocal terms. Writing in May 1806 to his friend and fellow officer Daniel Bissell at the end of the Mississippi Expedition of 1805–06, Pike announced, "I arrived her on the 30 Ulto. Having succeeded in the principal objects of my voyage, and explored the source of the Mississippi."[25]

Clark understood Pike's language, in no small part because he shared Pike's ambition for advancement within the federal system. Like Pike, Clark was busy, but not at the task of exploration. To the contrary, except for Pike none of Jefferson's explorers conducted a second expedition, and by 1807 Pike was out of the exploring business as well. Instead, most of Jefferson's explorers were fully engaged in the task of western government. The explorers were still keen on producing book-length accounts of their ventures and maps to chart out the West. They did so in part because they had been commanded to do so. But producing those accounts would also serve the long-term professional aspirations of the explorers.

Custis and Dunbar should have been eager to produce those books. Of all Jefferson's explorers, they displayed the greatest interest in scientific publication. After the Red River Expedition, however, Custis got as far from the West as he possibly could. He completed his medical training, began work on a botanical study that he never completed, and spent the rest of his life as a physician (and patrician) in North Carolina, thoroughly removed from the grand mission of western exploration.[26] Dunbar followed a similar path. He remained a committed scientist and a minor political presence in the Mississippi Territory, but he never led an expedition again. Equally important, aside from his occasional correspondence with Jefferson and with the American Philosophical Society, Dunbar removed himself from the grand project of mapping the Far West. He died in 1811 a wealthy man, a beneficiary of the tremendous profits being reaped by southwestern plantation agriculture.[27]

Jefferson still hoped the expeditions would bolster science in the United States and disprove European claims that the United States was and would remain a culturally underdeveloped nation. Most of the explorers, on the other hand, showed no intention of joining the American scientific community, and Jefferson made no effort to have them do so. Lewis, like Dunbar, joined the American Philosophical Society and seemed to enjoy the embrace of the nation's leading intellectuals. At the same time, Dunbar's residence in Mississippi and Lewis's distraction by other demands meant that their interactions with the organization were limited.

For Lewis, Clark, Pike, and Freeman, it was the challenge of governing the West that would dominate their lives and shape the way they eventually told the story of their brief careers as explorers. The reason was simple: governing the West was far more important than exploring it. Whatever Jefferson's personal scientific and commercial roles before 1803, the acquisition of Louisiana converted western exploration into a necessary first step toward governance.

The American effort to explore the West was, after all, short-lived. A particular set of circumstances created the political support for the federal government to sponsor a few expeditions over a brief period. Congress authorized minimal funds, and Jefferson was the only federal leader who showed any personal interest in the matter. In stark contrast, western government was among the most costly and time-consuming activities of the federal government. Creating new civil governments for whites, preserving the slave system in the Southwest, and asserting federal sovereignty over Indians was a matter of concern for every cabinet office and a subject of extensive debate in Congress. This project had begun in the Northwest Territory, where Clark first learned about federal governance and Indian policy. It continued in the Mississippi Territory that Andrew Ellicott, Thomas Freeman, and William Dunbar had helped define through the southwestern boundary survey of 1798. The project began anew with the Louisiana Purchase.[28]

This state of affairs may well explain the puzzling absence of James Madison in the planning for western exploration. After all, his State Department would be among the chief beneficiaries. Mapping the North American landscape would serve his efforts overseas to coordinate a successful resolution to the boundaries of the United States. Meanwhile, information on the people within those boundaries would serve his domestic responsibilities, for the State Department supervised civil government in the federal territories. But Madison himself was consumed with the daily realities of western government and had little time to spend on western exploration.[29]

In October 1806, less than a month after returning to St. Louis, Clark wrote a terse letter to Dearborn. "The included commission haveing answered the purpose for which it was intended," he wrote, "I take the liberty of returning it to you."[30] The document he enclosed was the commission as first lieutenant he had received immediately before the Lewis and Clark Expedition. He had preserved the commission carefully, but he resented its very existence. Clark concluded his letter by stating, "I have the honor to be with every Sentiment of the highest respect Your Most Obedient and Very humble Servent." This was a standard conclusion in letters in the early nineteenth century, but its content belied its tone. Clark had been deeply insulted at being forced to return to the army as a lieutenant rather than as the captain he had been in 1796, and he blamed the situation on Dearborn. He had no formal reason to return the commission, except to offer the closest thing he could to a rebuke of Dearborn. In the honor-bound culture that had produced both men, Dearborn would have understood Clark's message.

Yet Clark never used the word "resign." Once restored to military service, he apparently had no intention of leaving the army again. Instead, Clark proceeded east with Lewis, hoping to reap the personal rewards of a successful expedition. They brought with them a delegation of Indian chiefs, whose arrival in Washington enabled both parties to see themselves as victors. To the

chiefs, the visit to Washington reinforced their power at home while constituting a major concession by the United States, which preferred to leave Indian negotiations to officials in the West. To Lewis and Clark, however, the
arrival of the chiefs proved they had succeeded in their diplomatic mission.
During this exercise in diplomacy Clark left Lewis and the Indian chiefs to
visit his family in Kentucky, planning to rejoin Lewis in Washington. As he
traveled home alone Clark received a tribute in Fincastle, a growing settlement in southwestern Virginia. He delivered a public reply thanking his hosts,
adding, "The distinguished attention shown to me by the citizens of Fincastle & it's vicinity produces those emotions which I am unable to discribe."
Unable indeed, for Clark had always resisted the open expression of sentiment. Clark had been quick to admit the frustrations he encountered when
it came to writing about the world around him. Yet this moment centered
on him. It constituted the first public moment in which he emerged from
Lewis's shadow and was among the first moments in his life as a federal em-
ployee that Clark enjoyed personal glory. That he would struggle to find
words to express this moment made perfect sense.[31]

So, too, did the events that followed. It was during this sojourn that Clark
met Judith Hancock, a fifteen-year-old girl who was twenty-one years his junior. Known as Julia, she was the daughter of George Hancock, a wealthy
planter and two-term congressman. Did Clark arrive to court young Julia or
to meet with her father? In typical style, Clark never divulged the answer in
writing. The introduction to Hancock had come from a friend of Clark's who
had married Julia's older sister, which suggests that either answer could be
true. Regardless, meeting the Hancocks mattered to Clark, so much so that
he was willing to delay his arrival in Washington, forcing the sponsors of a
major celebration honoring Lewis and Clark to postpone the event. His reputation restored and his prospects enhanced by the expedition to the Far
West, Clark confidently set about courting this daughter of the Virginia gentry whose social status was more secure than his own.[32]

Clark finally reached Washington on January 18, 1807. As he informed his
brother Jonathan, the visit to the capital involved "formal visits to the heads
of departments and partaeing of the Sumptious far of maney of the members,
many of whom I have become acquainted with." He made no reference to
the scientific community or to the scientific concerns that mattered to Lewis,
instead discussing the political and military affairs that members of the Virginia gentry usually considered the appropriate subject of discussion during
a Washington visit. He also reported that a congressional committee "is ap-

pointed to bring in a bill giveing Compensation to the Party on the late Expedition."[33]

The arrival of Lewis and Clark in Washington was ideally timed to capitalize on Jefferson's search for a cadre of officials who could respond to the challenges he saw facing the United States in every quarter. Lewis was the first to
benefit. His successful leadership of the expedition concluded a five-year period during which he had transformed himself from a troublesome army officer with a penchant for violence into a reliable confidant of the president. In
February 1807 Jefferson nominated Lewis for governor of the Louisiana Territory. He had reasons for doing so that extended beyond his desire to reward
Lewis. Jefferson had become increasingly disenchanted with the current governor, General James Wilkinson, the man who had dispatched Pike on his two
expeditions. Rumors accusing the general of complicity in the Burr conspiracy
were already reaching Washington. Wilkinson responded to those rumors by
launching a relentless campaign to imprison suspected Burr conspirators in
St. Louis and later in New Orleans, an act which only further undermined his
reputation in Washington. The controversy came after a year in which Wilkinson had faced growing opposition in St. Louis, primarily from aspiring local residents who believed he was restricting power to friends and protégés like Pike.[34]

Rather than remove Wilkinson outright, Jefferson simply allowed his commission as governor to expire and selected Lewis as his successor. He conducted this business in the midst of a winter weekend. On Saturday, February
28, Jefferson sent one of the numerous letters he dispatched to the Senate listing nominees for federal appointment. "I nominate Meriwether Lewis, of
Virginia, to be Governor of the Territory of Louisiana" was the first item on
the list. Next, Jefferson nominated Clark for promotion to lieutenant colonel
in one of the army regiments stationed in the Territory of Orleans.[35]

The Territory of Louisiana was a vast mandate. In 1804, the federal government had created the Territory of Orleans, corresponding roughly to what
is now the state of Louisiana. Everything else the United States acquired
through the Louisiana Purchase became the Territory of Louisiana.

These nominations were hardly unique. They came in the midst of Jefferson's hurried efforts to meet the considerable demands of western government. In the same letter that announced the nominations of Lewis and Clark,
Jefferson also nominated three other western officials. When the Senate met
two days later, they voted in favor of all the civil appointments. The matter was
apparently so simple that the Senate record did not even record a vote. Clark's
case was another matter: the Senate voted 20–9 against his promotion.[36]

The reason for this outcome most likely resides not in the biographies of Lewis or Clark, but in the heated politics of army promotions. As Clark explained to his brother Edmund, the nomination "was rejected by the Senate on the Grounds of braking through a Principal. I am truly gratified to find that in this decision of the senate they as I am told unanimously agred that they would confirm any other nomonation in the gift of the government." That "Principal" was a time-honored system through which seniority in one rank commonly dictated advancement to the next. Clark's comments to his brother were typical of his style of writing. There was little revelation of the sort of irritation Clark displayed earlier over his commission as lieutenant.[37]

When the Senate finally filled the contested vacancy in December 1807, it chose Major Richard Sparks. There was, in fact, at least one major with seniority over Sparks: Zebulon Pike Sr. Old and partially disabled, the explorer's father had long been overlooked for promotion. To Zebulon Pike Jr., his father's injuries—suffered while in service to the nation—made him all the more deserving of promotion.[38]

Even as Clark lamented his lack of promotion within the army, the optimism for other possibilities he had shared with Edmund proved correct. The day after approving Lewis's appointment as governor and rejecting Clark's promotion to lieutenant colonel, Congress passed a bill awarding fifteen hundred dollars each to Lewis and Clark and 350 acres of land in Louisiana to their men as well as double pay for the length of the expedition. Dearborn had recommended that Clark's lower rank demanded that he receive less than Lewis, but Lewis himself was steadfast in securing both Jefferson's and Dearborn's approval for an equal distribution for himself and Clark.[39]

Jefferson was also apparently still keen on rewarding Clark and, equally important, exploiting his talents. Jefferson selected Clark to serve as the chief Indian agent for all the tribes in the Louisiana Territory with the exception of the Osage, who would be the concern of Pierre Chouteau, a member of the dominant merchant family in St. Louis, which enjoyed extensive contacts with the Osage.[40] On March 15, Lewis wrote to Clark with the additional news that he would soon receive "your commission as Brigadier General of the Militia of Louisiana."[41]

His appointment as Indian agent headquartered in St. Louis was a logical step for Clark. Nonetheless, it marked a definitive end to his military career. This time, however, he would not regret the decision, as he had in 1796. Clark now began a career within the western bureaucracy that would provide steady employment for the rest of his life.

Clark immediately left for St. Louis. Lewis remained in the East to consult with Jefferson and with the experts in Philadelphia about how best to proceed with the materials from the expedition. He attended meetings of the American Philosophical Society, sat for a portrait, and welcomed the attention he received as a nineteenth-century celebrity. Like Clark, Lewis also began courting. Lewis's correspondence does not reveal all the women whom he approached, but one of them was certainly the daughter of James Breckenridge. Like Hancock, Breckenridge was a planter and politician from southwestern Virginia. Unlike Julia Hancock, however, Lettissia Breckenridge seemed uninterested in her suitor, curtailing the sort of possibilities for a family of his own and for new social connections that Clark saw in his future.[42]

Lewis also made plans for the book he knew Jefferson expected him to publish. He looked to Philadelphia, and rightly so. Over the preceding decade Philadelphia had consolidated its status as the center of American cartographic publishing. Lewis chose the publishing house of C. and A. Conrad, which had published American editions of John Barrow's *Account of Travels into the Interior of Southern Africa*, a major travel narrative, and the Comte de Volney's *View of the Soil and Climate of the United States of America* (1804), a scientific text that Jefferson admired.[43]

Lewis and Conrad imagined a project entirely in keeping with the most ambitious goals of Jefferson and his Enlightenment cohort. This would be a massive three-volume work divided into two parts. The first part would be a traditional travel narrative that recorded the expedition in chronological sequence. Part two would address subjects ranging from geography to trade to Indian culture to "reflections on the subjects of civilizing governing and maintaining a friendly intercourse with those nations." Consuming all of the third volume, part two would be "confined exclusively to scientific research, and principally to the natural history of those hitherto unknown regions."[44]

To this Lewis added, "Detached from this work, there will be published on a large scale, as soon as a sufficient number of subscribers be obtained to defray the expence, LEWIS & CLARK'S MAP OF NORTH AMERICA." The relationship that Lewis described between the map and the book indicated the various ways in which Americans had approached the relationship between visual and textual descriptions of the landscape. In his response to other publishing ventures, Lewis had made clear that his experience and his alone would provide the most accurate representation of the landscape. He dismissed what other authors had to offer and emphasized the direct observations on geography, commerce, and Indians that would form the basis of his book.

In sharp contrast, the map would achieve its accuracy by including the material of others. The map would "be compiled from the best maps now extant, as well published as in manuscript, from the collective information of the best informed travelers through the various portions of that region, and corrected by a series of several hundred celestial observations, made by Captain Lewis during his late tour."[45]

Together, the book and the map would serve multiple purposes, for Jefferson and for Lewis and Clark. For Jefferson, they would provide the information to support his territorial pretentions and promote trade in the Far West, all the while helping develop a domestic scientific community to place the United States on a par with Europe. For Lewis and Clark, producing this work would fulfill the debt to Jefferson while further securing their own status within the leadership class of the United States.

Lewis was also in a rush to establish himself as the author of the official, definitive account of the expedition. In October 1806, only weeks after the expedition returned to St. Louis, a proposal was circulating "for Publishing by Subscription Robert Frazers Journal." Private Frazer had been one of the six journal writers on the expedition. The proposal estimated a book of four hundred pages, "published by permission of Captn. Meriwether Lewis."[46] Lewis immediately initiated a nasty editorial brawl with the publisher, David McKeehan, in which he attacked Frazer's credentials to produce a major published work, while McKeehan accused Lewis of being a petty tyrant who was unwilling to share acclaim with his subordinates.[47]

Lewis could have saved himself the trouble. Even if he could muzzle McKeehan, describing their experiences in the West was beyond the control of any of Jefferson's explorers. Unfamiliar with the intricacies of publishing either books or maps, their lives consumed by the daily tasks of federal governance, they would be hard-pressed to produce an image of the North American West. Instead, Americans continued to learn about the Far West from other sources. After newspapers had circulated the first news from Jefferson's expeditions, the diverse and diffuse set of men who had already begun representing the West would continue to do so. They had strong incentives to do so. The explorers—with their plans to publish new accounts of the West—suddenly threatened to render obsolete a generation of American publishing about the West. At the same time, however, those explorers also created new possibilities and, perhaps, a chance for new profits.

Consider the letter that Jabez Jackson wrote to Jedidiah Morse on December 19, 1806. A resident of Savannah, Georgia, Jackson was one of Morse's few southern friends. "I must congratulate you, on the arrival, at St. Louis, Louisiana, of Messrs. Lewis & Clarke, whose important discoveries in the Western Country, must open a wide field for you in your work, as regards the knowledge of those almost uninhabited Regions."[48] It was a remarkable letter, suggesting just how quickly news of the Lewis and Clark Expedition circulated, how Clark's name entered the picture, and how others immediately began to exploit that information. This was not "Capt. Lewis' expedition," as it had been called in 1805. Now William Clark's name was firmly attached, not only in the printed world but also in the minds of Americans like Jackson. Meanwhile, Jackson immediately appreciated how the information from that expedition could benefit Morse. Ever since Morse had lamented the decivilizing qualities of the Near West in his 1784 edition of *Geography Made Easy*, he had also been forced to acknowledge the absence of reliable, accurate information on the Far West. That had remained the case in subsequent editions of *Geography Made Easy* as well as in Morse's other major project, *The American Universal Geography*, a longer volume which shared a great deal with *Geography Made Easy* but which was intended for adults rather than schoolchildren.

What Jackson could not know was that the timing of Lewis's and Clark's arrival could not have been more useful to Morse. In December 1806, Morse was in negotiations with the Boston-based publisher of Manning and Loring about producing a special abridged version of *American Universal Geography*. "After having gone over the calculations . . . in a very careful and deliberate manner," they informed Morse, "we have made up our minds that it will be worth ten cents, each copy, for the priviledge of printg twelve thousand copies."[49]

Morse did not have time to include any new information in his 1807 version of *Geography Made Easy*. When it came to the Far West of upper Louisiana, he simply repeated language he had used in earlier editions that "the boundaries of Louisiana are not settled; its extent of course cannot be ascertained." His details on the Far West were still cobbled together from the same late eighteenth- and early nineteenth-century sources that Jefferson and Madison had consulted in the aftermath of the Louisiana Purchase.[50]

Mapmakers faced similar delays. Printers on both sides of the Atlantic continued to produce maps that generally preserved both the topography and the boundaries predating Jefferson's expeditions. More specifically, cartographers and publishers continued to reproduce existing maps that might hint at the Louisiana Purchase or the recent exploration of the West, but few of which

were actually the product of new printing plates. Much of the continental interior remained blank. Equally important, the boundaries of Louisiana varied radically.[51]

In the meantime, other publishers working primarily in the realm of print
and less committed to proving the authenticity of their sources were eagerly
describing the West in their own terms. They did so in much the same way
as the newspaper accounts. Cobbling together bits and pieces from *An Account of Louisiana*, the correspondence of individual explorers, and from Jefferson's public statements about the explorers' findings, these accounts in
1806 and 1807 all claimed to be the latest, most authoritative word on the Far
West.[52] Some of these accounts were entirely fraudulent, claiming to be the
official report that Jefferson's explorers were struggling to produce. The most
remarkable of these was a book from 1809 that combined Lewis's and Clark's
Fort Mandan report with details from the work of European explorers. Yet the
book had all the trademarks of a real travel narrative. And if you can't judge
a book by its cover, the cover of this book certainly suggested that it was the
real thing. Consider the title: *The Travels of Capts. Lewis & Clarke: by Order
of the Government of the United States, performed in the years 1804, 1805 &
1806, being upwards of three thousand miles, from St. Louis, by way of the Missouri and Columbia Rivers, to the Pacifick Ocean : containing an account of
the Indian tribes, who inhabit the western part of the continent unexplored,
and unknown before : with copious delineations of the manners, customs, religion, &c. of the Indians.*[53]

In the midst of all this publishing, only a few firsthand accounts of western
exploration were available to the public. McKeehan never published Frazer's
diary. But in 1807 he did release a book based on the journal of Patrick Gass,
one of Lewis's and Clark's sergeants. While never criticizing Lewis by name,
the Gass account did describe a far more democratic expedition than that
portrayed in either Lewis's or Clark's manuscript journals, the expedition's accomplishments being characterized as the result of teamwork and collaboration rather than of the bold leadership of the two captains. Gass's book, *A
Journal of the Voyages and Travels of a Corps of Discovery*, also began the
process of popularizing a name for the expedition—the Corps of Discovery—
that downplayed its leaders in favor of its entire membership. Only after the
colon that followed *Corps of Discovery* did the title read, *Under the Command
of Capt. Lewis and Capt. Clarke of the Army of the United States.*[54]

The printer whom McKeehan commissioned to produce Gass's book was
Zadok Cramer. A Pittsburgh printer and bookseller as well as an author and

publisher in his own right, Cramer released *The Ohio and Mississippi Navigator* in 1802. He reissued the book regularly in the years that followed.[55] A technical guide to travel through the Near West, the book also celebrated western settlement in the same terms John Filson had used two decades earlier. Cramer described a world of easy river transport, inexpensive land, and tremendous farming potential. Whereas Jefferson's explorers used "abundance" in the absence of detailed information, Cramer used it to emphasize the unbounded opportunities in the West. In his 1806 edition, Cramer reproduced *An Account of Louisiana*, the pamphlet of information Jefferson had released in 1803. In 1808, the cover of *The Navigator* announced an appendix describing "The Missouri and Columbia Rivers, as discovered by the voyage under Captains Lewis and Clark." The only sources Cramer mentioned by name were Gass's journal and Clark's letter from Fort Mandan to Jonathan.[56]

Yet even as Lewis and Clark lost control of the published account of the expedition, Clark saw particular benefits from all this publication. Whatever Dearborn may have done to subordinate Clark, American publishers had followed the lead of Lewis. By 1807, this was no longer "Capt. Lewis' expedition" or even, for that matter, the "Corps of Discovery" that Gass described. Instead, it was the Lewis and Clark Expedition. Clark could not have been more pleased.

"I THINK IT WOULD BE PRUDENT"

By the time the Lewis and Clark Expedition took form within the national consciousness, Clark had reached St. Louis and was busy with the daily realities of territorial governance. In his dual capacity as militia officer and Indian agent, Clark served two masters. As an official of the territorial system, he reported to the territorial governor and to his superior, the secretary of state. But as an Indian agent, Clark reported to the secretary of war, and in 1807 Dearborn still held that office. If there was any residual animosity, Clark did not display it in his correspondence. Like Lewis, Clark was hard at work securing his reputation within the strict hierarchy of federal appointment.

St. Louis in 1807 was a crucial factor in the broader federal effort to respond to the Louisiana Purchase. Since 1803 the United States had struggled to extend its sovereignty over the territory it had acquired from France. The focus of most of that attention remained on the Territory of Orleans, where the United States faced the greatest opposition from white residents, Indians, slaves, and free people of color.[57] But the Territory of Louisiana posed its own problems. Clark's mission was to normalize relations with the Indians west of the Mississippi. In St. Louis, however, he also found himself in the middle of the tense ethnic relations between the existing Francophone population and the growing number of Anglo-Americans. These tensions had threatened to explode during Wilkinson's term as governor, and the long delay in Lewis's assumption of the governorship further postponed any political resolution.

Clark immediately sought to establish himself not only as a public official, but also as a conduit for information between the Far West and the federal leadership in Washington. Much of this activity emerged through a correspondence with Dearborn, one in which neither man revealed any antagonism toward the other. Clark discussed the state of commerce and settlement. He reported scraps of information about Pike's Arkansas Expedition, although he was quick to doubt the rumors that Pike and his men had been killed by Indians. As Clark wrote in June 1807, "No certain accounts of Mr Pike, some Indians have said they left him two days from the Setlements of Santa Fee. No reliance can be placed on this information."[58] This letter was only part of Clark's effort to establish himself as an expert on the complex diplomatic landscape of the Far West, discussing the relationships among Indians, their contacts with whites, and the strategies the United States should pursue to make sovereignty a reality.[59]

Clark's strategy in Indian affairs was simple. He hoped to build commercial relationships with the most powerful and most distant Indians. He sought alliances with those closer at hand, especially those with whom the United States could negotiate from a position of strength. Finally, Clark was prepared to use threats and coercion with Indians who were both weak and close. Ideally, that sort of pressure would either convince Indians to vacate the lands coveted by white settlers or force them to join alliances against more powerful Indians. In the end, Clark's vision of sovereignty in the Far West rested on the assumption of Indian subordination.[60]

Despite Clark's concerted efforts to advance territorial policy and his own career, he was preoccupied by other matters. On June 7, 1807, Clark was drafting another letter to Dearborn. Reserving the draft for scrap paper, he repeatedly scribbled "Julia Hancock" and eventually "Julia Clark."[61] Six months later he left St. Louis for Virginia. William Clark and Julia Hancock were married on January 5, 1808, at the Hancock family plantation. Julia suddenly found herself taken away from her friends and family and from the place she

had called home her entire life. As was true of so many women from the
upper South, the need to secure stability within her new married family
meant westward migration.[62] Clark always displayed an abiding affection for
his in-laws, but he showed no hesitation in taking Julia with him to the West.
And the West where Clark imagined his future was not the Kentucky that
had attracted first his brother George Rogers Clark and later his parents. Clark
imagined his own future in St. Louis and saw it through the lens of appointment within the federal structure that governed the nation's western territories.

During Clark's absence, Lewis had finally arrived in St. Louis. When Clark
returned, he was among Lewis's few confidants in the territorial capital, where
Lewis struggled to ingratiate himself with the local political elite. Even as
Lewis and Clark took charge of the government of the Louisiana Territory,
they still found themselves consumed by mapmaking. Clark's primary task
was to produce the map that was supposed to combine all the information
from the expedition. And while Lewis had contracted to edit the book that
contained that map, the book would speak in Clark's voice. Of all the journal writers, Clark produced the most text. Indeed, the manuscript journals of
the expedition included the largest single collection of words Clark ever put
on paper.

Clark's emerging reputation as an authority on the West had already established him as a coveted contact within the competitive, entrepreneurial
world of cartographic publishing. In June 1807 Clark received an unsolicited
letter from John Jones, a New York entrepreneur who wrote of "an improvement I have made in the Art of Varnishing of Maps Drawings and of Paintings." Jones sought to curry favor with Lewis and Clark by informing them he
had heard of the "map of your late important discoveries permit me to congratulate you on such an event that I presume will not be only highly grati-
fying to the publick in general, but also of considerable importance to you."
It was a perceptive comment, and Jones knew why: "A great number [of maps]
have been sold . . . in this city . . . and I doubt not but from the very favourable
impression your new work has made on the citizens of this Wealthy City, and
I may say in all the principle cities of the United States."[63]

As Clark waited for Lewis to make progress on the book, he continued writing and drawing. Clark did not keep another major journal, but his new public offices and expanded social connections demanded that he become an
active correspondent. He wrote to cabinet officials in Washington, territorial
officials in the Louisiana Territory, new social contacts in St. Louis, and his

family scattered throughout Virginia and Kentucky.[64] Likewise, Clark did not conduct any mapping project on the scale of his effort to survey the Far West, but he did repeatedly depend on his capacity to draw maps as a way to reinforce the points he struggled to make in words. In September 1808, for example, he drew what he called "A Rough Draught & Plan of the Fort near Fire Prairie." It was the sort of strategic survey he had revealed in 1795 when drawing the Spanish outpost near the Chickasaw Bluffs. In characteristic style, Clark also kept a journal of his efforts. The outpost eventually became known as Fort Osage, a major fur-trading station on the Missouri River located near the frontier outpost that eventually became Kansas City.[65]

In all these efforts, Clark understood his written and visual work in practical terms, advancing the specifics of territorial policy while also establishing his reputation as a reliable official. Yet Clark was also engaged in the broader project of claiming the Far West for the United States. He knew as well as anybody that surveying provided the means through which Anglo-Americans established landownership. In the years after the Louisiana Purchase, the United States pursued a grand project of establishing its claims west of the Mississippi. There was more to this process than legal land title. Americans had long lamented their dependence on Europeans for the geographic knowledge of their own country. On the Lewis and Clark Expedition and in the years that followed, Clark described the West in ways that would eventually replace the work of Europeans with new, American knowledge.

5

CAREERS

Throughout much of his adult life, William Clark had written portions of an autobiography, not that he ever would have recognized it as such. To the contrary, he wrote and drew in ways that seemed to remove him from the picture. Yet these efforts were very much about him. Clark's autobiography appeared slowly in various journals as well as in the growing correspondence he sent to family members and government officials. That autobiography also appeared in numerous maps through which Clark situated himself in the history of the North American West.

If an autobiography is meant to create a portrait of an individual life or a portion of it, a portrait that needs to rise above any conflicting descriptions, then Clark was clearly engaged in an autobiographical project in 1813. As he had done so many times before, he drew a map. It was a rather hurried affair, reflecting none of the time and care he planned to devote to the grand map of the West he was supposed to produce after the Lewis and Clark Expedition. Instead, this map resembled the numerous local surveys of rivers and Indians that Clark had drawn during the course of the expedition (Figs. 19 and 20).

On a ten-by-sixteen-inch piece of paper Clark attempted to construct an overview of the strategic situation he faced in a region encompassing the Great Lakes as well as the Mississippi and Missouri rivers. The map displayed Clark's knowledge, his skills, and his activities. Details from Lake Michigan described the strategic situation in a region where William Henry Harrison, Clark's personal and professional associate for nearly twenty years, was in the midst of an extended war against Indians who, nineteen years after Fallen Timbers, had renewed their militant resistance to the United States. Clark's map implicitly repudiated a generation of American mapmakers who claimed that the federal government and Anglo-American settlers had conquered the

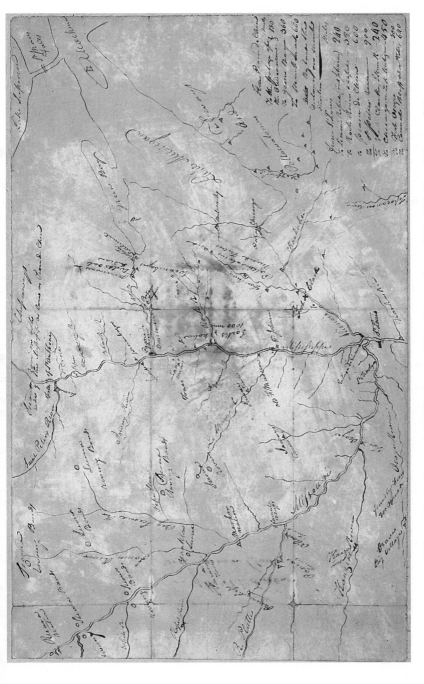

Figure 19. William Clark, *Plan of the N.W. Frontier* (1813). Geography and Map Division, Library of Congress.

Figure 20. Upper Mississippi River (above) and Lake Michigan (opposite), including Clark's estimate of geographic distances (details of Fig. 19).

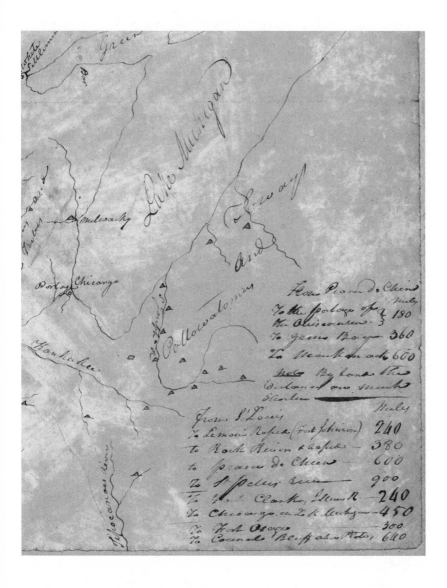

Northwest. John Filson put that story in print along with a map that described whites' control of the Ohio Valley. Clark's map of 1813 seemed more closely akin to the European maps that had described the Mississippi Valley as a contested frontier.

Clark's map came in the final stages of work on the book that would chronicle the Lewis and Clark Expedition. All of Jefferson's explorers found themselves in similar circumstances. William Dunbar, George Hunter, and Peter

Custis had already chosen to opt out of the federal system. Their silence about the West was all the more striking because, as highly literate men who defined themselves as scientists, they were far more qualified than Lewis, Clark, Freeman, or Pike to describe the West. Yet it was these four men who produced the written accounts of Jefferson's expedition.

In the years following his return to St. Louis, Clark's life often intersected with that of Jefferson's other explorers, including Lewis, Clark's immediate superior in St. Louis and also his closest friend. But Pike and Freeman too passed through William Clark's world in ways that were no less informative than Lewis's presence as Clark's closest friend. They did so in the midst of active, occasionally feverish efforts to create or protect the public reputations that would sustain their public careers. Driven by professional advancement rather than aesthetic concerns, operating on the frontiers of the Union rather than the urban community of scientists, rooted in the appointed system of patronage rather than the dynamic politics of election, these men hoped to create an image of the West through books and maps that would serve the nation as well as themselves.

THE FALL OF MERIWETHER LEWIS

Clark followed the careers of his fellow explorers, none more closely than that of Lewis. Clark watched in dismay as Lewis's career disintegrated. Charles Willson Peale, an American artist and naturalist who had helped train Lewis in 1803, informed his son, Rembrandt Peale, in November 1809, "Governor Lewis has distroyed himself."[1] It was an appropriately vague statement, for the particulars of Lewis's death in the fall of 1809 were only symptomatic of a broader process throughout which Lewis had destroyed a seemingly brilliant career with remarkable speed. In 1806, Lewis was ideally poised for rapid advancement within the federal system, and he was only too happy to let Clark ride on his coattails. In 1809, Lewis's downfall occurred in no small part because he found himself unable to write his way out of trouble.

Barely two years before writing of Lewis's demise, Peale had informed Jefferson that "Mr. Lewis is richly entitled to a place amongst the Portraits of the Museum, and I hope he will do me the favor of sitting as soon as he arrives here." Two months later, Peale was even more insistent: "I long to see Captain Lewis. I wish to possess his portrait for the Museum."[2] It was a remarkable compliment, for Peale intended his museum to surround visitors with

Figure 21. Charles Willson Peale, *Meriwether Lewis* (1807).
Independence National Historic Park.

portraits of great Americans, providing visual instruction in the qualities of
virtue, enlightenment, and leadership.[3]

Completed in 1807, Peale's portrait became the standard visage of Lewis.
The painting now illustrates Lewis for contemporary readers, but in the
process we have lost sight of the very specific role this portrait was supposed
to serve in its own time. Intended for public display, the portrait announced
Lewis as he imagined himself. Wearing the simple but dignified clothing of
a private citizen, Lewis was no longer a soldier but a leading American who
combined high public rank with personal modesty (Fig. 21). The book project he planned, to be based on the notes of the expedition, told the same
story, establishing Lewis as an enlightened thinker and a committed agent of
the federal government. If Peale's portrait would establish Lewis's image for

museum-goers in Philadelphia, the book would circulate his image throughout the country.

Peale began work on the portrait just as Lewis became the latest in a series of young Virginians to assume high office in the territorial government of the western frontier. Particularly striking were the similarities among four territorial governors: Lewis in the Territory of Louisiana, William Henry Harrison in Indiana, William C. C. Claiborne in the Territory of Orleans (the jurisdictional predecessor to the state of Louisiana), and Robert Williams in Mississippi. Despite their professional differences (Lewis and Harrison came from the army, while Claiborne and Williams had served in Congress), all four men were Virginians born between 1773 and 1775 into gentry families with deep roots in the political and military struggles of the Revolution. When these men found themselves facing declining circumstances in Virginia, their ambitions led them to seek opportunities in the West, and their unflagging loyalty to the Jefferson administration made them logical candidates for public office. The only exception to this pattern of Virginia appointments was William Hull, an aging Connecticut native who, since 1805, had served as governor of the Michigan Territory.

Like all territorial governors, these Virginians worked in a system that depended less on the popular support that sustained elected state governors than on the political support of their superiors in Washington, especially the president and secretary of state. Territorial governors ruled accordingly, often maintaining difficult relationships with their constituencies. Local elites eager to seek elected office chafed at the political limitations of the territorial system.[4]

Meriwether Lewis proved particularly unsuccessful at negotiating the politics of territorial leadership. Abandoning the easy camaraderie that had characterized the Lewis and Clark Expedition, Lewis often ruled by decree and bristled at every public criticism, immediately generating antagonism from his fellow appointees, from the French-speaking elite of St. Louis, and from ambitious Anglo-American newcomers.[5] Lewis's problems were not simply matters of style. The first Indian treaties he developed with Clark seemed to satisfy nobody, whites claiming that Lewis and Clark made too many concessions to Indians, and Indian chiefs claiming that the Americans would negotiate only with chiefs who seemed willing to cede land to the United States.[6]

As Lewis came under increasing public criticism, he also faced mounting financial problems. In an age of ambiguous boundaries between public and private life, Lewis invested his own money in a fur-trading venture that also enjoyed government privilege. Not only did this seem to confirm the accusations of his critics that Lewis sought personal enrichment, but when the St. Louis Missouri Fur Company failed to deliver a profit, Lewis found himself in personal debt. The governor was also the subject of various civil suits, most of them from private individuals who claimed that he had contracted them for government services for which they had never been paid.

At the crucial moment when criticism in the Louisiana Territory mounted and Lewis showed no signs of making progress in completing a book from his western expedition, Lewis found himself isolated and lacking support in Washington. Lewis had no close associates within Congress, and he enjoyed markedly tepid relations with Jefferson's cabinet. His only reliable ally had been Jefferson himself, which was just fine so long as Jefferson was president. But in 1809 Jefferson retired to Monticello, and Lewis found himself virtually alone, his only trusted ally being Clark.

Even more striking was the absence of any relationship at all—friendly or cold—with the new president, James Madison. The two men had undoubtedly met, if not before 1801 then certainly after Madison became secretary of state and Lewis became Jefferson's personal secretary. Neither man ever complained about the other, and both probably respected one another. Yet neither man wrote to the other during Lewis's tenure as Jefferson's secretary or during the planning of the Lewis and Clark Expedition, a stunning situation in a time when public officials were regular correspondents. The fact that they could easily meet in the federal capital does not explain the absence of correspondence. Jefferson and Madison maintained a voluminous correspondence, even when their offices were in neighboring buildings. In contrast, the earliest remaining piece of correspondence between Madison and Lewis comes from late in the Jefferson administration and is striking for its absence of detail. "You will find herewith inclosed an Account with a receipt annexed for my salary as governor of the Territory of Louisiana," Lewis wrote to Madison on June 28, 1807.[7]

Throughout this period Lewis attempted to write himself out of trouble by publishing the official account of the Lewis and Clark Expedition. As Lewis struggled to complete a book that would secure his reputation from a distance, he relied on a more common written tool available to territorial officials: formal reports to his superiors in Washington. Self-congratulatory reports on the progress in the Louisiana Territory mirrored the language of success in which all of Jefferson's explorers had written in the immediate aftermath of their expeditions and in the books they produced. As Lewis wrote in one of his few letters to Madison, "Before my appointment to the government of this territory, several of our white inhabitants had been murdered by the neighbouring Indians. The proper Agents had demanded the offenders of their respective tribes; but not in such preemptory terms as to procure their delivery. On my arrival, I immediately took efficient measures, and had the satisfaction, in a few months to deliver over these murderers to the civil authority, together with the evidences of their guilt."[8]

The breakdown of Lewis's efforts to sustain his reputation through the written word explains his abrupt decision to leave St. Louis in the fall of 1809. The proximate cause was a series of public purchases that the War Department refused to cover. Uncertain of his reputation in Washington and unable to adequately defend himself through writing, Lewis headed for the federal capital, hoping that direct contact with the administration would restore his reputation as a reliable leader of western government.[9] By September 15, 1809, Lewis had reached Chickasaw Bluffs, Tennessee, on the eastern bank of the Mississippi River, where fourteen years earlier Clark had confronted Manuel Gayoso de Lemos.

A month later Lewis was dead. He committed suicide on the night of October 10–11 at Grinder's Inn, located near Nashville. A long-circulating theory has proclaimed Lewis the victim of a murder plot, but this conclusion rests on a slim documentary record produced in Lewis's time and on a much larger need in our own time to believe that no man as strong as Lewis could succumb to suicidal feelings. The murder theory also conflicts with the men who knew him best. Observers throughout the United States who had worked with Lewis in various capacities all agreed he had taken his own life.[10]

Clark apparently never doubted it was suicide. He too was traveling east, following a more northerly route. He brought with him his wife, Julia, as well as their infant son, Meriwether Lewis Clark, born only eight months earlier. They were intent on proudly displaying the boy to family members in Virginia. Clark then planned to leave his wife and son with Julia's family as he proceeded to confer with his superiors in Washington. This would be his first set of meetings with the Madison administration, and Clark was eager to develop exactly the relationship with the new administration that had eluded Lewis.[11] The Clarks learned of Lewis's death when they reached Lexington. "We arrived here this evening all in the Same State of health we were when we parted with you," Clark informed his brother Jonathan, "but not in the Same State of Mind." He soon wrote again, informing Jonathan that "I am at a loss to know what to be as his death is a turble Stroke to me, in every respect. I wish I could talk a little with you just now."[12]

If murder fails to offer a satisfying explanation of Lewis's death, most discussions of suicide have their own problems. Interpretations from a broad range of perspectives have linked the death to causes ranging from alcoholism to substance abuse to mental illness to undue personal attacks by his critics to a lack of support from the Jefferson and Madison administrations. All of these factors did apply. Lewis was drinking to excess, he was taking heavy doses of laudanum to treat ill-defined diseases, his personal history did reveal erratic behavior that might comport with contemporary diagnoses of various mental illnesses, and he certainly faced criticism in both Washington and St. Louis. But these interpretations are no less apologetic, seeking to explain Lewis's suicide in a way that absolves him of his unsuccessful tenure as governor.

Such explanations of the suicide also tend to put the cart before the horse. The reasons Lewis was unsuccessful as governor and considered himself to be in such a state of crisis that he needed to take an unplanned trip to Washington to defend himself—let alone commit suicide along the way—make far more sense in the context of the publishing ventures and public aspirations that were at the center of Lewis's concerns. It was abundantly clear that as governor Lewis had failed to achieve the objectives of territorial policy. He was supposed to promote a stable political system; his shrill response to his opponents showed his failure to do so. He was supposed to establish a vigorous system of regional trade; his debts showed his failure there, too. He was supposed to establish federal sovereignty over Indians; in 1809, most tribes remained independent polities. The completion of all these goals—political development, commercial prosperity, and racial supremacy—were supposed to secure the Union in the West.

Then there was the matter of the book. In the wake of Lewis's suicide, Jefferson continued to hold out hope that Lewis had made significant progress on the manuscript. Indeed, he apparently expected something akin to a manuscript from the collection of materials that Lewis had brought with him. No sooner did news of his death reach Philadelphia than John Conrad, the publisher whom Lewis had contracted to produce the book, wrote to Jefferson in November 1809. Conrad was tentative and apologetic: "It is with much regret & some apprehension of incurring your Displeasure that we address you on this painfull subject so soon after the unfortunate circumstance that gives occasion for it. But the consideration that it is not alone our individual interests, but those of our country and of science." Conrad hoped Jefferson would inform him of whoever inherited responsibility for the project, since "Govr. Lewis never furnished us with a line of the M.S. nor indeed could we ever hear any thing from him respecting it tho frequent applications to that effect were made to him."[13]

Jefferson's initial reply was reassuring: "Be assured I shall spare no pains to secure the publication of his work, and when it may be within my sphere to take any definitive step reserving it, you shall be informed of it."[14] Perhaps so, but even Jefferson would come to express frustration with Lewis in the years following his death. Once Lewis's materials reached Washington, Jefferson fell silent. Lewis obviously had done little to organize his materials, let alone begin writing a manuscript.

Jefferson's comment to Conrad brought the discussion full circle, returning the verdict on Meriwether Lewis back to Charles Willson Peale's comment that "Governor Lewis has distroyed himself."[15] In making this claim, Peale most likely was using delicate terminology to state that Lewis had committed suicide. Nonetheless, he also captured just how much Lewis had destroyed himself as a public figure in the three years since the expedition. That self-destruction had occurred in the amorphous interchange between public policy and print culture. Lewis had failed to achieve the most basic principles of federal policy in the Louisiana Territory. He had also failed to write himself out of this situation through the production of a book that would remind Americans of his greatest success — leading the expedition of 1804–06 — or to produce letters and reports that sufficiently countered the written comments of his critics in the West.

Jefferson concluded that Clark had to protect Lewis's legacy. "I am waiting the arrival of Gen. Clarke," he informed Conrad, "expected here in a few days, to consult with him on the subject. his aid & his interest in the publication of the work may render him the proper depository to have it prepared & delivered over to you."[16] Clark treated the task as a debt of honor to Lewis, and Clark as much as Lewis believed in the Virginia gentry's code of honor. Besides, Clark was eager to see a book because he, too, believed it could help his career.[17]

THE HEROISM OF ZEBULON PIKE

During the same years in which Lewis struggled to make himself a frontier leader and suffered such disastrous consequences, Pike was engaged in a similarly ambitious project of narrative self-creation and professional advancement. In a brash, often self-complimentary tone, Pike described himself as a man of insurmountable determination and unflagging loyalty whose commitment to himself never overshadowed his commitment to his country. Pike often shared Clark's conviction that he had been wrongly denied the recognition he deserved. Unlike Clark, who endured those snubs in relative quiet, Pike converted them into yet another obstacle that he had overcome. And in the same way that the failure to produce a book contributed to Lewis's inability to defend his actions, Pike successfully produced the written and visual accounts designed to establish a clear picture of his achievements.

By 1808, Pike had joined Lewis and Clark in Missouri. Unlike Clark, whose military career had stalled, Pike had been promoted to major and was commanding troops in St. Louis.[18] Apparently Pike had no substantive contact with either Lewis or Clark. Part of the reason may rest in Pike's close association with General James Wilkinson, Lewis's troublesome predecessor as governor and a suspected Burr conspirator whom Lewis and Clark both decided to treat with suspicion. It may also rest in Pike's jealousy. Explaining the expenses of his expeditions to Wilkinson in 1806, Pike wrote, "I advert to the expences of my *two* Voyages (which I humbly conceive might be compared with the *one* performed by Captains Lewis & Clark) and the appropriations made for *their's*."[19] Pike resented the acclaim and rewards showered on Lewis and Clark.

Lewis and Pike both left St. Louis in 1809. Lewis began his desperate journey of professional self-defense in Washington, which ended with his suicide in Tennessee. Pike traveled to New Orleans and was promoted to lieutenant colonel.[20] Pike was also hard at work on a book. Rather than take the direct route down the Mississippi, Pike first took a lengthy sojourn to Annapolis, Maryland, to examine final editorial changes to the manuscript.[21] In 1810, Pike finally got the chance to announce himself on a national stage when he published *An Account of Expeditions to the Sources of the Mississippi: and through the western parts of Louisiana to the sources of the Arkansaw, Kans, La Platte, and Pierre Jaun Rivers: performed by order of the government of the United States during the years 1805, 1806, and 1807 and a tour through the interior parts of New Spain when conducted through these provinces by order of the captain-general in the year 1807.* This lengthy title introduced a one-volume account of Pike's two expeditions as well as his imprisonment in Mexico. In an early example of cross-marketing, an atlas with five maps of Pike's travels as well as charts of Indian populations and western commerce was available for purchase separately.[22]

Pike's publisher, C. and A. Conrad, seemed eager to corner the market on publishing the accounts of western exploration. Before Cornelius and Andrew Conrad attached their names, the firm was called John Conrad and Co., which only three years earlier had announced its contract to produce the official account of the Lewis and Clark Expedition. As they were completing Pike's volume, the Conrads learned of Lewis's suicide and his failure to make any progress on his book manuscript.

Like Lewis, Pike had himself painted by Charles Willson Peale. The two portraits, though clearly the work of the same artist, served different purposes and sent different messages. Unlike Lewis, whose portrait was destined for Peale's museum, the portrait of Pike appeared prominently in *An Account of Expeditions*. Whereas Lewis's dark clothing was almost invisible in a portrait meant to announce the subject as a modest civilian official, Peale's visage of Pike included a uniform of gold braid and shining buttons. It was a typical military portrait, the subject's clothing establishing both glory and accomplishment. Smiling faintly, Pike gazes, appropriately enough, at the title page, announcing his achievements on the frontier (Fig. 22).

In the year after the book's publication in 1810, Pike had the opportunity to seek his vengeance against the Spaniards and Indians alike, whom he had always identified as his foes in the West. When the United States annexed West Florida in the winter of 1810–11, Pike eagerly led his troops to seize Baton Rouge.[23] Months later, he dispatched troops to the western borderlands not only to evict white settlers who threatened the fragile peace there, but also to keep an eye on Spanish and Indian intentions. News of Pike's actions reverberated up the Mississippi Valley. Indian agents serving William Clark in the Louisiana Territory were particularly interested, eager to preserve a peace on the tense borderlands but equally pleased to see Pike assert American control over the territory.[24] Pike soon left the Territory of Orleans for the Indiana Territory, and in 1811 he commanded troops at the Battle of Tippecanoe under Clark's old friend William Henry Harrison. The Battle of Tippecanoe was a dubious victory for the United States. Harrison had his own career to advance, and he created an image of the battle that satisfied an American public eager for news of victory on the frontier.[25]

Then the very book Pike had written to secure his career threatened to destroy his reputation. In the fall of 1811, Alexander von Humboldt accused Pike of breaking the most time-honored rules of map production. A leading naturalist and explorer who enjoyed the admiration of intellectuals on both sides of the Atlantic, Humboldt had led an extensive tour through Spanish America from 1799 to 1803. In the years afterward, the Prussian-born Humboldt relocated to Paris, where he could immerse himself in the intellectual and cartographic communities that Americans had eyed with admiration and disdain. In 1805 he began to publish a massive account of his findings in natural history, geography, geology, and meteorology, an account he subsequently reissued in various languages, adding new information as he acquired it.[26] Humboldt also produced a map of the northwestern frontier of the Spanish empire in 1804 which bore a striking similarity to the maps that accompanied Pike's *Account of Expeditions* of 1810.[27]

David Bailie Warden, the American consul in Paris, reported to President Madison that Humboldt "accuses Major Pike of having copied a part of his map, without even the mention of his Name."[28] Warden was also a physician who had published books on subjects ranging from race to silk production, and Humboldt felt comfortable confiding his grievances to a fellow intellectual. Humboldt later wrote directly to Jefferson. As he explained, "Mr. Pike has taken, rather ungraciously, my report which he undoubtedly obtained in Washington with the copy of this map, and besides, he also extracted from it all the names." Humboldt leveled the same accusation at Aaron Arrowsmith, a cartographer whose 1795 map of North America had been vital to planning the Lewis and Clark Expedition. Jefferson had consulted the map to gather the latest knowledge on North American geography, while he saw the vast emptiness Arrowsmith left in the North American interior as evidence of the geographic ignorance that American explorers would correct. Humboldt claimed that Arrowsmith had sought to fill those gaps in later editions of his map by including information gleaned from Humboldt's work without any proper attribution.[29]

It was a potentially devastating accusation against both Pike and Arrowsmith. Humboldt enjoyed high esteem in American intellectual circles, not least of all that of Jefferson. Yet the accusations went unheeded by both Jefferson and Madison. Never particularly concerned with disputes among scientists, Madison had always seen landscape description as a practical way to advance western government and foreign policy. Madison ignored Humboldt's complaints altogether.

Besides, Madison had other matters on his mind, and he needed men like Pike. By the winter of 1811–12 the Madison administration had concluded that a military campaign against Canada was the only way to coerce change

Figure 22. Portrait of Zebulon Pike and title page from *An Account of Expeditions to the Sources of the Mississippi*. David Rumsey Map Collection, http://www.davidrumsey.com.

AN ACCOUNT OF EXPEDITIONS

TO THE *Wm Hayward*

Sources of the Mississippi,

AND THROUGH THE

WESTERN PARTS OF LOUISIANA,

TO THE SOURCES OF THE

ARKANSAW, KANS, LA PLATTE, AND PIERRE JAUN, RIVERS;

PERFORMED BY ORDER OF THE

GOVERNMENT OF THE UNITED STATES

DURING THE YEARS 1805, 1806, AND 1807.

AND A TOUR THROUGH

THE

INTERIOR PARTS OF NEW SPAIN,

WHEN CONDUCTED THROUGH THESE PROVINCES,

BY ORDER OF

THE CAPTAIN-GENERAL,

IN THE YEAR 1807.

BY MAJOR Z. M. PIKE.

ILLUSTRATED BY MAPS AND CHARTS.

PHILADELPHIA:

PUBLISHED BY C. & A. CONRAD, & Co. No. 30, CHESNUT STREET. SOMER-
VELL & CONRAD, PETERSBURGH. BONSAL, CONRAD, & Co. NORFOLK,
AND FIELDING LUCAS, Jr. BALTIMORE.

John Binns, Printer.....1810.

in British commercial policy. On June 18, 1812, Congress declared war on Great Britain, and experienced officers like Pike were in great demand. In the months afterward, Congress authorized a massive increase in the size of the army. Pike rose quickly through the ranks of the officer corps. By 1813, at the age of thirty-four, he was a brigadier general. As he commanded troops preparing for a dramatic maritime invasion across Lake Ontario, Pike believed his moment had finally arrived. Writing to his father, who had known so much frustration in his own military career, Pike proclaimed, "If success attends my steps, honor and glory await my name."[30] Pike was eager to take the lead as his men launched an assault on the Canadian town of York (present-day Toronto). At the height of the battle, Pike was mortally wounded by a shower of exploding stone masonry. He died within hours, apparently aware that the British were in retreat. Whatever Pike's final thoughts, a man so thoroughly immersed in military traditions and so committed to his own advancement might well have taken satisfaction in the fact that there was hardly a better way for a general to attach "honor and glory" to his name than to die in combat at the moment of victory.

Three months after Pike's death, Humboldt's letter of 1811 accusing Arrowsmith and Pike of cartographic plagiarism finally reached Jefferson after a three-year delay in its delivery.[31] At the height of his anti-British sentiments, Jefferson concluded "that their Arrowsmith should have stolen your map of Mexico, was in the piratical spirit of his country." In sharp contrast, Jefferson was hardly prepared to criticize one of the few military heroes in a war that had revealed widespread incompetence within the leadership of the U.S. Army. "I should be sincerely sorry if our Pike has made an ungenerous use of your candid communication here," Jefferson explained, "and the more so as he died in the arms of victory gained over the enemies of this country. Whatever he did was on a principle of enlarging knolege [*sic*] and not for filthy shillings and pence of which he made none from that book." Besides, Jefferson believed that Pike's description of the West was filled with "defective information" and would only motivate people to consult "the copious volumes of it with which you have enriched the world."[32]

Jefferson had previously shown little hesitancy to criticize what he considered the faulty surveying and cartography of Pike's book and his maps. In the wake of Pike's death, however, and especially in correspondence with a foreigner, things were different. The former president hoped to preserve the image that Pike had struggled so mightily to create.

THE EMPLOYMENT OF THOMAS FREEMAN

There is no portrait of Thomas Freeman. If he ever commissioned one, it has not survived. One thing is clear: Charles Willson Peale never painted Freeman. That Freeman's physical appearance remains a mystery is somehow appropriate, however, for it captures the place Freeman created for himself in the federal government. Unlike Lewis and Pike, who acted in ways typical of men aiming for high-level office in the civil and military branches of the federal government, Freeman sought only the regular pay and elevated status that separated a midlevel territorial official from the journeyman surveyor he had once been. He described the West accordingly.

In the years after the Red River Expedition, Freeman continued to follow the principles established by his mentor, Andrew Ellicott. Like Lewis, Clark, and Pike, Freeman stayed in the West. He continued in his role as a federal surveyor, and in 1811 he became chief surveyor for all the federal territory south of Tennessee. It was a daunting assignment consisting primarily of the Mississippi Territory, a vast region in which the competing claims of the federal government, Indian villages, American newcomers, and the existing white population with French and Spanish land claims led to endless disputes. But it was an appropriate destination for Freeman in that a decade earlier he had helped define the Mississippi Territory when he joined Ellicott on the southwestern boundary survey.[33]

Freeman was also on hand to protect the meager legacy of a fellow explorer. In November 1809, he was in Nashville, Tennessee, soon after Lewis committed suicide. Unaware that Clark was nearby in Kentucky, Freeman took charge of Lewis's few personal possessions before mailing them to Washington. That Freeman did so was a coincidence, and an ironic one at that. That Freeman was in the West was anything but ironic. His career remained in the West because that was where surveyors secured advancement within the federal system.[34]

In his efforts to describe the West, Freeman faced many of the same challenges from Indians and white settlers that had bedeviled federal officials throughout the territories. He supported the eviction of squatters just as he sought to extend the claims of white settlers. In both cases, he crafted surveys that were the foundation for legal property claims on an American model.[35] Throughout these years, surveyors like Freeman were the closest thing in the United States to an official mapping agency. In 1812 Congress authorized the creation of the General Land Office. Instead of a collection of scattered fed-

eral surveyors usually reporting to the Treasury Department, the United States
had now committed itself to a permanent bureaucracy to describe the western territory. Nonetheless, they rarely produced large regional maps, devot-
ing themselves instead to local surveys.[36]

Like most territorial officials, Freeman often complained about the inac-
curacy of existing surveys as well as about resistance from white settlers and
Indians alike. Unable or unwilling to make the sort of loud assertions and
protests that characterized the writing of Lewis and Pike, Freeman nonetheless struggled mightily to establish a reputation from a distance through the
same sort of surveying results he had produced on the Red River Expedition.
Writing to his superiors in Washington during the 1810s, Freeman repeatedly
referred to the maps he had completed and the boundaries he had surveyed.
The very landscape of the Southwest seemed to announce his success. As the
population grew, Congress divided the Mississippi Territory in half, creating
the new Alabama Territory in the East and providing a new set of surveying
challenges that guaranteed the ongoing employment of Thomas Freeman.
Soon after he began work in the Alabama Territory in 1817, for example, he
proudly informed Josiah Meigs, the commissioner of all federal lands, that "I
have the honor to inform you that I have had prepared for Sale 31. Townships in the Alabama District."[37] The letter quietly proclaimed Freeman's
achievements. So, too, did the maps he included. In the process of describing the southwestern landscape, numerous surveys and local maps also served
as testimony to Freeman's work.[38] Rarely referring to himself by name, Freeman nonetheless engaged in a form of narrative self-creation through the written word and visual representation.

The greatest threat to that reputation came in 1817, not from the squatters
of Mississippi but, appropriately enough, from a dispute over maps. Much
like Humboldt's complaints about Pike's work, the controversy that consumed
Freeman emerged from the vague rules of authorship in cartographic publishing.

The accusations against Freeman came from Maxfield Ludlow, a public
surveyor in Louisiana and a former subordinate of Freeman. As Ludlow told
the story, in 1812 Freeman approached him about a contract from Abraham
Bradley, himself a revealing figure in American landscape representation.
Bradley dabbled in cartography, first publishing a map of the United States
in 1796 that he periodically updated in the years afterward to incorporate both
shifting boundaries and new geographic information.[39] But Bradley was also
a long-serving assistant postmaster who, like Jefferson's explorers, wanted the

steady income of government patronage. Ludlow proposed that he and Freeman produce the map and split the profits with Bradley. The deal apparently
fell through, but Ludlow did publish a map of Louisiana and the Mississippi
and Alabama territories in 1815.[40]

Ludlow produced a second printing in 1817, apparently at the very moment
that Freeman was planning to publish a similar map for Bradley. When Ludlow learned of Freeman's plans, he charged Freeman with just about every
transgression imaginable. Not only was there the obvious copyright transgression, but Ludlow accused Freeman of misleading and then betraying a
trusting colleague. To this he added comments that Freeman was an in-
competent surveyor whose sloppy conduct broke the public trust. Ludlow
suggested the reason for this by claiming Freeman was "constantly absent on
feats of dissipation; an habitual drunkard." Ludlow's claims smacked of
Lewis's defensive response to the plans for Frazer's book a decade earlier. Fu-
rious at the apparent betrayal by trusted subordinates, both Lewis and Freeman not only asserted their authority over western description, but also
dismissed the accuracy of their competitors.[41]

Freeman himself apparently offered no public response to these accusations. He had complained about the conduct of an unnamed former clerk
during the 1810s, most likely Ludlow. Whether these were legitimate grievances on Freeman's part or preemptive criticism to explain any future attacks
by Ludlow is more difficult to determine. There is no record of a map published by Bradley that was created by Freeman. Meanwhile, Ludlow claimed
that the initial discussion with Freeman came in 1812, while Ludlow himself
had published a circular announcing his plans to produce a map as early as
1810. At the same time, this hardly eliminates the possibility that Ludlow believed Freeman intended to produce a map in 1817.[42]

The two surveyors manifestly hated each other, and the source of their ha-
tred was maps. Both men had staked their future on public employment as
surveyors, and Ludlow in particular seemed keen on joining the small number of men who made a living as published cartographers. Ludlow lost the immediate battle, for Freeman's reputation remained intact, as did his authority
as a public official. Yet Ludlow did complete his project, producing a massive forty-two-by-seventy-three-inch map that included much of the material
from his map of 1815.[43]

Freeman remained on the federal payroll, dispatched his reports to Washington, and continued to enjoy the quiet approval of his superiors. Unlike
Lewis and Pike, both of whom received published testimonials after their

deaths, the federal government had little to say about Freeman. Even Freeman's death was anonymous. Instead, the death of Thomas Freeman entered the public record of the federal government only when it came time to distribute his office to another aspiring surveyor. In January 1822, President James Monroe dispatched a brief note to the Senate nominating "Levin Wailes, to be Surveyor of the Public Lands south of the State of Tennessee, vice Thomas Freeman, deceased." This came in the midst of dozens of similar nominations during a week the president apparently devoted to making federal appointments.[44]

Freeman's very anonymity suggested just how common his efforts actually were. The United States had surveyors in every federal territory. None of them matched Freeman's involvement in western exploration, but most of them shared his quiet means of establishing a reputation from a distance. Describing the western landscape in words and pictures for them took the form of highly technical surveys. Those surveys were also the means through which men made the case for patronage.

THE RISE OF WILLIAM CLARK

In the years between his return from the Lewis and Clark Expedition in 1806 and his efforts to take charge of the book project following Lewis's death in 1809, Clark struggled to establish himself as a reliable senior official on the territorial frontier. Lewis's failures only highlighted Clark's skills. Clark observed Lewis's downfall with sadness and a certain bewilderment. Lewis's erratic political behavior and profligate financial management flew in the face of Clark's emotional restraint and financial thrift. Yet Clark lacked either the reputation or the influence to move up in the territorial hierarchy.

As the Madison administration began considering candidates to replace Lewis as governor of the Louisiana Territory, for example, Clark's name apparently never entered the discussion. Instead, officials considered a variety of other candidates, most of them elite Virginians.[45] In January 1810, Clark explained to his brother Jonathan that "no nomination for Govr. has taken place—many and a great maney of the ferst Standing has offerard ther Interest and expressed a wish fer me to be appointed, but I am afraid, and Cannot Consent if I was, no doubt would remain ___ I do not think myself Calculated to meet the Storms which might be expected."[46] It was a revealing passage, suggesting Clark's ambivalence about entering the highly politicized world of senior territorial office. His letter to his brother helps explain why.

Clark's bizarre spelling habits have long intrigued and amused his biographers, but they may have embarrassed Clark himself. He had joined the army at a time when even penmanship could be a criterion for assigning rank. Although spelling was hardly standardized, Clark was more inconsistent in his spelling than many of his contemporaries.[47]

Madison's eventual selection, Benjamin Howard, was the typical sort of man to take charge of the territorial West. Howard was born in western Virginia and became a successful lawyer and politician in Kentucky. He was elected to Congress in 1806 but resigned his seat in April 1810 to accept the offer to become governor of the Louisiana Territory. Meanwhile, Clark remained an Indian agent, a task that seemed to suit his limitations as well as his talents.

Clark also had his hands full meeting his promise to supervise completion of the book from the Lewis and Clark Expedition. When Clark reached Washington in the wake of Lewis's suicide, he inspected the contents of Lewis's trunks along with Isaac Coles, a well-connected Virginian serving as Madison's secretary. He was delighted to find Lewis's notes intact but, like Jefferson, was startled to learn just how little progress Lewis had made on producing a polished manuscript.[48] Clark then proceeded to Philadelphia, carrying a letter from Joel Barlow (an aspiring poet but also a well-connected diplomat) introducing Clark to Benjamin Rush, a physician and leading figure in Philadelphia's intellectual circles. Rush had trained both Lewis and Peter Custis. Still, Clark faced social challenges. Barlow recommended Clark to Rush only because he hoped "your men of Science" would be able to assist Clark in producing a book that he was patently unqualified to complete.[49]

Still intending to focus his own efforts on producing a map, Clark arranged for Benjamin Smith Barton to produce a scientific volume. This book would be a rough equivalent to the last of Lewis's proposed three-volume account of the Lewis and Clark Expedition. A physician by training, Barton was among the leading botanists in the United States as well as the long-serving vice president of the American Philosophical Society. Most important, in 1803 Barton had trained Lewis in botany and seemed the logical choice to supervise the publication of the scientific legacy of the Lewis and Clark Expedition. Meanwhile, Clark sought an editor who would accept the daunting task of extracting a single narrative from the mass of expedition journals. His first choice was William Wirt. Wirt was originally from Maryland, but his law practice brought him to Virginia, where he launched a political career that quickly attracted the attention and trust of the Jefferson administration. In

1807 Wirt had assisted with the prosecution of Aaron Burr. Wirt was also an occasional writer and in 1817 produced the first major biography of Patrick Henry. But Wirt's literary career was still in its infancy in 1810, and he quickly declined Clark's invitation.[50]

Clark next approached Nicholas Biddle, and so began one of Clark's only extended relationships with a member of the urbane literary society of the Northeast. If Clark exemplified how describing the West was the work of men who never considered themselves writers or artists, Biddle exemplified a certain type of man with literary ambition. Like Wirt and Barlow, Biddle enjoyed writing in a way Clark never did. Also like Wirt and Barlow, Biddle considered writing more of a hobby than a profession. All three men saw themselves primarily as public figures. Barlow held various diplomatic appointments. In 1817, the same year that Wirt published his biography of Patrick Henry, he also became James Monroe's attorney general. Biddle came from a wealthy family with deep roots in Philadelphia's elite. A gifted student, he had graduated from Princeton University at fifteen and by eighteen was crossing the Atlantic to serve as the secretary to John Armstrong, the U.S. minister to France. When he returned to the United States in 1807, Biddle began publishing the *Port-Folio,* a literary magazine, but he never lost sight of his political aspirations.

Biddle came from the tradition of gentlemen writers that remained a small community in the United States. In an age when elite American men were more likely to display their sophistication through their knowledge of science and politics, men with Biddle's literary interests were few and far between. Bookshelves stocked with nonfiction titles—biographies, histories, or for that matter geographies—were far more respectable than a collection of novels or poetry. While elite American men like Biddle did read fiction, their upbringing taught them that this was a genre more appropriate for women.[51]

If Biddle himself represents a telling example in American literary history, so, too, does his interaction with Clark. The relationship between the two men took shape through letters. In an age when letter writing was crucial to everyday life, many American men established themselves and their relationships with others in the masculine, seemingly impersonal language of letter writing, but this was particularly true of Biddle and Clark. In Clark's case, writing was also supposed to overcome distance, sustaining crucial professional relationships in the East.[52] For his part, Biddle never traveled west, preferring to move between his townhouse in Philadelphia and Andalusia, his family's country estate on the banks of the Delaware River. While Clark traveled repeatedly from St. Louis to the East Coast, he rarely went north of Washington.

When Clark initially approached him to edit a narrative of the Lewis and Clark Expedition, Biddle demurred. Recently elected to the Pennsylvania General Assembly, Biddle was more concerned with his budding political career than his literary interests. He also pleaded poor health. "I have neither health nor leisure to do sufficient justice to the fruits of your enterprize and ingenuity," he informed Clark. "You cannot be long however without making a more fortunate selection."[53]

Clark was undeterred. As he explained to Jonathan, "Docr. Barton will write the Scientific part, and I expect to get a Mr. Biddle to write the naritiv. The map I Shall improv on my Self."[54] Only after confirming C. and A. Conrad's commitment to publishing the project and Barton's decision to produce the scientific volume did Biddle relent. He immediately regretted the decision. Apparently he never complained to Clark, but he did vent his frustration to a Philadelphia confidant. "With my usual indolence I declined [Clark's offer]," Biddle confided in 1810 to David Bailie Warden, the man who in 1811 informed Madison of Humboldt's complaints about the Pike maps. "But after much more persuasion than the subject was worth I have consented. . . . I find it exceedingly troublesome, for not a word was prepared for the press by Captain Lewis. The papers are very voluminous."[55] After Jefferson and Clark, Biddle was only the latest to express frustration at Lewis's failure.

As Biddle immersed himself in the project, however, he revealed a growing enthusiasm that linked his literary inclinations to his political aspirations. For example, he asked Warden to procure a copy of Antoine-Simon Le Page du Pratz's *History of Louisiana*. He most likely hoped to use the book as a geographical reference, no doubt unaware how frustrated Jefferson and Madison had been only a few years before when they consulted French historical texts in pursuit of Louisiana's boundaries. Concluding that Lewis and Clark had provided material to correct the European texts rather than the other way around, Biddle eventually wrote to Secretary of State James Monroe, "You know I believe that I am preparing for publication Lewis & Clarkes' travels. Among other subjects of enquiry, they were desirous of finding some branch of the Missouri which, by reaching as far north as the Lake of the Woods, might enable us to rectify the error in the Treaty of 1794, relative to our northern boundary." Biddle celebrated his project as an important tool of federal policy as the United States continued its ongoing efforts to settle boundary disputes after decades in which American and British diplomats lamented the absence of geographic information.[56]

As soon as Biddle accepted the offer to edit the account of the Lewis and Clark Expedition, he consulted with the publisher and recommended that the book include a single "large connected map of the whole route & the adjacent country." Apparently, the brothers Cornelius and Andrew Conrad had thought twice about their decision to publish an atlas to accompany Pike's *An Account of Expeditions*. Most publishers preferred to save costs by including only a single map folded into their books, as in the case of the work of Jedidiah Morse. Ellicott had included multiple maps in his *Journal*, published in 1803, but they were contained within the book itself rather than in a separate volume like Pike's. Biddle explained that Conrad had promised to print a number of small-scale maps within the book to illustrate specific points of the journey. More important, Clark was free to create a map that could "embrace as many degrees of latitude as you think your Indian information will authorize you to make it, and on a scale perhaps somewhat larger than that which you have already made."[57]

These suggestions released Clark to complete work on his most important contribution to the book project and his most detailed self-portrait. Unschooled as an editor, uncomfortable as a writer, possessing none of Lewis's aspirations for scientific acclaim, Clark had eagerly accepted the task of producing a map. What he drew on a twenty-eight-by-fifty-inch piece of paper eventually became known as William Clark's Master Map of the North American West. A landmark piece of cartography, the map also announced Clark's achievements and his qualifications in terms no less clear than he hoped Biddle would use when explaining Clark's rank on the expedition. That map and the book that Biddle was editing would present him to a national audience. More crucially, it would establish his reputation from a distance in the place where it mattered most: Washington, D.C.

On December 20, 1810, Clark proudly informed Biddle, "I herewith inclose to you a map which I have drawn for my book, it is much more correct than any which has been before published, it is made on the same scale of the one you have, containing more country, I wish you to anex as much of it to the book as you think best, you will observe that I have not inclosed it in lines. the Ohio is not correct, mearly shows the river as they mouth."[58] Like so many other mapmakers, Clark left almost no record of how he actually produced his work. Yet certain details emerge from the object itself. The map was clearly in his own hand. Clark also surrounded the regions he had actually surveyed with information from numerous other sources, ranging from other published maps to conversations he had had with Indians during the Lewis and Clark Expedition.[59]

The result was a map of unprecedented detail and technical accuracy that continues to amaze cartographers to this day. Whatever its cartographic contributions, Clark's map remained an autobiographical document. It constituted his most personal effort to display his achievements and his skills to a national audience, but it was not the only one. In the summer of 1811 Biddle approached Clark with an unexpected opportunity to produce an autobiography in words as well. "There is one and only one more thing about which I wish you would give me information," Biddle wrote. "It is the exact relative situation in point of rank & command between Captain Lewis & yourself. I think you mentioned to me that your commision was that of Lieutenant of Engineers, which placed you completely on an equality with Captain Lewis who was & that in all other respects you were equal in command. a captain of infantry or artillery I am desirous of being correct and I will get you to state to me whether I have understood you precisely so as to avoid all error on that subject."[60]

"I did not think my self very well treated as I did not get the appointment which was promised me," Clark responded. What followed was an intriguing statement: "I was not disposed to make any noise about the business have never mentioned the particulars to any one, and must request you not to mention my disapointment & the cause to any one." Perhaps so, but the book-writing process provided the ideal means to set the record straight. Clark wrote an extensive overview of his military career in the 1790s. After a brief description of his efforts as a planter, Clark described Lewis's invitation to join the expedition and how he then "waited with some anxiety for the commision which I had reasons to expect (Capt. of Indioneers)."[61]

When he received only a second lieutenant's commission, "my feelings on this occasion was as might be expected." Clark made another cryptic reference to his decision to return his commission to Henry Dearborn in 1806 before concluding, "I do not wish that any thing relative to this coms.n or appointment should be inserted in my book or made known, for very perticular reasons, and I do assure you that I have never related as much on the subject to any person before. Be so good as to place me on equal footing with Capt. Lewis in every point of view without exposing any thing which might have taken place or even mentioning the commission at all."

It was a remarkable passage. Whatever his claims to the contrary, Clark went out of his way to give Biddle the means to craft a public rebuke of Dearborn. Perhaps Clark felt more secure because by 1811 Dearborn (who had left the cabinet at the end of the Jefferson administration) held the modest office of port collector in Boston. Clark made no effort to contact Dearborn when he returned to uniform as a major general commanding forces on the U.S.–Canadian border during the War of 1812. Dearborn proved a lackluster commander whose only major success in the War of 1812 was to command the forces engaged in the assault on York. One of his immediate subordinates was Zebulon Pike. Whereas the paucity of correspondence between Lewis and Madison reflected a cordial but impersonal relationship that helps explain Lewis's movements and actions in the fall of 1809, the complete silence between Clark and Dearborn seems less the result of their military assignments than of the long-simmering disputes related to Clark's military career.[62]

William Clark had finally arrived. As if to confirm the matter, in February 1811 the Senate renewed his commission as brigadier general in the territorial militia. The appointment was no small affair given Clark's numerous frustrations about promotion.[63] In 1807, Charles Willson Peale had painted what became the most familiar visage of Clark. But in 1810, Clark commissioned two other major portraits. In his portrait John Wesley Jarvis made Clark appear much older, his jowls sagging and his red hair growing thin. Meanwhile, Joseph Bush pictured Clark in the military uniform of a militia officer. Whether showing him wearing a formal suit and ruffled kerchief or a gold-fringed uniform, the paintings all announced Clark as the leading citizen he had become (Fig. 23).[64]

Yet portraits were never sufficient. Like his portrait of Lewis, Peale's painting of Clark can be misleading. The two works now quite literally face one another in most books on Lewis and Clark, quickly establishing Clark's image for a general public. Two centuries ago, however, portraits of Clark did little to project his image beyond either St. Louis or Philadelphia. He was busy creating his own self-portrait for mass production. And that portrait did not show his face. Instead, it was a map that would represent William Clark's world.

Even as Clark collaborated with Biddle to produce a book that established his reputation from a distance, he concluded that reputation alone was never sufficient. He repeatedly traveled east, usually to visit his family in Kentucky and Virginia before consulting with his superiors in Washington. He was on one of these trips in 1812 when he learned that the Louisiana Territory had ceased to exist and the United States was at war.

Figure 23. Charles Willson Peale, *William Clark* (1807–08).
Independence National Historic Park.

In May 1812, the Territory of Orleans became the state of Louisiana. To
prevent the obvious confusion that would have resulted from having a state
and a territory with the same name, Congress changed the Territory of
Louisiana to the Territory of Missouri. More important, though, Congress
was prepared to create a territorial house of representatives and provide for a
nonvoting delegate to the U.S. House of Representatives. It marked an important step toward statehood. Much as Clark might welcome the change,
the prospect put his political future at risk. As an Indian agent, he remained
a subordinate of the federal government. The creation of elected offices in
Missouri marked the beginning of a political system he had rarely encountered.[65]

The Madison administration sought these changes in part to build public
support in the West for the great challenge that was soon to come. In June

1812 the United States declared war on Great Britain. It was in the midst of a national mobilization for war that Biddle wrote to Clark with his own alarming news: "Mr. Conrad's difficulties have obliged him to surrender every thing to his creditors & give up business." It was a polite way of saying that the firm of C. and A. Conrad had gone bankrupt. Biddle was apologetic. He was also irritated, claiming "last winter I was prevented from going to the legislature chiefly by a desire to stay & superintend the printing yet notwithstanding all my exertion the publication has been prevented from time to time."[66]

Clark made an unplanned trip to Philadelphia in August, where he learned that Biddle was struggling to complete a new contract with another Philadelphia printer, Bradford and Inskeep. Apparently Biddle was not working fast enough for Clark, for in September Clark explained that he was consumed by "the situation of my publick duties" and could ill afford to spend any more time in Philadelphia. "Cant I perswade you to become Interested in Lewis & Clarks work," Clark implored Biddle. "I hope you will concent and under that hope I take the liberty of offering you the half of every profit arrising from it if you will attend to it, how it completed as far as it is possible."[67]

On that note, Clark left Philadelphia never to return. In the end, Biddle proved a reliable partner who managed to shepherd the project through the final stages of publication. He served as intermediary between Paul Allen, Biddle's editorial assistant at the *Port-Folio*, who finished the process of editing the journals; Samuel Lewis, who drew a copy of Clark's master map; Samuel Harrison, who engraved Clark's master map onto metal plates ready for mass printing; and Bradford and Inskeep. All the while he kept Clark apprised of their progress.

For his own part, Clark's interest waned as he focused on mobilizing western defenses. When the United States declared war on Great Britain, the Madison administration planned to pursue a quick war pitting American soldiers against British redcoats on the U.S.–Canadian border. This strategy proved a disaster, the conflict lasting far longer than the administration hoped and spreading in all directions. U.S. and British ships—both naval vessels and privateers—scoured the Atlantic and Pacific oceans. In addition to fighting the British, American forces faced a resurgent Indian resistance in the West. Meanwhile, Americans exploited the war to defeat beleaguered Spanish forces in the South and secure the long-sought American possession of the Gulf Coast. The war was both an international and interracial conflict, and Clark's entire life had taught him to understand western conflict in those terms. For his older brother George Rogers Clark, the American Revolution was a struggle between volunteers and Indians, not between the Continental Army and British regulars. In the 1790s, Clark had learned firsthand about the connections between diplomacy with Indians, Britain, and Spain. Clark had always understood the Lewis and Clark Expedition as an extension of these diplomatic concerns. He brought that experience with him as he developed strategies for what he considered the two wars in the West: one between the United States and Great Britain that began in 1812, the other a longer conflict between the territorial leadership and the Indians of the West.

As Clark struggled to combine borderland defense, landscape description, and narrative self-creation, Madison selected Benjamin Howard for a commission as brigadier general in the U.S. Army and command of all military operations in the Missouri Territory. Howard's appointment was the sort of assignment Clark had always sought, but if he resented the situation his extensive written record provides no indication of it. Besides, any resentment would have been short-lived. Howard's military commission also brought an end to his term as territorial governor, and with Congress in recess, Madison selected Clark as Howard's successor. The formal nomination went to the Senate on May 31, 1813. This time there were no impediments, the Senate granting approval two days later.[68] After a decade in which decisions by the Senate and secretaries of war had humiliated the status-conscious Clark, he now enjoyed unquestioned authority with the clear support of Washington. Unlike Howard, who could not hold both a general's commission in the army and his office of territorial governor, Clark remained the commanding general of the territorial militia, consolidating his status as the public figure in the territorial administration.

By the time Clark became a territorial governor, he was a practiced writer. The increasing demands of Indian policy forced him to become a regular correspondent with senior officials in Washington. As governor, he had to produce an even more polished prose. His conception of the proper tone for a governor's public pronouncements was a formal, authoritative style that shared more with the Federalist officials of the 1790s than with the new generation of democratic politicians who became particularly powerful in the West. But this only made sense, for Clark's notions of leadership were rooted in his experiences in the Northwest Territory during the 1790s. To Virginia-born military men like Clark, there could be no better model of leadership than George Washington, who always imagined that leaders needed to write in ways that showed their difference from average citizens, not their similarity.

Yet even as Clark found himself writing more, he never abandoned his practice of combining written and visual representations of the western landscape and its occupants. His analysis of the strategic situation often took shape in the form of maps that attempted to show the location and movements of Indians as well as possible locations for federal outposts. These were typical instruments of war planning, drawing on a long tradition of military cartography. But they were also the logical expression of Clark's representational skills, imposing a rational interpretive order onto the landscape that mimicked similar goals in everything from small surveys he made of his family's private property to the vastness of the national property he had shown in his master map.[69]

It was in these circumstances that Clark, in 1813, drew the map of the Great Lakes and the Mississippi and Missouri rivers that appears at the beginning of this chapter. The map charted U.S. settlements, military establishments, and possible Indian threats. It formed a visual component to one of Clark's first letters as governor. Writing to Secretary of State Monroe, Clark explained, "We have had a number of hostile parties of Indians Continuely on our Northern, & Eastern frontiers."[70] In a single page, the map conveyed Clark's strategic outlook for the entire region extending north from St. Louis. Some of this material came from a similar map of 1811. Drawn in the midst of the pan-Indian revival, the map attempted to show the possibilities of attack by the Indian forces of Tecumseh and Tenskwatawa (also known as the Shawnee Prophet), the brothers who had emerged as leaders of that movement. Meanwhile, notation on the back of the map recorded how Indians had traveled west from this region across the Mississippi to attack white settlers. The notes also included a list of "good Chiefs" and "Bade Chiefs." The Shawnee Prophet's name appears prominently among the bad chiefs.[71] Although Americans celebrated the Battle of Tippecanoe as a crushing defeat for the Indians, Clark knew better. As he drew his map in 1813, Clark continued to worry about an alliance that would link Indians to each other and to Great Britain.

In technical terms, Clark's map of the Great Lakes region was a pale shadow of his Master Map of the North American West from 1810. In fact, at the very moment Clark was drawing his crude illustration of the military situation in 1813 for his own use and that of the administration, Samuel Harrison was creating the detailed, elaborate engraving that would mass-produce Clark's map. Yet Clark conceived of the maps in similar terms, both personally and nationally. These were policymaking tools, like his written reports before and during the War of 1812. They were also autobiographical documents, creating a portrait of Clark in terms just as clear as Peale's painting of him.

In March 1814 Biddle wrote triumphantly, "I have at last the pleasure of informing you that the travels are published that they have sold very well I understand, and have been well thought of by the readers. Henceforward you may sleep upon your fame which must last as long as books can endure."[72] The book was late, and not simply because it had taken so much longer to produce than the published accounts of the other explorers. The book was too late to redeem Lewis's career and save his life. And now it was late in the sense it had failed to offer the professional advancement Clark had secured through other means.

Biddle's note to Clark contained the sort of supportive language that Biddle had long used in his correspondence with the explorer. It also exhibited the sort of overblown language that people had long used to celebrate writing. It was, in other words, the way writers discussed books. But Clark was no writer. He depended on the book, but in a way very different from the way writers imagined their thoughts and ideas extending across time. In September 1814, Clark responded to Biddle in ways that indicated both his fondness for the editor as well as his public concerns. He consoled Biddle and his wife, Jane, in the midst of tremendous personal grief. Jane's mother and infant daughter had died within less than a month of each other. "I do assure you," Clark wrote, "that I was extreemely concerned for the loss you have met with in your familey, my own feelings enable me to know what those of a fond parent must be towards his child." Clark informed Biddle that his copies of *History of the Expedition* had not arrived, although "I have borrowed a copy of my book which has reached this place but have not had time to read it as yet." He told Biddle of a recent trip he had taken up the Mississippi River to build a new fort, part of the more elaborate efforts to coordinate military strategy. While Clark was eager to read the book, the War of 1812 took top priority.[73]

When Clark finally found the time to read the book, he examined what proved to be an impressive physical object. Two leather-bound volumes contained close to one thousand pages. And neatly folded behind the cover of every copy was the twenty-seven-by-thirty-inch map pressed from the plates Harrison had engraved. Based on Clark's Master Map, it repeated many of the errors Clark had made. Nonetheless, the map stands up remarkably well, current cartographic technologies doing more to confirm Clark's representation than to challenge it. Clark would have been pleased, for he always understood his first responsibility to be a map that provided Americans with a precise measurement of the western landscape.[74]

Biddle and Clark continued to correspond on personal and business matters. In the spring of 1816 Biddle wrote with what he thought was bad news. The problems had begun the previous year when, like John Conrad and Co., Bradford and Inskeep declared bankruptcy. The publisher had completed production of *History of the Expedition* but was incapable of promoting the book locally, let alone nationally. Biddle blamed the situation on the economic woes brought about by the War of 1812. "I cannot express to you how much I am disappointed at the unfortunate result of this business," he informed Clark in May 1816. While Biddle intended these comments as a statement of condolence to Clark, he might as well have been referring to himself. Biddle had long regretted his decision to participate in an apparently endless project that seemed cursed by the suicide of one author, the bankruptcy of two publishers, and a war that consumed both Clark's energies and his own. Still serving in the Pennsylvania Senate, Biddle had to leave the state capital in Harrisburg for Philadelphia, where he hoped to make ongoing arrangements for selling the book. "I was in hopes," he wrote, "that after having sacrificed a great deal of time and some money (in traveling to Virginia)—after renouncing all claim for the trouble of almost two years I should at least have had the pleasure of seeing you enjoy something to reward for your long laborious & honorable services."[75]

Biddle was undoubtedly irritated, but he was also apologetic. He was also mistaken, for Clark had every reason to feel relief to the point of elation. Those feelings hardly came from *History of the Expedition*, for Clark shared Biddle's frustrations with a project that had yet to deliver on its promise to promote Clark's career as well as his finances. Rather, Clark was delighted by his circumstances as well as by his country's. In 1814, American and British officials negotiated a conclusion to the War of 1812. In 1815, before news of the Treaty of Ghent reached the United States and, more important, before the U.S. Senate ratified the treaty, American and British forces fought their last battles on land and sea. Indeed, one of the great ironies of the Battle of New Orleans is that this greatest of American victories came in January 1815, almost two months after the two parties had settled on peace terms. Americans now treat the Battle of New Orleans as the end of the War of 1812. But as British and American troops stopped fighting in the winter of 1815, peace in the West remained elusive. Indians had chosen sides in the war and formed alliances with the United States and Great Britain. Throughout 1815, Indians rejected a peace in which they had not participated, interpreting the treaty as yet another example of British betrayal similar to that in 1794, when the British decision to abandon the Indians at their weakest point in the aftermath of the Battle of Fallen Timbers had forced them to accept the terms of the Treaty of Greenville.

The war that concerned Clark—a conflict between Indians and white settlers—finally ended at one of the largest gatherings of Indian representatives in North America and one of the most important moments in U.S. negotiations. In July 1815, delegates from all the warring parties, including the United States, gathered at Portage des Sioux, near St. Louis. The negotiations that followed were tense and often frustrating. In addition to the overriding conflict between the United States and many of the Indians from the eastern Plains, Clark had constructed alliances with other Indians during the War of 1812 that had created intense antagonisms of their own. The gathering ended with all of the leaders—U.S. and Indian—forging the terms of a general peace. Although Indian leaders claimed victories of their own at Portage des Sioux, it was a resolution for which Clark was only too eager to take credit.[76]

The following summer Clark received a brief but elaborate document. Signed by President Madison and Secretary of State Monroe, it was a commission renewing his appointment as governor of the Missouri Territory. Clark saved the document, filing it away with a growing collection of official and private correspondence that he saved with assiduous care.[77] Clark continued to fret about *History of the Expedition,* but now his fears seemed to be more financial than political. Over a decade after the Lewis and Clark Expedition brought Clark back into the federal government, his status within that government finally seemed secure.

6

BOOKS

By the time *History of the Expedition* rolled off the presses in 1814, all of Jefferson's explorers were finished both with exploration and with writing books. But what had they created? What did those books and maps say about the North American West? A suggestion of the answer emerges from the difficult circumstances facing William Clark in 1816, a moment that indicated not only the content of those books and maps, but also the ways in which the production of those objects had a profound effect on the stories they told.

As Clark and Biddle tried to tie up the loose ends of *History of the Expedition*, Thomas Jefferson got impatient. In 1816 he informed Clark that he "had hoped to hear that something was doing with the astronomical observations, the Geographical chart, the Indian vocabularies, and other papers not comprehended in the journel published."[1] It was a gentle but insistent reminder that Jefferson had always intended the Lewis and Clark Expedition to produce a major scientific publication. In 1811, Jefferson had enthusiastically informed C. and A. Conrad that "I shall want 10. or 12. copies, unbound, as soon as it comes out." What followed inevitably was a suggestion of Jefferson's impatience: "When will that be? I had hoped . . . it would have been before now." He concluded with a statement of dubious sincerity. He told the publisher to "accept the assurances of my respect," but Jefferson did not respect the publishing skills of C. and A. Conrad, and he was plainly frustrated with everybody involved in this project that was so dear to his heart.[2]

Instead of the book Jefferson wanted, Biddle and Clark had produced a standard travel narrative unremarkable in its structure or in its claims. Jefferson was irritated by this state of affairs. Clark, who had spent much of his adult life trying not to irritate influential patrons, wrote back to explain the litany of delays and difficulties that had beset the project. Lewis's death, the collapse of two publishers, the challenges of coordinating efforts with an editor located almost a thousand miles away had all prevented the completion of the book in a timely manner or in the form that Jefferson expected. Besides, Clark thought his work was finished. He had no intention of writing another book, let alone a tome on scientific research. That was Benjamin Smith Barton's task. When Clark had come east after Lewis's suicide to help settle the disposition of the materials from the expedition, he had confidently left the production of a scientific volume in the capable hands of Barton, a talented naturalist and physician who shared Jefferson's commitment to the Enlightenment. The problem was that Barton died in 1815, and once again Clark became the caretaker of the materials of the Lewis and Clark Expedition. Clark apparently hoped Jefferson would take responsibility for the project. The former president was more interested in seeing it completed and was certainly more qualified to address matters of science. In fact, Clark had already made arrangements for Jefferson to receive the materials in the possession of both Biddle and Barton.

Clark preferred not to discuss the scientific volume at all with Jefferson, instead discussing matters of greater concern and greater familiarity. He focused on the status of white politics and Indian affairs in the Missouri Territory. He concluded by stating, "I am happy to have it in my power to say to you that I succeed in keeping the Indians of the territory in peace. . . . The dificuelties & responsibilities however were great, and in some instances I was compeled to vary from principal." Less than a year after the grand conference at Portage des Sioux had imposed an uneasy peace on the eastern Plains, Clark struggled to reconcile his desire to respect the commitments made to Indians with his responsibility to serve the interests of white settlers who eagerly moved onto Indian land.[3]

While Jefferson was pressing Clark to help produce a second book, Biddle was still trying to salvage the first. As Bradford and Inskeep liquidated their stock, they informed Biddle that if Biddle or Clark wanted the remaining copies of *History of the Expedition* they had to pay for them. Acting on Clark's behalf, Biddle negotiated a deal through which both men would be relieved of the financial losses for *History of the Expedition* in exchange for surrendering any claims to the copyright of its text. Clark in turn would receive copyright for "A Map of Lewis and Clark's Track," the map that accompanied the book, and Biddle made certain that Clark would also receive physical possession of the metal plates used to print the maps. Biddle included his correspondence with Bradford and Inskeep so that Clark could "see exactly how things stand, and make up your mind." But his recommendation was clear: take the deal.[4]

The decision facing Clark in 1816—whether to own hundreds of printed pages or a single map—served as a reminder that the published product of Jefferson's expeditions remained physical objects that told their own stories. Created through a combination of scientific interest, policymaking necessity, and professional self-advancement, these books were supposed to provide the grand description that would finally make sense of the Far West. They were supposed to provide policymakers with the great map that would guide their decisions and promote the national interest. They were also truly multimedia projects. Dense text, large-scale maps, small-scale surveys, and occasional illustrations showing specific scenes, landscapes, and people functioned together to describe the West and situate the explorers within the West.

The published results of Jefferson's expeditions also told a unifying set of stories. They told stories of conquest, as the emissaries of the United States successfully overcame tremendous challenges in the West. They described a landscape filled with animals, vast prairies, and well-stocked rivers. All this celebration would seem to suggest a simple process of expansion through which Americans quelled local unrest, secured Indian compliance, and provided the geographic knowledge that could establish a foundation for international boundary agreements.

Yet these books and maps are no less striking for the warnings they announced. At a time when public commentators had no predilection for subtlety, these narratives are striking for the absence of any reference to the explicit benefits of territorial expansion. Regardless of geography, leadership, or instructions, the explorers described the Far West as a place of considerable opportunities but also a landscape of tremendous danger. The West was a place of great challenges and great deserts. The instructions the explorers received, the models they followed, the purposes for which they imagined their information would be used, and the careers they hoped to build all combined to construct a dangerous western landscape of questionable benefit to Anglo-American settlers.

This hardly means the accounts of American explorers did not celebrate the American mission in the West, nor does it mean they lacked any comments on the possibility of western settlement. But these accounts contrasted sharply with the boosterism of so much of the literature on the Near West. The explorers in the Far West described a place that exceeded federal control, that should not beckon settlers, that was dominated by landscapes of questionable habitability. Rather than impose clarity, the books and maps generated by Jefferson's western expeditions suggested confusion and danger. The maps and other materials described not an empty western landscape awaiting settlement, but a crowded frontier, one with frightening occupants.

This is a matter of no small importance because writing about the West would eventually become all things to all people. Americans have discussed western accounts as literature, road maps for conquest, and expressions of the American self. The men who produced these materials saw them differently. They were producing policy documents that constructed a direct correlation between geographic knowledge and national interest. They were also producing testaments to their own achievement that would enable them to secure their futures as instruments of the western policy that they had helped to shape.[5]

BOOKS AND MAPS

Perhaps one can't judge a book by its cover, but the physical form of these reports from the West spoke volumes about their contents. That begins with their titles. They may be a mouthful, but they constitute a necessary first step in understanding how people went about describing the West.

Jefferson himself began the process of publication. In 1806 he released the material from the Hunter-Dunbar Expedition, Lewis and Clark's Fort Mandan report of 1805, and John Sibley's 1806 report from Natchitoches as *Message from the President of the United States, communicating discoveries made in exploring the Missouri, Red River, and Washita, by Captains Lewis and Clark, Doctor Sibley, and Mr. Dunbar; with a statistical account of the countries adjacent.* Later that year, Nicholas King produced his account based on the Freeman and Custis journals, entitled *An Account of the Red River, in Louisiana, Drawn up from the Returns of Messrs. Freeman & Custis to the War Office of the United States, who Explored the Same, in the year of 1806.* By 1807 Gass had published *Journal of the Voyages and Travels of a Corps of Discovery Under the Command of Capt. Lewis and Capt. Clarke, of the Army of the United States, from the mouth of the river Missouri through the interior parts of North America to the Pacific Ocean, during the years 1804, 1805 and 1806.* In 1810, Pike published *An Account of Expeditions to the Sources of the Mississippi: and through the western parts of Louisiana to the sources of the Arkansaw, Kans, La Platte, and Pierre Jaun Rivers: performed by order of the government of the United States during the years 1805, 1806, and 1807 and a tour through the interior parts of New Spain when conducted through these provinces by order of the captain-general in the year 1807.* All of these books preceded *History of the Expedition under the Command of Captains Lewis and Clark, to the sources of the Missouri, thence across the Rocky Mountains and down the river Columbia to the Pacific Ocean: Performed during the years 1804–5–6 by order of the government of the United States,* which made its long-overdue appearance in 1814.[6]

Jefferson's *Message* and Freeman's and Custis's *Report* were relatively brief documents (181 pages for Jefferson's *Message,* a mere 64 pages for Freeman's and Custis's *Report*) with simple paper binding. Pike, Gass, and Lewis and Clark took an entirely different approach. Bound in leather and advertising themselves as welcome additions to any personal library, those books came from the more general tradition of travel writing that included not only Andrew Ellicott and Thomas Hutchins, but a host of European travelers reaching back to the first published accounts of the European exploration of the New World. These books were massive by comparison to the *Message* and the *Report:* Gass's book was 262 pages, Pike's was a total of 503 pages, and the *History of the Expedition* was 523.

The titles also suggest how these books presented new information to Anglo-American observers. All of these books were fundamentally unoriginal in their means of presentation or, for that matter, in their analysis of data. That may seem like an odd conclusion, but the reasons it is odd are rooted more in contemporary concerns than in the publishing realities of the early Republic. After all, the study of writing has long sought to explain—indeed, to celebrate—the ways in which individual texts have pushed the English language in new directions, the ways in which literature has challenged common assumptions, and the ways literature has subverted political hierarchies. Even the most seemingly mundane forms of writing are worthy of study, not because they are, in fact, mundane, but rather because they contain some unseen form of subversion or innovation. Likewise, much of the mythology surrounding Jefferson concerns his quest for new knowledge and the revolutionary quality of his thinking. That image has only been reinforced by recent discussions of the "discoveries" later attributed to the Lewis and Clark Expedition as well as by the novel approach to science that Lewis outlined in his initial plans for the book he intended to write.

Jefferson's explorers did none of these things in the literature they produced. On the contrary, the explorers and their publishing partners struggled mightily to make certain their books followed the rules of western travel narratives. They certainly presented a wealth of new *information*. But their books and maps were nonetheless conventional in *form*. For Clark, the most important and original finding, the only one to truly change how Jefferson understood the West, simply confirmed existing worries about western government. *History of the Expedition* loudly proclaimed that there was no Northwest Passage. This statement crushed Jefferson's hopes for a simple process of overland trade to the Pacific. But European explorers had been making the same claim for years.

The decision facing Clark in 1816—to own copyright to a book or to a map—also serves as a reminder that describing the West remained a multimedia project, at least in the nineteenth-century sense of the term. How would Americans "see" the West? The accounts of Jefferson's expeditions all sold themselves with promises of new maps that would rewrite—or, more correctly, redraw—the image of the North American West, but it was on the matter of visual material that the published descriptions of the West most dramatically diverged. Jefferson's *Message* contained no visual material of any kind, instead referring readers to a map of the Ouachita River of 1804 by Nicholas King. King produced a similar map of the Red River that he released at the same time, but separately from, his edited *Account* of the Freeman and Custis Expedition.

These were local maps that promised revision rather than revolution. They could not have been more different from the map of the West that accompanied *History of the Expedition*. Advertisements for the book had promised a map of unprecedented accuracy and detail, a document which would forever change the way Americans thought about the West. Pike may have been a far less competent surveyor (which helps account for his equally faulty navigation), but his *Account* of 1810 had even greater cartographic ambitions, containing an entire atlas. Unlike the rather compact book, the large atlas contained five maps from his two expeditions as well as three detailed tables of Indian settlements and the fur trade.[7]

For all their detail, the maps were equally crude, especially in comparison to their European competitors. First and foremost, the maps of Jefferson's expeditions were black and white, without any of the labor-intensive hand coloring that elevated a map's value. Equally striking, the maps all lacked elaborate cartouches. Some of the first European reviews of *History of the Expedition* singled out the map for special criticism, not for its cartographic information but for its physical appearance, which appeared deficient, almost amateurish, by European standards.[8]

Yet for all these limitations, maps were the predominant visual medium through which Americans saw the Far West. The one exception was Gass's *Journal of the Voyages and Travels of a Corps of Discovery*, which included six illustrations depicting subjects ranging from Indian negotiations to the shooting of bears. These illustrations, crude even by American standards, were among the first representations of the landscape, the animals, and the plants of the Far West to be produced in the United States (Fig. 24). Together with the maps, they demonstrated how the American ability to see the West remained limited by the American capacity to publish visual material.

WRITERS AND EDITORS, LEADERS AND FOLLOWERS

In 1810 Clark began referring to the project that became *History of the Expedition* as "my book."[9] Pike did the same about his project.[10] This was never the case. The books and maps of western exploration were always collaborative projects involving explorers, editors, publishers, and cartographers. Add to this the fact that most of the accounts included material from multiple explorers, and the notion of a single author becomes even more problematic. Nonetheless, these books actually announced certain explorers as if they were authors. In doing so, they completed the process of associating the expeditions with their leaders. It was through the relationship between writers and editors as well as through the description of leaders and followers that the image of the American West began to emerge.[11]

References to the editors and publishers who played such a large role in producing these books were almost entirely missing from the final product. The books all announced that they were the work of the explorers, and for one simple reason: travel narratives drew their legitimacy by claiming to be the record of the travelers, not of the editors, printers, or cartographers. Again, one can judge a book by its cover, which always established the explorers as the authors. Consider the emergence of Clark's name. After years in which he struggled to garner some credit as Lewis's collaborator rather than his subordinate, the first page of the narrative in *History of the Expedition* introduced the expedition by stating that Jefferson's "private secretary, Captain Meriwether Lewis, and Captain William Clark, both officers of the Army of the United States, were associated in the command of this enterprise."[12] Jefferson's *Message* introduced "Captains Lewis and Clark, Doctor Sibley, and Mr. Dunbar" as the leaders of major federal initiatives. King produced a book "Drawn up from the Returns of Messrs. Freeman & Custis." Finally, given

Frontispiece   Page.220.

A Canoe striking on a Tree,

Page.95.

Captain Clark and his men shooting Bears.

Figure 24. Illustrations from Patrick Gass, *Journal of the Voyages and Travels of a Corps of Discovery Under the Command of Capt. Lewis and Capt. Clarke, of the Army of the United States, from the mouth of the river Missouri through the interior parts of North America to the Pacific Ocean, during the years 1804, 1805 and 1806* (Philadelphia: Mathew Carey, 1810 and 1812). Special Collections, Washington University in St. Louis.

Pike's eagerness for advancement and glory, it was no surprise that his name appeared prominently on the cover of his account in 1810, with Peale's portrait of Pike smiling as he peered at the title page.

The only book to assert from the start that these expeditions entailed the efforts of people besides their leaders was, appropriately enough, written by somebody who was not a leader. Gass's *Journal* referred to a venture by a "Corps of Discovery," not only introducing the public to a nickname that eventually became synonymous with the Lewis and Clark Expedition, but also reminding readers that those expeditions included men like himself.

Yet for all the ways in which titles and cover pages emphasized the explorers, equally solid rules about the content of the expedition narratives worked against any substantive reference to the explorers in the pages that followed. Although all of the published narratives listed the membership of the expeditions, usually at the start of the books, they rarely referred to them by name. Instead, the explorers were simply referred to as "they" or "the party" or "the expedition" or occasionally "we." At the same time the explorers ceased to be individuals, they also ceased to be groups, for the published accounts of Jefferson's expeditions offered few insights into the dynamics within the expeditions.[13] Explorers recovered their names only when they traveled alone, when they became lost, when they were injured, or when they died. And then the references always remained in the third person. Even Pike, who showed such confidence in announcing his accomplishments, accepted this editorial method. Yet Pike had no reason to worry, for several times on both expeditions he had indeed traveled alone, creating the ideal circumstances for a book that could discuss him as an individual.

This portrait of the explorers stood in stark contrast to the manuscript journals of the explorers. The explorers had shown no hesitancy in referring to themselves in the first person. Although they rarely described their personal feelings or interpersonal relations, they often began entries with "I" or "we." They recounted their activities, injuries, and illnesses. The manuscript journals also afford fleeting glimpses of the relationships among the explorers, again in contrast to the published accounts.

More than anything, it is this stance of impersonal observation that makes these accounts so frustrating to contemporary readers. They discuss travel and landscape in ways that are the opposite of almost every truism that emerged later about travel literature: that the book should be as much about the traveler as the journey, that the traveler should change in the process of making that journey, that the profound implications of travel should be recorded in equally profound or elegant prose. In this telling, the purpose of the account is to describe how the traveler returns from his journey transformed. *Moby-Dick* and, for that matter, *On the Road* exemplify the transformative impact of the journey on the traveler. In other words, travel needs to be about the self.

The notion that a travel account should be about the traveler goes a long way toward explaining how the record of Jefferson's expeditions is discussed today. Literary critics and general readers alike have tended to gravitate toward those accounts which make explicit reference to individual feelings. Not surprisingly, they have ignored the published accounts of early federal exploration almost entirely, preferring instead to focus on a highly selective reading of manuscript journals. Fortunately, there is always Meriwether Lewis. Nobody seems to epitomize this literary interpretation of western travel better than Lewis. His writing situates western exploration from the early Republic within a broader aesthetic tradition emphasizing the personal encounter between the individual and the landscape through the process of making a journey. Lewis has assumed a special place, and he had done so long before the bicentennial observations of the Lewis and Clark Expedition. The reason was simple: he was the embodiment of every aesthetic trope of both Enlightenment rationalism and romantic sentimentality. At least his manuscript journals suggested as much. Occasional passages in which Lewis described intense feeling—on his thirty-first birthday, on witnessing the Great Falls of the Missouri, on viewing the Continental Divide—have become standard fare for most scholars who have attempted to situate American western explorers within a broader narrative of cultural development.[14]

Such revealing analysis of self-expression has two problems. First, it is only through the most selective reading of books or the most limited examination of maps that western describers emerge as men concerned about the emotional relationship between a traveler and the surrounding landscape. Second, in the early Republic nobody read those passages. They never appeared in the published accounts of the Lewis and Clark Expedition, and it was almost a century before the manuscript journals were published. Equally important, none of the numerous other western explorers from Lewis's and Clark's generation made such literary digressions. Clark's style, often halting and ungainly, was the more common one in its emphasis of the observed rather than the observer.

If the explorers were going to announce themselves, it would have to be in subtle ways. It was an ironic state of affairs, for these men had been anything but subtle in their public behavior or in their writing. The result was a fusion of the authors' lived experiences, their understandings of federal policy, their personal goals, and the rules of landscape description they felt compelled to follow. All of these key concerns emerged in the way the explorers addressed Indians, the western environment, and the boundaries of North America. They discussed all three subjects with ambivalence and ambiguity. At one moment the United States had secured its authority over a West that presented tremendous opportunities; at another it faced unprecedented, almost insurmountable challenges.

INDIANS

In 1813, Clark had attempted to chart a military strategy in the West. He did so through his map of the Indians in the Great Lakes and the Mississippi and Missouri valleys as well as through his correspondence with officials in Washington. The following year, *History of the Expedition* tried to do the same. Indians had always been crucial to Clark's understanding of the West and to his representation of its landscape. Although all his accounts were rooted in racial supremacy, Indians appeared in conflicting ways. For every suggestion that Indians would give way to white settlement, there were other claims that Indians were a danger that remained firmly in place.

In strict narrative terms, the books of American explorers were about Indians. They were often about the landscape, periodically about science, and occasionally about the explorers themselves. But they always returned to Indians, both because the explorers had been instructed to describe Indians and because they encountered Indians at every turn. The explorers considered themselves free to observe and occasionally interpret Indians on just about every subject imaginable. They discussed Indians' agriculture and dining habits, politics and religion, sexual behavior and gender rules. In all these comments, the explorers drew ambivalent conclusions about American expansion. At one moment the books claimed Americans could look forward to an easy future of commanding the West, at others they claimed that Americans faced tremendous dangers.[15]

All of the published narratives described a crowded West. To American western explorers, Indians were at once compliant yet resistant, declining yet powerful. Whatever else they were, they were not the Indians of Benjamin Smith Barton or Jedidiah Morse. Throughout the late eighteenth century, scientific and religious writers located almost exclusively in the Northeast had written about Indians in increasingly sentimental terms. Hoping to capture an ethnographic picture of a race that seemed to be heading for rapid extinction, members of the American scientific community cast Indians as the unfortunate victims of their inferiority. Meanwhile, members of the American religious community believed that the very weakness of Indians made them ripe for conversion. For scientists and theologians alike, Indians were fundamentally unthreatening.[16]

Clark saw things differently. By 1814, he was a seasoned Indian negotiator, and *History of the Expedition* described an interracial diplomatic landscape in the Far West that he continued to navigate with great care. During the course of the expedition, Lewis and Clark personally changed from a superficial understanding of Indian culture that assumed violence and savagery at any moment to a more complicated view that was at once paternalistic and occasionally belligerent, yet often sympathetic. *History of the Expedition* was more simplistic, establishing Indians as childlike in their proclivity for violence and their absence of industrious civilization. Lewis and Clark occasionally wondered about the long-term fate of western Indians, and *History of the Expedition* periodically commented on "the unsteady movements and the tottering fortunes of the American Indians."[17] Nonetheless, Indians remained powerful players in the book's vision of the West. *History of the Expedition* did periodically suggest that weak or friendly Indians indicated that establishing the federal hold on Louisiana would be easy, but passages like this were the exception that proved the rule.

For example, in discussing events of September 1804, *History of the Expedition* claimed "there were so many Indians in the neighborhood we were in constant expectation of being attacked." In a passage from August 1805, the book explained that "to doubt the courage of an Indian is to touch the tenderest string of his mind." An effort to interpret Indian cave sketches sought to explain Indian culture while never once losing sight of the prospect of Indian violence: "Such sketches, rude and imperfect as they are, delineate the predominant character of the savage nations. If they are peaceable and inoffensive the drawings usually consist of local scenery and their favorite diversions. If the band are rude and ferocious, we observe tomahawks, scalping knives, bows, arrows, and all the engines of destruction."[18]

Indian power radiated from the text and maps of these books, with the images in the maps reinforcing the written message in the text. This was most striking on Clark's map, which filled in the Missouri and Columbia river val-

leys with dozens of Indian villages. The maps in Pike's atlas were more varied, and in revealing ways. In the territory the United States considered in-
disputably under its control—the Mississippi and Ohio river valleys, the
centers of white settlement in the territories of Orleans and Louisiana—Pike's
maps showed an exclusively Euro-American imprint consisting of towns, land
claims, and military forts. In the Southwest and the Rockies, however, Pike's
maps situated numerous villages in commanding positions. Nearby Spanish
outposts likewise detailed an alliance structure that preserved both Indian
power and Spanish influence (Fig. 25).

The explorers' commercial and ethnographic efforts further proclaimed
Indian populations and Indian power. *History of the Expedition* and Pike's
Account both included elaborate charts that sought to create a rough census
of western Indians, listing the population of individual villages while also trying to dissect the linguistic, diplomatic, commercial, and cultural connections between villages. The result was to estimate Indian populations in the
tens of thousands. These were hardly the scattered, disconnected Indians living in small numbers that the most optimistic pamphleteers had described in
1803–04.

Since 1776 American cartographers had attempted to remove Indians from
the cartographic record, replacing the image of a crowded, multiracial West
of European maps with a clearly delineated West of white governments. Jefferson himself had attempted to do so in 1784 through his Plan for Western
Government. Now the very explorers whom Jefferson had dispatched to the
West had put Indians back in the picture. In fact, if there was a model for
their maps, it was exactly the European maps of the late eighteenth century
that American policymakers had so eagerly rejected.

The heightened awareness of Indians hardly meant that the explorers assumed Indians would always control the West. Whatever their flashes of sympathy, American explorers remained racial supremacists. They were quick to
describe their own ability to negotiate friendly agreements with the Indians.
Likewise, they joined a chorus of European and Euro-American observers
who believed that disease and warfare, compounded by an uncivilized culture, put most Indians on a road to rapid extinction. Nonetheless, Freeman
and Custis described the Caddo of the Red River Valley as crucial players in
borderland diplomacy. Pike struggled to negotiate with a Pawnee leadership
that wielded undeniable power throughout much of the southern Plains.
Lewis and Clark described Indians who controlled commerce and politics
throughout the Missouri Valley.

Figure 25. Detail from "A Chart of the Internal Part of Louisiana . . . ," in *Atlas accompanying An account of expeditions to the sources of the Mississippi and through the western parts of Louisiana to the sources of the Arkansaw, Kans, La Platte, and Pierre Jaun rivers* (Philadelphia: C. and A. Conrad, 1810). Geography and Map Division, Library of Congress.

ENVIRONMENT

In his first attempts to write about the western landscape in 1789, Clark had observed "first-rate land" and "second-rate land" as he participated in the Kentucky volunteers' mission against the Wea Indians. As one of Jefferson's explorers, Clark engaged in the same process of evaluating the land on a continental scale. More than any subject, it was on matters of landscape that the books of Jefferson's western expeditions faced their limits. Just as the explorers described Indians as being both dangerous and inferior, so they described a landscape at once fertile and barren. The explorers could seem like boosters. At times the West, in their eyes, was a garden, its pastures ready for easy settlement by white farmers.[19] The writers described fertility, comfort, and agricultural opportunity, but all in a limited space, whether in the landscape itself or on the pages of a book. The signs of a welcoming West stood in vivid contrast to lands of meager resources and overwhelming impediments.

Nothing seems to reveal the possibilities in the West better than the notion of abundance. It appears—appropriately enough—abundantly throughout the published accounts of western exploration. Indeed, the word suggests a settler's paradise. That was certainly the way Filson had used the word when he listed the abundant resources awaiting settlers in Kentucky. A passage from *History of the Expedition* reported that "the game is as usual so abundant that we can get without difficulty all that is necessary."[20] It was the kind of comment that all the explorers made.

Nonetheless, scarcity and abundance were often side by side in the pages of these books. Soon after describing abundant game, *History of the Expedition* claimed "game is now more scarce" or "the buffalo have now become scarce," even as it claimed, "The wild roses are very abundant and now in bloom."[21]

The explorers' abundant use of "abundance" should not be misunderstood, however, for they used it in multiple ways. Even as they used the word to suggest the western bounty, it also became an admission of the explorers' limited capacity for observation. "Abundant," "immense," and "numerous" were among the terms all the explorers used when they were unable to adequately quantify what they saw. Abundance described both valuable resources and useless details. It was a far cry from Filson.

The caveats that applied to animals also applied to the soil. All of the explorers told stories of agricultural opportunities on the western Mississippi Valley and the eastern Plains. Freeman and Custis went out of their way to disprove any belief that the "clayey or marley soil" of the Red River would be "not desirable for cultivation; the fact however is otherwise: they are found to be more productive lands than the best Mississippi lands."[22]

Yet these celebratory passages are striking for their brevity and are offset by accounts of vast distances, inhospitable climates, and dangerous Indians. After all, if these books were supposed to stimulate settlement and development— as both Filson and Jefferson had attempted in their descriptions of Kentucky and Virginia—the authors and editors could have devoted an exaggerated amount of space to describing the most fertile landscapes. That certainly was the tradition in the promotional travel literature that Europeans had created for centuries.

The greatest opportunities were to be found less in agriculture than in trade. The books of western expeditions described a West that might be ideal for traders, trappers, and merchants, but not necessarily for farmers. "At the lower extremity of this lake," records *History of the Expedition*, "about 400 yards from the Missouri, and twice that distance from the Yellowstone, is a situation highly eligible for trading establishment."[23]

The most dire predictions came from Pike, who famously described the Southwest as a great desert. The notion of the Great American Desert soon entered the scientific literature, contributing to an active debate about whether the West was healthy and productive or harmful and barren.[24] In an attempt to make a virtue out of adversity, Pike concluded that "from these immense prairies may arise one great advantage to the United States, viz.: The restriction of our population to certain limits, and thereby a continuation of the Union." In this one brief passage Pike restated a generation of conventional wisdom about the expansion and survival of the United States. Rather than writing in language that presaged the ebullient expansionism of the 1830s and 1840s, he wrote with the guarded concern of the 1780s and 1790s.[25]

Exploring the marshy confines of the Red River Valley, Freeman and Custis could not have seemed further from the Great American Desert. Yet they, too, saw natural impediments to settlement. The weather itself was part of the problem, as they endured heat, humidity, and excessive downpours during the rainy summer of 1806. Worse still was the Great Raft, a massive collection of fallen trees that completely blocked the upper reaches of the Red River.[26] For decades American boosters had celebrated the providential quality of the North American waterways, which efficiently connected the most habitable portions of the United States. Americans continued to believe in a Northwest Passage in the face of evidence to the contrary specifically because they were already inclined to expect that rivers would naturally take form to serve an enterprising population. Freeman and Custis, on the other hand, described a region where nature itself sought to impede settlement.

In all their efforts to describe these circumstances, the explorers used the language they knew best. They drew on their experience as surveyors recording coordinates, army officers writing to their superiors, and scientists drafting technical reports. It was in their efforts to describe the physical environment that the explorers faced their greatest limitations as writers. For example, they employed "abundance" in the absence of more detailed quantitative data. What the writers of the narratives of the West did not do was use their emotional reactions as a way to convey landscape or experience. The books of western exploration occasionally, but only occasionally, attempted to describe the landscape in terms of sentiment rather than of technical detachment. And the books deployed those passages for highly pragmatic reasons. While most of Lewis's self-consciously sentimental journal passages disappeared from *History of the Expedition*, the book did contain a modified version of his reaction to the Great Falls. "He [Lewis] hurried with impatience and seating himself on some rocks under the centre of the falls, enjoyed the sublime spectacle of this stupendous object which since the creation had been lavishing its magnificence upon the desert, unknown to civilization," read the account of June 13, 1805. Yet this personalized text immediately yielded to a more typical passage: "The river immediately at its cascade is three hundred yards wide, and is pressed in by a perpendicular cliff on the left, which rises to about one hundred feet and extends up the stream for a mile; on the right the bluff is also perpendicular for three hundred yards above the falls."[27]

Pike's *Account* of 1810 had similar passages. "The appearance of the Falls was much more tremendous than when we ascended," Pike wrote of the Falls of St. Anthony. "The increase of water occasioned the spray to rise much higher, and the mist appeared like clouds. How different my sensations now, from what they were when at this place before!"[28] "My situation can more easily be imagined than described," read the *Account* when he became separated from his men while hunting for food on the Mississippi Expedition.[29] This was a common literary technique, an efficient way to let readers use their imaginations to summon a more powerful reaction than any writer could achieve. Yet this was a particularly appropriate phrase for Jefferson's explorers to use, for their journals as well as the books based on them all struggled to convey the landscape.

Far from being unique, these books bore the stamp of most western travel writing during the early Republic. In doing so, they directly refuted emerging literary trends in describing the landscape, trends that were already well established in Europe—especially Great Britain—and later became increasingly important in the United States.

By 1800 three highly important terms had come to dominate landscape description: the sublime, the picturesque, and the beautiful. The words were of paramount concern to novelists, poets, and painters on both sides of the Atlantic. Yet the narratives of Jefferson's expeditions avoided these terms altogether, at least as they were understood in literary circles. The sublime and the picturesque were almost entirely missing from either manuscript journals or the published accounts of Jefferson's western explorers. There was no beauty in Jefferson's *Message* or in King's *Report*. It may seem odd to even suggest as much, since words like "beautiful" rarely figure into scientific accounts. Yet these were the first published accounts to describe the Far West beyond the Mississippi, and they introduced terms that Americans used to understand the western domain. Beauty was certainly present in the later accounts of Gass, Pike, and Lewis and Clark, but the explorers used the term in ways that no self-respecting artist would accept.[30]

"Beautiful" was among the common adjectives the explorers deployed to describe the West, in large part because they used the term in so many ways. More than anything else, however, their understanding of that term was less a reflection of prevailing literary notions than of the fundamentally practical outlook of William Clark. The explorers went back and forth between the use of beautiful as a term to describe vistas that were somehow pleasing to the eye and a more specific use of the term to describe a place with the practical requirements for human settlement. *History of the Expedition* occasionally described situations like this: "The mountains which border as far as the Sepulchre rock, are high and broken, and its romantic views occasionally enlivened by beautiful cascades rushing from the heights, and forming a deep contrast with the firs, cedars and pines, which darken their sides."[31] But the book was just as likely to claim "the country continues level, rich, and beautiful; the low grounds are wide and, comparatively with the other parts of the Missouri, well supplied with wood."[32] The first passage describes a landscape that is emotionally stirring but almost physically inaccessible, definitively beautiful in traditional aesthetic terms. The second passage is almost dull by comparison but would appear beautiful to anybody like Clark, who treasured a plot of land well suited to farming.

The books of western exploration described the West in the language of surveyors, soldiers, and amateur scientists. They all discussed a reality in which Americans would move to the West. For those who entered commerce, there were considerable opportunities. For all others, the challenges would be greater.

BOUNDARIES

When Clark joined the federal administration in the Louisiana Territory in 1807, he sought to impose boundaries onto the eastern Plains. In his efforts to force the Osage Indians to cede territory southwest of St. Louis, he also hoped to continue a process of mapping the Louisiana Territory. It was on this matter of boundaries that the published record of western exploration revealed the greatest conflict. At one instant, the explorers claimed federal ownership of Louisiana that flew in the face of the reality in the West. At the next, they undermined federal sovereignty and federal claims. This conflict reflected the general ambivalence toward the West the explorers wrote in their journals. It also emerged from the tension between books and maps.

For decades, leaders of the United States had sought "clear and indisputable boundaries," the phrase the Continental Congress had first used in the 1770s and 1780s. Geographers like Jedidiah Morse, surveyors like Andrew Ellicott, and engravers like Samuel Lewis had been only too happy to oblige, producing maps that imposed boundaries onto the landscape. Those boundaries had always been more imagined than real, especially when it came to the West, a place of fluid borderlands and local rules. Imposing boundaries served a nationalist agenda, for it proclaimed the United States as a unified nation distinct from all others. Imposing boundaries could also serve expansionist agendas, for mapmakers had long used maps to lay claim to new territory.

The published maps of Jefferson's western expeditions did little to advance these agendas, creating instead a West of vague or nonexistent borders. Even those maps which made a stab at constructing Louisiana acknowledged that the land itself was home to populations who existed outside federal sovereignty. Clark's own Master Map of the North American West avoided political boundaries almost entirely. "A Map of Lewis and Clark's Track" divided Louisiana from Canada with almost invisible lines and tiny print. Just as big were notations indicating the location of Indian villages. The map also made no attempt to validate American claims to the southwest, imposing no line to delineate Louisiana and Spanish North America. Clark had created a map in which the Indian presence dominated the landscape or, more accurately, the printed page. Meanwhile, Clark's map made no explicit claim to the Oregon country, despite the fact that Jefferson himself had expressed his eagerness to see the United States gain a foothold in the Pacific trade (Fig. 26).[33]

The fact that Clark did not include boundaries hardly means he did not support American territorial claims. To the contrary, the very existence of his map provided the geographic information that was at the heart of Anglo-American property law. Clark's map did rename most of the rivers in the West (usually after members of the administration or of the expedition itself), a process that Lewis's and Clark's journals recorded in monotonous detail. Yet those names are far smaller on Clark's map than the labels for Indian settlements, a reversal of earlier maps produced in the United States that always superimposed the names of states and towns in large letters onto the smallest of labels for Indians. The maps of Pike's expeditions told a similar story. Only King's map from the Freeman and Custis Expedition attempted to impose a "clear and indisputable boundary," in this case between the Territory of Orleans and Spanish Texas.

It was also a far cry from the explicit ways in which maps asserted ownership. The absence of strong international boundaries is particularly striking in the maps of Jefferson's expeditions. After all, continental maps, especially those commissioned by governments, usually showed international boundaries in the strongest terms possible, in large part because they often sought to support territorial claims. Jefferson had dispatched his western expeditions to acquire the geographic information that would sustain exactly those claims. Then why the faint, vague, or nonexistent boundaries? These written and visual strategies hardly indicated that the American explorers had any sympathy for Indians or any opposition to American territorial claims. They were unapologetic racial supremacists and committed nationalists. The leaders of all these expeditions explored the West within extensive western careers that consisted primarily of efforts to consolidate the federal hold against all challengers, whether settlers, Indians, or Europeans.

TRIALS AND TRIUMPHS

What accounts for this state of affairs? Why would the first published accounts of the West issue such strong warnings for settlers? Why would the first maps fail to impose boundaries as the federal leadership saw fit? The image of the North American West created by the published accounts of Jefferson's expeditions responded to factors both simple and complicated. In simple terms, the very instructions the explorers took with them worked against maps that announced continental mastery. Yet those instructions also dovetailed with traditions of western exploration and the personal aspirations of the explorers themselves.

Figure 26. Detail from *A Map of Lewis and Clark's Track, Across the Western Portion of North America from the Mississippi to the Pacific Ocean* . . . (Philadelphia: Bradford and Inskeep, 1814). Geography and Map Division, Library of Congress. Compare the line and text indicating the "Boundary of Louisiana" to the text identifying

First and foremost, the explorers described the world as they had been instructed to do. Their journals and later their books devoted so much attention
to Indians, landscape, and geography because federal policymakers had made
clear just how important that information would be in the difficult task of
managing the expansion that came with the Louisiana Purchase. Just as those
instructions—whether they came from Jefferson, Henry Dearborn, or James
Wilkinson—bore so much in common, so too did the journals of the explorers. None of them were instructed to present plans for the immediate arrival
of white settlers, so none of them did. Instead, the explorers attempted to
compose a grand geography of the North American West. Some of that information concerned the landscape in ways drawn from natural history, but
most of the information served more pragmatic policymaking needs.

Equally revealing is what remains missing. While the Jefferson administration hoped that the western expeditions would provide information to help
boundary negotiations with Spain and Great Britain, nowhere did the explorers' instructions ask them to construct a political map that imposed
boundaries onto the landscape. Instead, the explorers interpreted the instructions to mean they should create templates onto which officials more
senior than themselves could impose the boundaries they wanted.

Where were the explorers in all this discussion of culture, landscape, and
diplomacy? Once again, their instructions provide part of the answer. In their
effort to fulfill their instructions, the explorers had begun a process of almost
entirely removing themselves from the story. In an effort to create books that
satisfied the norms of travel narratives, editors and publishers nearly completed the process. The explorers were in the books nonetheless, just not as
romantic individualists wandering through the West in search of themselves
or as Enlightenment rationalists in search of scientific truth. Instead, they
were rational individualists pursuing government objectives as well as opportunities for themselves.

The explorers proclaimed their presence most clearly in the successes they
attributed to their expeditions: success for leaders, for exploratory teams, and
for the United States. They did so in various ways, both implicit and explicit.
They did so despite the fact that every one of Jefferson's expeditions faced
certain obvious failures.

Pike was the most unapologetic in proclaiming his achievements as well
as his talents. But Lewis and Clark were not far behind. Freeman was, appropriately enough, more modest. The texts of their expeditions presented
all four men as specialists thoroughly prepared to handle the tasks of west-

ern government. Hunter, Dunbar, and Custis established different portraits. Their victories had been more cerebral, overcoming the ignorance of the western landscape and its inhabitants in ways that established the scientific credentials of three men who eagerly sought membership in a community of intellectuals.

Extending a message that the explorers first suggested in the preliminary reports that circulated before their expeditions were even complete, all of the narratives told of missions accomplished. That began with victories over the western landscape. The explorers celebrated their ability to withstand the challenges of western travel and their ability to strip the aura of geographic mystery from the West. Clark suggested as much the moment he reached St. Louis in September 1806. He declared, "We were completely successful." He was referring specifically to the task of locating "the most practicable rout which does exist across the continent." Clark composed the letter as a piece of personal correspondence, but it was published in a newspaper, suggesting that he hardly intended it to remain private.[34] Pike described the Mississippi Expedition in similar manner. "I will not attempt to describe my feelings on the accomplishment of my voyage," read his journal entry of February 1, 1806, "for this is the main source of the Mississippi."[35]

These assertions were only part of the explorers' effort to establish their reputation from a distance. These books all portrayed them as committed public servants who could properly interpret their instructions, even when separated from their superiors by tremendous distances.

History of the Expedition and Pike's narrative made similar claims about negotiations with Indians. Both accounts described repeatedly successful negotiations concluding with Indians accepting federal sovereignty or recoiling before the power of the expeditions. These passages were, of course, wrong. Indians continued to wield power throughout the Far West, while the small American exploring parties were emblematic of a federal government with only the most limited hold in the West. At the same time, however, the published accounts of those expeditions began a process of claiming that the United States was conquering Indians through the clever negotiation of its first emissaries.[36]

In the end, the books celebrated the explorers' ability to overcome challenges in ways that only reinforced the notion of the West as a dangerous and foreboding place. Instead of describing a calm passage from the Missouri to the Columbia as Jefferson had imagined in fantasies of the Northwest Passage, *History of the Expedition* and Gass's *Journal* told of endless mountains, scarce resources, and an unforgiving climate. Instead of describing agricultural opportunities at the headwaters of the Red River, Freeman and Custis detailed the contentious international situation that had forced them to abandon their expedition before it even reached its goal. Finally, Pike managed to combine the narrative components of both stories. He, too, described the harrowing conditions of the Rocky Mountains, detailing levels of fear and danger that Lewis, Clark, and Gass, never acknowledged. Pike had reasons for doing so that were rooted in his tale of overcoming obstacles, just as Lewis's and Clark's efforts to be scientists and implacable leaders led them to write otherwise. It was in the experience of facing western challenges that the explorers themselves began to emerge from the texts they created.

BIOGRAPHIES

In 1811 Biddle had written to Clark inquiring about "the exact relative situation in point of rank & command between Captain Lewis & yourself." Clark went out of his way to make certain Biddle understood not only that Lewis had treated him as cocaptain, but also that Clark considered himself entitled to the rank, Dearborn's opinion notwithstanding. Biddle gave Clark his wish, and in the simple statement that "captain Meriwether Lewis, and captain William Clarke, both officers of the army of the United States, were associated in the command of this enterprise," he put Clark's own identity in print.

The passage came on the first page of the narrative, seemingly before the real action got started. Yet Clark's own lengthy, emotional commentary on the matter suggested just how important it was. It was the fringes of these books — the introductions that preceded their narratives, the appendices and other documents which often appeared at the end, and the maps inserted at either end — that often provided the most detailed discussion of the explorers.

In letters to his closest relatives and to the most distant public officials, in private journals and public records, in words and in pictures Clark had always described himself primarily in professional terms and always with a close connection to federal policy. Rarely describing feelings, Clark instead discussed events: his personal financial investments, the state of Indian affairs, the government of the Louisiana Territory. This was Clark's style, but it was hardly unique. To the contrary, formality and public affairs were common stuff for the correspondence of men in the early Republic, especially men in public office. They generally eschewed sentiment, reserving it primarily for their correspondence with women, in large part because women themselves often believed that was the most appropriate material for their own writing.[37]

Since childhood, Clark had treated his efforts to describe the western landscape as opportunities to create an ongoing autobiography. Seeking to prove himself as knowledgeable, reliable, intrepid yet obedient, Clark's narrative persona was perfectly tailored to establish his capacity for public employment on the frontiers of the Union. Maps had always been part of that process. It was in this context that Clark's Master Map of the North American West was an autobiographical document. In a single page, it condensed the material of thousands of pages of manuscript journals. It described where Clark had gone, what he had seen, and what he had overcome. It showed a company of American explorers traveling through a territory filled with abundant Indians and towering mountains. The map did all this even as its mere existence displayed Clark's expertise.

But the map was never sufficient to tell Clark's story, and when Biddle had written to him with the simple request that he clarify his rank, Clark relished the opportunity to set the record straight about his status on the expedition and the indignity he had suffered from Dearborn. He made certain that *History of the Expedition* made clear that Clark deserved a commission as captain and that it was Lewis's and Clark's expedition, not simply "Captain Lewis' expedition," as it was first called in print.

The same principles applied to other explorers. Nicholas King may have excluded Freeman and Custis from his efforts to edit their journals, but he did describe both men in the biographical terms they preferred. Where *History of the Expedition* announced Clark as an army captain, *An Account of the Red River* announced, "The party employed to explore the Red River . . . consisted of Mr. Thomas Freeman. Surveyor . . . [and] Dr. Peter Custis." It was as a surveyor that Freeman had defined himself as an American, and it was as a surveyor that he drew his livelihood and status. Meanwhile, Custis was not yet a doctor when the expedition began, but it was through that title that he established himself as a man of science.[38]

Pike seemed to have taken a lesson in autobiographical methods straight from Andrew Ellicott. Like Pike's, Ellicott's 1803 narrative of the southwestern boundary survey contained not only a straightforward chronology, but also a collection of letters chronicling Ellicott's efforts to overcome the impediments he confronted in the form of the natural landscape as well as recalcitrant Spaniards. It was in letters to James Wilkinson that Pike reviewed his personal achievements and constantly stated his commitment to the national project of western government. It was in letters to Spanish officials that Pike proclaimed his resistance to his imprisonment and his unflinching defense of national honor. And it was in speeches to Indians that Pike announced his bravery in the face of savagery.

Lewis never had the chance to complete his autobiography. Only the practical concerns of publishing inspired the sort of public defense that had so eluded him in 1809. In August 1813, Jefferson received a letter from Paul Allen, Biddle's associate from the *Port-Folio* who supervised the final editorial work on *History of the Expedition*. Allen informed Jefferson that he believed *History of the Expedition* would be "more compleat by the addition of Gov Lewis biography." It was a last-minute addition to a book that was already well behind schedule. Nonetheless, Allen had "prevailed upon the Booksellers to procrastinate the volume. I wish very much to enliven the dulness of the Narrative by something more popular splendid & attractive."[39]

Allen got more than he bargained for. Jefferson responded enthusiastically, writing a lengthy essay that appeared almost verbatim in *History of the Expedition* as "Life of Captain Lewis."[40] Jefferson had long hoped that the entirety of the book could somehow provide one final public defense of Lewis, yet it was no simple task for Jefferson to chronicle Lewis's life, ending as it did in suicide and under the shadow of public criticism.

The structure and goals of the biography borrowed heavily from Mason Locke "Parson" Weems's biography of George Washington. That work had already appeared in numerous editions by 1813. Weems's greatest contribution to the Washington mythology was to create the story of a young George Washington chopping down a cherry tree. Weems idealized Washington in an effort to determine what a good American should be. Jefferson had read Weems's biography carefully, and in 1813 he borrowed from it to celebrate both Lewis and the United States.[41]

Like so many biographers of the early Republic, Jefferson considered any lengthy discussion either of Lewis's private life or of his life before the expedition to be both unnecessary and inappropriate. Instead, Lewis's background and childhood served to introduce a set of national virtues. First, Jefferson celebrated Lewis's father for his service in the Revolution and for his "good sense, integrity, bravery, enterprise, and remarkable bodily powers."[42] Jefferson then situated young Lewis within the bloody struggle for supremacy in the Near West during the 1790s, with valiant Americans fighting against the unholy alliance of bloodthirsty Indians and their corrupt British allies. Jefferson had good reason to see things this way. In 1813 the United States was once again at war with Great Britain and with western Indians. His conclusions were in no small part informed by reports from men like Clark, who warned of a British–Indian alliance that could spread destruction throughout the West.

Emulating Weems's cherry tree story, Jefferson then created a myth for Lewis. Whereas Weems's apocryphal story established Washington's unshakable honesty, Jefferson hoped to establish Lewis's fortitude: "When only eight years of age he [Lewis] habitually went out, in the dead of night, alone with his dogs, into the forest to hunt the raccoon and opossum. . . . In this exercise, no season or circumstance could obstruct his purpose." These qualities had reached their maturity by 1803, when Jefferson "had opportunity of knowing him intimately. Of courage undaunted; possessing a firmness and perseverance of purpose which nothing but impossibilities could deliver from its direction; careful as a father of those committed to his charge, yet steady in the maintenance of order and discipline; intimate with the Indian character, customs, and principles." In addition to these qualities, Lewis possessed "honest, disinterested, liberal, of sound understanding, and a fidelity to truth so scrupulous that whatever he should report would be as certain as if seen by ourselves."[43] Here were all the qualities of Washington, complete with two references to honesty, albeit without a story so powerful as the cherry tree. The reference to disinterest was particularly important. It was the specific quality that so many believed had enabled Washington to rise above pecuniary interests, and it was the absence of disinterest that Americans worried would lead to a more crass and corrupt political culture.[44]

It worked. Like the cherry tree, the nocturnal journeys of young Meriwether Lewis have survived. They have become a standard refrain of biographies in the two centuries since Lewis's death.[45]

Jefferson provided no details about the expedition itself, explaining that "from this time his journal, now published, will give the history of his journey to and from the Pacific ocean."[46] If the book itself provided a biography for Lewis from 1803 to 1806, Jefferson intended to make his discussion of Lewis's tenure as governor into one last example of the importance of high-minded disinterestedness. Lewis "found the territory distracted by feuds and contentions among the officers of the government, and the people themselves divided by these into factions and parties." Jefferson described St. Louis in terms that were both specific and metaphoric. As he watched the Federalist Party implode in the face of the Democratic-Republicans, Jefferson imagined a chance for the sort of unanimity he nostalgically associated with the

1770s and 1780s, while still fearing that rampant disputes would destroy the national fabric of the American people and the constitutional structure of the federal Union.[47]

Jefferson's solution to the national threat of fragmentation appeared in his discussion of Lewis's solution to the local challenges in St. Louis: "He determined at once to take no side with either, but to use every endeavor to conciliate and harmonize them. The even-handed justice he administered to all soon established a respect for his person and authority, and perseverance and time wore down animosities and reunited the citizens again into one family."[48] Ignoring the very real discord facing Lewis's administration, Jefferson described a scene of calm that testified to Lewis's talents as well as to a particular vision of politics. The family metaphor was especially important here. Advocates of union—especially Jefferson—had long deployed the notion of family to explain how the United States would work over time.

If this was the case, how could Jefferson explain Lewis's demise? Here he turned to psychology: "Governor Lewis had from early life been subject to hypochondriac affections. It was a constitutional disposition in all the nearest branches of his family." Jefferson claimed to have observed this disposition firsthand during Lewis's service as the president's secretary. Jefferson explained that Lewis "was in a paroxysm of one of these when his affairs rendered it necessary for him to go to Washington." When it came to the suicide itself, Jefferson avoided details while still sending powerful messages: "About three o'clock in the night he did the deed which plunged his friends into affliction and deprived his country of one of her most valued citizens, whose valor and intelligence would have been now employed in avenging the wrongs of his country. . . . It lost, too, to the nation the benefit of receiving from his own hand the narrative now offered."[49]

Jefferson used Lewis's death to once again sing the praises of a specific form of public service, a form which seemed especially vital in 1813. The War of 1812 had led men like Jefferson to question the emerging leadership within the United States, as senior military personnel pursued disastrous campaigns on the U.S.–Canadian border and senior civil officials at the state and national levels failed to support the Madison administration's war planning.

Jefferson's biography of Lewis, a brief passage requested as an afterthought to include in a much longer book, set the pattern for how Americans understood western exploration. Lewis's family, his childhood excursion to the wilderness, his commitment to science, his friendship with Clark are less the stuff of legend than of biography. Like Weems, Jefferson imagined an idealized American with physical bravery, one whose masculinity was both tested and developed in either the military struggle of the Revolution (as in the cases of Washington and Lewis's father) or the struggle to explore and govern the West (as in the case of Lewis).

THE BOOK AND THE PLATES

Clark still had to decide the fate of *History of the Expedition*. Biddle had written to him on the urgent matter of whether he wanted to own the abstract legal copyright of the book or the cold physical object of the plates to print "A Map of Lewis and Clark's Track." Clark did not keep Biddle waiting for long. Nor did it seem a difficult choice to make. Always worried about his finances, Clark did not question Biddle's claim that Clark would see more revenue from "A Map of Lewis and Clark's Track" than from *History of the Expedition*. Besides, Clark was personally invested in that map, based as it was on the Master Map that was entirely his own work. In December 1816 Clark accepted the deal, adding, "I am realy sorry that you have been at so much trouble in acting for me." Clark chose the plates.

Clark also thanked Biddle for his detailed discussion of the dreadful financial condition of the project. It proved useful in Clark's correspondence with Lucy Marks, Lewis's mother. An aging widow who had outlived two husbands, Lucy Marks had long struggled financially and apparently believed that she had somehow been swindled out of the money from sales of the book. Clark informed Biddle, "This measure is important to me as it enables me to satisfy the old lady who I have reasons to believe has been persuaded that profit arrising from that work has been received."[50] That information was no less useful in satisfying Jefferson. Clark knew Jefferson was equally worried about Lewis's family, so in 1817 he informed the former president of the news he had given Marks. As he had done the year before when Jefferson first prodded Clark on the matter of a second book, Clark avoided a substantive discussion of Lewis's scientific materials. Instead, he again covered matters with which he felt more confident: the state of affairs in territorial administration: "The population of this Territory is rapidly increasing and very widely extending itself, the Lands on the Missouri having greatly the advantage as respects fertility of soil & health, draws the greatest emigration in that direction."[51]

This remarkable statement seemed completely at odds with the book and the map Clark had so recently seen through to completion. He described western settlement without any reservations and celebrated the fertility of the western landscape, doing so only three years after the release of *History of the Expedition*, with its dire commentary on western conditions. The apparent disjuncture between the two statements made sense to Clark, however, for he accepted the notion that definitions of the West, or rather the Wests, could change. *History of the Expedition* described a Far West well beyond the Missouri Territory. It was in the upper Missouri Valley, the northern Plains, and the Rockies that Clark saw infertile lands, powerful Indians, and difficult passages. In 1803 the land that became the Missouri Territory was already a gateway, but in this case a gateway to an unwelcoming West that Clark had described with grave concern. By 1817 the Missouri Territory had joined the Near West, and Clark had helped make this transformation happen.

Other forms of landscape description also suggested how Clark made his peace with Missouri. In addition to the Master Map of the North American West he had completed in 1810 and the strategic maps of western defenses he had drawn in 1813, Clark had accumulated numerous survey maps of his own Louisiana Purchase. The Clark family had always bet its future on speculation in western lands, and William Clark was no exception. Throughout the 1810s, he acquired lots of various sizes throughout the territory he governed. Given the unpredictability of western speculation, Clark was quite literally gambling on Missouri's future.

As far as Clark was concerned, the great project of mapping the West was over. The books resulting from Jefferson's expeditions had described the landscape, even as so many participants in those expeditions continued to serve in a federal government that used the information from the expeditions to enact policy in the Far West.

Whatever Jefferson's desire to produce a second book, he had no more motivation than Clark. Lewis's dream of a major scientific work based on the Lewis and Clark Expedition remained an elusive goal. The materials from the expedition soon scattered to various individuals and institutions. Clark focused his own attention on the Missouri Territory.

But Clark kept the Master Map. In 1818 the Clark family moved into a new house, an imposing brick structure in downtown St. Louis. Clark hung the Master Map in his office and consulted it as he planned Indian policy. He showed the map to travelers seeking detailed geographic information. He also preserved the map as an autobiographical statement of what he had achieved in the West.

Part III

A WORLD TRANSFORMED

7

Return to the West

In 1820, William Clark had it all. He had built the family, the career, and the reputation that had so long eluded him. If *History of the Expedition* had failed to deliver on its financial promise, Clark was nonetheless pleased to have published his comprehensive map of the West. More important, though, Clark no longer needed that project in the way he had only a few years earlier. As the leading citizen of the Missouri Territory, his status seemed secure. Happily married with a growing family and living in a manner that satisfied his gentry pretensions, Clark, in his midforties, had finally arrived.

And then he lost everything. The losses began in February 1818, when George Rogers Clark died after years of alcoholism, declining health, and residual bitterness over failed opportunities that left him dependent on family members in Kentucky. William Clark mourned his brother, unaware that far worse was yet to come in 1820. In short order Julia Clark was dead and William Clark was no longer governor. These upheavals came to a catastrophic conclusion less than a year later. In September 1821, Clark's youngest child, seven-year-old Mary Margaret Clark composed a simple letter to her father: "I am a good girl and read and write every day." Three weeks later, she too was dead.[1]

How did he feel? It is the most basic question of any biography, or at least of biography as it has come to be defined. The remaining evidence provides almost no indication, and what little there is comes more from the comments of those who surrounded Clark than from Clark himself. And yet Clark had hardly stopped writing. It was simply that what he wrote provided few indications of his feelings. There was more to this than avoidance or denial, the easiest explanations to apply in our post-Freudian culture. Rather, Clark wrote as he always had. Facing an uncertain future as a recently widowed resident of the state of Missouri, Clark returned to the tasks he knew best: Indian negotiation, land speculation, and the task of landscape description that connected the two. After all, Clark had regularly kept journals, but not diaries. He recorded what he did, rarely what he felt. In this, he was a typical man of the early Republic.

Clark drafted one of those pieces of representative writing in September 1815. Only four months after Clark had helped broker an uneasy peace on the eastern Plains at Portage des Sioux, he wrote about Indian affairs to William Crawford, who had recently taken office as secretary of war. Clark began by addressing the chronic problem of white settlers moving onto Indian land in defiance of the edicts issued by territorial officials. Clark's short-term solution was to warn the settlers against the move. In the long term, however, he wanted to negotiate a cession of the land "which would connect the Settlements of this Territory with the States of Louisiana, covering a Country which the Indians set but little value." Struggling to describe the situation in words, Clark added, "The inclosed Sketch or Map will afford you a better view of the country, and extend of population, than can be shewn in a letter."[2] Twenty years after his encounter with the Spanish at Chickasaw Bluffs, Clark still considered his words inadequate to the task of describing intercultural contact. Pictures were needed to fill the gap.

Unfortunately, Clark's "sketch" disappeared in the War Department archives. Only the letter remains. The Far West that Clark described in his letter and in the missing map of 1815 remained a place of ambiguous benefit. It might be less dangerous, but it was hardly edenic. An unpleasant climate, questionable agricultural potential, uncertain mineral resources, and widespread Indian power continued to pervade the written and visual description of the West. Clark believed that managing expansion still required an aggressive public policy combined with an effort to continue mapping unknown territory and remapping the demographic landscape to meet national objectives.

Yet even as the Mississippi River divided Near West from Far West, Clark himself was contributing to a process through which Americans could claim the Far West as their own and articulate a process of orderly expansion and the benefits that would come from it. As in the past, this was a process that combined diplomacy, Indian policy, and the cultural production of western description. In 1821 the creation of the state of Missouri upset Clark's career just as his private life reached its low point. Nonetheless, even as Clark struggled to find his future in Missouri, creating that state suggested how William Clark's world could move into the Far West.

THE END OF THE MISSOURI TERRITORY

All of these tragedies hit Clark in short order. The greatest problem Clark faced was a simple one: he never saw it coming. There was more to this than the sudden death of his wife and daughter. Clark's shifting political prospects showed just how little he understood about the political transformation at work in the United States. He had spent his adult life trying to make himself into a good republican citizen. The Virginians who had been his models— George Rogers Clark, Thomas Jefferson, George Washington—were all products of an American Revolution almost a half century away. As much as any place in the United States, the Missouri Territory was home to the sort of changes at work in the United States in the years after the War of 1812. Missouri experienced a revolution in demography, economy, and politics. Missouri also stood at the epicenter of a broader embrace of expansion in all its forms. Even as Clark set about recording these changes for his superiors in Washington, he never fully understood their implications.

In 1817, James Monroe, fresh from his victory in the presidential election of 1816, coined the expression "Era of Good Feelings" to describe the times. Clark shared Monroe's sentiment that the end of war in Europe and the Americas, the declining power of Indians in the eastern Plains, and the collapse of the Federalist party might finally bring about peace and prosperity in both the East and the West. Clark considered himself an immediate beneficiary. He knew he enjoyed considerable popularity, in sharp contrast to the men who had preceded him as territorial governor.

Throughout the late-1810s, Clark's private life seemed to mirror his public affairs. After the birth of Meriwether Lewis Clark in 1808, four other children followed in quick succession during the 1810s: William Preston in 1811, Mary Margaret in 1814, George Rogers Hancock in 1816, and John Julius in 1818. Clark also assumed responsibility for a growing coterie of relatives and dependants. When Clark's profligate brother-in-law, James O'Fallon, deserted Clark's sister, William Clark assumed the role of patron for Fanny Clark O'Fallon's two sons, John and Benjamin, bringing them to Missouri and launching their careers. If the task proved challenging, Clark enjoyed the unwavering gratitude and support of the O'Fallons.[3] Another of Clark's protégé's reconnected him to the Lewis and Clark Expedition in revealing ways. In

1811 Clark received a visit from Sacagawea and Toussaint Charbonneau. Charbonneau, the child of a French father and an Indian mother, had both disappointed and irritated Clark while serving as a translator on the expedition. His teenage wife, Sacagawea, however, had proven invaluable at crucial moments on the expedition, all the while caring for the infant son, Jean-Baptiste, who had been born during the winter at Fort Mandan. From the end of the expedition in 1806 until their visit in 1811, this family rejoined the multiracial population of the Missouri Valley. When Charbonneau and Sacagawea departed from St. Louis in 1811 to return to the upper Missouri Valley, they left Jean-Baptiste in Clark's care. As in so many other situations, Clark left no record of his feelings on the matter or of his reaction to news in 1812 that Sacagawea had died and Charbonneau had no intention of returning to care for his son. All that remains are records showing that Clark paid for Jean-Baptiste's education in the decade that followed. Clark made his peace with Charbonneau and later helped secure work for him in the Missouri fur trade.[4]

In the same way that Clark considered himself responsible for Jean-Baptiste's welfare, he always convinced himself that he was acting in the best interest of western Indians. Clark believed he had always negotiated with Indians in good faith and secured for them the best agreements that were available within the prevailing circumstances of the 1810s. Clark also considered himself the Indians' defender. Yet he also remained a pragmatic advocate of the federal policy of racial supremacy. Through alliance and commercial dependence, he sought to strip friendly Indians of their autonomy. Clark effectively exploited these circumstances to establish himself as the overseer for all negotiations in the region. In 1818, for example, Clark proudly informed Secretary of War John C. Calhoun that he had "with much difficulty succeeded in bringing about a peace between the Osages and Cherokees. As it was thought by both parties that no treaty they could make would be considered as reciprocally binding upon them, unless it should be ratified and confirmed in my presence, I invited both Tribes to send a deputation of Eight or ten of their principal Men to meet in council at this place."[5] When Indians refused to accept those relationships, Clark deftly manipulated intervillage rivalries to force Indians into alliances with the United States as a defense against their local adversaries. "It must be admitted," he explained, "that the encourageing of War among the Indian Tribes, is cruel, but the situation of this Country has been such, that I found myself compelled to promote a War amongst the Indians."[6]

Clark's description of himself took visual form in his most dramatic portrait, a painting by Chester Harding completed in 1820. It was a massive, full-length portrait, just over seven by five feet. Harding portrayed Clark as a statesman, posed in classical formality, clothed in black, and standing in a well-appointed room of a type that was rare in frontier Missouri. In other words, this was hardly the image of an explorer (Fig. 27). It was instead typical of American portraiture for men who sought to portray themselves as the embodiment of social, political, or economic power. As a long-serving territorial governor and Indian agent, Clark sought to present himself as a figure of stability and civilization. As a board member on various banks, as a member of a Masonic lodge, Clark had established himself alongside the communities of French- and English-speaking elites.

Even though Harding's portrait represented Clark at the height of his authority, Clark's political world was in danger. During the 1810s, thousands of Americans descended on the Ohio and Mississippi valleys. Propelled by declining economic prospects in the East and attracted by the same appealing accounts of the Near West that had first brought the Clarks to Kentucky, Americans flooded the Missouri Territory. Those numbers only increased in 1819, when a nationwide economic collapse brought a quick end to Monroe's Era of Good Feelings. As the population of the Missouri Territory swelled, residents—especially politically ambitious ones frustrated by the limitations of the territorial system—eagerly awaited the transition to statehood. Clark himself expressed enthusiasm for the change. But the question remained: could William Clark survive statehood? More specifically, could he survive election? Despite a lifetime in public office Clark had never secured the consent of the governed at the ballot box. In this he was typical of many territorial officials, men whose entire careers had relied on patronage from above rather than election from below.

That background may well help explain why Clark proved so politically tone-deaf to the circumstances in Missouri—and the nation at large—in 1820. First, Clark was completely blindsided by the debate over slavery that enveloped the discussion of Missouri statehood. As a young man, he had observed firsthand as Kentucky entered the Union without controversy in 1792, followed four years later by Tennessee. Meanwhile, the system first created for the Northwest Territory had established a procedure for attaining statehood rapidly throughout the West. Six territories had already become states (Ohio in 1803, Louisiana in 1812, Indiana in 1816, Mississippi in 1817, and Illinois and Alabama in 1819), and none had faced much opposition in Congress.

Figure 27. Chester Harding, *William Clark* (1820). Collections of the St. Louis
Mercantile Library at the University of Missouri–St. Louis.

Clark expected that Missouri would follow the same smooth path to state-hood. When Congress considered the matter in 1819, however, members of the House and Senate who opposed the expansion of slavery attempted to impose restrictions that would require any state constitution to include a pro-hibition against slavery. The matter festered in Washington, unleashing ex-actly the sort of loud argument about slavery that American politicians had always sought to avoid. The most pessimistic feared the event would destroy the union. Congress only managed to resolve the issue through the Missouri Compromise, which allowed for the admission of the free state of Maine and the slave state of Missouri and the imposition of the Mason-Dixon Line as a dividing line for future slave and free states.[7]

Clark seemed unprepared for this controversy, the result of his southern roots, his western experiences, and his misunderstanding of how Americans had come to conceive of expansion. Clark had always worried about the ten-sions between East and West, not North and South. As a child of the Virginia gentry, he never questioned the appropriateness of slavery. He was a slave-holder himself and had helped encourage the growth of slavery in Missouri. Clark treated slaves in the same paternalistic terms as Indians. The case of the slave York exemplifies his outlook and his inability to perceive the explosive political content of slavery. Among the most famous stories of the Lewis and Clark Expedition is that York achieved a rough parity with other members of the expedition and that Clark promised to grant him freedom in exchange for his service. Whether the story is true or not, Clark certainly did not free York. More important, when York protested, Clark took offense. Only after years of protest did York finally secure his freedom.[8]

Accordingly, Clark never grasped the effort to restrict slavery in Missouri, nor for that matter did he fully understand the groundswell of support for its expansion. Since 1776, a coalition of planters, southern politicians, and slave traders had seen clear benefits to the expansion of slavery into the Southwest. This is not to say they always endorsed *territorial* expansion. Some, like Jef-ferson and Madison, worried about the capacity of the United States to govern new territory. Others worried about the prospects of slave revolt on western frontiers, where the institutions of slavery were their weakest.[9] None-theless, in the 1810s and early 1820s a younger generation was keen to push the boundaries of slavery. This cohort included Americans who hoped to extend the reach of slavery within existing boundaries. It also included the growing colony of American settlers in Spanish and, later, Mexican Texas, many of whom had arrived to seek a new frontier for slavery. Among the founders of the American colony in Texas were two former Missourians, Moses Austin and his son, Stephen. They had left Missouri in the late 1810s, driven away by a series of lawsuits that emerged from their questionable dealings in business and land speculation. For his part, Clark considered the Austins trouble-makers within the Missouri Territory, and he was only too happy to see them leave.[10]

When Congress finally approved Missouri statehood, Clark initially balked at the prospect of running for governor. Then he disappeared: in the summer of 1820 he left Missouri for Virginia. His reasons were simple and sentimen-tal. Julia Hancock Clark had become ill, apparently suffering from breast can-cer. Assuming she would recover under her family's care, Clark traveled with her to Virginia. He then returned to St. Louis, and on June 25, 1820, Clark wrote from St. Louis to inform Thomas Forsyth, a fellow Indian agent, that "I have become a candidate for the place of governor." Two days later, un-beknown to her husband hundreds of miles away, Julia Clark died.[11]

Though his campaign was barely under way, Clark immediately left for Fotheringay, the Hancock family plantation, arriving a month after Julia's death. Clark then returned to Missouri and entered the first and only election of his life. What followed was a disaster as Clark took one political misstep after another. First, he publicly preserved his loyalty to the old French elite of St. Louis, a group that faced growing resentment from the Anglo-American migrants who, by 1820, constituted the majority of the electorate. Second, Clark had no effective response to critics who charged he had sided with In-dians at the expense of white settlers. Clark could not respond in large part because he had, in fact, so rarely sided with Indians, pursuing a policy in-stead that was designed to eliminate Indian power and clear Indians from the lands most coveted by whites. Third, Clark was outmaneuvered by a younger generation of politicos in Missouri. All three factors indicated the same thing: William Clark did not understand democracy. More specifically, he did not understand the democratic political culture taking shape in the United States and reaching its extreme on the frontiers of the union. In this democratic world, politicians appealed directly to their constituencies, often by casting themselves as friends of the people who would vigorously represent their in-terests. In sharp contrast, Clark had been raised in a republican political cul-ture in which elected officials had always claimed they had a responsibility to represent the best interests of the people, even if that meant disagreeing with them. The territorial system itself had only reinforced these principles. On the assumption that territorial residents were politically immature, federal appointment of governors was supposed to protect them from the whims of the electorate.[12]

Added to all this was Clark's emotional distraction and absence during much of the campaign because of Julia's death. These personal developments were contributing factors, however, not deciding ones. Clark proved completely incapable of responding to his critics in the rough-and-tumble world of nineteenth-century frontier politics. In the end, Alexander McNair defeated Clark by an overwhelming margin, 6,576 to 2,656.[13]

In February 1821, with Missouri statehood approved but the new government not yet in place, John Scott, the territorial delegate to Congress, informed Secretary of State John Quincy Adams that "Governor William Clark of Missouri desires to know what situation in the eye of the General Government he now occupies." Since the state of Missouri had been carved out of the larger Louisiana Territory, "it is now necessary for him to know whether the Government considers him still in office, within the state of Missouri? or whether in office as to that portion of Country out of the lines of the State? or both? And also that he have some directions as to the disposition he is to make of the Public acts, records, and documents which would properly belong to the State. An early reply will oblige him."[14]

The uncertainty of Clark's future was made all the more unpleasant as Clark considered his cohort of Virginians in the territorial administration. His old friend William Henry Harrison was elected to Congress in 1816 and joined the Senate three years later. William C. C. Claiborne was elected the first governor of Louisiana in 1812 after serving as the only appointed governor of the Territory of Orleans. Like Harrison, Claiborne was elected to the Senate but died on the eve of his departure for Washington in 1817. Both men began their appointed tenures with accusations of aloof leadership in which disinterestedness seemed more closely akin to unrepresentativeness. Yet both men had overcome these obstacles in the pursuit of electoral success. Clark, however, was never able to make the leap from reliable appointee to elected leader.[15]

On March 21, 1821, Missouri entered the Union as the twenty-fourth state, and the office of territorial governor ceased to exist. Clark was already hardpressed for money. He had invested poorly in various banking and commercial schemes, and he knew it would be years before his speculation in western lands would see a profit. In the meantime, his only steady revenue would come from his appointment as an Indian agent, and he had no way of knowing if that patronage would continue.[16]

REVISITING THE FAR WEST

During the years that Missouri became the focal point of a national argument over slavery, the content of written and visual materials seeking to understand the West experienced its own internal battle. In the 1810s and the early 1820s, a slew of new publications by American authors sought to describe the Far West and to situate it alongside the rest of the country. The same promotional language that John Filson had used to attract people to Kentucky appeared in material for settlements in the trans-Mississippi West. Meanwhile, other Americans continued in the tradition of Clark and Jefferson's other explorers, describing the West as a dangerous place with an inhospitable climate. As always, however, this debate was not entirely about expansion. Instead, the familiar forces—professional aspirations, technological limitations, written and visual conventions—continued to inform the ways in which Americans imagined the Far West. Equally important, the shifting cultural representations of the West coincided with changes in the ways Americans policymakers situated the West in the domestic political economy and foreign policy.

That was certainly the case for Major Stephen Harriman Long, who led five surveying expeditions into the Far West. In 1819–20, Long's Yellowstone Expedition retraced the route of Lewis and Clark up the Missouri River to the Rocky Mountains before returning on Pike's route down the Arkansas River. Long's Great Lakes Expedition of 1823 sought to correct Pike's erroneous claims about the sources of the Mississippi River. Those two expeditions resulted in major published accounts that continued the tradition of describing the Far West as a place filled with Indians who remained relatively independent and who might become violent at any moment.[17] The Teton Sioux, among the great villains of the Lewis and Clark narrative, remained the stereotypical violent savages. Long's Yellowstone account described the Tetons taking revenge for an assault on one of their villagers. They "immediately attacked the assailant, felled him in his turn to the earth, gashed his body with the spear of his war-club and left him for dead. This is a strong evidence of the determination of the savages, as they are called, to protect those whom they consider under their guardianship."[18]

The accounts of Long's expeditions also confirmed what Jefferson's explorers had concluded about the landscape itself. The books used "abundance" less to suggest a bounty for settlers than to announce numbers too large to estimate or enumerate. Those books described isolated regions of fertility and the potential for white settlement, but they also described arduous passages. The northern Plains were a place of bleak grasslands while the southern Plains were the deserts that Pike had described.[19]

Yet even if Long drew the same conclusions, his work and that of his contemporaries emerged from a very different set of concerns and identities. Unlike Lewis, Clark, Pike, or Freeman, Long was a bookish figure who sought to combine a career in government employment with long-standing intellectual pursuits. A New Hampshire native born in 1784, Long was a college-educated mathematician who by 1809 was a school principal. He joined the army during the War of 1812 and in 1816 became one of the army's three topographical engineers, with an immediate promotion to major. Long's expeditions included a team of experts, among them a zoologist, a botanist, and a geologist. He also had three men dedicated to describing the land: Major Thomas Biddle, who kept a written journal; Titian Ramsay Peale (a son of Charles Willson Peale), who sketched the flora and fauna under the title of assistant naturalist; and Samuel Seymour, who painted the western landscape.[20]

Another scientist and explorer, named Henry Rowe Schoolcraft, was also imposing a new scientific stamp onto western exploration. A precocious intellect from New York, Schoolcraft began publishing a series of scientific studies and travel accounts in 1819. In 1832, it was Schoolcraft who finally identified the source of the Mississippi River, a generation after disputed claims on the matter had undermined negotiations for the Jay Treaty.[21] Long and Schoolcraft were the first in a growing number of American traveler scientists trying to understand the western landscape. Many of them were still testing age-old European tales of outlandish animals and natural resources. Others were responding to Jefferson's western explorers, who had questioned the fertility of the Far West without possessing the scientific training or knowledge to convince readers they were equipped to draw any conclusions.[22]

Like the earlier western describers, Long and Schoolcraft depended on federal employment. Long remained in the U.S. Army for most of his adult life, and Schoolcraft became a long-serving Indian agent. Nonetheless, they reversed the relationship that Clark and his contemporaries saw between federal employment and western description. For Long and Schoolcraft, federal employment provided the means to write about the West, whereas Jefferson's explorers considered writing about the West a means to advance federal careers. Some Americans continued to see publication as a way to advance western careers or to generate additional revenue. That was certainly the case for

Amos Stoddard, an army officer who served alongside Clark in St. Louis, and Henry Marie Brackenridge, a Pittsburgh attorney who built political careers in both Louisiana and Missouri before returning to Pennsylvania. Both published accounts of the West that suggested modest productivity from western land rather than exaggerated accounts of unlimited potential.[23]

The maps that accompanied this new set of books on the Far West reflected those concerns, focusing on topography and hydrology rather than on populations or international boundaries. The same held true for the experts who accompanied Long, some of whom pursued the long-term scientific careers that the likes of William Dunbar and Peter Custis had sought earlier. Edwin James, who edited the official account of Long's Yellowstone Expedition, wrote constantly about his desire to secure gainful employment as a scientist. Thomas Say, Long's zoologist, published the leading texts on North American entomology. Finally, western exploration established Schoolcraft as a major figure in American geology.[24]

Long and Schoolcraft were among the first in a series of American scientists to argue about possibilities in the Far West. Eventually, their conclusions were challenged by scientists and settlers who concluded the West contained unprecedented opportunities for settlement.[25] In the 1820s, however, the official accounts of major federal expeditions did not share the claims that boosters had attached to the Near West. Equally important, Long and Schoolcraft had their own reasons to describe the West in detached terms. Once again, there were few references to sublime, picturesque, or beautiful landscapes of the type more common to writers schooled in classical aesthetics. Eager to prove themselves as scientists, these new explorers wrote with rationality rather than with sentiment and with statistical data rather than emotional reactions.

Yet the Far West was hardly lacking in boosters. During the 1810s the descriptions of the Far West as a dangerous, inhospitable place faced their first serious challenge in the form of books, pamphlets, and travel narratives. Some of these were published in the West, the work of western residents eager to celebrate their region.[26] Others were the work of travelers who found much to admire in the West. Among the admirers was John Bradbury, who published his *Travels in North America* in 1817. Discussing the enormous potential for settlement, Bradbury claimed that "nothing so strongly indicates the superiority of the western country, as the vast emigrations to it from the eastern and southern states."[27] Bradbury and others like him based their claims less on what they knew about the Far West than on the precedent of the Near

West. They claimed that the ease people experienced in settling Ohio and Indiana suggested the same prospects for the land west of the Mississippi, even as they acknowledged just how little they knew about the Far West. Perhaps so, but books like Bradbury's were helping to attract settlers to the Far West.

Many of these accounts drew on arguments that Americans had first made in the pamphlets advocating congressional approval of the Louisiana Purchase in 1803–04 but used them in a very different way. In those pamphlets, Americans had rarely celebrated expansion for its own sake, discussing fertility in the Far West as an afterthought, a secondary benefit after the more important process of securing control of the Mississippi. By the 1810s, however, Americans were beginning to shift those claims to the forefront. In his travel narrative of 1819, for example, William Darby reminded Americans that in 1803–04 advocates for the Louisiana Purchase "were of accord . . . that the surplus produce of all our states and territories, situated upon the tributary streams of the Mississippi, must find a vent by that great outlet." Now he extended that argument to the Great Lakes. Claiming that "Detroit is now a place of extensive commerce," he predicted that trade would extend throughout the West and into Canada, benefiting settlers on both sides of the border.[28]

These positive accounts of the Far West were closer to public opinion than the comments of Clark, Long, or Schoolcraft. White settlers were eager to descend on the Far West, and Clark's loss in the election of 1820 reflected their irritation with public officials who sought to restrain expansion. During the 1810s and 1820s Americans even sought to upset the time-honored fur-trading system. Most important, they hired Anglo-American trappers. This approach broke with over a century of tradition in which Indians trapped animals before bartering with Europeans for the sale of their pelts. A growing cohort of white mountain men competed openly with Indians, eventually displacing them as the source of beaver and other valuable pelts. Meanwhile, mounting tensions between Indian villages and the declining power of the old French trading families prevented an organized response to the Anglo-American economic challenge. John Jacob Astor, a German-born merchant who arrived in the United States in 1784, emerged as the dominant figure in this process. Astor created his first fortune when the Jay Treaty opened trade on the Great Lakes. Without ever leaving his home in New York, he became the preeminent American fur trader on the Pacific Coast in the wake of the Louisiana Purchase. He established a permanent outpost at the mouth of the Columbia River called Fort Astoria and eagerly lobbied the federal leadership to pursue a claim to the Oregon Country. In fact, topographical details from the first reports from Astoria found their way onto Clark's Master Map of the West.[29]

Astor sought to promote his ventures with a lobbying campaign in Washington and a publicity campaign throughout the nation. His efforts joined a cultural battle to describe the West that was already under way. That battle occurred in maps as much as in words.

Most travel narratives and promotional materials of the 1810s and 1820s continued the tradition of inserting a single, folded, black-and-white map, supplemented occasionally by a few additional illustrations interspersed within the text. Only the books of Long's expeditions included substantive illustrations. The account of the Yellowstone Expedition included five Indian scenes, three views of the Rocky Mountains, and one reconstruction of an illustrated bison robe. The account of Long's expedition in 1823 contained two illustrations of village life and five landscapes as well as two pages of drawings of shells from the inland waterways (Fig. 28).

These illustrations afford only the smallest glimpse of the visual record from Long's expeditions. Samuel Seymour, the artist for the expedition, made watercolors that never found their way into either book. Meanwhile, the books excluded Titian Ramsay Peale's work altogether, despite the fact that Peale had completed numerous detailed drawings of the plants and wildlife of the Far West. As records of an expedition that produced copious visual material, the books are striking for their paucity of illustration. The reason was simple: mass producing illustrations was extremely expensive.

The absence of Peale's artwork says as much about twentieth- and twenty-first-century scholarship as it does about nineteenth-century publishing. At first glance, the Long expedition becomes the first artistic venture to the West. Titian Ramsay Peale was the son of Charles Willson Peale, the scientist, artist, and intellectual who had been so important in framing the Lewis and Clark Expedition. That family connection has always been attractive to historians. Suddenly the work of father and son creates a history of American exploration founded on science and enlightened art.[30] Perhaps so, but the American public never saw much of that artistry. The problem is that Peale's drawings are so compelling and his family is so important that he overshadows Seymour in most of the histories of Long's expeditions. Peale's illustrations serve a role very similar to the manuscript journals of the Lewis and Clark Expedition. Those seductive passages from the journals suggest a deeply emotional and sentimental way of writing at work in the early nineteenth century. But like

J. Seymour delin.

F. Kearney sculp.[t]

View of the Rocky Mountains on the Platte 50 miles from their Base.

Figure 28. Samuel Seymour, "View of the Rocky Mountains on the Platte, 50 miles from their Base," illustration from Edwin James, *Account of an Expedition from Pittsburgh to the Rocky Mountains: Performed in the Years 1819 and '20, by Order of the Hon. J.C. Calhoun, Sec'y of War, Under the Command of Major Stephen H. Long . . .* (Philadelphia: H. C. Carey and I. Lea, 1822). Special Collections, Washington University in St. Louis.

Peale's drawings, those passages never made it into the public record. They were not the means by which a larger American public encountered the West, and they suggest just how much the conventions of writing and the realities of publishing came together to shape those western images.[31]

As a result, heading into the 1820s it was still maps, not landscape paintings, scientific illustrations, or still-life portraits, that dominated the visual representation of the North American West. But in the same way that print culture contained discrete forms of expansionist celebration, so, too, did maps. That was certainly the case for A *Map of the United States of America with the Contiguous British and Spanish Possessions*, a landmark piece of cartography published in 1816 by John Melish. It was a far cry from the Master Map of the North American West Clark had produced only a few years before, yet Melish was utterly dependent on Clark and Jefferson's other explorers (Fig. 29).

Clark's map, published only two years earlier, described the West as a dangerous place, a place without boundaries and crowded with Indian villages. Melish copied Clark's topographical details even as he told a very different story of the West. There were few Indian villages to be seen anywhere, let alone the sort of population statistics that Clark had situated so prominently on his map. Melish's use of boundaries was no less revealing. Instead of the contested western frontier described in the words and maps of Jefferson's expeditions, Melish imaged a West of clearly defined borders and clearly delineated power. Put simply, the West was American. By European tradition that long predated the United States, imposing boundaries onto the landscape was a first step in claiming that landscape. This outlook applied on the local level in the tedious process of land surveying just as it did in the grand contests of monarchs and empires. In the Americas, mapmakers had imposed boundaries to make claims seem real, denying the power of local residents— often Indians—or the claims of other countries.[32] By 1815 Americans possessed the cartographic literacy to understand Melish's map. The United States had unquestionable claims and unquestioned authority on a western landscape occupied by Indians in small numbers and possessing limited power.

Yet in spite of all these differences, Melish's map was a product of Jefferson's expeditions. As much as anybody, Melish began the process of sharing Clark's world with a larger public. Indians may have been removed from the picture, but the topography of the West came straight from "A Map of Lewis and Clark's Track." Meanwhile, Melish's description of the Southwest just as clearly borrowed from the maps in Pike's *Atlas* of 1810. Combined as never before, re-created with new detailed flourishes, and overlaid with an arresting

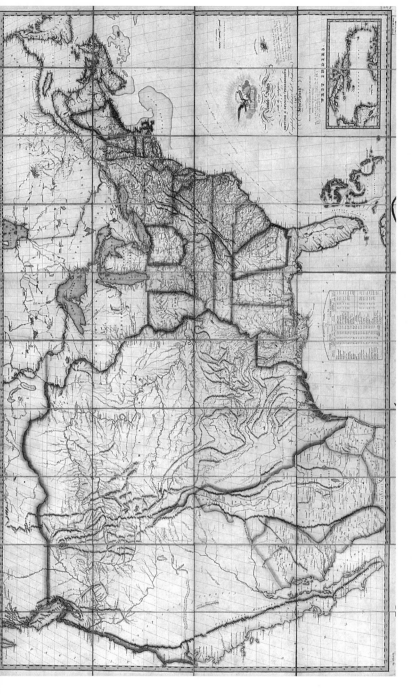

Figure 29. John Melish, *Map of the United States of America with the Contiguous British and Spanish Possessions* (Philadelphia, 1816). Geography and Map Division, Library of Congress.

use of color, Melish's map of 1816 finally created what American policymakers had sought for a generation. The United States had a single map of the North American West detailing the strategically vital waterways and borderlands. But Melish himself was hardly operating at the policymakers' request. Instead, the changes in publishing technology and in attitudes toward expansion had shifted the way Americans saw the Far West.

Even as men like Melish recirculated the material created by Clark, Clark himself continued to worry about the future. Stripped of his powers as governor, Clark spent the 1820s focusing on the task that had defined much of his life after 1803: negotiation with the Indians. He did so at a moment when the federal government was pursuing new strategies toward territorial expansion, changes Clark himself helped to realize. He did so in large part as a public official, but also as a western describer. Clark's map and the book he and Biddle produced became one of a series of tools available to federal policymakers during the 1820s. Those policymakers responded much as they had in the 1790s: they relied on the representation of the western landscape to achieve their goals. They used the work of public officials and the published work of private individuals whenever it served their purpose. Yet they also rejected that material as well, hoping to impose new boundaries onto the landscape.

Since 1803 the United States had acquired territory east of the Mississippi through a series of incursions into Spanish West Florida. After 1815, however, the moment seemed ripe for the United States to revise its policy in the Far West. With Napoleon deposed for good, Britain and the United States at peace, and the Spanish crown desperate to hold onto its American colonies, the United States was finally able to pursue a broad-based foreign policy that included the resolution of long-standing border disputes. Meanwhile, with Indian power collapsing in the Mississippi Valley, the eastern woodlands, and the eastern Plains, Indian agents like Clark could impose their own terms onto the negotiations. As Clark sought to establish new boundaries between American settlers and Indians, boundaries that included massive land cessions by the Indians, Secretary of State John Quincy Adams sought to establish boundaries with the European claims in North America.

In his efforts to define the United States, Adams expressed his ambivalence toward expansion. Generally uninterested in the matters of territorial governance and Indian affairs that had been so important to his predecessors in the State Department, Adams worried about a West beyond the control of the federal government. Likewise, in the Missouri Crisis Adams immediately recognized the capacity of expansion to ignite a vicious argument about slavery.[33] Nonetheless, he was prepared to take an aggressive stance toward both Spain and Great Britain. Whatever his concerns, Adams was far more confident in the pursuit of territory in the Far West than his predecessors. Peace in 1815 finally created the opportunity to resolve old disputes with Britain, while the outbreak of revolution in Latin America enabled the United States to pursue a more aggressive policy with the beleaguered Spain. In 1812, on the eve of war with Britain, the United States had relinquished Fort Astoria (Astor's outpost on the Pacific), and, implicitly, its claims to the Oregon Country. Only five years later, Adams dispatched the sloop-of-war *Ontario* to reestablish the U.S. claim on the Pacific Coast. The commanding officer, James Biddle, was the brother of Nicholas Biddle, Clark's collaborator in producing *History of the Expedition*. Adams took this action in no small part because John Jacob Astor wielded his considerable influence among leading politicians to make the case for expansion in the Pacific Northwest.[34]

In 1817 the United States and Britain launched a joint surveying effort to establish a final boundary between the United States and Canada. In 1794, the Jay Treaty had proposed just such an expedition, but the ongoing tensions between the United States and Great Britain rendered the project impossible. The man in charge of the American team was none other than Andrew Ellicott, almost twenty years removed from leading the southwestern boundary survey and fourteen years from providing Lewis with his rushed training in surveying and mathematics. In the intervening years, Ellicott stayed true to his goal of securing public patronage through landscape description. When the government of Pennsylvania removed him from the position of secretary of the land office in 1811, Ellicott rebounded quickly by securing an appointment as professor of mathematics at West Point. A colleague appointed that year was Stephen Long, who soon launched his own career exploring the West, one that produced both books and maps. For his part, Ellicott returned to West Point following the U.S.–Canadian boundary survey and continued to teach mathematics until his death from a stroke in 1820.[35]

At West Point, Ellicott and Long helped train the first generation of men who identified themselves exclusively as cartographers for the federal government. Meanwhile, the Treasury Department's General Land Office employed a growing number of men who created careers for themselves surveying the federal domain. They followed in the tradition of Thomas Freeman, for whom the creation and settlement of the Mississippi and Alabama territories had provided abundant work as a surveyor.[36]

These men helped survey a United States of increasingly well-defined borders. In 1818 American and British negotiators used this growing body of geographic knowledge to establish a boundary between the United States and Canada. Still unable to resolve the Oregon question, they left the territory in jurisdictional limbo, a strange state of affairs for international treaties, which usually sought to confirm clear title to land.[37] The following year Spanish and American negotiators finally agreed on the southern boundaries of the United States. Spain ceded all of the Florida Peninsula and the Gulf Coast, which amounted to little more than acknowledging the fact that the United States had already seized most of that territory in the preceding decade. The United States and Spain also fixed a boundary between Texas and Louisiana, eliminating the vagueness that Jefferson's explorers had acknowledged in their maps only a few years earlier. Ratified in 1821, the Transcontinental Treaty ended eighteen years of dispute over the boundaries of the Louisiana Purchase.[38]

In the midst of this diplomatic flurry, the private citizens who had long produced maps and travel accounts found themselves in ambiguous circumstances. They aspired to be players in the process only to be frustrated. They produced maps for their own purposes only to find those materials serving as policymaking instruments. They thereby became agents of empire without even knowing it. In other words, they continued to occupy much the same role they had played since 1776. Driven by their own diverse motivations, the men who drew, wrote, engraved, and published descriptions of the West were linked in numerous but complex ways to the policymaking process on both sides of the Atlantic.

That was certainly the situation with American geographers and cartographic publishers. The creation of new states in the 1810s and the changes to national borders were both a frustration and a golden opportunity. Making substantive alterations to the engraved printing plates used in making maps was almost impossible, forcing mapmakers to choose between the expense of commissioning new plates and using outdated ones as the nation's borders changed. Most chose the latter. Geographers likewise produced books that described states and territories undergoing regular change. Yet these circumstances also enabled authors, mapmakers, and publishers to regularly produce new editions of their work, all the while claiming that it was essential for Americans to purchase the latest, most accurate representation of the country.[39]

Still others sought to advance their projects through the policymakers themselves, something that Ellicott and Thomas Hutchins had done decades earlier. In 1816, for example, Melish sent Jefferson a copy of his *Map of the*

United States of North America for much the same reason map publishers had long written to presidents: to increase sales through endorsement by a public figure. Jefferson complimented Melish for "giving a luminous view of the comparative possessions of the different powers in our America." But Jefferson also appreciated the way maps told stories, adding that "it is on account of the value I set on it that I will make some suggestions." He was worried that Melish would underestimate American claims in the Floridas due to the "usurpations of Spain on the East side of that river [the Mississippi]"[40]

Jefferson had good reason to be concerned, for he knew just how much maps had served as ammunition in the diplomatic battles for territory. Melish's map became the primary source for Adams in 1818 as he struggled to coordinate boundary negotiations with Britain and Spain. Adams recorded in his private journal that when the Spanish delegation "asked whether we had been more yielding than heretofore, I showed him, upon Melish's map, the extent of U.S. claims." Adams literally drew a line on his copy of Melish's map, which he presented to the Monroe administration as a way to frame their diplomatic strategy.[41]

THE CREATION OF THE STATE OF MISSOURI

John Quincy Adams no longer concerned himself with William Clark, or for that matter with Missouri. He demonstrated only limited interest in Indian affairs, and, with the end of territorial rule, Adams's State Department relinquished its responsibility for daily governance. In 1821 Secretary of War John C. Calhoun rescued Clark's career. With the territory of Missouri eliminated by statehood and the vast Indian agency he supervised being subdivided, Clark was in danger of losing almost all of his income. But Calhoun valued Clark. In July 1820, at the height of Clark's personal suffering and political setbacks, Calhoun had written to Clark to "sympathize most sincerely with you in the death of your amiable partner, which I see announced by the papers." In 1821 Calhoun renewed Clark's commission as an Indian agent with only minor alterations to his mandate.[42]

Preserved as a federal appointee, the widower Clark felt surrounded by children. Still mourning the death of his wife and daughter, Clark found himself busily caring for many others: the four surviving children of his marriage with Julia; Jean-Baptiste Charbonneau, who turned sixteen in 1821; and his nephews, John and Benjamin O'Fallon, both adults but still eager for Clark's assistance.

Clark had no intention of raising the children on his own. In November 1821, just past the customary year of grieving for his first wife and a scant two months after the death of young Mary Margaret, Clark married Harriet Kennerly Radford. Clark had known Harriet for years, for she was the cousin and close friend of Julia Hancock Clark. Harriet had married Dr. John Radford and come to Missouri under circumstances very similar to Julia's arrival with Clark in 1808. Widowed with two children of her own, she had been married to Clark for almost two years when she bore the first of three more children. Again, the names the children were given were telling: Jefferson, Edmund (named for one of Clark's brothers), and Harriet. Jefferson, born in 1824, lived to the ripe age of seventy-six, but Edmund and Harriet both died in infancy.

Well into his fifties, Clark was the father of eight children born over a seventeen-year period. All the surviving evidence suggests that Clark assumed Harriet would take charge of this growing brood in a blended family that may now seem difficult to keep straight but which would have been altogether common in the nineteenth century, when death and remarriage were regular events in many families.

Clark approached his more fictive kin in other ways. Jean-Baptiste remained in the care of the priests at a Jesuit academy in St. Louis, his tuition paid by Clark. Meanwhile, in the O'Fallon boys Clark had a pair of full-grown foster sons. He guided their careers, but he also relied on their support. John O'Fallon had already returned the favor by helping Clark in the election of 1820, and Benjamin O'Fallon remained a loyal subordinate as an Indian agent in the 1820s.

Meanwhile, Clark's description of the West continued to inform federal policymakers. In 1823 Adams was still trying to resolve the thorny issue of the Oregon Country. In addition to the British, Adams now faced Russian claims. "I was very much absorbed in the examination of this Northwest Coast question," he recorded in the extensive journal he kept throughout much of his adult life. Like Jefferson twenty years earlier, he looked to western description to resolve the diplomatic challenges: "My time is swallowed up in the examination of Cook's Third Voyage, Coxe's Russian Discoveries, Humboldt, Mackenzie, Lewis and Clarke, and the Annual Register for 1790, for research into this question." In the end, he believed "I find proof enough to put down the Russian argument; but how shall we answer the Russian cannon?"[43]

It was a passage typical of Adams, whose memoirs are filled with moments of humor. He embraced the challenge of writing in a manner very much at odds with Clark's fumbling prose and unpredictable spelling. Yet both men approached the task of writing in similar ways. After all, they were writing journals, not diaries. Clark and Adams both wrote in the same dispassionate, impersonal manner that American men had long used to describe themselves and that American travelers also used to describe the West.

In 1824 Clark added yet another title to his list of federal appointments: surveyor general for the states of Missouri and Illinois as well as the newly created Territory of Arkansas. It was an appropriate appointment, drawing on Clark's regional experience and his technical expertise. It also suggested Clark's future in the state of Missouri. Western states like Missouri and Illinois still possessed vast areas of public land. It fell to men like Clark to map that land and prepare it for sale, whether to state governments, land speculators, or individual settlers. Preparing land for white settlement—either through mapping the land itself or by extinguishing competing claims—was no less important to the creation of Missouri than the state's difficult, unruly birth in Washington in the bitterness of the Missouri Crisis.

In his letter of 1815 to William Crawford, Clark had attempted to describe an arrangement "which would connect the Settlements of this Territory with the States of Louisiana." Into the 1820s that arrangement had become increasingly clear, not only in the land cessions of Indians but also in the growing number of Anglo-American settlements across the Mississippi. The very successes of the two institutions Clark served in the 1810s—the territorial system of the State Department and the Indian system of the War Department—had made these developments possible, eroding Indian power and providing an orderly system of white settlement. Within these years, the territorial boundaries of the United States had remained limited, and only in the Oregon Country did the federal government attempt to extend its reach. Yet Americans were finding the means to accommodate themselves to the West in ways that would enable them to welcome not only the demographic expansion of white settlers, but also the geographic expansion of the United States.

8

MOVING THE FAR WEST

In old age William Clark found himself surrounded by men trying to describe the West. Clark occasionally met those men. They visited him, sought his advice, and even found themselves at odds with the aging gatekeeper in St. Louis. Some of the most welcome visitors reminded Clark of the way in which western description had elevated him from the descending ranks of the Virginia gentry to the leading ranks of the western government. They consulted Clark's Master Map of the American West. They peppered Clark with questions about the topography and demography of the Far West. And they sought his permission, for as the senior Indian agent of the Far West he could offer the hospitality of western villages or prohibit travelers from interacting with Indians.[1]

Despite this status, Clark's world was under assault. In the realms of politics and public administration that he knew best, Clark seemed increasingly irrelevant. The very successes he had achieved in Indian policy made Indians appear far less threatening. In turn, Indian officials seemed far less important. The democratic political culture that had contributed to Clark's loss in the gubernatorial election of 1820 continued to spread in ways that made old Jeffersonians like him uncomfortable. Meanwhile, as maps reached their technological fulfillment, maps and travel narratives competed as never before with new forms of written and visual representation.

In Clark's childhood, three men had captured the way writing, mapping, and governing the West came together. Thomas Jefferson, John Filson, and Jedidiah Morse had all struggled to situate the West in a larger national story, and Clark's own outlook emerged in response to the models they established. By the 1830s, all three men were dead, their roles replaced by four others: Thomas Hart Benton, George Catlin, Washington Irving, and Henry Schenck

Tanner. These four men looked to Clark as a model in their efforts to represent the West. Yet all of them soon broke from Clark's outlook. And if Jefferson, Filson, and Morse established the world in which Clark operated, Benton, Catlin, Irving, and Tanner showed just how much had changed. That change took its most dramatic form in the ways people imagined the boundary between the Near West and the Far West. To many Americans, that line quite literally moved west in the 1820s and the 1830s. Historians have long shown how the frontiers of white and Indian settlement, territorial control, and intercultural contact shifted during this period. Stephen Aron and William Foley have specifically chronicled those processes in Missouri.[2] But how did the line change in the print and visual culture that sought to explain the American West? Benton, Catlin, Irving, and Tanner together provide an answer.

There was no single letter, no single map that connected Clark to Benton, Catlin, Irving, and Tanner. Instead, it was a series of written and visual works by all of them that captured not only the arguments about the West, but also the transformation in the ways Americans went about describing themselves and their country.[3] These four men joined Clark in asking the question that had been raging since the 1770s: Would expansion, in particular expansion into the Far West, bring benefits or destruction? Clark himself had been contradictory, at once warning about western dangers even as he pursued a western future for himself and his family. After years in which the printed and visual culture of the United States was out of step with the expansionist ambitions of many American citizens, the men who surrounded him showed how the representation of the Far West finally came into alignment with public opinion. In the process, Americans redefined the West. That process also signaled the transition from the early American Republic to the antebellum era.

HENRY SCHENCK TANNER

Clark had always conceived of how to represent the United States through the visual medium of mapmaking. This applied in localities, where surveys imposed order onto the landscape and transformed the natural environment into private property. It applied as well to the grand subject of the North American Continent, where maps explained the property of nations. In the 1820s and 1830s, the goal of a grand map for North America, with the United States controlling geographic knowledge itself, finally became a reality. The

United States developed a profitable cartographic publishing industry with a reputation for accuracy that displaced its European competitors. The maps they produced also told a very different story from the one Clark had told throughout his life. The new technological capacity of American mapmaking combined with a new nationalist content to create maps that made expansion appear logical and successful. Henry Schenck Tanner played a crucial role in this process. He helped establish the new preeminence of American mapmaking. Equally important, he helped solidify Clark's place in that mapmaking pantheon even as he became the latest western describer to redefine the West in ways very different from Clark's vision.

Sales of *History of the Expedition* may have been disappointing, but American cartographers acquired copies of "A Map of Lewis and Clark's Track" and copied its details in their own work. Tanner was one of the first cartographers to express any gratitude to Clark. There is no evidence he ever met Clark, but he clearly believed he was operating in the shadow of Clark and the other western describers. "Having explored [the Missouri] and the Columbia rivers," Tanner explained in 1823, "and in general effected nearly all the objects of the enterprise, the party returned . . . after an absence of two years."[4]

A talented engraver originally from New York, Tanner moved to Philadelphia in 1812 to work for John Melish. It was Tanner who, along with John Vallance, engraved Melish's *Map of the United States of America* in 1816. In 1819 Tanner left Melish to launch his own engraving firm with Vallance as well as his brother, Jonathan Tanner, and Francis Kearney (who had also engraved the illustrations for the 1822 account of Long's Yellowstone Expedition). The new company's first project was its most ambitious: *A New American Atlas*, released in five parts from 1819 to 1823 and then republished in its entirety in 1825, was a landmark in American cartography. The maps themselves were exceptional in every way. First and foremost, Tanner was the first American cartographer to offer a multipage atlas that presented the entire United States on a uniform scale. Second, he made greater use of color than any American mapmaker who preceded him.[5]

Adding to the superb visual quality of his maps, an eighteen-page essay on sources and methods appeared at the beginning of Tanner's atlas. This was a rarity in an age when cartographers simply copied other maps and included brief references to the latest "sources" or "authorities." His atlas contained "a topographical representation of the United States, infinitely superior, as it regards correctness and detail, and every way equal in style, to any European publication of the kind." To this he added that "our geography is so rapidly progressive, that no European publication can keep pace with our improvement and the extension of our settlements."[6] Such boasting was not unfounded. Tanner was at the vanguard of an era of unprecedented productivity in American cartography, an era in which Europeans increasingly deferred to Americans when it came to mapping North America.[7] Tanner attributed much of the American ascension in geographic knowledge to the federal efforts to explore the West. And Tanner's vision was expansionistic. As he had done with Melish's map of North America, Tanner included the Oregon Country clearly within the United States, in direct refutation of the agreement in 1818 between U.S. and British negotiators to postpone any final decision on the matter (Fig. 30).

Tanner offered an equally revealing vision of domestic politics. Nowhere was it more lucid than in his representation of the world that concerned Clark throughout the 1820s: the confluence region connecting the Missouri and Mississippi rivers as well as the states of Missouri, Illinois, and Kentucky. In a single map of Missouri and Illinois, Tanner displayed his mastery of black-and-white cartographic detail and the practical use of color (Fig. 31).

Here was the future of the Far West as Clark liked to imagine it, extending from the local to the national level. It was also the West that Clark himself was still creating when, in 1824, he secured appointment as surveyor general for Missouri, Illinois, and the Arkansas Territory. Onto the topographical foundation Tanner had superimposed the land grids that federal officials like Clark had surveyed to facilitate speedy, uncontested land sales. Encompassing the grids were counties, the local administrative and political units that were the signs of a self-governing polity. Finally, there were the states themselves. Illinois and Missouri appeared as friendly neighbors, the Mississippi River constituting a natural boundary between the two.

Tanner's map of Illinois and Missouri was the most accurate topographical representation that any publisher had ever produced. All of his state maps benefited from the growing number of federal, state, and local surveys commissioned over the preceding half century, including the work of the new cohort of surveyors in the army and the General Land Office. But when it came to lived reality in these two states, Tanner could not have been less accurate. Missouri was in the midst of loud, occasionally violent land disputes as settlers, speculators, and attorneys battled with each other and with neighboring Indian villages. Meanwhile, at the very moment Tanner was producing his atlas, the Mississippi River was becoming less a conduit between Missouri

Figure 30. "North America," from Henry Schenck Tanner, *A New American Atlas, containing maps of the several States of the North American union* (Philadelphia: Henry Tanner, 1822). David Rumsey Map Collection,

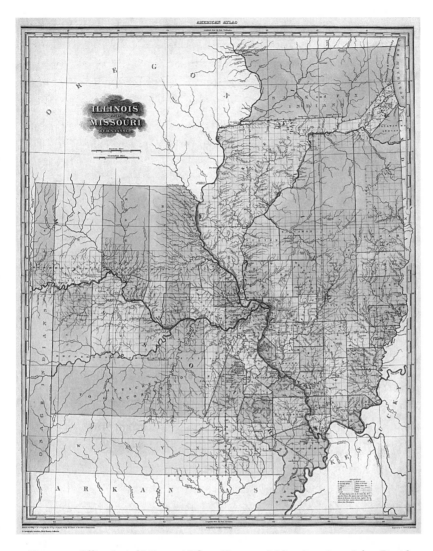

Figure 31. "Illinois and Missouri," from Tanner, *A New American Atlas.* David
Rumsey Map Collection, http://www.davidrumsey.com.

and Illinois than an emerging barrier between freedom and slavery. That sectional conflict was entirely missing from Tanner's map, in which the states resided comfortably, side by side.

Through his atlas Tanner continued the long tradition of visualizing federalism through maps. Like that of so many other American mapmakers, Tanner's work engaged in a process of claiming the West for the United States and normalizing it in the American imagination. In the 1790s, European cartographers had shown the Near West as a region of contest in which whites and Indians overlapped and no system of government truly reigned supreme. The first American cartographers told a similar story.

By the 1830s, American cartographic publishing told a very different story, one of the progressive and relentless extension of the federal system itself. Maps like Tanner's imposed clear borders onto the national landscape. Those maps also reinforced the claims of travel narratives, statistical reports on the West, and emigrant guides. Tanner himself produced a variety of books that described the Near West as a place of fertile fields for those who wished to settle there as well as a place of roads, rivers, and eventually railroads for those who wished to travel farther west. When it came to the Far West, Tanner's guides described abundance, but not in the same way Clark or Long had used the term. Instead, Tanner described the abundant agricultural potential of the new settlements beyond the Mississippi River.[8]

This new vision of a West under federal control applied as well to a growing number of urban maps that showed emerging western cities like Cincinnati, New Orleans, and the St. Louis of William Clark. Urban maps had long announced places as developed and civilized. Europeans had used them for that purpose. So, too, had Americans, who created maps showcasing cities like Boston, Philadelphia, and New York as proof that Americans could create a sophisticated culture in the New World. The new urban maps of the Far West did the same thing. Showing cities and listing civic institutions, they could make even the most struggling settlement look like a well-organized, vibrant, cosmopolitan center.[9]

These claims were hardly surprising since so many of these maps were themselves produced in the West. Clark's adoptive home of St. Louis, for example, which possessed only a few printing presses when he arrived in 1807, by the 1820s was home to a growing printing community that reflected the rapid growth in the city's population. During the 1820s and 1830s St. Louis printers produced books, emigrant guides, and atlases that all celebrated the city's growth and its future.[10]

The capacity for reimagining the Far West was especially clear in "Map of the United States of North America with parts of the adjacent countries," published in *An American Atlas* in 1833 (Fig 32). The map was the work of David Burr, recently the topographer for the U.S. Post Office and the latest in a long line of public officials hoping to establish themselves as published mapmakers. Like Clark, Freeman, and Freeman's nemesis, Maxfield Ludlow, Burr was keen to make a profit in the global map trade. The map announced the Far West as Jefferson had first imagined it in 1784 when he illustrated his Plan for Western Government, with new states entering the Union with the sort of "clear and indisputable boundaries" that Congress had first attempted to establish during the American Revolution. The new states of Louisiana, Arkansas, and Missouri had emerged from the western landscape, linked seamlessly to the older states in the East. Building on a model established by Melish and Tanner, the national boundaries of the United States were equally clear, a far cry from the ambiguous international borderlands in the maps of Jefferson's explorers.

The representation of these states through maps provided the visual claim that expansion could indeed proceed in an orderly manner. In the 1810s and 1820s, territorial governors like Clark, William Henry Harrison, and William C. C. Claiborne had made their bid for elected office by claiming to have created a model of orderly expansion. Now maps had converted those political claims into visual form, quite literally showing how the United States had grown without the chaos, violence, and disunion that critics had long associated with expansion.

Finally, Burr's map situated Indians on the landscape in ways that actually reinforced the claim to federal sovereignty. Located just beyond Missouri and Arkansas were the new homes imposed onto Indians by the federal government in the 1820s and 1830s and often facilitated by the negotiations of Clark. Unlike the powerful, ill-defined, freely moving Indians Clark had described decades earlier, these Indians were bounded, occupying territory selected for them and controlled by the federal government.

The publisher of Burr's map was John Arrowsmith, the nephew of the cartographer whose work on North America had informed Jefferson's planning for western exploration in 1803. In contrast to Aaron Arrowsmith's map, with its vast empty spaces beyond the Mississippi and only the vaguest international boundaries, John Arrowsmith portrayed a West that was clearly known and clearly bounded. And whereas Aaron Arrowsmith had based his map primarily on European sources, John Arrowsmith relied on Americans for his details. By the time Jefferson died in 1826, Americans had indeed assumed leadership in the representation of the North American landscape, the result of federal and state surveys as well as of the growing capacity of American cartographic publishing.[11]

These new maps also divided the Far West. In 1803 Americans considered the Far West to be all points beyond the Mississippi, specifically, the territory acquired through the Louisiana Purchase. It was not simply that the land was

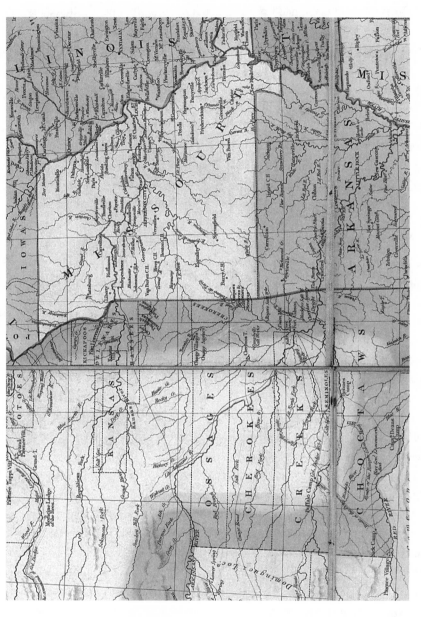

Figure 32. David H. Burr, *Map of the United States of North America with Parts of the Adjacent Countries . . .* (detail) (London: 1839). Geography and Map Division, Library of Congress.

contained by that single treaty, but also that, for all its regional variation, the Far West was a place of Indian power, dubious fertility, and limited government authority. The maps of the 1830s now described the space immediately beyond the Mississippi as a region where white power had replaced Indian power, white settlers found fertility rather than a desert, and the federal government had successfully created new states to replace older systems of governance. Points further west, however, were still up for grabs.[12]

GEORGE CATLIN

In 1830 Clark drew a picture of a new house he planned to build in downtown St. Louis. It was no fanciful drawing but a characteristically technical sketch.[13] It was one of a series of sketches he had made throughout his lifetime, whether it was the Spanish galley in 1795 or the Grand Tower in 1803. The following year Clark met somebody with greater artistic ambitions, a Pennsylvania native named George Catlin. The two men shared a fascination with Indian culture. Yet they understood Indian policy in very different ways, ways that reflected their cultural differences. In Catlin and in his own family, Clark encountered an increasingly romantic culture that expressed itself toward Indians in ways both sentimental and violent. And in the same way that American cartographic publishing reached new heights in the 1820s and 1830s, the Indian policy Clark had pursued on behalf of the Jeffersonians reached its own fulfillment, with horrific consequences, in the age of Andrew Jackson.

Catlin arrived in St. Louis at the beginning of a career that would establish him as one of the leading figures in American art. He began as a self-trained painter working the portrait trade in Philadelphia, only to move to New York in the 1820s just as that city was beginning to supplant Philadelphia as the center of the arts in the United States. Convinced that the Indians of North America were doomed to extinction, Catlin intended to create a written and visual record for a white posterity. In 1831 Catlin arrived in St. Louis, boldly announcing that "nothing short of the loss of my life shall prevent me from visiting their country, and of becoming their historian." Clark was happy to help. For years he had built a collection of Indian artifacts, and he was eager to show this museum, as he called it, to Catlin. Catlin admired Clark, and in 1832 he painted the last major portrait of Clark, presenting him as an aging but distinguished figure in subdued colors and interior surroundings rather than in the open spaces through which Clark had so often traveled.[14]

Their shared interests notwithstanding, Clark was an agent of the very destruction Catlin found so upsetting. Writing to Secretary of War Henry Barbour in 1826, Clark explained that "while strong and hostile it was our policy
and duty to weaken them; now that they are weak and harmless, and most of
their lands fallen into our hands, justice and humanity require us to cherish
and befriend them."[15] Clark's long view of federal Indian relations presaged
both the policy and the outlook toward Indians that soon took hold throughout the country. In 1830 Congress passed the Removal Act. President Andrew
Jackson, who had called for the legislation in the first place, eagerly signed it
into law and aggressively pursued its implementation. The new policy of removal formally required the relocation of Indians to the Far West. Although
concerned primarily with Indians east of the Mississippi, officials in Washington made clear to Clark that removal also applied to Indians in Missouri
and in the other new states carved from the Louisiana Purchase. Throughout
the 1830s Clark supervised the process of evicting Indians from Missouri and
transporting Indians through Missouri en route to points father west.[16]

Removal marked a new level of cruelty on the part of the federal government, yet the policy constituted the logical extension of the way many Americans conceived of Indians and of the West. After all, George Rogers Clark
built an army of men who imagined their futures in a Near West without Indian power. Meanwhile, the federal government had never sided with Indians against the territorial aspirations of white settlers. Too often, removal is
associated primarily with Jackson, not only because he was the dominant political figure of the 1830s but also because his fame rested in no small part on
his military campaigns against Indians in the 1810s. Yet Jackson became such
a vocal advocate of removal because he knew it was immensely popular. Jackson also saw himself as a pragmatist on the matter, in contrast to Jefferson
and his contemporaries, all of whom expressed a deep commitment to Indians that they quickly abandoned in the interest of white settlement and federal control. Removal therefore marked a distinction in tactics rather than a
revolution in goals. Clark certainly understood it as such, for removal reflected policies he had pursued for decades.[17]

Removal also continued a process of appropriating and redefining the language people had used to explain expansion a generation earlier. In 1803–
04, American pamphleteers had suggested that the Far West could become
a home for Indians and former slaves. At the time, this was a benefit of con-
venience, a way to justify the broad extent of the Louisiana Purchase. By the
1830s, Americans acted as if American policymakers had planned things that

way from the start. Federal leaders came to see the Far West as the logical relocation center for Indians, a practical benefit to expansion that few policymakers had contemplated only a few decades before.

Yet if removal indicated a continuity of policy, it nonetheless indicated a
critical change in modes of expression. And this was no small affair, for the
terms Americans used to describe Indians had an immediate impact on the
ways they acted toward them. Advocates of removal like Jackson as well as
critics like Catlin discussed Indians in a manner very different from Clark. It
was an odd state of affairs, for Jackson was actually three years older than
Clark. Yet Jackson grasped the generational changes in American politics and
culture in a way that Clark could not. Whereas Jeffersonians like Clark sought
to describe Indians in the rationalizing language of the Enlightenment, Jack-
sonians often described racial conflict in the terms of the passionate, honor-
bound culture of antebellum America.

Those differences were apparent in Clark's correspondence with his
nephew, Benjamin O'Fallon. By 1819 Clark had secured an appointment for
O'Fallon as an Indian agent. Among O'Fallon's first assignments was to join
the contingent of nearly one thousand troops who accompanied Long's Yellowstone Expedition of 1819–20, a massive contingent of soldiers whose express task was to intimidate the Indians of the lower Missouri Valley.[18] In the
years that followed, O'Fallon worked under the direct supervision of his
uncle. They were committed to the same policy, but they described it in very
different terms. O'Fallon was more likely to accuse Indians of gross atrocities
and to draw direct linkages between his own personal honor and that of his
country. In characteristically overstated prose, in 1823 O'Fallon described an
Indian attack on federal troops as "the most shocking outrage to the feelings
of humanity ever witnessed by civilized man—unexampled in the annals of
the World. As those inhuman monsters will most probably be made to atone
for what they have done by a great effusion of their blood, I shall (however
painful it may be) endeavour to restrain my feelings." This was language typical of O'Fallon, and it shared a great deal with Jackson's tendency to treat the
actions of Indians and foreign powers as affronts to his personal honor as well
as to that of the nation. In sharp contrast, Clark had little difficulty restraining his feelings. For O'Fallon, doing so was not only a personal challenge, but
also a questionable activity in an era when passionate expression in writing
was increasingly the norm.[19]

Clark was not without a temper of his own. Throughout his adult life he
was quick to take offense at those he considered ungrateful for his efforts on

their behalf, primarily Indian leaders and slaves.[20] Nonetheless, Clark never wrote in the melodramatic terms used by O'Fallon, whose approach to Indian policy shared more with Jackson than with Clark. Clark shared Jackson's commitment to racial supremacy, which helps explain why Jackson kept Clark in office. At the same time, Clark worried about the capacity of white settlers to cause interracial conflict. Jackson, on the other hand, never doubted the right of white settlers to assert their own land claims. That attitude reached its extreme when the Supreme Court rejected the state of Georgia's efforts to evict the Cherokee. Jackson lambasted the Court for its failure to understand the inherent right of settlers to seize the land they needed and refused to implement the Court's ruling.

Catlin came to Missouri in the midst of a federal policy that was rapidly displacing Indians. In his efforts to chronicle the plight of western Indians, Catlin displayed a fundamentally sentimental paternalism toward Indians. In this he was not alone. In the years preceding his death in 1826, Jedidiah Morse demonstrated a newfound interest in promoting the missionary societies that sought to civilize western Indians. In the 1830s artists like Catlin and clerics like Morse all sought to save the Indians from the ravages of interracial violence. Jefferson himself had shown a similar attitude throughout much of his life, but those goals had always gone by the wayside as Jefferson the policymaker serving his white constituency overshadowed Jefferson the intellectual seeking to understand Indian culture or Jefferson the philanthropist attempting to protect Indians. Yet if Catlin saw himself as an opponent to Jacksonian removal, it was only the conquest of Indians that made sentimentalism possible. In this, he was typical of so many whites who defended Indians only once they ceased to appear threatening or ceased to occupy land that whites sought for themselves. Likewise, the same effusive emotion that O'Fallon displayed in his letters shaped Catlin's passionate empathy for the Indians' plight.

In 1837 Catlin returned to the East with a massive collection of notes, artifacts, and drawings. Those materials described places Clark had visited on the Lewis and Clark Expedition and Indian chiefs whom Clark had met in his varied negotiating efforts. Catlin proudly selected an exhibition of 310 paintings for display in New York, including portraits, group paintings, and landscapes. Catlin was also hard at work on a book that would capture the Indian world in print, including both ethnographic text and illustrations based on his paintings.

Catlin was not alone in these efforts to mass produce a written and visual account of Indians. In 1836, Thomas McKenney published the first volume of *The History of the Indian Tribes of North America,* a book he cowrote with James Hall. Clark quickly purchased a copy, for he and McKenney were long-time associates. From his office at the War Department, McKenney supervised all Indian trade from 1816 until 1824, when he took charge of the new Bureau of Indian Affairs. McKenney expressed a sentimental interest in Indians, even as he supervised their subjugation and suffering. In 1827, after participating in a negotiating mission to the Great Lakes, McKenney published a traditional travel narrative. Written in an impersonal yet self-promoting manner, McKenney's narrative chronicled his ability to negotiate major land settlements with Indians. It was, in other words, a typical travel narrative by a federal official. Yet McKenney also considered himself a friend to the Indians, and in the War Department he built an exhibit of artifacts as a tribute to a dying race.[21]

In 1830, just as Clark was ready to establish himself as a trustworthy agent of the removal policy, Jackson summarily dismissed McKenney, primarily to punish him for supporting, first, John C. Calhoun and, later, John Quincy Adams. Once out of office, McKenney applied the same combination of self-advancement and patronizing racial philanthropy to *History of the Indian Tribes.* He first made plans for a major study of North American Indians in the 1820s. When the project fell behind schedule he received an inquiry from one of the early subscribers, Nicholas Biddle, a man who knew all too well about publishing delays. His literary career long over, in 1832 Biddle was president of the Bank of the United States and was engaged in a losing battle to defend the institution against Jackson's efforts to destroy it.[22]

History of the Indian Tribes of North America described Clark's world in the visual terms that Catlin himself hoped to produce. The first two volumes consisted primarily of short biographical profiles of Indian chiefs, each accompanied by a portrait. The third volume included a final set of portraits within a lengthy essay on the history and future of Indians. McKenney and Hall proudly announced on the cover that the project was "Embellished with one hundred and twenty portraits," each one averaging just over ten by fourteen inches. It was an unprecedented achievement in American illustrated publishing. McKenney not only situated Lewis and Clark within his narrative of Indians, but even included portraits of the chiefs whom Clark had faced as adversaries on the eastern Plains, exemplified by the accompanying portraits of Tenskwatawa (the Shawnee Prophet) and Black Hawk (Fig. 33). Clark himself had derided both men as threats to federal policy, as had McKenney while in public office. Out of office, McKenney chronicled their lives with a com-

Figure 33. Portraits of Tenskwatawa and Black Hawk from
Thomas McKenney and James Hall, *History of the Indian
Tribes of North America* (Philadelphia, F. W. Greenough, 1838–
44). Special Collections, Washington University in St. Louis.

bination of racial condescension and respect of the sort that Jefferson had
shown toward Indians in *Notes on the State of Virginia.*

Together, McKenney and Catlin helped introduce a subgenre of Indian
portraiture that became increasingly popular in the mid-nineteenth century.
The sentimental care for Indians McKenney showed, like that of Catlin and
a growing collection of Americans and Europeans describing the West in the
1820s and 1830s, rested on the assumption that the "History of the Indians"

MA-KA-TAI-ME-SHE-KIA-KIAK
BLACK HAWK A SAUKIE BRAVE

PUBLISHED BY F. W. GREENOUGH, PHILADª

was, in fact, coming to an end. Maps of the 1820s and 1830s confirmed this story by showing Indians confined to territories designated by the United States and by announcing that while Indians might still live, their histories as independent peoples were over. Albert Gallatin, who served as Jefferson's and Madison's secretary of the treasury, had joined the crowd studying Indian extinction. In 1836 he completed his own map of Indian tribes. This was a historic map, however, showing where Indians had lived and predicting their inevitable decline.[23]

Yet Gallatin was wrong, as were McKenney and Catlin. In the Rocky Mountains, in the Great Basin of the Southwest, and along the Pacific Coast, Indians continued to govern the land despite the best efforts of European or

American governments to prevent them from doing so. The line between federal power and Indian power, a line that subdivided the Far West, corresponded with the world envisioned by the new maps of the 1820s and 1830s. Federal power over Indians in the Far West went only so far, and men like Catlin and McKenney showed little sympathy for the Comanche, the Apache, and the other Indians who continued to assert sovereignty over their territory. Tanner had told a similar story. While he imagined clear claims in the West, he nonetheless created maps in which the limits of federal authority extended only so far into the Far West.[24]

The growth in detailed color maps like Tanner's and the release of illustrated books like McKenney's *History of the Indian Tribes of North America* was no coincidence. McKenney's illustrations were not engravings, long the mainstay of mapmakers, but the result of the new technology of lithography. In much the same way that American cartographic publishing lagged behind that of Europe, so too did American lithography. Europeans developed lithography in the late eighteenth century, while the first American lithographs were not published until 1818. The city that produced those American lithographs was Philadelphia. The location made sense given Philadelphia's preeminence in illustrated publishing, including its leadership in cartographic publishing. Most lithographs were created by painting an image onto a smooth stone tablet with specialized inks. The most immediate impact of lithography was to eliminate the labor-intensive process of engraving. Equally important, lithographs could be easily corrected and could produce color illustrations with greater speed and consistency than the older technique of individually painting illustrations. Publishers soon took full advantage of lithography, releasing a flood of illustrated books in the United States. Such books helped propel the new visual representation of Indians that was so crucial to the way whites understood the West.[25]

Lithographs also reinforced the image of western cities already being created by maps. Among the most talented lithographers was John Caspar Wild, a Swiss-born artist who came to the United States in 1832. He published a series of illustrated books on the United States, most of them focusing on cities. In addition to the cities of the eastern seaboard that had long fascinated Europeans, Wilde visited Cincinnati and St. Louis. He portrayed these western locales as thriving cities. If their buildings were not so tall as those of their eastern counterparts, they nonetheless appeared to be vibrant centers of commerce and development, hardly the retrograde places of vice and degeneration that critics had described. Wild's urban scenes directly competed with the growing number of urban maps, claiming to enable Americans to see a city as if they were actually there, rather than representing cities from the abstract aerial perspective of maps.[26]

Lithography arrived not a moment too soon as far as Catlin was concerned. His grand traveling exhibition chronicling the dying race of western Indians never drew enough people to offset its considerable expenses. As a result, he became the latest western describer to put his hopes in federal support, beginning a fruitless campaign to convince Congress to purchase his paintings. Desperate for revenue, Catlin was hard at work on a book that he hoped would be the latest word on Indian culture. Written in the same ethnographic language as that employed by Schoolcraft and Long, *Manners, Customs, and Condition of the North American Indians* was finally released in 1841. Unlike those earlier accounts, which contained a limited number of black-and-white visual materials, Catlin's book contained close to three hundred black-and-white engravings and twenty-five color lithographs.

Although Catlin continued to paint and write about West, he remained in the East. Clark never saw him again, and rightly so, for the two men lived in very different worlds. Clark was convinced that Indians should remain the object of a concerted, efficient system of removal, their futures described through the rational language of government reports, recorded in maps. Catlin imagined a different, illustrated future that would describe an Indian past.

WASHINGTON IRVING

Clark's and Catlin's collaboration took place just as the latest set of tragedies in Clark's personal life struck. John Julius Clark, the youngest child of Julia Hancock Clark, died at the age of thirteen in September 1831. Worse was yet to come. Harriet Clark suddenly took ill and died on Christmas Day, 1831, almost eleven years to the day after Clark's first wife. In one of those rare moments when Clark expressed sentiment in writing, he confided to his oldest son, Meriwether Lewis Clark, "My spirits are low and my course indecisive." In the midst of these sorrows, Washington Irving came into William Clark's world, and the encounter between the two men demonstrated the titanic shifts at work in American print and visual culture.[27]

When Irving visited Clark in 1832 he was already a successful writer and on the cusp of producing the novels and essays like "Rip Van Winkle" and "The Legend of Sleepy Hollow" that would make him a landmark figure in American literature. Eager to meet the explorer, former governor, and Indian agent, he found Clark to be an engaged and gracious host, one who gave no outward signs of the personal losses he had suffered the preceding year. Unlike Catlin, who visited Clark at his new house downtown, Irving traveled to the small plantation Clark maintained outside St. Louis. In his journal, Irving recorded the encounter in notation even more sparse than Clark had used in his journals of the Lewis and Clark Expedition. Nonetheless, Irving knew how to describe Clark's arrival in dramatic terms. He began by writing, "The Govs. Farm. small cottage—Orchard bending & breaking with loads of fruit." Irving listed slaves of various ages engaged in diverse tasks. Only after setting the scene did he record, "Genl arrives on horseback with dogs. . . . Gun on his shoulder. . . . Gov Clark fine healthy robust man. tall about 56—perhaps more. His hair, originally light, now grey falling on his shoulders."[28]

This was hardly the visage Clark had attempted to create for himself as a leader of substance and sophistication. Instead, Irving preferred to see Clark as a romanticized frontiersman. Emerging from the literary culture of the Northeast, Irving thought this an attractive and familiar image. Only Irving's final observations, that Clark was "Frank—intelligent," fit with the persona Clark had attempted to build in the preceding quarter century.

Irving had just returned to the United States after seventeen years overseas. He came to St. Louis as a member of the party accompanying Count Albert-Alexandre de Pourtales, one of a growing number of European nobles who had become fascinated with the American West.[29] This was hardly Clark's first encounter with a person entertaining literary aspirations. In 1830 Clark received a letter from his oldest son, Meriwether Lewis Clark. Writing from West Point, the young cadet informed his father of efforts to form "an American Institute . . . [of] Societies . . . throughout the US composed of persons who are disposed to aid as much as in their power the literary character of the country. These societies to have a general head located in a Society called the associate Society at West Point, composed of Cadets, to which the Officers and Professors of the institution are members." Meriwether Lewis Clark believed the society "would be doing the country a service in contributing to the removal of the English Literary Yoke from the neck of our Scientific & Literary worthies substituting an honourable & useful encouragement to merit & a blast to false pretentions."[30]

Clark probably wished his son would stay focused on his studies. That was certainly the sort of fatherly advice he had dispensed to his children. Clark himself showed no real interest in the literary development his son considered so important. The correspondence of father and son revealed a generational divide in American letters in particular and American cultural production in general. It was a divide that Irving knew only too well. In the world of printed and visual culture, the United States underwent a transformation no less important than the shifts in politics and policy. In the same way that Benjamin O'Fallon spoke on behalf of the emotional content of Indian policy at work in the age of removal, Meriwether Lewis Clark expressed an impassioned, overstated commitment to the nation's literary future that Irving attempted to make real.

During the middle decades of the nineteenth century, many of the novelists, poets, and painters who eventually defined one of the most productive periods in American art and literature came into their own. Irving and the likes of Nathaniel Hawthorne, Ralph Waldo Emerson, and Henry David Thoreau formed a group of highly influential American writers. The role they played in American culture is partly a story of their time and partly one of subsequent generations. In their own time, they enjoyed varying degrees of success within literary circles, with critics, and with the public at large. By the twentieth century, however, they had been embraced by diverse audiences as brilliant writers who had helped transform the English language. In particular, their celebration by academics and educators guaranteed that many Americans would learn what constituted great writing through these figures of antebellum America.[31]

In sharp contrast to these literary giants of the mid-nineteenth century, writers of the early Republic exist primarily as the object of scorn or as foils to demonstrate the far greater creativity of the antebellum era. Many of these writers—Clark included—embraced convention, and much of the print culture they consumed was nonfiction. Great literature, however, has come to be defined by fiction that defies convention, and the early Republic produced few works of fiction, novels especially, that have stood the test of time.[32]

Clark's writing exemplifies what makes the literary history of the early Republic so frustrating to subsequent readers. Clark modeled himself on a style of writing that evolved from training in science, the military, and public administration. It was also the dispassionate language of the American version of the Enlightenment. One of the striking changes in American letter writing in the antebellum era was the rise of sentimental prose. Likewise, one of the most dramatic changes of the antebellum era was, appropriately enough, a shift toward dramatic writing itself, especially when it came to the ways in which Americans wrote about their relationships with nature. In the era of

Thoreau and Emerson, the natural world became a place of wonder. Most important, it became a transforming mirror that shaped people and revealed their inner selves. It was, looking back from the antebellum era, a literary world that Lewis himself had briefly entered in a few entries in the manuscript journals of the Lewis and Clark Expedition. Those entries discussed Lewis's feelings, primarily in response to the emotional impact he experienced in viewing grand western vistas. That Lewis would deploy this language of nature reflected the fact that Thoreau and Emerson were hardly the first people to write this way. Describing the natural world was, after all, one of the most common literary pursuits. Likewise, Americans in the antebellum era were often adopting the literary tropes that European, especially British, writers had developed in the late eighteenth and early nineteenth centuries. It was in these decades that the concern for the sublime, the picturesque, and the beautiful came to dominate how Americans sought to represent the western landscape.[33]

The meeting of Irving and Clark further reveals not only the linkages back to Clark's world, but also the view forward to the romanticism and sentimentality of Jacksonian America. Like Irving, many of the leading figures of nineteenth-century American literature—Emerson, Mark Twain, Herman Melville—began their careers as travel writers, in either the United States or Europe. They often borrowed from long-standing traditions of travel writing that western explorers like Clark had also appropriated for their own work. Yet all of these authors tired of the genre, finding the world of technical nonfiction frustrating in its limitations. Emerson and Thoreau explored nature in a way that none of Jefferson's explorers ever attempted. Twain eventually wrote about journeys, but he did so in novels, which enabled him to explore both individuals and nations in ways that conventional travel writing did not allow.[34]

The changes in American letters had a direct counterpart in American visual arts. The United States was hardly lacking in artists and writers, but during the antebellum era the country produced a crop of painters, many of them landscape artists, with ambitions to match those of American novelists. They, too, were attempting to understand expansion, and during the antebellum era they came to celebrate the capacity of the nation to extend across the continent.[35] Once again, the relationship between Clark and Catlin is a revealing case in point. When Catlin launched his exhibition in 1837, his ambitions extended beyond his effort to show the Indians of the West. Catlin also sought acceptance as an artist. That he would enjoy that recognition in the 1830s and in New York made sense. In the same way that Catlin imagined an Indian world very different from the one Clark had described, he entered a literary and artistic community that described the West in terms that were entirely alien to Clark and the first western describers. Deploying the same romantic, personal, deeply emotional language that Jackson and Benjamin O'Fallon had applied to Indian affairs, these writers and artists saw themselves as being at the vanguard of an era of American creative greatness.

Catlin considered himself the equal of the likes of Henry Rowe Schoolcraft, and would have called himself an ethnographer if such a term had existed at the time. At the same time, Catlin identified himself as an artist, and he attempted to cement that status in his efforts to represent the American West. His compositional elements—perspective, elevation, scale—conspicuously deployed all the techniques of European landscape artists. The same applied to his Indian portraits, in which he staged Indian chiefs in much the same way he had staged the subjects of his portraits in Philadelphia and New York. But Catlin faced his own set of challenges. The mountains, valleys, rivers, and villages of New York and New England—the typical subjects of American landscape artists—all conformed to European models. The Far West was another matter altogether. Catlin had to paint a very different landscape, where the rivers and plains were more often horizontal than vertical. Equally important, whereas the Hudson River painters celebrated what they saw as the democratic progress of white society, Catlin sought to commemorate an Indian society that may have possessed a sentimental appeal, but that many whites still saw as a vestige of their nation's contact with an uncivilized past.[36]

Romantic expression was hardly the creation of the United States in the antebellum era, let alone of Benjamin O'Fallon and Andrew Jackson. Sentimentalism and romanticism had been a driving force in European letters, arts, and culture since the eighteenth century. Meanwhile, sentimental and romantic writing had existed beforehand in the United States. Crucially, though, Americans had deployed these forms of representation to a much smaller degree during the early Republic, whether compared to Europe or to antebellum America. And that is where the style of Jackson and O'Fallon or Catlin and Irving proves so revealing. It reflected the broader shift separating the early Republic from the antebellum era. These two eras—the early American Republic and the antebellum era—which otherwise seem like abstract labels imposed onto the past, instead indicate real changes in the ways people understood and described the world around them.[37]

In addition to undergoing stylistic changes, American writers and artists were engaged in their own nationalist projects. Extending Meriwether Lewis Clark's call to cast off the "English Literary Yoke," these Americans believed that only through their own aesthetic creation could Americans become truly independent from Europe. They felt particularly strongly that Americans should take charge of describing America, whether that meant the landscape or its inhabitants.[38]

It can be seductive to situate Clark and the other early western describers alongside the later cadre of American writers and artists. Yet while Clark himself was an unapologetic nationalist, his nationalism was rooted in republican politics and Enlightenment rationalism, not in the sentimental romanticism of the antebellum era. The nationalism he pursued was a pragmatic commitment to the preservation of the Union through policy, not the celebration of the nation through art. Other western describers of Clark's generation had taken the same approach. Their books and maps celebrated the capacity of republican government, not artistic creation.[39] Jefferson had engaged in exactly the same sort of nationalist project in *Notes on the State of Virginia*, celebrating the American landscape as a way of celebrating Americans themselves. Few shifts better demonstrated the move from Enlightenment to romanticism than the way in which landscape artists of the antebellum era assumed the mantle of nationalist expression from the likes of Jefferson. Abandoning the formalized rationalism of Jefferson's written and visual representation of the land, these artists—along with American writers—proclaimed that the best way to understand America was through the heart rather than the head.

Increasingly the representation of the American landscape in general— and the West in particular—assumed a romantic quality during the antebellum era that was entirely unfamiliar to the more practically minded Clark and the people who surrounded him. James Fenimore Cooper did so in the Leatherstocking novels, one of which, *The Prairie*, was set in the territories of the Louisiana Purchase. Cooper was the son of a leading speculator in upstate New York who eventually lost everything in the volatile business of land speculation. Alan Taylor's superb study of Cooper's father, *William Cooper's Town*, shows just how much Cooper's literary pursuits in the antebellum era emerged from a particular set of stories about frontier settlement in the early Republic. James Fenimore Cooper moved to New York City but always perceived the capacity of the frontier to generate a powerful narrative.[40]

So, too, did Davy Crockett. Later immortalized as a frontiersman and hero of Texas independence, Crockett also had a lucrative side business as a writer. Unlike Lewis, Clark, and Pike, who all sought to establish themselves as serious, sophisticated servants of the federal government unchanged by life on the frontier, Crockett cultivated a different image by calling attention to his simple origins and frontier vernacular. Nothing captured the linkages—and the differences—more clearly than Crockett's description of bear hunting. "In the fall of 1825," Crockett wrote in his autobiography, "I turned out to hunting, to lay in a supply of meat." Deploying the colloquial phrasing that federal explorers eschewed for impersonal language, Crockett claimed, "I know'd that when they were fat, they were easily taken, for a fat bear can't run fast or long. But I asked a bear no favours, no way, further than civility." What follows is a bloodfest in which Crockett kills dozens of bears, all the while using the folksy language that became so closely associated with Crockett that Walt Disney replicated the language over a century later when Crockett became the subject of an immensely popular TV show. The Walt Disney Company actually produced only five episodes of what was more a miniseries than a true television series, but the image of Crockett that Disney created in the 1950s became one of the most evocative symbols of the nation's western history. Over a century earlier, the real-life Crockett, like James Fenimore Cooper, knew how to deploy the excessive achievements of the frontier for either drama or humor.[41]

Crockett and Cooper were both ambitious men like Clark, but writing enabled them to follow those ambitions in very different directions. Cooper reveled in his stature as a leader of New York's literary community.[42] Crockett, a former Tennessee congressman, threw himself into the Texas independence movement, joining a form of revolutionary politics that could not have been further from the aspirations of Jefferson's explorers, who sought advancement within respectable institutions. Cooper and Crockett also sought to create a western counterpart to the idea of a nation with cultural roots located entirely in the Northeast. They saw the nation's identity emerging on frontiers, especially western frontiers.

But the question remained: what was more accurate? Could Americans see the West better through a map that showed the landscape as it was, or in a painting that showed landscape and people as if a viewer was actually there to see it? Likewise, could Americans best understand the western experience through a traditional travel narrative, an ethnographic account like Schoolcraft's, or a rollicking work of humor like Crocket's essays?

As a growing number of artists from the United States and Europe ven-

Figure 34. George Catlin, *Bull Dance, Mandan O-kee-pa Ceremony* (top) and *Beautiful Prairie Bluffs above the Poncas, 1050 Miles Above St. Louis* (bottom), both from 1832.

tured into the Far West, their work sought to tell the story of the West in a way that a map could not. Consider the place that Clark helped introduce to an American audience: the upper Missouri Valley. Clark had situated the region and its occupants on the map, but Catlin showed both the river and the Mandan villages in vivid color and elaborate detail. Consider as well the title of one of them: *Beautiful Prairie Bluffs above the Poncas, 1050 Miles Above St. Louis.* Clark never concerned himself with beauty, and if Catlin was often concerned with other matters as well, as an artist he considered it his task to capture the beauty of the natural world (Fig. 34).

By the 1830s the staid language of travel narratives and scientific accounts faced enormous competition from the new fictional and semifictional accounts of the West. In 1838 Edmund Flagg attempted to drag the travel narrative into the age of romantic individualism when he published a book entitled (appropriately enough) *The Far West, or, A Tour Beyond the Mountains.* It appeared to be similar to the sort of books that Jefferson had read in planning a grand survey of the West, or the sort of book that Clark and his fellow explorers had produced in the 1810s. Yet Flagg's work was the product of a new world of landscape representation. As Flagg explained, "In the early summer of '36" he embarked upon "a ramble over the prairies of the 'Far West,' in hope of renovating the energies of a shattered constitution." Flagg came at the invitation of a newspaper editor in Louisville, and he passed through the Kentucky of the Clark family and eventually reached St. Louis. Flagg employed some of the same disparaging comments on the western entropy that Jedidiah Morse had lamented in 1784. "The commerce of the Eastern seaports and that of the Western Valley are utterly dissimilar," he explained, describing a world where people moved at a slower pace and showed little concern for tight schedules. Despite this behavior, however, he claimed that commerce was booming throughout the Ohio and Mississippi valleys. Flagg also joined a growing chorus that saw enormous potential in the Far West. He believed the earliest settlers in St. Louis had been "attracted by the beauty of the country, the fertility of its soil, the boundless variety of its products, the exhaustless mineral treasures beneath its surface, and the facility of trade in the furs of the Northwest." Flagg had actually reversed the priorities that informed the first Europeans, who were far more concerned with the fur trade than with farming, and they showed little concern for the beauty of the landscape. But Flagg was deeply concerned with aesthetics: "There are few objects more truly grand—I had almost said sublime—than the powerful steamer struggling triumphantly with the rapids of the Western waters."

He considered those waters truly beautiful and believed the landscape itself contributed to successfully "renovating the energies of a shattered constitution."[43]

Flagg even recounted tales of William Clark. There were no references to the Lewis and Clark Expedition, but rather to the work as an Indian agent that had defined Clark's life in the thirty years since the expedition. Flagg claimed that "no more interesting or picturesque episode has occurred in the history of Christian missions in the New World, than the famous visit made in the autumn of 1831 to General William Clark at St. Louis by the Flathead chiefs seeking religious instruction for their people." He likewise recounted the way "the old general" negotiated the release of a naturalist who, while traveling through the West, had offended his Indian guests.[44]

Flagg's account showed that even the stodgy travel narrative could adjust to the new romantic language of the self in the natural landscape. But Clark apparently could not. If Irving imagined Clark as a great frontiersman rather than a senior administrative official, similarly Clark seems to have ignored developments in literature and the arts.

Irving shared Flagg's assessment of the West. In September 1832 he wrote to his sister from Independence. Founded only five years earlier, the town was located on the Missouri River near the western border of Missouri. "Many of these Prairies of the Missouri are extremely beautiful," Irving wrote. Beautiful indeed, for Irving deployed the term as Flagg did six years later, infused with the aesthetic language of antebellum creative arts rather than the eighteenth-century traditions of travel writing. Irving believed "the fertility of all this Western Country is truly astonishing. The Soil is like that of a garden and the luxuriance and beauty of the forests exceed any that I have seen." Irving expressed a combination of excitement and trepidation that "we have gradually been advancing however towards rougher and rougher life . . . and shall soon bid adieu to civilization." His writings sought to move the Far West in the same way that Tanner's maps and Catlin's paintings did. Independence, Missouri, was as far as Irving would go. He made a quick passage through the Arkansas Territory and by December was back in Washington.[45]

Irving never returned to the West, but he immediately began writing about it. He used the trip as the foundation for *A Tour on the Prairies*, a book based less on the American tradition of western travel than on his own experience as an American traveling overseas. The book impressed John Jacob Astor, the politically connected entrepreneur who was hard at work building a fur-trading empire in the West. He commissioned Irving to write a history that would promote his expansionist commercial ventures in the Far West. Strapped for funds, Irving eagerly accepted, and in 1836 published a semifictional western account entitled *Astoria*. Finally, in *The Adventures of Captain Bonneville*, a novel he published in 1837, Irving invented his own western vision. Based loosely on a real officer in the U.S. Army, *The Adventures of Captain Bonneville* was a tale of high adventure in the Far West. Following a model already established by the likes of Cooper and Crocket, Irving told a story of physical challenges and racial conflict. He populated his story with all the stock characters of nineteenth-century westerns. Irving had his own struggles with westward expansion, occasionally criticizing the speculative bonanza at work on the frontiers of the Union. Nonetheless, he helped normalize the western adventure tale within the nation's literary development. Irving was always eager to find a profitable literary venture, and his brief flirtation with western accounts placed him alongside a growing number of authors who found there was a large audience for frontier adventures.[46]

In the process, Irving became only the latest in a series of authors to situate the West in the American imagination. Like Tanner and Catlin, however, he had helped move the boundary of the Far West to the point where the settlements of the Mississippi gave way to the "rougher and rougher life" that he would describe in books but avoided in person.

THOMAS HART BENTON

In the 1830s the mapping of property had become a family business for the Clarks. In April 1834 William Preston Clark wrote to his father with pride that he was "over head and ears in business." As he explained the situation, "I laid off a town in the lowest part of the reserve for the town made by yourself & Dr. Martin. The squares are laid off so as to range the ____ with the hills—running back as far as the old Town extends."[47] His father understood these technicalities, and he was pleased. Only twenty-two years old, William Preston Clark was among his father's trusted contacts in western Kentucky. Clark may have long worried about the dangers of unchecked expansionism, but in his correspondence with his son as well as with other friends and family, Clark showed himself to be among the greatest beneficiaries of western expansion. And as much as anybody, Clark understood just how much describing the West remained inseparable from owning the West.

Ever since he arrived in St. Louis as a territorial official in 1807, Clark had acquired every lot he could. To this end he pushed his credit to its limit. Although he eventually owned thousands of acres in Missouri and Kentucky, he considered himself nearly penniless and dependent on his salary as Indian agent to cover his daily expenses. In this he suffered the anxieties of many other land speculators including, for that matter, present-day real estate investors. A return on his investment had to wait until he could sell the land at a profit. And the real increase in land values depended on something beyond the control of any speculator. Land prices responded to simple forces of supply and demand, and only the influx of settlers could bring about a rapid increase in land values.[48]

By the time William Preston Clark wrote to his father in 1834, William Clark was a well-practiced land speculator. William Preston wrote from Paducah, a place of William Clark's creation. The settlement came into existence, as so many in the region had, as a trading center that connected neighboring Indian villages to white settlements. Located at the confluence of the Tennessee and Ohio rivers, it was home to few permanent residents but a place of abundant activity and trade. William Clark brought that world to an end in 1827, when he secured a deed for the territory. Deploying all the skills he had developed in two decades of negotiating with Indians and white settlers alike, he convinced Indians and whites to vacate the land. The details of those negotiations remain a mystery, but Clark drew on a well-tested strategy of convincing frontier residents that it was in their best interest to stake their claims in new territory. He entrusted his son and namesake to develop the family's claims in Paducah and sell the land to new settlers.

In his efforts to develop Paducah, Clark himself had become a western booster, and nobody expressed the concerns of western boosters more loudly than Thomas Hart Benton. For all the concerns of territorial expansion that he had expressed in certain circumstances, Clark had banked his future and that of his family on the expansion of white settlers. Yet he did so in the characteristic measured tones he had expressed throughout his life.

Not so Benton, a longtime associate and occasional friend whom Clark usually trusted but never fully understood. Whereas Catlin and Irving visited Clark as they passed through St. Louis, Benton remained in St. Louis but passed over Clark in the heated politics of antebellum America. Where Clark expressed an ambivalence toward expansion loaded with internal contradictions, Benton helped forge a political consensus that finally brought policy-making squarely in line with a new vision of expansion into the Far West.

A native of North Carolina, Benton built his political career as one of Jackson's protégés in Tennessee. After Jackson and Benton suffered a violent falling out in 1813, Benton moved to St. Louis, where he established a legal practice and edited the *Missouri Enquirer,* one of the first newspapers west of the Mississippi. In 1817 Clark invited Benton to join him on the board of trustees trying to create a system of public schools in St. Louis. Like boards in so many antebellum cities, this one was less successful at actually creating schools than it was at bringing established elites in contact with striving newcomers on the rise. Benton later defended the territorial governor against local critics. Benton even became a supporter of Clark's bid for governor, but he would go only so far. Clark fumbled to make republican politics work in democratic Missouri, but Benton immediately grasped the new political order. He became one of Missouri's first senators and quickly established himself as a major force in Washington.[49] As Benjamin O'Fallon confided to a friend in 1826, "You know that I never have been in the snug bosom of Colo. Benton—in the private walks of life we have never confided any thing to each other—But as a public man, around our great council fire, I have always admired, and as a Missourian have always been proud of him . . . He is (in my opinion) a considerable man, a useful man, our all, our shield in Congress."[50]

In the years that followed, among Benton's primary political objectives was to secure the expansion of the United States into the Far West. He sought expansion in all its forms: the territorial expansion of U.S. boundaries, the extension of western trade, and the growth of slavery into western territory.[51] Like Clark, Benton's personal interest meshed with his vision of national interest. For Clark the land speculator to see a profit on his investments, Clark the Indian agent and public surveyor needed to remove Indians and establish clear lines of property. For Benton the editor, a growing readership and advertising revenue depended on the growth of St. Louis and the presence of captivating news stories like expansion. Always astute in matters relating to local conditions, Benton also became a speculator, recognizing the potential bonanza in western land.

If Clark was a product of early St. Louis in the early Republic—a small town dominated by the interchange between Indians, Francophone merchants, and American newcomers—Benton was helping re-create St. Louis in the antebellum era as a bustling metropolis dominated by Anglo-American settlement and trade. On the eve of statehood in 1820, the U.S. census found that St. Louis County was home to ten thousand people. Twenty years later, that number had more than tripled to thirty-five thousand. In the social, political, and economic climate of antebellum St. Louis, men like Benton were eager to situate Missouri at the center of a broader national growth reaching in all directions.

Over a half century ago, Henry Nash Smith, one of the founders of American studies, astutely perceived Benton's connections to an expansionist sentiment at work in the late antebellum era.[52] As Smith demonstrated, Benton imagined himself the heir to Jefferson. He also joined a growing chorus to appropriate the arguments that came in the wake of the Louisiana Purchase, reinterpret that language, and apply it to justify expansion. In the same way that advocates of removal concluded that the Louisiana Purchase had provided the ideal place to relocate Indians, expansionists like Benton believed the purchase had providentially created new opportunities for white citizens of the United States. He celebrated Jefferson for demanding a right to control the Mississippi and for sending Lewis and Clark to explore the water routes to the Pacific. Benton then proclaimed the importance of extending that maritime trade. Finally, Benton established a more elaborate justification for expansion on the foundation of national necessity and national honor. "Woe to the statesman that undertakes to surrender one drop of its water, one inch of its soil," Benton wrote of his own expansive definition of Louisiana in an editorial for the *Missouri Inquirer*. To this he later added, "It is time that western men had some share in the destinies of this Republic." The two statements were never far apart. Westerners had been among the loudest voices demanding a federal government that protected further white settlement in the West.[53]

Benton's prediction soon rang true. By the 1830s, western interests indeed had their voice. From 1803 to 1837, ten new states entered the Union, all of them western states originally constituted as federal territories. Although population differences meant that older states still dominated the House of Representatives, the fractious politics of antebellum America meant that politicians could ill afford to lose the support of the western Congressional delegation. Meanwhile, men from these new states occupied twenty of the forty-six seats in the U.S. Senate.

The new western politics was never limited to voting strength. As early as 1820, Clark had learned the hard way what happened when would-be politicos ignored the increasingly democratic political culture of frontier states. It was no mere coincidence that many of the dominant political figures of the 1830s were themselves westerners. Although many of them had patrician impulses of their own, they also learned how to portray themselves as men of the people and particularly as men who understood the needs of western settlers.

Jackson understood all these political pressures. But he was not alone in emerging from the West to command national politics. William Henry Harrison, Clark's friend since their army service in the 1790s, was hardly a man of the people. An aristocrat by birth, Harrison had a style that was always one of aloof authority. Yet he rose quickly in national politics, primarily by tying himself to western concerns. Harrison solidified his image as an Indian fighter, transforming the Battle of Tippecanoe in the public imagination from a near-draw into an important victory that set the stage for his eventual defeat of Tecumseh and the Indian resistance movement in the Northwest. Harrison immediately translated that military victory into electoral victory as a congressman and senator from Ohio.[54]

By 1836, Harrison was prepared to become the northern version of Jackson, running on behalf of the newly formed Whig Party. Harrison lost the race to Martin Van Buren, Jackson's vice president and partner in creating the Democratic Party. The Whigs learned from their mistakes, however, launching a more effective campaign for Harrison that unseated Van Buren in 1840. The fact that Harrison died scarcely a month after taking office has rendered him something of a joke. In his time, however, Harrison stood alongside Jackson as a symbol of the rising political power of the West, the democratic political culture of the West, and the way that conquering Indians in the West could advance a public career.[55]

The success of all these western candidates always hinged on their capacity to build support in the more populace East. Nonetheless, they succeeded in helping place western interests—primarily the displacement of Indians—at the center of federal policymaking. Equally important, they helped establish a series of western archetypes at the center of American political culture and national identity.

For Benton, the annexation of Oregon and Texas, combined with the promotion of settlement in the central Plains, identified a new western political interest in the 1830s and 1840s. In the process, Benton extended the political definition of the Far West, just as Tanner, Catlin, and Irving had done in other areas of culture. Emerging from the Missouri that Clark had helped to create, Benton took the lead in propelling western interests to the center of national interests. But he was able to do so because American mapmakers, painters, and writers were all re-creating the West in ways that fit an expansionist political agenda.

Clark never joined this chorus, but his actions and those of his family explain the tide of political support for western expansion. His plan to provide for his children rested on access to western land. As the youngest son of a large family, he had learned firsthand how expansion created new opportunities. When William Preston Clark wrote from Paducah that he was "over head and ears in business," he wrote on behalf of a generation of Americans who were ready to seek their future in the West.

WILLIAM CLARK

In the midst of all these American efforts to describe the West, it was a Frenchman who produced the book that now dominates discussions of how best to describe America. In 1835 Alexis de Tocqueville published *Democracy in America*. Like so many Europeans, he was fascinated by the society that had formed in the United States in the decades since independence.

Tocqueville also marveled at the pace of white expansion into the West. Replicating the claims of John Filson, Tocqueville explained that "at the end of the last century, bold adventurers began to penetrate into the valleys of the Mississippi . . . Hitherto unknown societies sprang up in the wilderness overnight." Describing the world Jefferson hoped to create in 1784, Tocqueville wrote, "States that had been nameless only a few years before took their place in the American Union." Describing the circumstances as they were in 1830, Tocqueville wrote that "in the West it is possible to observe democracy pushed to its ultimate extreme."[56] Perhaps so, but in that process of democratization westerners had discarded William Clark.

Tocqueville concluded that "from Maine to the Floridas, and from the Missouri to the Atlantic Ocean, the people is held to be the legitimate source of all power." But what about the world beyond the Missouri? What about the Far West? Tocqueville never ventured to the Mississippi River save for a brief visit to New Orleans, still home to a vibrant Francophone culture that was more familiar to Tocqueville than the increasingly Anglo-American St. Louis. But describing the Far West was indeed the project of a growing number of authors, many of whom celebrated western possibilities in a way Jefferson's explorers never had. Some of these accounts had been written or published in the new western cities, created by authors and editors hoping to promote regional development or simply responding to their irritation at the moral outrage of easterners casting disparaging comments on the West.[57]

In the twentieth century, Tocqueville became enormously popular among writers of all stripes who sought to understand American culture and the American past. But by the time he published *Democracy in America* in 1835,

Americans had taken charge of their country's image, and they were propelling it into the Far West. Henry Tanner remained a profitable map publisher. George Catlin was preparing to return east and showcase his own vision of the West. Washington Irving was hard at work on *Astoria*. And Thomas Hart Benton was eagerly following the independence movement in Texas.

William Clark may have been familiar with all four men to varying degrees, but he was entirely disconnected from the movements they helped lead. In the 1830s, his attention seems to have been focused on Paducah, where he continued to acquire as much land as he could.[58] Nonetheless, Clark remained crucial to Tanner, Catlin, Irving, and Benton. Mapmakers continued to appropriate Clark's information for their own work. A growing number of illustrated histories of Indians included accounts of Clark's work as an explorer and Indian agent. Western politicians continued to imagine a democratic future in the new states that Clark and other territorial officials had helped to build.

Most important, the Far West might remain a distant periphery in the national geography, but it had assumed a central location in national culture. Clark himself had helped move the Far West, in large part through his efforts to map the western landscape and to relocate Indians. He began that process when mapmaking in the United States suffered from enormous limitations, but nonetheless enjoyed enormous cultural power. This mapmaking moment had created Clark even as Clark helped to create some of the most important maps in the nation's history. Nor had the importance of mapping the West vanished. In the 1830s, Americans continued to explore the West, and they also continued to produce maps, travel narratives, and geographies. But the mapmaking moment was over.

CONCLUSION: A WESTERN HISTORY

One of the last things William Clark wrote was his will. His health failing, Clark attempted to put his affairs in order in a seven-page document executed on April 14, 1837. Yet he recovered, as he had so often before. Washington Irving had described Clark as a "fine healthy robust man," mistaking the sixty-two-year-old of 1832 for a man "about 56." Clark returned to work, in large part because he could ill afford to retire. He continued to worry that his investments, primarily in western lands, would never substitute for the regular salary he received as an Indian agent.

This time, however, the recovery did not last long. Clark's condition varied in the months that followed. Family members were worried. Clark's health collapsed again in the spring of 1838, and he soon moved in with his oldest son, Meriwether Lewis Clark. Always on the lookout for money, Clark rented rooms in the house he had vacated. One of the tenants was a young army officer named Robert E. Lee, who had arrived in St. Louis to supervise engineering projects on the Mississippi waterfront.

William Clark died in his son's house on September 1, 1838.

Americans quickly sought to commemorate Clark. The residents of St. Louis did so at an elaborate funeral on September 3. A generation after the voters of Missouri had soundly rejected Clark as their leader in the election of 1820, in death they granted him the deferential respect he so clearly had hoped to achieve throughout his life. In Washington, Thomas Hart Benton lamented Clark's death, but quickly turned to the practical matters of patronage by nominating Joshua Pilcher to succeed Clark as Indian agent.[1] And in the nation at large, accounts of Clark's life appeared in various newspapers, describing his death as the end of an era of the nation's western history.[2] At public events and in print, Americans hoped to explain Clark and the

West. In the end, however, it was Clark's will, the document he had concluded in April 1837, that best chronicled not only the world that preceded Clark's death, but the world that emerged in the years that followed. It connects the western future Clark imagined as a child in Kentucky to the western history he joined in death.[3]

Clark divided his property among his four surviving sons: Meriwether Lewis, William Preston, Jefferson Kearney, and George Rogers Hancock. Four other children (Mary Margaret and John Julius, born to Julia Hancock Clark and Edmund and Harriet, born to Harriet Kennerly Radford Clark) had died before their father. Clark remained a widower after Harriet's death in 1831. This, combined with the absence of any surviving daughters, prevented the often complex arrangements of female inheritance. Clark left nothing to Harriet's two children from her marriage to John Radford.

Clark's will was entered in St. Louis Probate Court nine days after his death. Among the first tasks of the court was to conduct an assessment of Clark's personal property. A final listing from 1840 indicated what an affluent but cash-strapped citizen of Missouri might own. A rifle (perhaps the one Washington Irving described in his meeting with Clark) and hunting knife had a combined value of twenty dollars. Clark's copy of Thomas McKenney's *Indians of North America* was worth twenty-eight dollars, the price reflecting the considerable expense of mass-producing an illustrated book in the early days of lithography. There was a mahogany chest of drawers worth ten dollars, a set of silver spectacles worth three dollars, and a carpet worth fifteen dollars. Finally, Clark's possessions provided a visual story of conquering the frontier. In addition to a large portrait of himself (ten dollars), Clark had portraits of his brother, George Rogers Clark (three dollars), and of Daniel Boone (five dollars). Clark also had an engraving of Meriwether Lewis, with an assessed value of a mere twelve-and-a-half cents. This made sense, for simple portraits like the one of Lewis were among the least expensive mass-produced engravings, and they would always cost less than hiring a painter to produce a portrait. Many of the men who built careers engraving maps began by engraving illustrations, including the portraits of famous Americans. But that price difference—Clark's ten-dollar portrait and Lewis's twelve-cent portrait—captured what had become of their public image.

By the time Americans celebrated the bicentennial of the Lewis and Clark Expedition, Meriwether Lewis had eclipsed William Clark, and biographers described Lewis as everything from a pioneering leader to a talented scientist to a gifted writer. In the years after his death, however, Lewis had become a cautionary tale. If some Americans—most notably Thomas Jefferson—had set out to emphasize Lewis's accomplishments, the mere fact of his suicide worked against his becoming a model for other Americans.

After Clark's funeral in 1838 it became clear that settling his will would not be a speedy affair. Most of his property consisted of land in Missouri and Kentucky, and for a man who had so meticulously sought to measure the western landscape, Clark had apparently acquired land with surveys of questionable accuracy. In this he was hardly unique, for Americans were constantly at odds over the boundaries separating one land claim from another. Even as they waited to receive that inheritance, Clark's heirs eagerly threw themselves into land speculation. The most successful proved to be John O' Fallon, Clark's nephew, the brother of the Indian agent who had written to Clark with so much Jacksonian passion. John O'Fallon did not stand to inherit any of Clark's property, but he had learned about the value of land from Clark. An ambitious land speculator, O'Fallon eventually became one of the wealthiest men in Missouri. Like so many shrewd speculators in the antebellum era, he invested in railroads and purchased land through which the railroads passed, diversifying from farmland, which had been Clark's primary investment.

The possibilities for Clark's descendants in the West had come about in large part through the successful policy of driving Indians from the Mississippi Valley and attracting white settlers. But connecting one to the other had never been automatic. Whites considered Indian removal a prerequisite for western settlement, but they concluded the West was a safe place because the printed word and the published picture told them it was. The promotional literature of the Far West—emigrant guides, travel narratives, local histories—all successfully convinced thousands of Americans that the West was safe, that the land was fertile, and that opportunities abounded. The production of this material reached a fever pitch throughout the antebellum era, as new ways were invented to attract unsuspecting settlers. That material rested on a foundation that John Filson had helped establish in the Near West during the 1780s, emphasizing the successful conquest of Indians and the enormous benefits that came with landownership. Both stories tapped into deeply felt assumptions about what it meant to be American. Americans continued to believe that owning land was a precondition for individual freedom and national liberty. Likewise, Americans believed that conquest of Indians had defined them as a people.[4]

In the midst of all this activity, Clark's probate file swelled with new surveys, depositions, and administrative records. By the time the Probate Court closed the file in 1849, over five hundred pages chronicled the legacy of William Clark. In that decade, much of Clark's world had ceased to exist.

That change began with the shifting role of the maps that populated Clark's probate file. If local land surveys remained as valuable as ever, maps were losing much of their cultural capital. Maps continued to tell the story of the successful expansion of the United States into the West. Federal surveying expeditions and private land surveys combined to create a growing corpus of land representation that private publishers like Henry Tanner continued to appropriate for their profit. Yet even as the number of maps grew, they continued to face competition from the growing industry in illustrated representations of the West. John Caspar Wild's lithographs of St. Louis were only among the first in a slew of visual celebrations of westward expansion.

The most famous of these illustrators was the firm of Currier and Ives, which produced thousands of illustrations celebrating the nation's future in the West. Founded in 1835, Currier and Ives was ideally poised to capitalize on the new technologies of publication and the new sentiment of antebellum America. Their illustrations sent clear messages, whether they were showing idealized western farms or railroads carrying American settlers to a new future beyond the western horizon. In the half century that followed, the firm dominated the visual representation of the American experience. Maps may have told a story of orderly expansion by a unified nation that wielded clear authority, but those messages were always beneath the surface. Illustrations like those of Currier and Ives were never so subtle. Instead, they proclaimed the clear message of American civilization expanding into the West. Photographs eventually displaced lithographs as the primary form of visual representation, but only after decades in which the technological limitations of black-and-white photography guaranteed that colorful lithographs presented a more compelling and, to many people, a more accurate image of the West.[5]

Americans hardly stopped producing maps and travel narratives. To the contrary, maps remained immensely important materials in both practical and cultural terms. Likewise, western travel would become a mainstay of American writing throughout the nineteenth and twentieth centuries. In fact, many of those travel writers often saw themselves as heirs to a tradition of writing established in no small part by Lewis and Clark. At the same time, maps and traditional travel narratives of the sort that William Clark produced and consumed continued to lose the power to explain the West that they had enjoyed in the early Republic. Throughout the antebellum era, new literary

styles, especially fiction, and new visual forms, especially mass-produced illustration, displaced maps and travel narratives as the media that described
the West and explained it to American audiences.

All of these changes enabled Americans to domesticate the Far West during the antebellum era, at least in cultural terms. Americans increasingly
came to believe that they owned and controlled the West. This remained the
case despite the fact that Indians continued to wield power throughout much
of the Southwest, the Rocky Mountains, the upper Missouri Valley, and the
Pacific Coast. Only in the 1870s, with a modern army forged by the Civil
War, did the United States possess the means to compel the surrender of the
Indians and their final removal from the coveted lands of the Far West. The
history of the nineteenth century was one in which the opportunities gained
by white settlers became possible only through the conquest of people and
landscape.[6]

These changes occurred not only in the ways settlers sought to acquire
land as individuals, but also in how the United States acquired land as a nation. In the years separating Clark's death and the settlement of his probate
file, the United States had transformed its boundaries. In 1845 the annexation of Texas not only increased the national domain, but also validated the
efforts of Texas revolutionaries like Davy Crockett, who had successfully extended both Anglo-American freedom and African American slavery into the
Far West. Equally important, in 1846 Great Britain relinquished its claims to
the Oregon Territory after more than four decades of competing and confusing claims. That same year, the United States launched a war against Mexico that added a vast new western territory that extended to the Pacific, all
the while enjoying tremendous public support. These events helped keep
Americans transfixed by the West, aided by a popular culture that created a
series of archetypal stories, heroes, and villains that remained vividly powerful throughout the nineteenth and twentieth centuries.[7]

If the Mexican War occurred during a period of greater enthusiasm for expansion, it nonetheless revived the same fears Americans had felt a generation
earlier. With the acquisition of territory came the acquisition of people. More
specifically, many Americans worried that the Hispanic residents of the
Southwest would be unable to become good citizens, just as they had worried
about Francophone Louisianans. These anxieties had numerous roots: age-
old fears about the dangers of expanding empires, ethnic chauvinism among
Anglo-Americans who doubted the political capacity of people of Spanish or
mixed Spanish-Indian ancestry; religious tensions as the Protestant majority

of the United States concluded that Catholicism had prevented Mexicans from learning the basics of republican government.

As a result, at first glance these moments of expansion in the 1830s and 1840s seemed merely to repeat Clark's experience after the Louisiana Purchase. Once again, the United States faced the challenge of governing unfamiliar territory. Once again, the federal government dispatched expeditions to explore the West (one of the first of these was led by Thomas Hart Benton's son-in-law, an ambitious army officer named John C. Frémont). Once again, the West commanded public attention and cultural production. But the circumstances and the representation of expansion in the 1840s were different from those of a half century before. Most federal policymakers had enthusiastically thrown themselves into expansion. Some Americans were critical, but they were in the minority.

The changes in print and visual culture that coincided with the territorial acquisitions of the 1840s help answer a series of crucial questions. If Americans explained expansion in such shrill, often uncertain terms in the early Republic, how then to explain the change in the years that followed? How did the United States become the nation of Manifest Destiny, a Republic in which for many people expansion not only ceased to be a threat but became a positive good and eventually a necessity for the survival of the Republic? Some of the answers reside in the realm of print and visual culture. The comprehensive travel narratives and the meticulous maps that had been the primary way Americans learned about the West gave way to more fanciful characterizations in pulp novels and landscape portraiture. Well before public commentators even deployed the term "Manifest Destiny," the West had become a place of high adventure and sublime vistas. It was a place where Americans both sought and asserted conquest over people and over landscape itself.

But this was never solely a story of print culture propelling public opinion. This was also a story of democracy and market forces driving real changes in the written and visual descriptions of the West because western landscape description finally caught up with American public opinion in the 1830s and 1840s. After all, white settlers by the thousands had voted with their feet, making clear that they were willing to pursue their future in the West. They had done so for decades. I emphasize this point because the difficulty of embracing expansion in western representation hardly meant that American citizens rejected expansion. To the contrary, Clark himself was an unquestioned beneficiary of expansion. But that served only to emphasize the complexity at work in the nation's printed and visual culture, which for decades had proven far more suspicious of expansion than the public at large or even than men like Clark who helped fashion the image of the West.

Equally important, policymaking circumstances had changed in ways no less dramatic than the cultural circumstances. In 1803 Federalists and Democratic-Republicans alike considered expansion profoundly challenging to domestic governance, and they proceeded on a course of guarded expansionism. During and after the Mexican War, members of Congress and the administration seemed far less concerned with those fears. Many were enthusiastic about the potential for expansion, in part because they knew the United States had successfully expanded over the preceding decades. Meanwhile, the opposition to expansion emerged from very different fears. Critics focused their attention on a moral critique of the war or on the expansion of slavery. Few focused on the capacity of the United States to govern new people or new territory.[8]

Jefferson had expressed his belief that the United States should be an "empire of liberty." It is among Jefferson's most captivating phrases, both for those seeking to celebrate his commitment to liberty and for those seeking to condemn his creation of empire. Separated from the different cultural circumstances of the antebellum era, Jefferson's empire of liberty still appears imperialistic, but perhaps not so expansionistic. It also appears far less planned, responding instead to a variety of disparate forces, including policymaking priorities and institutional imperatives.

Crucial to understanding these changes is keeping culture in its context. An equally important policymaking reality confirmed what Americans were writing and drawing about the western landscape. Clark proves particularly relevant here, not only in his role as a policymaker but as a suggestion of the linkages between policymaking and cultural expression. The internal and external threats that many had feared in 1803 seemed gone a generation later. In many ways, these changes were real. The Union *did* survive despite the sudden and dramatic growth in both geography and demographic diversity. The United States *did* establish governments in the Far West that had successfully created new states with republican government and racial supremacy intact. The United States *did* face fewer threats at home and abroad. In other words, there were real counterparts to the printed and visual celebration of expansion. The anxieties that so many authors attempted to deny in the pamphlets of 1803–04 were no longer felt a generation later. From the antebellum era, the arguments of 1803–04 seemed visionary rather than guarded.

Some Americans would continue to oppose expansion, but the foundation of those protests had also changed. In some cases, the rise of commercial exploitation in the West would lead Americans to emphasize the importance of rivers over the benefits of the land itself. Still others feared that expansion in the North or South would deliver lopsided political power to free or slave states. Those critics included John Quincy Adams and Abraham Lincoln, men of profoundly different eras who nonetheless served together in Congress. Repudiated in the presidential election of 1828, Adams eventually won election to the House of Representatives, suffering a fatal stroke on the House floor in 1848, moments after shouting in protest about the Mexican War. Lincoln was also a member of the House, serving only a single term and speaking out loudly against the Mexican War.[9]

Yet if some public officials criticized particular elements of expansion, the strongest opposition to expansion per se was the work of critics who defined themselves as writers or artists, not as public officials. When George Catlin finally released *Letters and Notes on the Manners, Customs, and Conditions of the North American Indians* in 1841, the frontispiece depicted Catlin painting the portrait of an Indian chief, a far different visage from Charles Willson Peale's portrait of a dashing army officer that Pike had included in his narrative of 1810. The book included a map, but it was a physically small object designed to establish points of reference; it was overwhelmed by the numerous examples of Catlin's artistry that appeared throughout the book. Likewise, in *Astoria* Irving vacillated in his attitude toward western commercial development, but he considered these issues from the perspective of a novelist, deriving his narrative personae as a writer. Ralph Waldo Emerson and other writers who moved in the intellectual and literary circles of the Northeast worried about the moral implications of commercialism run amok in the Far West. Meanwhile, Henry David Thoreau went to jail rather than pay taxes to support the Mexican War.[10]

There is something attractive in those opponents to expansion, especially from a twenty-first-century perspective. They opposed enslavement and imperialism. They opposed the war with Mexico that resulted in the subjugation of Mexicans and Indians alike. And at first glance, the anti-expansionists of the 1840s seem to be the obvious extension of those who had criticized expansion in earlier decades. Yet there was a clear break at work here. Divorced from the policymaking imperatives and professional aspirations that had shaped earlier forms of western description, novels and landscape paintings could fashion both landscape and identity in very different ways. In the end, they would displace the cultural power of travel narratives and maps, but they would nonetheless keep the notion of the journey and the vision of the West at the center of the American experience.

The opponents of expansion were in conflict with a national political leadership that shared the eagerness of many white settlers for additional territory. Proslavery advocates saw a renewed future for the peculiar institution in the West; free soil advocates created their own portrait of landscape for white families freed from the economic inequalities created by slavery. They also recognized the stakes for Congress. Advocates on both sides knew the creation of new western states as free or slave could create congressional majorities for either side, while others imagined that the creation of new western states, if managed properly, could preserve a numerical balance of free and slave states that might, in turn, preserve the Union.

Among the most vocal advocates of expansion was John L. O'Sullivan, a writer and newspaper editor. When he popularized the phrase "Manifest Destiny" in 1845, he saw himself as an actor in a western history that reached back to 1776.[11] By that point, however, American print and visual culture had made an enormous leap. With expansion already established as being within the realm of the possible, Americans would begin considering it necessary. O'Sullivan's phrase has come to define the way Americans situate expansion within a broader national history. Yet O'Sullivan did not simply *reflect* an expansionist outlook. He knew as well as anybody that the use of the phrase "Manifest Destiny" was supposed to *create* a public consensus in support of expansionism. If O'Sullivan and others like him believed it was self-evident that the United States should extend to the Mississippi, they also knew that they still needed to convince the American public.[12]

The linkage between the written and visual records of expansion was particularly clear in a map which sought to keep pace with the transformation of the national landscape and of national culture. In 1833, Joseph Churchman published *Rudiments of National Knowledge*. In its general goals, the book would have looked very familiar to Jedidiah Morse. Like *Geography Made Easy*, Churchman's primer sought to teach American youngsters not only about global geography, but also about their nation. Churchman also advertised his book as one appropriate "to enquiring foreigners." Churchman included in *Rudiments of National Knowledge* a remarkable map of the United States, the so-called Eagle Map of 1833 (Fig. 35).

The map situated the eagle over the national landscape to teach lessons both practical and providential. Geographies had long used visual and

Figure 35. J. Churchman, *The Eagle Map of the United States* (Philadelphia: E. L. Carey and A. Hart, 1833). David Rumsey Map Collection, http://www.davidrumsey.com.

mnemonic devices to aid students in the rote memorization so typical of early American education. The eagle provided the ideal means to do so. Yet the Eagle Map also told a story of the United States. It announced a national landscape that seemed to overlap perfectly with the national symbol, as if territorial expansion were almost preordained by the eagle, an object which itself represented national greatness. With its wings extending clear to the Pacific, the eagle quite literally extended the reach of the United States, this during a period in which Americans were becoming increasingly comfortable with territorial expansion. The publisher was none other than E. L. Carey and Hart, a firm which had gone under various names and had published geographies by Jedidiah Morse, some of the first atlases produced in the United States, and the official narratives of Stephen Long's expeditions. The firm's founder, Mathew Carey, had even advised Nicholas Biddle on what to do with *History of the Expedition* after the collapse of Bradford and Inskeep.

In William Clark's world, maps had been a dispassionate way to measure the opportunities and threats of North America. Churchman's map answered an obvious question that emerged in the antebellum era. Was there any way to make a romantic map that would keep pace with the increasingly romantic quality of American written and visual culture? The answer seemed to be yes, but only by superimposing the eagle so clearly that it obscured the traditional map that lay beneath.

Clark died in the midst of these developments, and Americans immediately began a process of situating his actions as well as his words and drawings in a larger national history. In 1838, obituaries appeared throughout the country. Most of them mentioned Clark's role in the Lewis and Clark Expedition, but they also emphasized his career in the decades afterward. Still others emphasized Clark's stature as an expert on Indians. He emerged as less an explorer than one of the long-serving officials who had helped secure federal control in the Far West.

Meanwhile, after a lifetime describing the West in words and pictures, Clark's written and visual work scattered. Much of his correspondence as a public official went to the National Archives, sandwiched between the volumes of material that chronicled the federal effort to govern an expanding nation. Clark's contributions to the journals of the Lewis and Clark Expedition went to a variety of public and private collections. Eventually, the Missouri Historical Society received not only a cache of expedition materials, but also the largest single collection of materials from Clark and his family.

It would be decades before Clark once again became known primarily as an explorer. *History of the Expedition Under Captains Lewis and Clark* was republished periodically during the nineteenth century, but never with much success. Only Elliot Coues's edition of 1893, heavily annotated with the scientific knowledge acquired over the intervening decades, enjoyed a wide print run. In contrast, in 1905 Reuben Gold Thwaites released a seven-volume edition of the journals, beginning a process through which Americans learned about the Lewis and Clark Expedition by reading their manuscripts rather than the published account that appeared in the early Republic. This project came in a career during which Thwaites committed himself to reminding Americans of how they had described the West. He edited numerous editions of old accounts from the West, including the monumental thirty-two-volume *Early Western Travels, 1748–1846*. This single collection introduced American readers to a broad range of published travel narratives, including the work of Clark's contemporaries. Other editors followed suit, publishing many of the old manuscript accounts of trappers, traders, and mountain men.

Meanwhile, Thwaites's edition of Lewis's and Clark's expedition journals became the foundation for numerous editions that followed throughout the twentieth century, in the process re-creating William Clark as an explorer, the cocaptain to Meriwether Lewis, rather than a territorial governor or Indian agent. The current authoritative edition of the expedition journals, produced by an editorial team at the University of Nebraska under the leadership of Gary Moulton, is unique for its depth of detail and also because it was compiled from original manuscript journals; most other editors chose simply to republish Thwaites's material. At the same time, this definitive edition further solidified Clark's reputation as an explorer.

Thwaites and other editors at the beginning of the twentieth century operated during an era in which Americans were eager to evaluate their western history. Barely a decade earlier, Frederick Jackson Turner had issued his frontier thesis, in which he argued that the experience of conquering the West had imbued the United States with distinctive democratic institutions and a unique culture. In doing so, he was arguing with a generation of historians who believed the roots of national culture lay in Europe or those who, as the intellectual heirs to Jedidiah Morse, had written a history in which the nation's development and its virtues emanated from the Northeast, particularly from New England. Like Thwaites, Turner lived in Wisconsin, a state which had told its own history as part of a Near West where white settlers had established freedom and opportunity. Turner and Thwaites also wrote in the aftermath of the Spanish-American War, in which the United States finally abandoned its last inhibitions toward expansion, acquiring territories on a global scale. Again, some Americans (including Turner himself) expressed concerns with this new imperialism, but such preoccupations had only limited impact on a federal policy that, over the course of the twentieth century, became increasingly comfortable with extending the federal government's power to ever more distant locations.[13]

Throughout the twentieth century, western exploration and settlement continued to play a crucial role in the ways Americans told their national story. The record of western exploration finally had its great showcase in the bicentennial commemoration of the Lewis and Clark Expedition, a nationwide event that lasted from 2003 to 2006 and generated immense popular interest. Even the event's organizers admitted to be being surprised at the response. Indeed, interest in the bicentennial of the Lewis and Clark Expedition eclipsed the bicentennial of the Louisiana Purchase, in part because the expedition was a grand story of human adventure, whereas the purchase seemed to be a historical event having little direct contact with individuals' experiences.

These bicentennial events were replete with maps that showed the course of explorers, the transfer of land, the territorial claims of Indians and Europeans. In other words, in 2003 maps were still doing what they did in 1803. They continued to describe the western landscape. They also continued to locate the West in the American imagination. The mapmaking moment that had propelled the life of William Clark was long over, but the power of maps that he understood so well had hardly disappeared.

NOTES

INTRODUCTION

1. Martin Brückner, *The Geographic Revolution in Early America: Maps, Literacy, and National Identity* (Chapel Hill: University of North Carolina Press, 2006); Wayne Franklin, *Discoverers, Explorers, Settlers: The Diligent Writers of Early America* (Chicago: University of Chicago Press, 1979); Stephen Greenblatt, *Marvelous Possessions: The Wonder of the New World* (Chicago: University of Chicago Press, 1991); Thomas Hallock, *From the Fallen Tree: Frontier Narratives, Environmental Politics, and the Roots of a National Pastoral, 1749–1826* (Chapel Hill: University of North Carolina Press, 2003); Susan Scott Parrish, *American Curiosity: Cultures of Natural History in the Colonial British Atlantic World* (Chapel Hill: University of North Carolina Press, 2006).

2. Jeremy Adelman and Stephen Aron, "From Borderlands to Borders: Empires, Nation-States, and the Peoples in Between in North American History," *American Historical Review* 104 (1999), 814–41; Stephen Aron, *American Confluence: The Missouri Frontier from Borderland to Border State* (Bloomington: Indiana University Press, 2006).

3. Jay H. Buckley, *William Clark: Indian Diplomat* (Norman: University of Oklahoma Press, 2008); William E. Foley, *Wilderness Journey: The Life of William Clark* (Columbia: University of Missouri Press, 2004); Landon Y. Jones, *William Clark and the Shaping of the West* (New York: Hill and Wang, 2004). As a biographical subject, Clark long wallowed in the shadow of his close friend Meriwether Lewis. But Foley's, Buckley's, and Jones's studies of Clark offer complementary yet distinct interpretations.

4. Entitled simply *The Journals of the Lewis and Clark Expedition*, the collection contains thirteen volumes. The collection presents a rather sprawling portrayal of the expedition. Most readers have encountered the journals through condensed editions that usually eliminate the numerous redundancies and occasional inconsistencies of the manuscript journals in favor of an effort to create a single, cohesive

narrative of the expedition. Meanwhile, numerous single-volume editions have condensed materials from the journal into a more manageable size.

5. Walter Hesford, "'Do You Know the Author?' The Question of Authorship in *Wieland*," *Early American Literature* 17 (1982), 239–38; Leon Jackson, "Jedidiah Morse and the Transformation of Print Culture in New England, 1784–1826," *Early American Literature* 34 (1999), 2–31; Grantland S. Rice, *The Transformation of Authorship in America* (Chicago: University of Chicago Press, 1997).

6. Thomas R. Hietala, *Manifest Design: Anxious Aggrandizement in Late Jacksonian America* (Ithaca: Cornell University Press, 1985); James P. Ronda, *Astoria and Empire* (Lincoln: University of Nebraska Press, 1990); Adam Rothman, *Slave Country: American Expansion and the Origins of the Deep South* (Cambridge: Harvard University Press, 2005).

7. For the role of expansionism in the early American republic and the antebellum era, see Hietala, *Manifest Design*; Reginald Horsman, *Expansion and American Foreign Policy* (East Lansing: Michigan State University Press, 1967); Reginald Horsman, *Race and Manifest Destiny: The Origins of American Racial Anglo-Saxonism* (Cambridge: Harvard University Press, 1981), 85–90; Drew R. McCoy, *The Elusive Republic: Political Economy in Jeffersonian America* (New York: Norton, 1980); Patricia Nelson Limerick, *The Legacy of Conquest: The Unbroken Past of the American West* (New York: Norton, 1987), 58; Frank Lawrence Owsley, Jr., and Gene A. Smith, *Filibusters and Expansionists: Jeffersonian Manifest Destiny, 1800–1821* (Tuscaloosa: University of Alabama Press, 1997); John Carlos Rowe, *Literary Culture and U.S. Imperialism: From the Revolution to World War II* (Oxford: Oxford University Press, 2000); Richard Slotkin, *The Fatal Environment: The Myth of the Frontier in the Age of Industrialization, 1800–1890* (New York: Atheneum, 1985), 63–76; Henry Nash Smith, *Virgin Land: The American West as Symbol and Myth* (Cambridge: Harvard University Press, 1950); Robert W. Tucker and David C. Hendrickson, *Empire of Liberty: The Statecraft of Thomas Jefferson* (New York: Oxford University Press, 1990), 96–97.

8. For efforts to synthesize expansion and frontier contact, see Gregory H. Nobles, *American Frontiers: Cultural Encounters and Continental Conquest* (New York: Hill and Wang, 1997); Limerick, *The Legacy of Conquest*.

9. James E. Lewis, Jr., *The American Union and the Problem of Neighborhood: The United States and the Collapse of the Spanish Empire, 1783–1829* (Chapel Hill: University of North Carolina Press, 1998); J. C. A. Stagg, "James Madison and the Coercion of Great Britain: Canada, the West Indies, and the War of 1812," *William and Mary Quarterly*, 3d ser., 38 (1981), 3–34; Robert Lawson-Peebles, *Landscape and Written Expression in Revolutionary America: The World Turned Upside Down* (Cambridge: Cambridge University Press, 1988), 156–60; Angela L. Miller, *The Empire of the Eye: Landscape Representation and American Cultural Politics, 1825–1875* (Ithaca: Cornell University Press, 1993).

10. The connection between expansion and landscape description in the United States

has long been the province of scholars examining western exploration. More than anybody, William Goetzmann studied the connections between exploration and western government. See William H. Goetzmann, *Army Exploration in the American West, 1803–1863* (New Haven: Yale University Press, 1959); id., *Exploration and Empire: The Explorer and the Scientist in the Winning of the American West* (New York: Knopf, 1966); id., *New Lands, New Men: America and the Second Great Age of Discovery* (New York: Viking, 1986). Meanwhile, scholars of European culture have examined the linkages between mapmaking, travel writing, and the construction of empires. See William Patterson Cumming, *British Maps of Colonial America* (Chicago: University of Chicago Press, 1974); Matthew H. Edney, *Mapping an Empire: The Geographical Construction of British India, 1765–1843* (Chicago: University of Chicago Press, 1997); J. I. Little, "Canadian Pastoral: Promotional Images of British Colonization in Lower Canada's Eastern Townships during the 1830s," *Journal of Historical Geography* 29 (2003), 189–211.

11. For examples in literary criticism, see Charles Batten, *Pleasurable Instruction: Form and Convention in Eighteenth-Century Travel Literature* (Berkeley: University of California Press, 1978); Stephen Dow Beckham et al., *The Literature of the Lewis and Clark Expedition: A Bibliography and Essays* (Portland, Ore.: Lewis and Clark College, 2003); Albert Furtwangler, *Acts of Discovery: Visions of America in the Lewis and Clark Journals* (Urbana: University of Illinois Press, 1993); Bruce Greenfield, *Narrating Discovery: The Romantic Explorer in American Literature, 1790–1855* (New York: Columbia University Press, 1992); Amy Kaplan, *The Anarchy of Empire in the Making of U.S. Culture* (Cambridge: Harvard University Press, 2002); Stephanie LeMenager, *Manifest and Other Destinies: Territorial Fictions of the Nineteenth-Century United States* (Lincoln: University of Nebraska Press, 2004); Shelley Streeby, *American Sensations: Class, Empire, and the Production of Popular Culture* (Berkeley: University of California Press, 2002). For examples in art history, see Albert Bettex, *The Discovery of Nature* (New York: Simon and Schuster, 1965); S. Peter Dance, *The Art of Natural History: Animal Illustrators and Their Work* (Woodstock, N.Y.: Overlook Press, 1978); Barbara Novak, *Nature and Culture: American Landscape and Painting, 1825–1875* (New York: Oxford University Press, 1995); Barbara Novak, *American Painting of the Nineteenth Century: Realism, Idealism, and the American Experience* (New York: Praeger, 1969); John R. Stilgoe, *Common Landscape of America, 1580 to 1845* (New Haven: Yale University Press, 1982); Barbara Maria Stafford, *Voyage into Substance: Art, Science, Nature, and the Illustrated Travel Account, 1760–1840* (Cambridge: MIT Press, 1984).

12. For selected examples from places that are of primary concern to this book, see Aron, *American Confluence*; James Brooks, *Captives and Cousins: Slavery, Kinship, and Community in the Southwest Borderlands* (Chapel Hill: University of North Carolina Press, Omohundro Institute of Early American History and Culture, 2002); James P. Ronda, *Lewis and Clark Among the Indians* (Lincoln: University of Nebraska Press, 1988); Richard White, *The Middle Ground: Indians, Empires, and Re-*

publics in the Great Lakes Region, 1650–1815 (Cambridge: Cambridge University Press, 1991).

13. Gregory H. Nobles, "Straight Lines and Stability: Mapping the Political Order of the Anglo-American Frontier," *Journal of American History* 80 (1993), 9–35; Alan Taylor, *Liberty Men and Great Proprietors: The Revolutionary Settlement on the Maine Frontier, 1760–1820* (Chapel Hill: University of North Carolina Press, 1990); id., *William Cooper's Town: Power and Persuasion on the Frontier of the Early American Republic* (New York: Norton, 1995).

14. Brückner, *The Geographic Revolution in Early America*; Hallock, *From the Fallen Tree*; Miller, *Empire of the Eye*; Paul William Mapp, "European Geographic Ignorance and North American Imperial Rivalry: The Role of the Uncharted American West in International Affairs, 1713–1763" (Ph.D. diss., Harvard University, 2001); John R. Short, *Representing the Republic: Mapping the United States, 1600–1900* (London: Reaktion, 2001).

15. J. B. Harley, "Maps, Knowledge, and Power," in *The Iconography of Landscape: Essays on the Symbolic Representation, Design, and Use of Past Environments*, ed. Denis E. Cosgrove et al. (Cambridge: Cambridge University Press, 1988); J. B. Harley et al., *Mapping the American Revolutionary War* (Chicago: University of Chicago Press, 1978); D. W. Meinig, ed., *The Interpretation of Ordinary Landscapes: Geographical Essays* (New York: Oxford University Press, 1979); D. W. Meinig, *The Shaping of America: A Geographical Perspective on 500 Years of History*, vol. 1: *Atlantic America, 1492–1800* (New Haven: Yale University Press, 1986); Short, *Representing the Republic*.

16. John Logan Allen, *Lewis and Clark and the Image of the American Northwest* (New York: Dover Publications, 1991 [1975]); Smith, *Virgin Land*. The West's role in American culture remains a subject of intense interest. For selected examples with diverse concerns, see Leonard Engel, ed., *The Big Empty: Essays on Western Landscapes as Narrative* (Albuquerque: University of New Mexico Press, 1994); Dan L. Flores, *Horizontal Yellow: Nature and History in the Near Southwest* (Albuquerque: University of New Mexico Press, 1999); William H. Goetzmann and William N. Goetzmann, *The West of the Imagination* (New York: Norton, 1986); James McGuire, *A Literary History of the American West* (Fort Worth: Texas Christian University Press, 1987); Martha A. Sandweiss, *Print the Legend: Photography and the American West* (New Haven: Yale University Press, 2002).

17. Donald Jackson, *Thomas Jefferson and the Stony Mountains: Exploring the West from Monticello* (Urbana: University of Illinois Press, 1981).

18. For examples, see James P. Ronda, *Beyond Lewis and Clark: The Army Explores the West* (Tacoma: Washington State Historical Society, 2003); id., "Coboway's Tale: A Story of Power and Places Along the Columbia," in *Power and Place in the North American West*, ed. Richard White et al. (Seattle: University of Washington Press, 1999), 1–30; id., *The Exploration of North America* (Washington: American Historical Association, 1992); id., *Jefferson's West: A Journey with Lewis and Clark* (Charlottesville:

Thomas Jefferson Foundation, 2000); id., *Lewis and Clark Among the Indians*; James P. Ronda, ed., *Revealing America: Image and Imagination in the Exploration of North America* (Lexington, Mass.: D. C. Heath, 1996); James P. Ronda, *Thomas Jefferson and the Changing West: From Conquest to Conservation* (Albuquerque, St. Louis: University of New Mexico Press, Missouri Historical Society Press, 1997); James P. Ronda, ed., *Voyages of Discovery: Essays on the Lewis and Clark Expedition* (Helena: Montana Historical Society Press, 1998). See also Carolyn Gilman, *Lewis and Clark: Across the Divide* (Washington: Smithsonian Books, 2003), which takes the Lewis and Clark Expedition as the point of departure for a profound, far-reaching reconsideration of how best to interpret the physical artifacts of western cultural production. Studies of American Indian cartography have been equally illuminating. See G. Malcolm Lewis, ed., *Cartographic Encounters: Perspectives on Native American Mapmaking and Map Use* (Chicago: University of Chicago Press, 1998); Mark S. Monmonier, *Drawing the Line: Tales of Maps and Cartocontroversy* (New York: H. Holt, 1995); Gilman, *Lewis and Clark: Across the Divide*, 135–58.

PROLOGUE

1. For Clark's home and office, see Foley, *Wilderness Journey*, 188.
2. William Clark, *A Map of Part of the Continent of North America* . . . (1810), Beinecke.
3. For Clark's efforts to produce both a manuscript and published map based on the Lewis and Clark Expedition, see Allen, *Lewis and Clark and the Image of the American Northwest*, 378–90; Foley, *Wilderness Journey*, 187–88.
4. Karen Pearson, "The Nineteenth-Century Colour Revolution: Maps in Geographical Journals," *Imago Mundi* 32 (1980), 9–20; Mary Sponberg Pedley, *The Commerce of Cartography: Making and Marketing Maps in Eighteenth-Century France and England* (Chicago: University of Chicago Press, 2005).
5. These field notes have been magnificently reproduced in *The Journals of the Lewis and Clark Expedition*.
6. Allen, *Lewis and Clark and the Image of the American Northwest*, 160–65; Gilman, *Lewis and Clark: Across the Divide*, 148–51; William Preston, "The Accuracy of the Astronomical Observations of Lewis and Clark," *Proceedings of the American Philosophical Society* 144 (2000), 168–91.
7. Pedley, *The Commerce of Cartography*.
8. Allen, *Lewis and Clark and the Image of the American Northwest*, 74–126; Jackson, *Thomas Jefferson and the Stony Mountains*, 132–54.
9. Gilman, *Lewis and Clark: Across the Divide*, 138–48.
10. G. Malcolm Lewis, "Indicators of Unacknowledged Assimilation from Amerindian Maps on Euro-American Maps of North America: Some General Principles Arising from a Study of La Vérendrye's Composite Map, 1728–29," *Imago Mundi* 38 (1986), 9–34.

11. Nobles, "Straight Lines and Stability," 9–35.

12. Hallock, *From the Fallen Tree*.

13. For Lewis's other work, see Mathew Carey, *Carey's American Atlas* (Philadelphia: Mathew Carey, 1795).

CHAPTER 1. A WESTERN FUTURE

1. William Clark, Journal of Hardin's Campaign and Journal of General Scott's Journey, *Clark Family Collection*, MoHist, box 11.

2. Stephen Aron, *How the West Was Lost: The Transformation of Kentucky from Daniel Boone to Henry Clay* (Baltimore: Johns Hopkins University Press, 1996); Gregory Dowd, *A Spirited Resistance: The North American Indian Struggle for Unity* (Baltimore: Johns Hopkins University Press, 1992), 47–90; White, *The Middle Ground*, 366–412.

3. Foley, *Wilderness Journey*, 2–10; Jones, *William Clark and the Shaping of the West*, 12–13.

4. Lowell Hayes Harrison, *George Rogers Clark and the War in the West* (Lexington: University Press of Kentucky, 2001); White, *The Middle Ground*, 368–78.

5. For the past two decades, some of the most fascinating scholarship on the American Revolution has concerned the way Anglo-Americans joined the revolutionary movement because they believed the call for independence was a direct response to their local needs. For examples from Virginia, Kentucky, and the trans-Appalachian backcountry, see Aron, *How the West Was Lost*, 47–53; Ronald Hoffman et al., eds., *An Uncivil War: The Southern Backcountry During the American Revolution* (Charlottesville: University Press of Virginia, 1985); Rachel N. Klein, *Unification of a Slave State: The Rise of the Planter Class in the South Carolina Backcountry, 1760–1808* (Chapel Hill: University of North Carolina Press, 1990), 47–77; Albert H. Tillson, Jr., *Gentry and Common Folk: Political Culture on a Virginia Frontier, 1740–1789* (Lexington: University Press of Kentucky, 1991).

6. Thomas Jefferson to George Rogers Clark, 29 January 1780, *The Papers of Thomas Jefferson*, ed. Julian P. Boyd et al. (Princeton: Princeton University Press, 1950–), 3:273–77; Jefferson to George Washington, 26 September 1780, *Papers of Thomas Jefferson*, 3:664–66.

7. Thomas Perkins Abernethy, *Western Lands and the American Revolution* (New York: D. Appleton-Century, 1937); Herbert E. Sloan, *Principle and Interest: Thomas Jefferson and the Problem of Debt* (Oxford: Oxford University Press, 1995).

8. Jefferson's fascination with the West is the stuff of legend and the subject of intense study. The subject figures in almost every Jefferson biography. For selected examples of work focusing on Jefferson's concerns about the West, see Dan Flores, *Jefferson and Southwestern Exploration: The Freeman and Custis Accounts of the*

Red River Expedition of 1806 (Norman: University of Oklahoma Press, 1984); Lawrence S. Kaplan, *Thomas Jefferson: Westward the Course of Empire* (Wilmington: SR Books, 1999); Peter S. Onuf, *Jefferson's Empire: The Language of American Nationhood* (Charlottesville: University Press of Virginia, 2000); Ronda, *Thomas Jefferson and the Changing West.*

9. Dumas Malone, *Jefferson the Virginian* (Boston: Little, Brown, 1948), 32.

10. Joshua Fry and Peter Jefferson, *A Map of the Most Inhabited Part of Virginia Containing the Whole Province of Maryland with part of Pensilvania, New Jersey and North Carolina* (London: Thos. Jefferys, 1755), GMD, LOC.

11. Nobles, "Straight Lines and Stability," 17–21. For selected examples of European maps that struggled to represent the trans-Appalachian and trans-Mississippi West, see Elias Durnford, *Reference to the Lands Surveyed and Granted on the River Mississippi and Parts adjacent* (1770), GMD, LOC; Thomas Pownall, *The Provinces of New York, and New Jersey; with part of Pensilvania and the province of Quebec* (Frankfort upon the Mayn: Harry Lodowick Broenner, 1777), GMD, LOC; *Amérique Septentrionale avec les Routes, Distances en Miles, Villages et Etablissements François et Anglois, par le Docteur Mitchel* (Paris, 1777), GMD, LOC; Harry Liebersohn, *Aristocratic Encounters: European Travelers and North American Indians* (Cambridge: Cambridge University Press, 1998).

12. Jackson, *Thomas Jefferson and the Stony Mountains,* 86–97.

13. Thomas Jefferson, *Notes on the State of Virginia,* in *Jefferson Writings,* ed. Merrill D. Peterson (New York: Library of America, 1984), 127–28; Frank L. Dewey, *Thomas Jefferson, Lawyer* (Charlottesville: University Press of Virginia, 1986).

14. Peter S. Onuf, *The Origins of the Federal Republic: Jurisdictional Controversies in the United States, 1775–1787* (Philadelphia: University of Pennsylvania Press, 1983), 42–44, 99–100; Robert F. Berkhoffer, Jr., "The Northwest Ordinance and the Principle of Territorial Evolution," in *The American Territorial System,* ed. John Porter Bloom (Athens: Ohio University Press, 1969), 45–55.

15. *Journals of the Continental Congress, 1774–1789* (Washington: U.S. Government Printing Office, 1904–37), 26:110–20; *Papers of Thomas Jefferson,* 6:571–80; Peter S. Onuf, *Statehood and Union: A History of the Northwest Ordinance* (Bloomington: Indiana University Press, 1987), 50–53.

16. David Hartley, *Hartley–Jefferson Map of the United States East of the Mississippi River* (1784), David Hartley Papers, Clements Library, University of Michigan.

17. Jefferson, notes on Plan for Western Government, 1784, *Papers of Thomas Jefferson,* 27:601; Jefferson to Thomas Hutchins, 24 January 1784, *Papers of Thomas Jefferson,* 27:737; Jefferson to Reverend James Madison, 20 February 1784, *Papers of Thomas Jefferson,* 6:544–50; G. K. van Hogendorp to Jefferson, 22 May 1784, *Papers of Thomas Jefferson,* 7:284; Jefferson to John Page, 20 July 1785, *Papers of Thomas Jefferson,* 8:417–18.

18. Nothing reflects the power of visual representation more clearly than the way historians regularly discuss the Plan for Western Government by creating the map

that Jefferson did not. Imposing an orderly grid onto the West, these contemporary maps ignore the fact that Jefferson himself crafted a written description of territories in the West specifically because the absence of reliable surveys prevented him from creating a better map. Most books and articles and, more recently, the Powerpoint slides for public and academic talks use a map first introduced by the editors of the *Papers of Thomas Jefferson* in a lengthy editorial note discussing the Plan for Western Government. But those same editors also acknowledged that "no satisfactory delineation of Jefferson's cluster of six states lying along the Ohio river can be made on a modern map" because Jefferson's own understanding of the western geography was so far out of synch with subsequent geography. Facing a more abstract map that maintains the proportional rectangles of Jefferson's plan is an attempt to superimpose Jefferson's literal definitions onto a contemporary map. The result is a series of multifaceted shapes of varying sizes that look anything but orderly. See *Papers of Thomas Jefferson*, 6:588–92.

19. Anthony F. C. Wallace, *Jefferson and the Indians: The Tragic Fate of the First Americans* (Cambridge: Belknap Press of Harvard University Press, 1999), 163.

20. Andro Linklater, *Measuring America: How an Untamed Wilderness Shaped the United States and Fulfilled the Promise of Democracy* (New York: Walker, 2002), 74–88; Onuf, *Statehood and Union*, 19–25; Carstensen Vernon, "Patterns on the American Land," *Publius* 18 (1988), 31–39.

21. Andrew R. L. Cayton, *The Frontier Republic: Ideology and Politics in the Ohio Country* (Kent: Kent State University Press, 1986), 8–9.

22. Scholars have frequently chronicled Anglo-American land speculation in the late eighteenth and early nineteenth centuries. It was among the most common forms of financial investment and a subtle yet powerful influence on politics and social relations. The most comprehensive and sweeping investigation of the subject in the South and the early West remains Abernethy, *Western Lands and the American Revolution*.

23. John Filson, *The Discovery, Settlement and Present State of Kentucke* (Wilmington: James Adams, 1784).

24. Ibid., 11. For an informative reading of *History of Kentucke*, see Hallock, *From the Fallen Tree*, 56–74.

25. Ibid., 5.

26. Ibid., 15, 20, 25.

27. Ibid., 10.

28. Ibid., 28–29.

29. Ibid., 49.

30. Ibid., 72.

31. Ibid., 77–78.

32. Philip Joseph Deloria, *Playing Indian* (New Haven: Yale University Press, 1998).

33. John Mack Faragher, *Daniel Boone: The Life and Legend of an American Pioneer* (New York: Holt, 1992), 164–66.

34. This was apparently Pursell's only major published map. Pursell remains something of a mystery, leaving no record of his training or experience. While his map of Kentucky was widely distributed and featured prominently as a source for numerous other maps, none of the major map collections in the United States indicate that Pursell himself created other maps. Likewise, Pursell does not feature in the correspondence surrounding Filson's publication or record or in the work of other cartographers.

35. Thomas Hallock has produced an illuminating analysis of the ways in which Anglo-Americans sought to superimpose themselves and their nation onto the landscape, inscribing their names in ways that would replace European empires, Indians, and in some cases the environment itself. See Hallock, *From the Fallen Tree.*

36. John Filson to Washington, 30 November 1784 and 8 February 1785, *George Washington Papers* (Washington: Library of Congress Microfilm Collection).

37. Washington to Filson, 16 January and 15 March 1785, *George Washington Papers.*

38. Cayton, *The Frontier Republic*, 13–14; Philander Chase, "A Stake in the West: George Washington as Backcountry Surveyor and Landholder " in *George Washington and the Virginia Backcountry*, ed. Warren R. Hofstra (Madison: Madison House, 1998), 159–94; Edward J. Redmond, "Mapping from Mount Vernon, 1747–1799," paper presented at the Early American Cartographies Conference, Newberry, Chicago, 2006.

39. Morse has a special appeal to both historical geographers and literary critics. Well aware of and well connected with a variety of literary-minded elites in the Northeast, Morse usually is seen as a secondary but nonetheless important figure in the development of American culture. For example, see Joseph A. Conforti, *Imagining New England: Explorations of Regional Identity from the Pilgrims to the Mid-Twentieth Century* (Chapel Hill: University of North Carolina Press, 2001); Michael J. Everton, "The Courtesies of Authorship: Hannah Adams and Authorial Ethics in the Early Republic," *Legacy* 20 (2003), 1–21; Jackson, "Jedidiah Morse and the Transformation of Print Culture in New England, 1784–1826," 2–31; Lawson-Peebles, *Landscape and Written Expression in Revolutionary America*, 62–73; Short, *Representing the Republic*, 107–26.

40. Aside from specific studies of Morse's involvement in geography and literature, his life remains the subject of a series of aging biographies. For example, see Richard J. Moss, *The Life of Jedidiah Morse: A Station of Peculiar Exposure* (Knoxville: University of Tennessee Press, 1995).

41. Drew R. McCoy, "James Madison and Visions of American Nationality in the Confederation Period: A Regional Perspective," in *Beyond Confederation: Origins of the Constitution and American National Identity*, ed. Richard Beeman et al. (Chapel Hill: University of North Carolina Press, 1987), 226–58; David Waldstreicher, *In the Midst of Perpetual Fetes: The Making of American Nationalism, 1776–1820* (Chapel Hill: University of North Carolina Press, 1997), 246–95.

42. Martin Brückner, "Lessons in Geography: Maps, Spellers, and Other Grammars

of Nationalism in the Early Republic," *American Quarterly* 51 (1999), 331–34; Jill Lepore, *A is for American: Letters and Other Characters in the Newly United States* (New York: Alfred A. Knopf, 2002).

43. Jedidiah Morse, *Geography Made Easy* (New Haven: Meigs, Bowen and Dana, 1784), 5–26. For the nationalist content of Morse's geographies and similar books, see Brückner, *The Geographic Revolution in Early America*, 114–21; Short, *Representing the Republic*, 107–26.

44. William Altman to Jedidiah Morse, 14 May 1795, *Morse Family Papers, 1779–1868*, Yale University, box 2, folder 34; Dr. Fisher to Morse, 23 July 1795, *Morse Family Papers*, box 2, folder 36. The family correspondence is preserved in various archives, but two collections dominate. The largest single collection is, appropriately enough, located at Yale University; a second, substantially smaller collection, is located at the New-York Historical Society.

45. The map appears to draw most extensively from John Mitchell, *A Map of the British and French Dominions in North America* . . . (London: 1755), GMD, LOC; Thomas Pownall, *A New Map of the Whole Continent of America, Divided into North and South and West Indies with a descriptive account of the European possessions, as settled by the definitive treaty of peace, concluded at Paris Feby. 10th. 1763* (London: 1777), GMD, LOC.

46. Morse, *Geography Made Easy*, 41. The only state to rival New England's regional supremacy was Pennsylvania, primarily owing to the achievements of one man, William Penn. Morse especially praised Penn for instituting policies that were guided by wisdom, fair to Indians, and adequately responsive to the concerns of white settlers. See ibid., 58.

47. Ibid., 63, 68.

48. Joyce O. Appleby, *Capitalism and a New Social Order: The Republican Vision of the 1790s* (New York: New York University Press, 1984); Cathy D. Matson and Peter S. Onuf, *A Union of Interests: Political and Economic Thought in Revolutionary America* (Lawrence: University Press of Kansas, 1990), 92–94; McCoy, *The Elusive Republic*; Miller, *Empire of the Eye*, 34–35.

49. Morse, *Geography Made Easy*, 112–13.

50. The European and Euro-American belief in Indian laziness has been a central concern to a vast literature on intercultural contact, European science, and federal policy. For example, see Robert F. Berkhofer, *The White Man's Indian: Images of the American Indian from Columbus to the Present* (New York: Vintage Books, 1979); Terry Jay Ellingson, *The Myth of the Noble Savage* (Berkeley: University of California Press, 2001); Liebersohn, *Aristocratic Encounters*; John F. Moffitt and Santiago Sebastián, *O Brave New People: The European Invention of the American Indian* (Albuquerque: University of New Mexico Press, 1996); Bernard W. Sheehan, *Seeds of Extinction: Jeffersonian Philanthropy and the American Indian* (Chapel Hill: University of North Carolina Press 1973), 102–05; Wallace, *Jefferson and the Indians*, 180–203.

51. For the way various forms of print and visual culture achieved symbolic representations of the federal union, see Brückner, *The Geographic Revolution in Early America*; Waldstreicher, *In the Midst of Perpetual Fetes*.

52. Reuben T. Durrett, *John Filson, the First Historian of Kentucky* (Louisville: Printed for the Filson Club by J. P. Morton and Co., 1884); John Walton, *John Filson of Kentucke* (Lexington: University of Kentucky Press, 1956), 95–115.

53. John Filson, *Histoire de Kentucke, Nouvelle Colonie à l'ouest de la Virginie* (Paris: Buisson, 1785); id., *Reise nach Kentucke und Nachrichten von Dieser neu Angebaueten Landschaft in Nordamerica* (Leipzig: C. Weigel und Schneider, 1790).

54. John Filson, *Adventures of Colonel Daniel Boon* (Philadelphia: 1787); id., *A Topographical Description of the Western Territory of North America* (New York: Samuel Campbell, 1793).

55. Walton, *John Filson of Kentucke*, 116–26.

56. Cayton, *The Frontier Republic*.

57. Morse to Jedidiah Morse Sr., 8 January 1785, *Morse Family Papers*, box 1, folder 6. See also Morse to Jedidiah Morse Sr., 4 May, 23 May, and 8 June 1785, *Morse Family Papers*, box 1, folder 7.

58. Morse to Daniel Jones, March 1785, *Morse Family Papers*, box 1, folder 6. See also Morse to Jedidiah Morse Sr., 15 March 1785, *Morse Family Papers*, box 1, folder 6.

59. Jedidiah Morse, *The American Geography, or, A view of the present situation of the United States of America . . .* (Elizabethtown: Shepard Kollock 1789).

60. *Bailey's Pocket Almanac, Being an American annual register, for the year of our Lord 1785* (Philadelphia: Francis Bailey, 1784).

61. Faragher, *Daniel Boone*, 246.

62. Gilbert Imlay and Cornelius Tiebout, *A Topographical Description of the Western Territory of North America . . .* (New York: Samuel Campbell, 1793), 47.

63. Foley, *Wilderness Journey*, 8, 13.

64. For Anglo-American notions of landownership, see William Cronon, *Changes in the Land: Indians, Colonists, and the Ecology of New England* (New York: Hill and Wang, 1983), 65–81; Taylor, *Liberty Men and Great Proprietors*.

65. Foley, *Wilderness Journey*, 4–5. For the linkage between education and refinement in the eighteenth century, see Richard L. Bushman, *The Refinement of America: Persons, Houses, Cities* (New York: Knopf: Distributed by Random House, 1992).

66. Clark, mathematic notebook and arithmetic copy book, *Clark Family Collection*, box 11; Brückner, "Lessons in Geography," 311–34.

67. Clark, "Journal of Hardin's Campaign and Journal of General Scott's Journey," *Clark Family Collection*, box 11.

CHAPTER 2. THREE TREATIES, ONE NATION

1. Clark to Anthony Wayne, undated, *Clark Family Collection*, box 11, folder 4.

2. *Clark Family Collection*, box 11, folder 4.

3. Continental Congress to John Adams, 14 August 1779, *Journals of the Continental Congress, 1774–1789,* 14:958–60; Congress to Benjamin Franklin, 15 June 1781, *The Papers of Benjamin Franklin,* ed. Leonard Woods Labaree et al. (New Haven: Yale University Press, 1959–), 35:166–67.

4. For the notion of treaties as legal documents, see Peter S. Onuf and Nicholas G. Onuf, *Federal Union, Modern World: The Law of Nations in an Age of Revolutions, 1776–1814* (Madison: Madison House, 1993), 7–8; David C. Hendrickson, *Peace Pact: The Lost World of the American Founding* (Lawrence: University Press of Kansas, 2003).

5. Mitchell, *A Map of the British and French Dominions in North America . . .*

6. Robert Gough, "Officering the American Army, 1798," *William and Mary Quarterly,* 3d ser., 43 (1986), 460–71; William B. Skelton, *An American Profession of Arms: The Army Officer Corps, 1784–1815* (Lawrence: University Press of Kansas, 1992), 12–33.

7. Dowd, *A Spirited Resistance,* 90–116; Rothman, *Slave Country,* 92–16; Claudio Saunt, *A New Order of Things: Property, Power, and the Transformation of the Creek Indians, 1733–1816* (Cambridge: Cambridge University Press, 1999), 164–66; White, *The Middle Ground,* 433–68.

8. Samuel Flagg Bemis, *Pinckney's Treaty: America's Advantage from Europe's Distress, 1783–1800* (New Haven: Yale University Press, 1960), 31–34, 104–05, 126–31; Lewis, *The American Union and the Problem of Neighborhood,* 15–17.

9. Thomas Pownall, *A New Map of North America* (London: Robert Sayer, 1783), GMD, LOC; *Carte des Etats-Unis d'Amérique, et du cours du Mississippi . . .* (Paris: Esnats et Railly, 1784), Edward E. Ayer Collection, Newberry; *Bowels's New one-sheet map of the United States of America with the territories belonging to Great Britain and Spain* (London: Bowles and Carver, 1795), GMD, LOC; John Stockdale, *Part of the United States of North America* (London: J. Stockdale, 1800), GMD, LOC; F.L. (Franz Ludwig) Güssefeld, *Charte der XV Vereinigten Staaten von Nord-American nach Murdochischer projection* (Weimar, 1800), GMD, LOC; *Carte du Mississipi et de ses embranchemens* (Paris: 1802), GMD, LOC.

10. Mitchell, *A Map of the British and French Dominions in North America . . .*

11. *Amérique Septentrionale* (1777).

12. Jefferson to Edward Bancroft, 2 February 1786, *Papers of Thomas Jefferson,* 9:299–300; James Lyons to Jefferson, 27 February 1786, *Papers of Thomas Jefferson,* 9:302; Jefferson to William Stephens Smith, 10 August 1786, *Papers of Thomas Jefferson,* 10:211–13; Jefferson to Abbé Morellet, 12 August 1786, *Papers of Thomas Jefferson,* 10:225–26.

13. Chase, "A Stake in the West"; Redmond, "Mapping from Mount Vernon."

14. Washington to the Senate, 9 February 1790, *The Papers of George Washington: Presidential Series,* ed. W. W. Abbot et al. (Charlottesville: University Press of Virginia, 1987–), 5:117.

15. Benjamin Workman, *Elements of Geography* (Philadelphia: M'Culloch, 1790);

Carey, *Carey's American Atlas; A Map of the United States* (Philadelphia, 1795), Newberry; Abraham Bradley, *Map of the United States* (1796), GMD, LOC.

16. R. C. McGrane, "William Clark's Journal of General Wayne's Campaign," *Mississippi Valley Historical Review* 1 (1914), 422.

17. Lord Grenville to John Jay, 4 September 1794, *American State Papers: Documents, Legislative and Executive, of the Congress of the United States* (Washington: Gales and Seaton, 1832–61), Foreign Relations, 1:491.

18. *Treaties and Other International Agreements of the United States of America 1776–1949*, ed. Charles E. Bevans (Washington: Government Printing Office, 1971), 5:17.

19. A clear sign of where historians situate the Jay Treaty is the fact that recent studies have tended to focus on the treaty's connection to domestic politics rather than international relations. For example, see Jerald A. Combs, *The Jay Treaty: Political Battleground of the Founding Fathers* (Berkeley: University of California Press, 1970); Todd Estes, *The Jay Treaty Debate, Public Opinion, and the Evolution of Early American Political Culture* (Amherst: University of Massachusetts Press, 2006); Jeffrey L. Pasley, *The Tyranny of Printers: Newspaper Politics in the Early American Republic* (Charlottesville: University Press of Virginia, 2001), 91–95; Waldstreicher, *In the Midst of Perpetual Fetes*, 142–52.

20. Surveying the boundary between the United States and Canada remained a difficult, contentious project long after the Jay Treaty. See J. P. D. Dunbabin, "Red Lines on Maps: The Impact of Cartographical Errors on the Border Between the United States and British North America, 1782–1842," *Imago Mundi* 50 (1998), 105–25.

21. Dowd, *A Spirited Resistance*, 113; Alan D. Gaff, *Bayonets in the Wilderness: Anthony Wayne's Legion in the Old Northwest* (Norman: University of Oklahoma Press, 2004); John Sugden, *Blue Jacket: Warrior of the Shawnees* (Lincoln: University of Nebraska Press, 2000), 176–87; Wiley Sword, *President Washington's Indian War: The Struggle for the Old Northwest, 1790–1795* (Norman: University of Oklahoma Press, 1985), 291–328.

22. McGrane, "William Clark's Journal of General Wayne's Campaign," 429.

23. *Indian Affairs: Laws and Treaties* (Stillwater: OSU Library Digital Publications, 1999), 2:39–41.

24. Clark to Wayne, undated, *Clark Family Collection*, box 11, folder 4.

25. *Treaties and Other International Agreements of the United States of America 1776–1949*, 11:516–25.

26. William Short to Jefferson, 30 September 1795, *Papers of Thomas Jefferson*, 28:490; Duke de la Alcudia, notes on the convention with the United States, 25 September 1795, *American State Papers*, Foreign Relations, 2:540–42.

27. Andrew Ellicott to Washington, 24 March 1796, *George Washington Papers*; Ellicott to Jefferson, *Papers of Thomas Jefferson*, 24:664; Thomas Hutchins, *A General Map of the Country on the Ohio and Muskingham showing the situation of the Indian-towns with respect to the Army under the command of Colonel Bouquet . . . in 1764*

(1765), GMD, LOC; *An Historical Account of the Expedition Against the Ohio Indians, in the year 1764* . . . (Philadelphia: W. Bradford, 1765); Thomas Hutchins, *A Topographical Description of Virginia, Pennsylvania, Maryland and North Carolina* . . . (Boston: John Norman, 1787); Jefferson, report on boundaries with Indians, 10 March 1793, *Papers of Thomas Jefferson*, 25:354–56. Linklater, *Measuring America*, 74–77.

28. "A sketch of W. Clark's Trip Down the Ohio Sep. ad 1795," *Clark Family Collection*, box 11, folder 4; Andrew Ellicott, *The Journal of Andrew Ellicott, Late Commissioner on Behalf of the United States During Part of the Year 1796, the Years 1797, 1798, 1799, and part of the year 1800* . . . (Philadelphia: Thomas Dobson, 1803).

29. Foley, *Wilderness Journey*, 40.

30. Manuel Gayoso de Lemos, passport for William Clark, 18 June 1798, *Clark Family Collection*, box 11, folder 4. For Clark's movements in 1796–98, see Foley, *Wilderness Journey*, 41–46.

31. William Clark Notebook, 1798–1801, *Western Historical Manuscript Collection*, Missouri State Historical Society.

CHAPTER 3. EXPANSION

1. Clark to Meriwether Lewis, 18 July 1803, *Letters of the Lewis and Clark Expedition, With Related Documents 1783–1854*, ed. Donald Jackson (Urbana: University of Illinois Press, 1978), 1:110.

2. Clark's correspondence during the spring and summer of 1803 remains limited, in stark contrast to that of Lewis, who was producing a voluminous correspondence related to planning the expedition. The major published and manuscript collections of Clark's writings during these months make no reference to the Louisiana Purchase until after he wrote to Lewis. Likewise, the extant copies of Kentucky newspapers did not report on the Louisiana Purchase before July 18.

3. For the passage by the Grand Tower, see *The Journals of the Lewis and Clark Expedition*, ed. Gary E. Moulton et al. (Lincoln: University of Nebraska Press, 1983), 2:111–12.

4. Harrison, *George Rogers Clark*, 107.

5. The importance of the Mississippi River, and the particular way in which Kentuckians mobilized to articulate their concerns, remains a common theme in the history of U.S. foreign policy during the Jefferson administration. For selected examples, see Alexander DeConde, *This Affair of Louisiana* (New York: Charles Scribner's Sons, 1976); Lewis, *The American Union and the Problem of Neighborhood*, 14–16; Arthur Preston Whitaker, *The Mississippi Question, 1795–1803* (New York: C. Appleton-Century, 1934).

6. Jefferson to George Rogers Clark, 4 December 1783, *Papers of Thomas Jefferson*, 6:371; George Rogers Clark to Jefferson, 8 February 1784, *Papers of Thomas Jefferson*, 15:609.

7. Jefferson's attitudes toward science and political economy are the subject of a vast scholarly literature. For selected examples as they relate to trade and exploration, see Matson and Onuf, *A Union of Interests*, 17–19, 149–50; Onuf, *Jefferson's Empire*, 68–70; Ronda, *Astoria and Empire*, 42–43; Alan Taylor, "Jefferson's Pacific: The Science of Distant Empire, 1768–1811," in *Across the Continent: Jefferson, Lewis and Clark, and the Making of America*, ed. Douglas Seefeldt et al. (Charlottesville: University of Virginia Press, 2005), 16–44.

8. Gilman, *Lewis and Clark: Across the Divide*, 51–62; Taylor, "Jefferson's Pacific," 16–44.

9. Lewis to Clark, 19 June 1803, *Letters of the Lewis and Clark Expedition*, 1:60.

10. Stephen A. Ambrose, *Undaunted Courage: Meriwether Lewis, Thomas Jefferson, and the Opening of the American West* (New York: Simon and Schuster, 1996), 46–74; Foley, *Wilderness Journey*, 40–46.

11. Andy Trees, "Private Correspondence for the Public Good: Thomas Jefferson to Elbridge Gerry, 26 January 1799," *Virginia Magazine of History and Biography* 108 (2000), 217–55.

12. The best overviews of the process through which the United States acquired the Louisiana Purchase are DeConde, *This Affair of Louisiana*, 161–80; John Kukla, *A Wilderness So Immense: The Louisiana Purchase and the Destiny of America* (New York: Knopf, 2003).

13. Peter J. Kastor, *The Nation's Crucible: The Louisiana Purchase and the Creation of America* (New Haven: Yale University Press, 2004), 40–43; Kukla, *A Wilderness So Immense*.

14. Clark to Lewis, 21 August 1803, *Letters of the Lewis and Clark Expedition*, 1:117.

15. Jerry W. Knudson, "Newspaper Reaction to the Louisiana Purchase, 'This New, Immense, Unbounded World,'" *Missouri Historical Review* 43 (1969), 182–213; Betty Houchin Winfield, "Public Perception and Public Events: The Louisiana Purchase and the American Partisan Press," in *The Louisiana Purchase: Emergence of an American Nation*, ed. Peter J. Kastor (Washington: CQ Press, 2002), 38–50.

16. For examples of these pamphlets, see *Analysis of the Third Article of the Treaty of Cession of Louisiana* (Washington: 1803); Samuel Brazer, *Address, Pronounced at Worcester, on May 12th: 1804 in commemoration of the cession of Louisiana to the United States* (Worcester: Sewall Goodridge, 1804); David A. Leonard, *An Oration, Delivered at Raynham, Massachusetts, Friday, May 11th, 1804, on the Late Acquisition of Louisiana, at the Unanimous Request of the Republican Citizens of the County of Bristol* (Newport: Oliver Farnsworth, 1804); Allan Bowie Magruder, *Political, Commercial, and Moral Reflections on the Late Cession of Louisiana to the United States* (Lexington: D. Bradford, 1803); Orasmus Cook Merrill, *The Happiness of America: An Oration Delivered at Shaftsbury, on the Fourth of July* (Vermont, 1804); David Ramsay, *An Oration on the Cession of Louisiana to the United States . . .* (Charleston: W. P. Young, 1804); St. George Tucker, *Reflections on the Cession of Louisiana to the United States* (Washington: Samuel Harrison Smith,

1803); W. M. P., A Poem on the Acquisition of Louisiana Respectfully Dedicated to the Committee Appointed for the Celebration of that Great Event in this City (Charleston: Query and Evans, 1804).

17. Brazer, Address, Pronounced at Worcester, 6.

18. Peter J. Kastor, "'What Are the Advantages of the Acquisition?': Inventing Expansion in the Early American Republic," American Quarterly 60 (2008), 1013–17.

19. James Madison to James Monroe, 14 February 1804, The Papers of James Madison: Secretary of State Series, ed. Robert J. Brugger et al. (Charlottesville: University Press of Virginia, 1986–), 6:477.

20. For example, see A Correct Map of the United States of North America, Including the British and Spanish territories, carefully laid down agreeable to the Treaty of 1784 (London: 1797), Newberry; Map of the United States, Canada and . . . (London: R. Phillips, 1799), Edward E. Ayer Collection, Newberry; J. Luffman, A Map of North America (London: 1803), GMD, LOC; Carte des Etatus du centre, de l'ouest et du sud des Etats-Unis (1804), Everett D. Graff Collection, Newberry. See also Alfred E. Lemmon et al., eds., Charting Louisiana: Five Hundred Years of Maps (New Orleans: Historic New Orleans Collection, 2003).

21. Allen, Lewis and Clark and the Image of the American Northwest, 127–57; Gilman, Lewis and Clark: Across the Divide, 2–26; Jackson, Thomas Jefferson and the Stony Mountains, 120–24.

22. Aaron Arrowsmith, A Map Exhibiting all the New Discoveries in the Interior Parts of North America . . . (London: A. Arrowsmith, 1802), GMD, LOC.

23. William Faden, The United States of North America, with the British territories and those of Spain (London, 1793), GMD, LOC; Mitchell, A Map of the British and French Dominions in North America. . . .

24. Thomas Hutchins, An Historical Narrative and Topographical Description of Louisiana and West-Florida: Comprehending the River Mississippi with its Principal Branches and Settlements . . . (Philadelphia, 1784).

25. Jefferson, notes on the boundaries of Louisiana, 1803, Thomas Jefferson Papers, Washington: Library of Congress Microfilm Collection.

26. Ibid.

27. Jefferson to William Dunbar, 13 March 1804, Thomas Jefferson Papers.

28. "Clark's List of Questions," [1804], Letters of the Lewis and Clark Expedition, 1:157–61.

29. Caspar Wistar to Jefferson, 13 July 1803, Letters of the Lewis and Clark Expedition, 1:108.

30. Wistar to Jefferson, 6 October 1803, Letters of the Lewis and Clark Expedition, 1:133; Jefferson to Lewis, 3 October 1803, Letters of the Lewis and Clark Expedition, 1:133.

31. Jefferson to Lewis, 16 November 1803, Letters of the Lewis and Clark Expedition, 1:137–38.

32. Thomas Jefferson Papers. The queries appear in various stages in The Jefferson Papers, dated to July 1803.

33. James Wilkinson to Henry Dearborn, 27 July 1805, *The Journals of Zebulon Montgomery Pike*, 1:229–30. See also Wilkinson to Dearborn, 25 August 1805, *The Journals of Zebulon Montgomery Pike, with Letters and Related Documents*, ed. Donald Dean Jackson (Norman: University of Oklahoma Press, 1966), 1:232–33.

34. Jefferson to Thomas Freeman, 14 April 1804, *Papers of Thomas Freeman, 1796–1807*, Manuscript Division, LOC.

35. Wilkinson to Zebulon Pike, 30 July 1805, *The Journals of Zebulon Pike*, 1:3.

36. Jefferson to William Henry Harrison, 27 February 1803, *Jefferson Writings*, 1, 118. For relevant discussions of Jefferson's attitudes toward Indians in relation to the Lewis and Clark Expedition, see Jackson, *Thomas Jefferson and the Stony Mountains*, 203–20; Christian B. Keller, "Philanthropy Betrayed: Thomas Jefferson, the Louisiana Purchase, and the Origins of Federal Indian Removal Policy," *Proceedings of the American Philosophical Society* 144 (2000), 39–66; Ronda, *Lewis and Clark Among the Indians*, 4–9; Sheehan, *Seeds of Extinction*.

37. Arthur H. DeRosier, *William Dunbar: Scientific Pioneer of the Old Southwest* (Lexington: University Press of Kentucky, 2007); Flores, *Jefferson and Southwestern Exploration*, 49–54; Jeffrey S. Hanor, "The Dunbar–Hunter Expedition (1804–1805): Early Analyses of Spring Waters in the Louisiana Purchase," *Ground Water* 45 (2007), xvi–xx.

38. Dunbar to Jefferson, 14 July 1800, *Thomas Jefferson Papers*; Jefferson to Dunbar, 12 January 1801, *Thomas Jefferson Papers*; Jefferson to William C. C. Claiborne, 13 July 1801, *Papers of Thomas Jefferson*, 34:560–61; Jefferson to Dunbar, 17 July 1803, *Thomas Jefferson Papers*.

39. Jefferson to Dunbar, 3 March 1803, *Thomas Jefferson Papers*; Jefferson to Dunbar, 17 July 1803, *Thomas Jefferson Papers*; Dunbar to Jefferson, 22 August 1801, 5 January and 21 October 1803, *Thomas Jefferson Papers*; Dunbar to John Vaughan, 21 March and 25 November 1802, *Thomas Jefferson Papers*; William Dunbar and Thomas Jefferson, "Description of a Singular Phenomenon Seen at Baton Rouge, by William Dunbar, Esq. Communicated by Thomas Jefferson, President A. P. S," *Transactions of the American Philosophical Society* 6 (1809).

40. Flores, *Jefferson and Southwestern Exploration*, 59–62.

41. Manuel Gayoso de Lemos maintained an extensive correspondence with Dunbar throughout 1797 and 1798. See *Henry Raup Wagner Collection of Mexican Comisión de Limites papers, 1747–1834*, Yale Collection of Western America, Beinecke.

42. Ellicott to Jefferson, 6 March 1803, *Letters of the Lewis and Clark Expedition*, 1:23–24.

43. Ellicott, *The Journal of Andrew Ellicott*.

44. Jefferson to Dearborn, 13 August 1803, *Thomas Jefferson Papers*.

45. Clark's lack of promotion and Lewis's insistence on treating Clark as a coequal is a core piece of the Lewis and Clark story. For details of this moment in biographies of both men, see Ambrose, *Undaunted Courage*, 97–99; Foley, *Wilderness Journey*, 70–71. For the army's promotion system, see Theodore J. Crackel, *Mr. Jefferson's*

Army: Political and Social Reform of the Military Establishment, 1801–1809 (New York: New York University Press, 1987); Skelton, *An American Profession of Arms*.

46. *The Journals of the Lewis and Clark Expedition*, 2:227.

CHAPTER 4. EXPLORERS

1. *The Journals of the Lewis and Clark Expedition*, 4:285, 304.

2. Most of these letters are contained in *Letters of the Lewis and Clark Expedition*, 1:220–31. Additional letters from Clark to his brother Jonathan were recently discovered at the Filson Historical Society. See Clark to Jonathan Clark, April 1805, *Dear Brother: Letters of William Clark to Jonathan Clark*, ed. James J. Holmberg (New Haven: Yale University Press, 2002), 84–86.

3. Harrison was an immensely important figure in his time, yet historians have generally ignored him. He has finally received a modern biographical treatment in Robert M. Owens, *Mr. Jefferson's Hammer: William Henry Harrison and the Origins of American Indian Policy* (Norman: University of Oklahoma Press, 2007).

4. *The Journals of the Lewis and Clark Expedition*, 3:268.

5. *Connecticut Journal* (New Haven), 31 October 1805; *Newburyport Herald* (Newburyport), 5 November 1805; *The Farmers' Cabinet* (Amherst), 5 November 1805; *Northern Post* (Salem), 14 November 1805; *New Hampshire Sentinel* (Keene), 16 November 1805; *The Green Mountain Patriot* (Peacham), 26 November 1805.

6. Clark to Jonathan Clark, April 1805, *Dear Brother*, 84–115.

7. *Political Observatory* (Walpole), 20 July 1805.

8. The best discussion of newspaper accounts of the expedition is Betty Houchin Winfield, "Public Perception of the Expedition," in *Lewis and Clark: Journey to Another America*, ed. Alan Taylor (St. Louis: Missouri Historical Society Press, 2003). For a more general discussion of newspapers and the circulation of information, see Richard R. John, *Spreading the News: The American Postal System from Franklin to Morse* (Cambridge: Harvard University Press, 1995); Pasley, *The Tyranny of Printers*.

9. *Middlebury [VT] Mercury*, 24 July 1805; *Providence [RI] Phoenix*, 20 July 1805; *Political Observatory*, 20 July 1805.

10. Scholars in a broad range of fields have focused particular attention on the ways in which Lewis and Clark described Indians and the limitations of that analysis. For selected examples from a diverse set of disciplinary perspectives, see Gilman, *Lewis and Clark: Across the Divide*; Frederick E. Hoxie and Jay T. Nelson, eds., *Lewis and Clark and the Indian Country: The Native American Perspective* (Urbana: University of Illinois Press, 2007); Alvin M. Josephy and Marc Jaffe, eds., *Lewis and Clark Through Indian Eyes* (New York: Knopf, 2006); Ronda, *Lewis and Clark Among the Indians*; Thomas P. Slaughter, *Exploring Lewis and Clark: Reflections on Men and Wilderness* (New York: Alfred A. Knopf, 2003).

11. *Washington Federalist*, 27 March 1805. For other examples, see *Enquirer* (Rich-

mond), 23 March 1805; *Daily Advertiser* (New York), 26 March 1805; Salem [Mass.] *Gazette*, 2 April 1805; *City Gazette And Daily Advertiser* (Charleston), 5 April 1805.

12. Trey Berry et al., eds., *The Forgotten Expedition, 1804–1805: The Louisiana Purchase Journals of Dunbar and Hunter* (Baton Rouge: Louisiana State University Press, 2006), 31.

13. Pike to Wilkinson, 18 April 1806, *The Journals of Zebulon Montgomery Pike*, 1:268–69.

14. Pike to Daniel Bissell, 3 May 1806, *General Daniel Bissell Papers*, St. Louis Mercantile Library, University of Missouri–St. Louis; *Republican Star* (Easton), 21 October 1806.

15. Jefferson to Lewis, 20 June 1803, *Letters of the Lewis and Clark Expedition*, 61–66.

16. Jefferson to Comte de Volney, 11 February 1806, *Letters of the Lewis and Clark Expedition*, 1:291.

17. Jefferson to the House of Representatives, 19 February 1806, *Letters of the Lewis and Clark Expedition*, 1:298–300.

18. Marquis de Casa Calvo to Pedro Cevallos, 30 March 1804, *Letters of the Lewis and Clark Expedition*, 1:173–74; Nemesio Salcedo to Casa Calvo, 8 October 1805, *The Journals of Zebulon Pike*, 2:111–12; David J. Weber, *The Spanish Frontier in North America* (New Haven: Yale University Press, 1992), 279–82, 291–301.

19. *Eastern Argus* (Portland), 16 October 1806; *Massachusetts Spy* (Worcester), 28 July 1807; *Berkshire* [Mass.] *Reporter*, 8 August 1807; *United States' Gazette* (Philadelphia), 28 August 1807.

20. Ned Blackhawk, *Violence Over the Land: Indians and Empires in the Early American West* (Cambridge: Harvard University Press, 2006), 112–18; Kastor, *The Nation's Crucible*, 68–70.

21. For Burr's intentions, see Nancy Isenberg, *Fallen Founder: A Life of Aaron Burr* (New York: Viking, 2007), 272–365; Roger G. Kennedy, *Burr, Hamilton, and Jefferson: A Study in Character* (Oxford: Oxford University Press, 2000), 233–59; Lewis, *The American Union and the Problem of Neighborhood*, 31–34; Merrill D. Peterson, *Thomas Jefferson and the New Nation: A Biography* (Oxford: Oxford University Press, 1970).

22. Bradford Perkins, *Prologue to War: England and the United States, 1805–1812* (Berkeley: University of California Press, 1968); Burton Spivak, *Jefferson's English Crisis: Commerce, Embargo, and the Republican Revolution* (Charlottesville: University Press of Virginia, 1979).

23. Clark to Jefferson, 1 April 1805 (draft), *Letters of the Lewis and Clark Expedition*, 1:226; Clark to Jefferson, 3 April 1805, *Letters of the Lewis and Clark Expedition*, 1:230–31.

24. *Enquirer*, 11 April 1805; Pike to Bissell, 3 May 1806, *General Daniel Bissell Papers*, University of Missouri–St. Louis: St. Louis Mercantile Library; Pike to Wilkinson, 5 July 1807, *The Journals of Zebulon Pike*, 2:238.

25. Pike to Bissell, 3 May 1806, *The Journals of Zebulon Pike*, 1:274.

26. Flores, *Jefferson and Southwestern Exploration*, 309.

27. Berry et al., eds., *The Forgotten Expedition*, xxxii–xxxiii.

28. For details of territorial government, see Berkhoffer, "The Northwest Ordinance"; Cayton, *The Frontier Republic*; Kastor, *The Nation's Crucible*; Rothman, *Slave Country*.

29. For Madison's role in territorial government after the Louisiana Purchase, see Kastor, *The Nation's Crucible*.

30. Clark to Dearborn, 10 October 1806, *Letters of the Lewis and Clark Expedition*, 1:347.

31. Clark to the Citizens of Fincastle County, 8 January 1807, *Letters of the Lewis and Clark Expedition*, 1:359.

32. The best account of Clark's movements in 1806–07 are in Foley, *Wilderness Journey*, 154–57.

33. Clark to Jonathan Clark, 22 January 1807, *Dear Brother*, 119.

34. Crackel, *Mr. Jefferson's Army*, 111–15; William E. Foley, *The Genesis of Missouri: From Wilderness Outpost to Statehood* (Columbia: University of Missouri Press, 1989), 162–66.

35. *Journal of the Executive Proceedings of the Senate of the United States of America* (Washington: Duff Green, 1828), 2:53.

36. *Senate Executive Journal*, 2:54.

37. Clark to Edmund Clark, 5 March 1807, quoted in Foley, *Wilderness Journey*, 158; Skelton, *An American Profession of Arms*, 47–55.

38. *Senate Executive Journal*, 2:62.

39. Dearborn to Joseph Alston, 14 January 1807, *Letters of the Lewis and Clark Expedition*, 1:363–64. The appropriation followed a torturous path through Congress, only to end with approval but no official entry in the legislative record. For a detailed account, see Ambrose, *Undaunted Courage*, 413–15.

40. Dearborn to Pierre Chouteau, 3 March 1807, *The Territorial Papers of the United States*, ed. Clarence Edward Carter (Washington: Government Printing Office, 1934–75), 14:107–08.

41. Lewis to Clark, 15 March 1807, *Clark Family Collection*, box 11, folder 17.

42. Ambrose, *Undaunted Courage*, 421–30.

43. John Barrow, *An Account of Travels into the Interior of Southern Africa* (London: T. Cadell, Jun., and W. Davies, 1801); C. F. Volney, *A View of the Soil and Climate of the United States of America* . . . (Philadelphia: J. Conrad, 1804).

44. *National Intelligencer* (Washington), 14 March 1807, reprinted in *Letters of the Lewis and Clark Expedition*, 2:395.

45. Reprinted in *Letters of the Lewis and Clark Expedition*, 2:396.

46. *The Journals of the Lewis and Clark Expedition*, 345–46.

47. *National Intelligencer*, 14 March 1807; David McKeehan to Lewis, 7 April 1807, *Letters of the Lewis and Clark Expedition*, 2:399–407.

48. Jabez Jackson to Morse, 19 December 1806, *Morse Family Papers*, box 4, folder 109.

49. Manning and Loring to Morse, 31 December 1806, *Morse Family Papers*, box 4, folder 109.

50. Jedidiah Morse, *Geography Made Easy: Being an Abridgment of the American Universal Geography* (Boston: J. T. Buckingham for Thomas and Andrews, 1807), 260. For the identical language, see the 1806 edition by the same publisher.

51. Aaron Arrowsmith, *A Map of the United States of America* (New York, 1810), GMD, LOC; Nathaniel Atcheson, *Extract from Mitchell's map* (London: 1808), GMD, LOC; Nicholas King, *Map of the Red River in Louisiana from the Spanish Camp where the Exploring Party of the U.S. was met by the Spanish troops to where it enters the Mississippi, reduced from the protracted courses and corrected to the latitude* (Philadelphia: F. Shallus, 1806), GMD, LOC; P. Lapie, *Etats-Unis de L'Amérique Septentrionale* (Paris: Adam and Giraldon, 1810), GMD, LOC; Samuel Lewis and William Harrison, *A Map of the United States: Compiled Chiefly from the State Maps and other Authentic Information* (Philadelphia: Matthew Carey, 1809), GMD, LOC; John M'Culloch, *A Concise History of the United States: From the Discovery of America, till 1807: with a correct map of the United States* (Philadelphia: John M'Culloch, 1807); Carlton Osgood, *New Map of the United States of America Including art of Louisiana Drawn from the latest authorites* (Boston, 1806), GMD, LOC; Pierre Tardieu, *United States of Nth. America; carte des Etats-Unis de l'Amérique Septentrionale* (Paris, 1808), GMD, LOC.

52. Zadok Cramer, *The Navigator* (Zadok Cramer, 1806); id., *The Navigator: Containing Directions for Navigating the Monongahela, Allegheny, Ohio and Mississippi Rivers . . .* (Pittsburgh: Z. Cramer, 1808).

53. *The Travels of Capts. Lewis and Clarke: by Order of the Government of the United States, performed in the years 1804, 1805 and 1806, being upwards of three thousand miles, from St. Louis, by way of the Missouri and Columbia Rivers, to the Pacifick Ocean: containing an account of the Indian tribes, who inhabit the western part of the continent unexplored, and unknown before: with copious delineations of the manners, customs, religion, andc. of the Indians* (Philadelphia: Hubbard Lester, 1809).

54. Patrick Gass, *A Journal of the Voyages and Travels of a Corps of Discovery: Under the Command of Capt. Lewis and Capt. Clarke of the Army of the United States, from the Mouth of the River Missouri Through the Interior Parts of North America to the Pacific Ocean, during the years 1804, 1805 and 1806 . . .* (Pittsburgh: Zadok Cramer, 1807).

55. Zadok Cramer, *The Ohio and Mississippi Navigator . . .* (Pittsburgh: Zadok Cramer, 1802); id., *The Navigator* (1808); id., *The Navigator: Containing Directions for Navigating the Monongahela, Allegheny, Ohio, and Mississippi Rivers, with an ample account of these much admired waters . . .* (Pittsburgh: Cramer, Spear, and Eichbaum, 1811).

56. Cramer, *The Navigator* (1806).

57. Kastor, *The Nation's Crucible.*

58. Clark to Dearborn, 1 June 1807, *Territorial Papers of the United States*, 14:127.

59. Clark to Dearborn, 18 May 1807, *Territorial Papers of the United States*, 14:125.
60. Aron, *American Confluence*, 139–44; Jones, *William Clark and the Shaping of the West*, 165–68; Francis Paul Prucha, *The Sword of the Republic: The United States Army on the Frontier, 1783–1846* (New York: Macmillan, 1969), 98–102. The most recent and thorough analysis of Clark's Indian policy during this period is Buckley, *William Clark: Indian Diplomat*, 65–82.
61. Clark, draft letter to Dearborn, 8 June 1807, *Clark Family Collection*, box 11, folder 17.
62. Joan Cashin, *A Family Venture: Men and Women on the Southern Frontier* (Oxford: Oxford University Press, 1991).
63. John T. Jones to Clark, 13 June 1807, *Clark Family Collection*, box 11, folder 17.
64. There is no comprehensive collection of Clark's correspondence during this period. The largest and most revealing collection of his writings is in the following sources: *Clark Family Collection; Dear Brother; Territorial Papers of the United States*, vols. 13–15.
65. Clark, "A Rough Draught and Plan of the Fort near Fire Prairie," October 9, 1808, *Clark Family Collection*, box 11, folder 17; Kate L. Gregg, ed., *Westward with Dragoons: The Journal of William Clark on his Expedition to Establish Fort Osage, August 25 to September 22, 1808* (Fulton, Mo.: Ovid Bell Press, 1937).

CHAPTER 5. CAREERS

1. Charles Willson Peale to Rembrandt Peale, 17 November 1809, *Letters of the Lewis and Clark Expedition*, 2:469.
2. Peale to Jefferson, 24 December 1806, *Thomas Jefferson Papers*; Peale to Jefferson, 10 February 1807, *Letters of the Lewis and Clark Expedition*, 2:373.
3. Paul R. Cutright, "Lewis and Clark: Portraits and Portraitists," *Montana: The Magazine of Western History* 19 (1969), 38.
4. Cayton, *The Frontier Republic*, 70–80; id., *Frontier Indiana* (Bloomington: Indiana University Press, 1996), 194, 236–39; Kastor, *The Nation's Crucible*, 149–50; John Wunder, "American Law and Order Comes to the Mississippi Territory: The Making of Sargent's Code, 1798–1800," *Journal of Mississippi History* 38 (1976), 131–55.
5. Studies of Lewis surged in the years between the immense success of Stephen Ambrose's *Undaunted Courage* and the Lewis and Clark Bicentennial. Written for academic and public audiences alike, many of these studies have as their central concern the apparent contrast between Lewis's success as a leader of the expedition and his political problems as territorial governor. Most of this work has explained those problems in biographical terms rather than by considering the particular notions of leadership and behavior that informed the political culture of the early republic. My approach to Lewis's behavior and his sense of public display emerges from recent scholarship on political culture focusing on notions of character and reputation in the early republic. See Joanne B. Freeman, "Dueling as Politics: Rein-

terpreting the Burr–Hamilton Duel," *William and Mary Quarterly*, 3d. ser., 53 (1996); Jan Lewis, "'The Blessings of Domestic Society': Thomas Jefferson's Family and the Transformation of American Politics," in *Jeffersonian Legacies*, ed. Peter S. Onuf (Charlottesville: University Press of Virginia, 1993), 109–46; Trees, "Private Correspondence for the Public Good."

6. Aron, *American Confluence*, 142–44; Buckley, *William Clark: Indian Diplomat*, 77–78; Jones, *William Clark and the Shaping of the West*, 164–70; Kathleen DuVal, *The Native Ground: Indians and Colonists in the Heart of the Continent* (Philadelphia: University of Pennsylvania Press, 2006), 202–03.

7. Lewis to Madison, 28 June 1807, *Territorial Papers of the United States*, 14:131.

8. Lewis to Madison, 27 August 1809, *Territorial Papers of the United States*, 14:293.

9. Lewis to William Eustis, 18 August 1809, *Territorial Papers of the United States*, 14:292.

10. The particulars of Lewis's death remain a mainstay of every biographical treatment and have generated a small subfield of people investigating the specific questions of why Lewis might have committed suicide or who might have attempted to murder him. The most thorough discussion of the details surrounding Lewis's death and the competing explanations that surround it are in John D. W. Guice et al., *By His Own Hand? The Mysterious Death of Meriwether Lewis* (Norman: University of Oklahoma Press, 2006).

11. Clark to Jonathan Clark, 12 January 1810, *Dear Brother*, 233–34.

12. Clark to Jonathan Clark, 30 October 1809, *Dear Brother*, 224; Clark to Jonathan Clark, 8 November 1809, *Dear Brother*, 226.

13. John Conrad to Jefferson, 13 November 1809, *Letters of the Lewis and Clark Expedition*, 2:469.

14. Jefferson to Conrad, 13 November 1809, *Letters of the Lewis and Clark Expedition*, 2:474–75.

15. Peale to Peale, 17 November 1809, *Letters of the Lewis and Clark Expedition*, 2:469.

16. Jefferson to C. and A. Conrad and Co., 23 November 1809, *Letters of the Lewis and Clark Expedition*, 2:475.

17. Clark to Jonathan Clark, 12 January 1810, *Dear Brother*, 233.

18. *Senate Executive Journal*, 2:86, 151.

19. Pike to Wilkinson, 24 October 1806, *The Journals of Zebulon Pike*, 2:157; Clark to Dearborn, 18 May 1807, 14:122–25.

20. *Orleans Gazette* (New Orleans), 15 September 1809.

21. Pike to Conrad, 1 September 1809, *The Journals of Zebulon Pike*, 2:358–59.

22. Zebulon Montgomery Pike, *An Account of Expeditions to the Sources of the Mississippi: and through the western parts of Louisiana to the sources of the Arkansaw, Kans, La Platte, and Pierre Jaun Rivers* . . . (Philadelphia: C. and A. Conrad, 1810); Zebulon Montgomery Pike and Gouverneur Kemble Warren, *Atlas Accompanying an Account of Expeditions to the Sources of the Mississippi and Through the western parts of Louisiana* . . . (Philadelphia: C. and A. Conrad, 1810).

23. Leonard Covington to Eustis, 4 December 1810, *Letters Received by the Secretary of War: Registered Series*, reel 35, C-276; Covington to Eustis, 12 December 1810, *Letters Received, Registered Series*, reel 35, C-303; Pike to Eustis, 19 January 1811, *Letters Received, Registered Series*, reel 39, P-212; Pike to Eustis, 19 January 1811, *Letters Received, Registered Series*, reel 39, P-216; Fulwar Skipwith, articles of agreement for surrendering West Florida to the United States, 3 March 1811, *Miscellaneous Letters of the Department of State*, reel 24.

24. George Sibley to Amos Stoddard, 2 April 1812, *George Champlain Sibley Collection*, MoHist, box 1.

25. Cayton, *Frontier Indiana*, 222–25; Dowd, *A Spirited Resistance*, 139–41.

26. Alexander von Humboldt and Aimé Jacques Alexandre Goujaud Bonpland, *Voyage de Humboldt et Bonpland; voyage aux régions équinoxiales du nouveau continent* (Hildesheim, N.Y.: G. Olms, 1971).

27. Von Humboldt eventually included this map in an extensive atlas published in Germany in 1810 and in France the following year. For recent considerations of Humboldt's work, see Chunglin Kwa, "Alexander von Humboldt's Invention of the Natural Landscape," *European Legacy* 10 (2005), 149–62; Aaron Sachs, *The Humboldt Current: Nineteenth-Century Exploration and the Roots of American Environmentalism* (New York: Viking, 2006).

28. David Bailie Warden to Madison, 2 December 1811, *The Papers of James Madison: Presidential Series*, ed. Robert A. Rutland et al. (Charlottesville: University Press of Virginia, 1986), 4:48.

29. Alexander von Humboldt to Jefferson, 20 December 1811, *The Journals of Zebulon Pike*, 2:377.

30. Quoted in John Upton Terrell, *Zebulon Pike: The Life and Times of an Adventurer* (New York: Weybright and Talley, 1968), 233.

31. *The Thomas Jefferson Papers* collection at the Library of Congress includes the final page of this letter. As he so often did with his incoming correspondence, Jefferson scribbled both the date of the letter and the date of its arrival. As Jefferson wrote, "Humboldt Baron de Paris Dec.20.11. recd Jul.31.13."

32. Jefferson to Humboldt, 6 December 1813, *The Journals of Zebulon Pike*, 2:387–88.

33. *Senate Executive Journal*, 2:159.

34. Memorandum of Lewis's personal effects, 23 November 1809, *Letters of the Lewis and Clark Expedition*, 2:470–72.

35. *Letter from the Secretary of the Treasury transmitting a report prepared in obedience to a resolution of the first instant, requesting information touching any settlement contrary to law, on the public lands in the county of Madison in Mississippi territory* (Washington: Roger Chew Weightman, 1809).

36. Malcolm J. Rohrbough, *The Land Office Busines: The Settlement and Administration of American Public Lands, 1789–1837* (New York: Oxford University Press, 1968), 109–36.

37. Freeman to Josiah Meigs, 7 July 1817, *Territorial Papers of the United States*, 18:116.

38. Meigs to Freeman, 15 May 1816, *Territorial Papers of the United States*, 6:684–85; Israel Pickens to Freeman, 18 August 1817, *Territorial Papers of the United States*, 6:799.

39. Bradley, *Map of the United States (1796)*; Abraham Bradley, *Map of the United States: exhibiting the post-roads, the situations, connexions and distances of the post-offices, stage roads, counties and principal rivers* (Philadelphia: Caldcleugh and Thomas, 1804), GMD, LOC; Abraham Bradley, *Map of the United States: exhibiting the post-roads, the situations, connexions and distances of the post-offices, stage roads, counties and principal rivers* (Philadelphia: Caldcleugh and Thomas, 1812), David Rumsey Map Collection, http://www.davidrumsey.com; Abraham Bradley, *Map of the United States Intending Chiefly to Exhibit the Post Roads and Distances (1836)*, Cartographic Collection, RG 28, Library Map Collection, NARA.

40. Maxfield Ludlow, *A Map of the State of Louisiana with part of the state of Mississippi and Alabama Territory (1815)*, Map Collection, Sterling Memorial Library, Yale University.

41. Maxfield Ludlow, *To the Public* (Natchez, 1817).

42. Maxfield Ludlow, *Prospectus for publishing by subscription A map of the state of Louisiana, with a part of the State of Mississippi and Alabama Territory (1810)*.

43. Maxfield Ludlow, *A Map of the State of Louisiana . . .* (Charles W. Warnick, J.F., 1817), GMD, LOC.

44. *The Public Statutes at Large of the United States of America* (Boston: Charles C. Little and James Brown, 1845), 3:263.

45. Jefferson to Madison, 30 November 1809, *The Papers of James Madison: Presidential Series*, 2:95; Madison to Jefferson, 11 December 1809, *The Papers of James Madison: Presidential Series*, 2:95; William Cocke to Madison, 30 October 1809, *The Papers of James Madison: Presidential Series*, 2:51. See also John Dawson to Madison, 16 November 1809, *The Papers of James Madison: Presidential Series*, 2:71; James Taylor to Madison, 23 November 1809, *The Papers of James Madison: Presidential Series*, 2:75–76.

46. Clark to Jonathan Clark, 12 January 1810, *Dear Brother*, 233–34.

47. Gough, "Officering the American Army, 1798," 466.

48. Much like Jefferson's first secretary, Meriwether Lewis, Coles suffered from an unpredictable temper. In January 1810 Coles attacked Congressman Roger Nelson of Maryland, who had "attacked [Coles's] character." Coles soon left the office. His successor, his brother Edward, would prove more levelheaded and eventually become one of Madison's closest confidants. See Isaac Coles to Jefferson, 5 January 1810, *Letters of the Lewis and Clark Expedition*, 2:486–87; *The Papers of James Madison: Presidential Series*, 2:151 n1–3; Drew R. McCoy, *The Last of the Fathers: James Madison and the Republican Legacy* (Cambridge: Cambridge University Press, 1988), 157–61.

49. Joel Barlow to Benjamin Rush, 11 January 1810, *Letters of the Lewis and Clark Expedition*, 2:488.

50. Clark to William Meriwether, 26 January 1810, *Letters of the Lewis and Clark Expedition*, 2:490–91; Anya Jabour, *Marriage in the Early Republic: Elizabeth and William Wirt and the Companionate Ideal* (Baltimore: Johns Hopkins University Press, 1998), 59–62, 84–86.

51. For the gendered nature of reading habits, see Cathy N. Davidson, *Revolution and the Word: The Rise of the Novel in America* (New York: Oxford University Press, 1986), 45–50, 91–98. For the attitudes and identities of writers, see Catherine O'Donnell Kaplan, *Men of Letters in the Early Republic: Cultivating Forums of Citizenship* (Chapel Hill: Published for the Omohundro Institute of Early American History and Culture, Williamsburg, Virginia, by the University of North Carolina Press, 2008); Bryan Waterman, *Republic of Intellect: The Friendly Club of New York City and the Making of American Literature* (Baltimore: Johns Hopkins University Press, 2007).

52. For the role of letter writing, see Michael Warner, *The Letters of the Republic: Publication and the Public Sphere in Eighteenth-Century America* (Cambridge: Harvard University Press, 1990); Trees, "Private Correspondence for the Public Good," 217–55.

53. Nicholas Biddle to Clark, 3 and 17 March 1810, *Letters of the Lewis and Clark Expedition*, 2:495–96. Overshadowed in literary circles by writers of far greater talent and significance just as he was overshadowed in politics by his nemesis, Andrew Jackson, Biddle remains the subject of limited analysis. The only substantive biography of him is now half a century old. See Thomas P. Govan, *Nicholas Biddle, Nationalist and Public Banker, 1786–1844* (Chicago: University of Chicago Press, 1959).

54. Clark to Jonathan Clark, 8 March 1810, *Dear Brother*, 236.

55. Biddle to Warden, 7 July 1810, *Letters of the Lewis and Clark Expedition*, 2:555.

56. Biddle to Monroe, 6 June 1811, *Letters of the Lewis and Clark Expedition*, 2:567.

57. Biddle to Clark, 7 July 1810, *Letters of the Lewis and Clark Expedition*, 2:550–54.

58. Clark to Biddle, 20 December 1810, *Letters of the Lewis and Clark Expedition*, 2:565.

59. Allen, *Lewis and Clark and the Image of the American Northwest*; Gilman, *Lewis and Clark: Across the Divide*, 138–63; Preston, "The Accuracy of the Astronomical Observations of Lewis and Clark," 168–91; Seymour I. Schwartz and Ralph E. Ehrenberg, *The Mapping of America* (Edison, N.J.: Wellfleet, 2001), 227–28.

60. Biddle to Clark, 8 July 1811, *Letters of the Lewis and Clark Expedition*, 2:569.

61. Clark to Biddle, 15 August 1811, *Letters of the Lewis and Clark Expedition*, 2:571–72.

62. Richard Alton Erney, *The Public Life of Henry Dearborn* (New York: Arno Press, 1979), 269–328; J. C. A. Stagg, *Mr. Madison's War: Politics, Diplomacy, and Warfare in the Early American Republic, 1783–1830* (Princeton: Princeton University Press, 1983), 165–67, 284–86.

63. *Senate Executive Journal*, 2:164–66; Eustis to Clark, 8 March 1811, 14:443.

64. Cutright, "Lewis and Clark: Portraits and Portraitists," 41–49. Carolyn Gilman has offered the most revealing analysis of the way portraits and clothing informed

Clark's efforts at public self-creation. See Gilman, *Lewis and Clark: Across the Divide*, 206–08.

65. *Statutes at Large*, 2:743.

66. Biddle to Clark, 4 July 1812, *Letters of the Lewis and Clark Expedition*, 2:577.

67. Clark to Biddle, 5 September 1812, *Papers of Nicholas Biddle* (Washington: Library of Congress Microfilm Collection).

68. *Senate Executive Journal*, 2:349.

69. William Clark, *Plan of the N.W. Frontier* (1813), GMD, LOC.

70. Clark to Monroe, 31 July 1813, *Territorial Papers of the United States*, 14:691.

71. *[Map of the region south and west of Chicago and Fort Dearborn]* (ca. 1811), GMD, LOC.

72. Biddle to Clark, 23 March 1814, *Biddle Papers*.

73. Clark to Biddle, 16 September 1814, *Letters of the Lewis and Clark Expedition*, 599–600; Govan, *Nicholas Biddle*, 42–44.

74. The most detailed and revealing evaluation of the map's precision is Allen, *Lewis and Clark and the Image of the American Northwest*, 382–94.

75. Biddle to Clark, 12 March 1815, *Letters of the Lewis and Clark Expedition*, 2:604–05; Biddle to Clark, 29 May 1816, *Letters of the Lewis and Clark Expedition*, 2:613–15.

76. Aron, *American Confluence*, 159; Buckley, *William Clark: Indian Diplomat*, 110–11; Jones, *William Clark and the Shaping of the West*, 226–31.

77. Governor's commission, 16 June 1816, *Clark Family Collection*, box 12, folder 10.

CHAPTER 6. BOOKS

1. Jefferson to Clark, 6 September 1816, *Thomas Jefferson Papers*.

2. Jefferson to C. and A. Conrad, 24 April 1811, *The Papers of Thomas Jefferson: Retirement Series*, ed. J. Jefferson Looney (Princeton: Princeton University Press, 2004), 3:582.

3. Clark to Jefferson, 10 October 1816, *Letters of the Lewis and Clark Expedition*, 2:623–25.

4. Biddle to Clark, 21 October 1816, *Letters of the Lewis and Clark Expedition*, 2:627. See also Mathew Carey to Biddle, 26 December 1816, *Letters of the Lewis and Clark Expedition*, 2:627.

5. The West as a region and western travel as an American experience have long been a central concern of American literature. Equally important, they have long been a concern to scholars of American literature. A few recent examples, many of which provide more thorough overviews of scholarly interpretations, include Kathleen Boardman and Gioia Woods, eds., *Western Subjects: Autobiographical Writing in the North American West* (Salt Lake City: University of Utah Press, 2004); Reginald Dyck and Cheli Ruetter, eds., *Crisscrossing Borders in Literature of the American West* (New York: Palgrave Macmillan, 2009); Martin Padget, "Claiming, Corrupt-

ing, Contesting: Reconsidering 'The West' in Western American Literature," _American Literary History_ 10 (1998), 378–92; Susan J. Rosowski, _Birthing a Nation: Gender, Creativity, and the West in American Literature_ (Lincoln: University of Nebraska Press, 1999); John Seelye, "Captives, Captains, Cowboys, Indians: Frames of Reference and the American West," _American Literary History_ 7 (1995), 304–19; Sara L. Spurgeon, _Exploding the Western: Myths of Empire on the Postmodern Frontier_ (College Station: Texas A&M University Press, 2005); John L. Thomas, _A Country in the Mind: Wallace Stegner, Bernard De Voto, History, and the American Land_ (New York: Routledge, 2000).

6. _Message from the President of the United States, communicating discoveries made in exploring the Missouri, Red River, and Washita, by Captains Lewis and Clark, Doctor Sibley, and Mr. Dunbar; with a statistical account of the countries adjacent. February 19, 1806_ (Washington: A. and G. Way, 1806); _An Account of the Red River, in Louisiana, Drawn up from the Returns of Messrs. Freeman and Custis to the War Office of the United States, who Explored the Same, in the year of 1806_ (Washington, 1806); Gass, _A Journal of the Voyages and Travels of a Corps of Discovery; An Account of a Voyage up the Mississippi River: From St. Louis to its Source, Made Under Orders of the War Department, by Lieut. Pike, of the United States Army, in the years 1805 and 1806_ (Washington, 1807); Pike, _An Account of Expeditions; History of the Expedition under the Command of Captains Lewis and Clark, to the sources of the Missouri, thence across the Rocky Mountains and down the river Columbia to the Pacific Ocean: Performed during the years 1804–5–6 by order of the government of the United States_ (Philadelphia: Bradford and Inskeep, 1814).

7. Unlike _History of the Expedition,_ in which the progression from Clark's Master Map to the published _Map of Lewis and Clark's Track_ is relatively clear, ascertaining the provenance of Pike's maps is frustrating in the extreme. Anthony Nau, himself a shadowy figure whom James Wilkinson apparently kept as his personal military mapmaker, produced one of Pike's maps. Nicholas King produced another. But when and how these maps came into being remains a question that even Donald Jackson, the gifted scholar of Jefferson's expeditions and the most thorough analyst of Pike's materials, could not answer. _The Journals of Zebulon Pike,_ 2:451–64.

8. William E. Foley, "Lewis and Clark's American Travels: The View from Britain," _Western Historical Quarterly_ 34 (2003), 313–24.

9. Clark to Benjamin Smith Barton, 28 May 1810, _Papers Regarding the Lewis and Clark Expedition, 1803–1816,_ Albert and Shirley Small Special Collections Library, University of Virginia; Clark to Biddle, 24 January 1811, _Letters of the Lewis and Clark Expedition,_ 2:565–66; Clark to George Shannon, 20 April 1811, _Letters of the Lewis and Clark Expedition,_ 2:566; Clark to Biddle, 15 August 1811, _Letters of the Lewis and Clark Expedition,_ 2:571; Clark to Biddle, 16 October 1816, _Letters of the Lewis and Clark Expedition,_ 2:626.

10. Pike to Conrad, 7 June 1812, _The Journals of Zebulon Pike,_ 2:378–79.

11. The problematic notion of authorship has been the subject of intense study among literary critics. Much of this work has sought to problematize the notion that a single writer ever really controls his or her text given the broad cultural influences that determine how people write. But the case of these expedition narratives suggests the more practical and explicit limitations of authorship, since the books and maps of western exploration were the product of numerous individuals whose specific actions remain elusive. For studies of authorship in the early republic, see Hesford, "'Do You Know the Author?'" 239–48; Jackson, "Jedidiah Morse and the Transformation of Print Culture in New England, 1784–1826," 2–31; Rice, *The Transformation of Authorship in America.*

12. *History of the Expedition,* 1:1.

13. The accounts were never entirely silent. *History of the Expedition* discussed generally amicable relations among the explorers, punctuated by periods of restive discontent during the winters of 1804–05 and 1805–06. Likewise, Gass's *Journal* provides glimpses of life among the enlisted men who accompanied Lewis and Clark. Finally, Pike's two accounts offer passing celebrations of the camaraderie among the men he commanded and occasional commentary on the suffering of men who got lost. Nonetheless, these passages are the exception rather than the rule and prove particularly unsatisfying to modern readers hoping to obtain glimpses into the private lives and unguarded moments of Americans engaged in exploration.

14. For the particular focus on these passages, see Ambrose, *Undaunted Courage,* 279–81; Furtwangler, *Acts of Discovery,* 23–25, 131–33; Greenfield, *Narrating Discovery,* 84–112; Lawson-Peebles, *Landscape and Written Expression in Revolutionary America,* 205–07.

15. In the two centuries that have followed, researchers of all sorts have sifted through that commentary with gusto. Given the challenges of studying American history, the records of western exploration have provided morsels of information. Scholars have long acknowledged the cultural lenses that distorted the explorers' abilities to understand Indians, but even those limitations have proven useful when it comes to understanding the ways in which Europeans and Euro-Americans understood race. For selected scholarship that has used these travel narratives as a means to research Indians, see Gilman, *Lewis and Clark: Across the Divide*; Josephy and Jaffe, eds., *Lewis and Clark Through Indian Eyes*; Ronda, *Lewis and Clark Among the Indians*; Elizabeth Vibert, *Traders' Tales: Narratives of Cultural Encounters in the Columbia Plateau, 1807–1846* (Norman: University of Oklahoma Press, 1997).

16. Robert E. Bieder, *Science Encounters the Indian, 1820–1880: The Early Years of American Ethnology* (Norman: University of Oklahoma Press, 1986), 12–15; Joanna Brooks, *American Lazarus: Religion and the Rise of African-American and Native American Literatures* (Oxford: Oxford University Press, 2003), 56–60; Amy DeRogatis, *Moral Geography: Maps, Missionaries, and the American Frontier* (New York: Columbia University Press, 2003); Parrish, *American Curiosity*; Sheehan, *Seeds of*

Extinction; Wallace, *Jefferson and the Indians*, 133–40. These selections from the early republic form part of a much larger scholarly literature covering the Americas more generally from the moment of contact through the present day. Eventually embodied in a single phrase—the Noble Savage—the sentimentalization of Indians in the early republic was part of a larger literary project that complemented European and later Euro-American policies of conquest.

17. *History of the Expedition*, 1:129.

18. Ibid., 1:96, 176–77, 372.

19. The pastoral qualities of the American West have long concerned scholars, but the best analysis of the West as a garden in the work of western explorers remains Allen, *Lewis and Clark and the Image of the American Northwest*.

20. *History of the Expedition*, 1:216.

21. Ibid., 1:226, 229.

22. *An Account of the Red River*, 9.

23. *History of the Expedition*, 1:197.

24. Scholars have long situated environmental conclusions at the center of their analysis of American attitudes toward the West. Over fifty years ago, Henry Nash Smith concluded that Americans were hesitant to celebrate an arid landscape. More recently, Stephanie LeMenager has emphasized how commercial and literary visions combined to celebrate navigable waterways at the expense of arid plains. See Smith, *Virgin Land*; LeMenager, *Manifest and Other Destinies*; Conevery Bolton Valencius, *The Health of the Country: How American Settlers Understood Themselves and Their land* (New York: Basic Books, 2002).

25. Pike, *An Account of Expeditions*, appendix to part 2, page 8.

26. *An Account of the Red River*, 12–14. Despite repeated efforts by governments and private individuals to achieve its destruction, the Great Raft would restrict Red River commerce well into the nineteenth century. Only the development of steam power enabled Henry Miller Shreve to construct specially designed boats that could ascend the Red River and extract the logs constituting the Great Raft. The first major town above the Great Raft, Shreveport, Louisiana, bears his name. See Peter Zachary Cohen, *The Great Red River Raft* (Niles, Ill.: A. Whitman, 1984); Flores, *Jefferson and Southwestern Exploration*, 135 n22.

27. *History of the Expedition*, 1:260–61.

28. Pike, *An Account of Expeditions*, 1:92.

29. Ibid., 1:42.

30. Much of the scholarship on western landscape description has claimed that western explorers responded to these aesthetic concerns for the sublime, the picturesque, and the beautiful. For example, see Percy G. Adams, *Travel Literature and the Evolution of the Novel* (Lexington: University Press of Kentucky, 1983); Furtwangler, *Acts of Discovery*, 23–51, 192–200; Lawson-Peebles, *Landscape and Written Expression in Revolutionary America*; Andrew Wilton and T. J. Barringer, *American Sublime: Landscape Painting in the United States, 1820–1880* (Princeton:

Princeton University Press, 2002), 11, 57–58. Yet almost all the examples come from Meriwether Lewis, and those references are from entries in his manuscript that Biddle either removed or extensively edited.

31. *History of the Expedition*, 2:242.

32. Ibid., 1:208.

33. A *Map of Lewis and Clark's Track, Across the Western Portion of North America from the Mississippi to the Pacific Ocean* . . . (Philadelphia: Bradford and Inskeep, 1814), GMD, LOC.

34. *Palladium* (Frankfort), 9 October 1806. The recipient of the letter does not appear in the newspaper article duplicating Clark's letter. Scholars have concluded it was most likely George Rogers Clark.

35. Pike, *An Account of Expeditions*, 66. Pike's claim actually proved incorrect, since his expedition failed to identify the actual headwaters of the Mississippi.

36. Pike, *An Account of Expeditions*, 1:163–64.

37. For discussions of letter writing and politics, see Andrew Burstein, *The Inner Jefferson: Portrait of a Grieving Optimist* (Charlottesville: University Press of Virginia, 1995); Trees, "Private Correspondence for the Public Good," 217–55; Warner, *The Letters of the Republic*. The discussion of gender and writing remains a problematic subject. Scholars have often taken for granted that men and women wrote differently. This remained the case in large part because even as the call for a greater attention to women's experiences challenged fundamental assumptions about the past, much of that work began by discussing different themes in women's writing, assuming that those differences reflected very real differences of opinion and experience. More recently, scholars have problematized this work by exploring the way in which gendered distinctions in writing were themselves products of the social construction of gender. This proved particularly powerful on matters of sentiment, with women believing it was appropriate to write about feelings while men considered it appropriate to write about action.

38. *An Account of the Red River*, 3.

39. Paul Allen to Jefferson, 18 August 1813, *Thomas Jefferson Papers*.

40. Jefferson to Allen, 20 August 1813, *Thomas Jefferson Papers*.

41. Mason Locke Weems, *A History of the Life and Death, Virtues and Exploits of General George Washington* (Philadelphia: John Bioren, 1800); Scott E. Casper, *Constructing American Lives: Biography and Culture in Nineteenth-Century America* (Chapel Hill: University of North Carolina Press, 1999), 67–79.

42. *History of the Expedition*, viii.

43. Ibid., xii.

44. Ibid., ix–xi; Gordon Wood, "Interests and Disinterestedness in the Making of the Constitution," in *Beyond Confederation: Origins of the Constitution and American National Identity*, ed. Richard R. Beeman et al. (Chapel Hill: University of North Carolina Press, 1987), 69–112.

45. The way subsequent biographers addressed Lewis's life as well as his death is the sub-

ject of Megan Lindsay, "Of Interpretations Unlimited: Meriwether Lewis and American Collective Memory" (Honors Thesis, Washington University in St. Louis, 2003).

46. *History of the Expedition*, xx.

47. Ibid., xxi.

48. Ibid., xxi.

49. Ibid., xxii–xxiii.

50. Clark to Biddle, 28 December 1816, *Letters of the Lewis and Clark Expedition*, 2:629. The original letter is dated 1817, but Donald Jackson made the convincing case that the date is most likely inaccurate. The letter may indeed have been completed in 1816 but actually signed and dated in 1817, which may well account for an inadvertent error.

51. Clark to Jefferson, 1 February 1817, *Letters of the Lewis and Clark Expedition*, 2:630.

CHAPTER 7. RETURN TO THE WEST

1. Mary Margaret Clark to Clark, 12 September 1821, *Clark Family Collection*, box 13, folder 8.

2. Clark to William Crawford, 30 September 1815, *Territorial Papers of the United States*, 15:177.

3. For Clark's efforts to secure federal patronage for one of these boys, Benjamin O'Fallon, see Monroe to Clark, 11 March 1816, *Clark Family Collection*, box 12, folder 9; Clark to John C. Calhoun, 24 May 1818, *The Papers of John C. Calhoun*, ed. Robert L. Meriwether et al. (Columbia: University of South Carolina Press, 1959), 2:306–08.

4. W. Dale Nelson, *Interpreters with Lewis and Clark: The Story of Sacagawea and Toussaint Charbonneau* (Denton: University of North Texas Press, 2003), 70–80.

5. Clark to Calhoun, October 1818, *Territorial Papers of the United States*, 15:454.

6. Clark to Alexander Dallas, 28 August 1817, *Territorial Papers of the United States*, 15:301. See also Clark to George Graham, 15 May 1817, *Territorial Papers of the United States*, 15:260–61.

7. Historians have long treated the Missouri Crisis as a pivotal moment in the nation's history, but it has rarely been the subject of focused study. The two book-length studies are Glover Moore, *The Missouri Controversy, 1819–1821* (Lexington: University of Kentucky Press, 1954); Robert Pierce Forbes, *The Missouri Compromise and Its Aftermath: Slavery and the Meaning of America* (Chapel Hill: University of North Carolina Press, 2007).

8. Robert B. Betts, *In Search of York: The Slave Who Went to the Pacific with Lewis and Clark* (Boulder: Colorado Associated University Press, 1985).

9. Herbert Aptheker, *American Negro Slave Revolts* (New York: International Publishers, 1974); Rothman, *Slave Country*.

10. Gregg Cantrell, *Stephen F. Austin, Empresario of Texas* (New Haven: Yale University Press, 1999), 55–62, 76–85.

11. Foley, *Wilderness Journey*, 219–20.
12. William Foley has written two superb overviews of the first elections in the state of Missouri. See Foley, *The Genesis of Missouri*, 283–302; Foley, *Wilderness Journey*, 219–25. The shift to an increasingly democratic political culture is the subject of a vast scholarly literature that has dominated the discussion of the early republic and the antebellum era for nearly a generation. For selected examples of the work discussing the move from republican to democratic political styles, see Kenneth Cmiel, *Democratic Eloquence: The Fight for Popular Speech in Nineteenth-Century America* (New York: W. Morrow, 1990); Daniel Walker Howe, *What Hath God Wrought: The Transformation of America, 1815–1848* (Oxford: Oxford University Press, 2007), 282–84; Taylor, *William Cooper's Town*, 235–79; Wood, "Interests and Disinterestedness," 69–112; id., Wood, *The Radicalism of the American Revolution* (New York: Knopf, 1992).
13. Foley, *Wilderness Journey*, 224.
14. John Scott to John Quincy Adams, 27 February 1821, *Territorial Papers of the United States*, 15:705.
15. Kastor, *The Nation's Crucible*, 149–52, 223–24; Owens, *Mr. Jefferson's Hammer*, 247–50.
16. Foley, *Wilderness Journey*, 175–79, 227.
17. David Kaser, *Messrs. Carey and Lea of Philadelphia: A Study in the History of the Booktrade* (Philadelphia: University of Pennsylvania Press, 1957), 20–34.
18. Edwin James, *Account of an Expedition from Pittsburgh to the Rocky Mountains: Performed in the Years 1819 and '20, by Order of the Hon. J. C. Calhoun, Sec'y of War, Under the Command of Major Stephen H. Long* . . . (Philadelphia: H. C. Carey and I. Lea, 1822), 161–62.
19. James, *Account of an Expedition from Pittsburgh to the Rocky Mountains*, 101–03.
20. Stephen H. Long to Calhoun, 20 April 1819, *Papers of John C. Calhoun*, 4:31–33. See also Long to Calhoun, 24 December 1818, *Papers of John C. Calhoun*, 3:422–24.
21. Henry Rowe Schoolcraft, *A View of the Lead Mines of Missouri* . . . (New York: Charles Wiley, 1819); id., *Journal of a Tour into the Interior of Missouri and Arkansaw* (London: Sir R. Phillips, 1821); id., *Narrative Journal of Travels through the Northwestern Regions of the United States* . . . (Albany: E. and E. Hosford, 1821); id., *Travels in the Central Portions of the Mississippi Valley* . . . (New York: Collins and Hannay, 1825); id., *Narrative of an Expedition Through the Upper Mississippi to Itasca Lake* . . . (New York: Harper, 1834); id., *The Rise of the West, or A prospect of the Mississippi Valley: A poem* (New York: W. Applegate, 1841).
22. Valencius, *The Health of the Country*.
23. H. M. Brackenridge, *Views of Louisiana: Together with a Journal of a Voyage up the Missouri River, in 1811* (Pittsburgh: Cramer, Spear, and Eichbaum, 1814); Amos Stoddard, *Sketches, Historical and Descriptive, of Louisiana* (Philadelphia: Mathew Carey, 1812).

24. James, *Account of an Expedition from Pittsburgh to the Rocky Mountains*; Thomas Say, *American Entomology, or Descriptions of the Insects of North America . . .* (Philadelphia: S. A. Mitchell, 1824); Harry B. Weiss and Grace M. Weiss, *Thomas Say, Early American Naturalist* (Springfield, Ill.: C. C. Thomas, 1931).

25. Valencius, *The Health of the Country*.

26. Andrew Miller, *New States and Territories, or, The Ohio, Indiana, Illinois, Michigan, North-western, Missouri, Louisiana, Mississippi and Alabama, in their real characters, in 1818* (1819).

27. John Bradbury, *Travels in the Interior of America, in the years 1809, 1810, and 1811 . . .* (Liverpool: Sherwood Neely and Jones, 1817), 317.

28. William Darby, *A Tour from the city of New-York, to Detroit, in the Michigan territory, made between the 2d of May and the 22d of September, 1818 . . .* (New York: Kirk and Mercein, 1819), 188.

29. Richard M. Clokey, *William H. Ashley: Enterprise and Politics in the Trans-Mississippi West* (Norman: University of Oklahoma Press, 1980); Jay Gitlin, *The Bourgeois Frontier: French Towns, French Traders, and American Expansion* (New Haven: Yale University Press, 2009); William R. Nester, *From Mountain Man to Millionaire: The "Bold and Dashing Life" of Robert Campbell* (Columbia: University of Missouri Press, 1999), 13–81; Ronda, *Astoria and Empire*; Tanis C. Thorne, *The Many Hands of My Relations: French and Indians on the Lower Missouri* (Columbia: University of Missouri Press, 1996), 177–208; David J. Wishart, *The Fur Trade of the American West, 1807–1840: A Geographical Synthesis* (Lincoln: University of Nebraska Press, 1992).

30. Richard Rhodes, *John James Audubon: The Making of an American* (New York: Alfred A. Knopf, 2004), 148–49; Michael L. Tate, *The Frontier Army in the Settlement of the West* (Norman: University of Oklahoma Press, 1999), 3–4.

31. For the role of Seymour and Peale, see Kenneth Haltman, *Looking Close and Seeing Far: Samuel Seymour, Titian Ramsay Peale, and the Art of the Long Expedition, 1818–1823* (University Park: Pennsylvania State University Press, 2008); Gary Allen Hood, *After Lewis and Clark: The Forces of Change, 1806–1871* (Tulsa: Gilcrease Museum, 2006).

32. Nobles, "Straight Lines and Stability," 9–35.

33. Lewis, *The American Union and the Problem of Neighborhood*, 134–36; Lynn H. Parsons, *John Quincy Adams* (Madison: Madison House, 1998), 159–63; William Earl Weeks, *John Quincy Adams and American Global Empire* (Lexington: University Press of Kentucky, 1992), 191–93.

34. Ronda, *Astoria and Empire*, 310–15.

35. Catharine Van Cortlandt Mathews, *Andrew Ellicott, His Life and Letters* (New York: Grafton Press, 1908), 227–48.

36. Rohrbough, *The Land Office Business*, 109–36; Frank N. Schubert, *The Nation Builders: A Sesquicentennial History of the Corps of Topographical Engineers, 1838–1863* (Washington: U.S. Army Corps of Engineers, 1988), 3–26. For selected ex-

amples of western survey maps commissioned by the federal government, see William Rector, *Sketch of the western half of the continent of North America between latitudes 35° and 52° N.; originally drawn under the inspection of William Rector, U.S. Surveyor for Missouri., and Illinois, and by him presented to the General Land office, January 21, 1818* . . . (1818), Cartographic Collection, RG 77, Civil Works Map File, NARA; Board of Commissioners, *United States, outline map showing the waters and roads of the* (1818), Cartographic Collection, RG 77, Civil Works Map File, NARA; *Reconnaissance of the Mississippi and Ohio rivers* . . . (1821), Cartographic Collection, RG 77, Civil Works Map File, NARA; Joshua Meigs, *Survey of eastern and southeastern Missouri* (1821), Cartographic Collection, RG 77, Headquarters Map File, NARA; Edward Browne, *Indian land survey in Missouri* (1822), Cartographic Collection, RG 77, Headquarters Map File, NARA; *Map of eastern half of the United States showing locations of military posts and boundaries of states and territories* . . . (Manuscript Map, 1825), Cartographic Collection, RG 92, Post and Reservation File, NARA.

37. Dunbabin, "Red Lines on Maps," 117–19; *Treaties and Other International Agreements of the United States of America 1776–1949*, 12:57–60. For details of the 1818 treaty, see Bradford Perkins, *Castlereagh and Adams: England and the United States, 1812–1823* (Berkeley: University of California Press, 1964).

38. For American diplomacy in the 1810s, see Lewis, *The American Union and the Problem of Neighborhood*; Ernest R. May, *The Making of the Monroe Doctrine* (Cambridge: Belknap Press of Harvard University Press, 1975); Weeks, *John Quincy Adams and American Global Empire*; Perkins, *Castlereagh and Adams*.

39. Lewis C. Beck, *A Gazetteer of the States of Illinois and Missouri* . . . (Albany: C. R. and G. Webster, 1823); E. Dana, *Geographical Sketches on the Western Country: Designed for Emigrants and Settlers* . . . (Cincinnati: Looker, Reynolds Printers, 1819); Timothy Flint, *Recollections of the Last Ten Years, passed in occasional residences and journeyings in the valley of the Mississippi, from Pittsburgh and the Missouri to the Gulf of Mexico, and from Florida to the Spanish frontier: in a series of letters to the Rev. James Flint, of Salem, Massachusetts* (Boston: Cummings, Hilliard, 1826); Benjamin Harding, *A Tour through the Western Country, A.D. 1818 and 1819* (New London: Samuel Green, 1819). For an indication of the change in geographies, see Daniel Adams, *Geography or a Description of the World* (Boston: West and Blake, 1814); Richard Brookes, *General Gazetteer* (London: Johnson and Clarke, 1809); id., *General Gazetteer Improved* (Philadelphia: Johnson and Warner, 1812); Jacob Abbot Cummings, *School atlas to Cummings' geography* (Boston: Cummings and Hilliard, 1813).

40. Jefferson to John Melish, 31 December 1816, *Thomas Jefferson Papers*.

41. *Memoirs of John Quincy Adams, Comprising Portions of His Diary from 1795 to 1848*, ed. Charles Francis Adams (Philadelphia: J. B. Lippincott, 1874), 4:161.

42. Calhoun to Clark, 20 July 1820, *Territorial Papers of the United States*, 15:629.

43. *Memoirs of John Quincy Adams*, 6:159.

CHAPTER 8. MOVING THE FAR WEST

1. Clark to Henry Atkinson, 25 March 1833, Clark, permit to pass through Indian country, 2 April 1833, both in *Edward E. Ayer Collection*, Newberry.
2. Aron, *American Confluence*, 229–43; Foley, *The Genesis of Missouri*, 283–302.
3. For the broad shifts at work in the antebellum era, see Howe, *What Hath God Wrought*.
4. Henry Schenck Tanner, *A New American Atlas, containing maps of the several States of the North American union* (Philadelphia: Henry Tanner, 1823), 6.
5. Ibid.; Short, *Representing the Republic*, 146–54.
6. Tanner, *A New American Atlas (1823)*, preface.
7. Walter William Ristow, *Maps for an Emerging Nation: Commercial Cartography in Nineteenth-Century America* (Washington: Library of Congress, 1977), 19–29.
8. Henry Schenck Tanner, *Memoir on the Recent Surveys, Observations, and Internal Improvements in the United States* . . . (Philadelphia: Published by the author, Mifflin and Parry, 1829); ibid., *The American Traveller, or, Guide through the United States* . . . (Philadelphia: Henry Schenck Tanner, 1834).
9. For example, see E. Dupré, *Atlas of the city and county of St. Louis, by congressional* (1838); *Topographical map of the city of Cincinnati, from actual survey* (Doolittle and Munson, 1841), GMD, LOC; I. Tanesse, *Plan of the city and suburbs of New Orleans* (New York, New Orleans: Charles Del Vecchio; P. Maspero, 1817), GMD, LOC.
10. Jeffrey S. Adler, *Yankee Merchants and the Making of the Urban West: The Rise and Fall of Antebellum St. Louis* (Cambridge: Cambridge University Press, 1991); Adam Isaac Arenson, "City of Manifest Destiny: St. Louis and the Cultural Civil War, 1848–1877" (Ph.D. diss., Yale University, 2008); James Neal Primm, *Lion of the Valley: St. Louis, Missouri, 1764–1980* (St. Louis: Missouri Historical Society Press; Distributed by University of Missouri Press, 1998 [1981]), 110–49.
11. For example, see Lewis Robinson, *An Improved Map of the United States of America* (1825), GMD, LOC; D. H. Vance and A. Finley, *Map of North America Including all the Recent Geographical Discoveries* (1826), GMD, LOC; J. H. Young and M. Malte-Brun, *United States* (Philadelphia: 1828), GMD, LOC; J. H. Young, *Mitchell's Travellers guide through the United States* (Philadelphia: S. Augustus Mitchell, 1832).
12. Steven Aron describes a similar process of moving the frontier in political, economic, and demographic terms. See Aron, *How the West Was Lost*, 230–38.
13. *Clark Family Collection*, box 14, folder 1.
14. Cutright, "Lewis and Clark: Portraits and Portraitists"; Kathryn S. Hight, "'Doomed to Perish': George Catlin's Depictions of the Mandan," *Art Journal* 49 (1990), 119–24; Harold McCracken, *George Catlin and the Old Frontier* (New York: Dial Press, 1959).
15. Clark to James Barbour, 1 March 1826, *Clark Family Collection*, box 14, folder 13.

16. Jay Buckley offers the most thorough investigation of Clark's role in the long-term U.S. policy of Indian relocation. For the specifics of Jacksonian removal, see Buckley, *William Clark: Indian Diplomat*, 192–203.

17. The development of removal remains one of the well-studied topics in the history of American Indian policy. For selected studies emphasizing the continuities of federal policy, see Horsman, *Race and Manifest Destiny*; Wallace, *Jefferson and the Indians*; Anthony F. C. Wallace, *The Long Bitter Trail: Andrew Jackson and the Indians* (New York: Hill and Wang, 1993); Richard White, *The Roots of Dependency: Subsistence, Environment, and Social Change among the Choctaws, Pawnees, and Navajos* (Lincoln: University of Nebraska Press, 1983). Clark's Indian policy is most thoroughly explored in Buckley, *William Clark: Indian Diplomat*; Jones, *William Clark and the Shaping of the West*, 296–301. See also Aron, *American Confluence*, 212–15; J. Wendel Cox, "A World Together, a World Apart: The United States and the Arikaras, 1803–1851" (Ph.D. diss., University of Minnesota, 1998).

18. *Senate Executive Journal*, 3:184, 411, 472; *American State Papers*, Indian Affairs, 2:225–26; Roger L. Nichols, *General Henry Atkinson, A Western Military Career* (Norman: University of Oklahoma Press, 1965), 56–68.

19. Benjamin O'Fallon to Clark, 23 June 1823, *Benjamin O'Fallon Letter-book, 1823–1829*, Yale Collection of Western Americana, Beinecke, 1:11–12. For similar comments, see O'Fallon to William Ashley, 20 June 1823, *O'Fallon Letter-book*, 1:6–8; O'Fallon to John Daugherty, 1 February 1824, *O'Fallon Letter-book*, 1:53–56.

20. Foley, *Wilderness Journey*, 166–69, 244–47; Jones, *William Clark and the Shaping of the West*, 164–71.

21. Thomas Loraine McKenney, *Sketches of a Tour to the Lakes, of the character and customs of the Chippeway Indians, and of incidents connected with the Treaty of Fond du Lac* (Baltimore: F. Lucas, 1827); Herman J. Viola, *Thomas L. McKenney: Architect of America's Early Indian Policy, 1816–1830* (Chicago: Sage Books, 1974).

22. Govan, *Nicholas Biddle*, 193–222.

23. Albert Gallatin, *Map of the Indian tribes of North America, about 1600 A.D. along the Atlantic, and about 1800 A.D. westwardly* (Washington, 1836), GMD, LOC.

24. Blackhawk, *Violence Over the Land: Indians and Empires in the Early American West*, 145–75; Pekka Hämäläinen, *The Comanche Empire* (New Haven: Yale University Press, 2008).

25. Bryan F. LeBeau, *Currier and Ives: America Imagined* (Washington: Smithsonian Institution Press, 2001); Felix H. Man, *Artists' Lithographs: A World History from Senefelder to the Present Day* (New York: Putnam, 1970); John William Reps, *Saint Louis Illustrated: Nineteenth-Century Engravings and Lithographs of a Mississippi River Metropolis* (Columbia: University of Missouri Press, 1989); Ristow, *Maps for an Emerging Nation*, 19–22.

26. John William Reps, *John Caspar Wild: Painter and Printmaker of Nineteenth-Century Urban America* (St. Louis: Missouri Historical Society Press, Distributed by University of Missouri Press, 2006).

27. Clark to Meriwether Lewis Clark, 29 December 1831, *Clark Family Collection*, box 8, folder 8.

28. Washington Irving, *Journals and Notebooks*, ed. Nathalia Wright (Madison: University of Wisconsin Press, 1969), 5:60–61.

29. For Irving's visit, see Andrew Burstein, *The Original Knickerbocker: The Life of Washington Irving* (New York: Basic Books, 2007), 261–62; Peter Antelyes, *Tales of Adventurous Enterprise: Washington Irving and the Poetics of Western Expansion* (New York: Columbia University Press, 1990), 150.

30. Meriwether Lewis Clark to Clark, 16 February 1830, *Clark Family Collection*, box 14, folder 1.

31. F. O. Matthiessen, *American Renaissance: Art and Expression in the Age of Emerson and Whitman* (London: Oxford University Press, 1941). For more recent studies, see Walter Benn Michaels and Donald E. Pease, eds., *The American Renaissance Reconsidered* (Baltimore: Johns Hopkins University Press, 1985).

32. For recent studies on the novel in the early American republic, see Elizabeth Barnes, *States of Sympathy: Seduction and Democracy in the American Novel* (New York: Columbia University Press, 1997); Davidson, *Revolution and the Word*; Stephen Shapiro, *The Culture and Commerce of the Early American Novel: Reading the Atlantic World-System* (University Park: Pennsylvania State University Press, 2008); Karen Ann Weyler, *Intricate Relations: Sexual and Economic Desire in American Fiction, 1789–1814* (Iowa City: University of Iowa Press, 2004).

33. Beth Lynne Lueck, *American Writers and the Picturesque Tour: The Search for National Identity, 1790–1860* (New York: Garland Publishing, 1997); Miller, *Empire of the Eye*, 10–11.

34. Kris Fresonke, *West of Emerson: The Design of Manifest Destiny* (Berkeley: University of California Press, 2003); Heidi Aronson Kolk, "The Discriminating Cicerone: Class, Cultural Identity and Social Performance in Nineteenth-Century Travel Narratives" (Ph.D. diss., Washington University in St. Louis, 2003).

35. Miller, *Empire of the Eye*.

36. Brian W. Dippie, *Catlin and His Contemporaries: The Politics of Patronage* (Lincoln: University of Nebraska Press, 1990); Hight, "'Doomed to Perish': George Catlin's Depictions of the Mandan," 119–24; David Mazel, "'A Beautiful and Thrilling Specimen': George Catlin, the Death of Wilderness, and the Birth of the National Subject," in *Reading the Earth: New Directions in the Study of Literature and Environment*, ed. Michael P. Branch (Moscow: University of Idaho Press, 1998).

37. Kristin Boudreau, *Sympathy in American Literature: American Sentiments from Jefferson to the Jameses* (Gainesville: University Press of Florida, 2002); Andrew Burstein, *Sentimental Democracy: The Evolution of America's Romantic Self-Image* (New York: Hill and Wang, 1999); Lynn M. Festa, *Sentimental Figures of Empire in Eighteenth-Century Britain and France* (Baltimore: Johns Hopkins University Press, 2006); Mark Phillips, *Society and Sentiment: Genres of Historical Writing in Britain, 1740–1820* (Princeton: Princeton University Press, 2000).

38. Theo Davis, *Formalism, Experience, and the Making of American Literature in the Nineteenth Century* (Cambridge: Cambridge University Press, 2007); Miller, *Empire of the Eye.*

39. Nationalism in the early republic has lately been the subject of a revealing and prolific scholarly literature. For selected examples, see Liah Greenfeld, *Nationalism: Five Roads to Modernity* (Cambridge: Harvard University Press, 1992); Kastor, *The Nation's Crucible*, 21–25; Onuf, *Jefferson's Empire*; Andrew W. Robertson, "'Look on This Picture . . . And on This!': Nationalism, Localism, and Partisan Images of Otherness in the United States, 1787–1820," *American Historical Review* 104 (2001), 1263–80; Len Travers, *Celebrating the Fourth: Independence Day and the Rites of Nationalism in the Early Republic* (Amherst: University of Massachusetts Press, 1997); Waldstreicher, *In the Midst of Perpetual Fetes.*

40. Taylor, *William Cooper's Town.*

41. Davy Crockett, *A Narrative of the Life of David Crockett* (Philadelphia, Baltimore: E. L. Carey and A. Hart; Carey, Hart, 1834), 174–75.

42. Taylor, *William Cooper's Town*, 402–27.

43. Edmund Flagg, *The Far West, or, A Tour Beyond the Mountains . . .* (New York: Harper and Brothers, 1838), iii, 117–18, 115.

44. Ibid., 14, 283.

45. Washington Irving, *Letters*, ed. Ralph M. Aderman et al. (Boston: Twayne Publishers, 1978), 2:725.

46. For Irving's western accounts, see Antelyes, *Tales of Adventurous Enterprise*; Greenfield, *Narrating Discovery*, 113–64; Guy Reynolds, "The Winning of the West: Washington Irving's 'A Tour on the Prairies,'" *Yearbook of English Studies* 34 (2004), 88–99.

47. William Preston Clark to Clark, 10 April 1834, *Clark Family Collection*, box 14, folder 4.

48. Aron, *American Confluence*, 164–69.

49. A prominent figure in most studies of antebellum politics, Benton himself has been the subject of only limited close study. See William Nisbet Chambers, *Old Bullion Benton, Senator from the New West: Thomas Hart Benton, 1782–1858* (Boston: Little, Brown, 1956); Elbert B. Smith, *Magnificent Missourian: The Life of Thomas Hart Benton* (Philadelphia: Lippincott, 1958).

50. O'Fallon to W. C. Lane, 12 December 1826, *O'Fallon Letter-book*, 2:175–78.

51. Thomas Hart Benton, *Selections of Editorial Articles from the St. Louis Enquirer on the subject of Oregon and Texas, as originally published in that paper in the years 1818–19 . . .* (St. Louis: Missourian, 1844); Chambers, *Old Bullion Benton*, 83–89, 265–79; Hietala, *Manifest Design*, 36–38.

52. Smith, *Virgin Land*, 19–34.

53. Quoted in Chambers, *Old Bullion Benton*, 83.

54. Owens, *Mr. Jefferson's Hammer.*

55. Howe, *What Hath God Wrought*, 486–87.

56. Alexis de Tocqueville, *Democracy in America* (New York: Library of America, 2004), 58.
57. Samuel R. Brown, *Western gazetteer; or emigrant's directory* (Auburn: H. C. South-wick, 1817); Flint, *Recollections of the Last Ten Years*; Samuel Augustus Mitchell, *Mitchell's traveller's guide through the United States, containing the principal cities, towns, &c, alphabetically arranged; together with the stage, steam-boat, canal, and railroad routes, with the distances, in miles, from place to place* (Philadelphia: Mitchell and Hinman, 1837); J. H. Young, *The Tourist's Pocket Map of the State of Illinois, exhibiting its internal improvements, roads, distances, and c.* (Philadelphia: S. A. Mitchell, 1838).
58. *Clark Family Collection*, box 15, folder 7.

CONCLUSION

1. Chambers, *Old Bullion Benton*, 233–34.
2. Ibid. For selected newspaper entries, see *Daily Commercial Advertiser* (St. Louis), 28 September 1838; *New Hampshire Sentinel*, 26 September 1838; *New-Bedford Mercury* (New Bedford), 21 September 1838.
3. William Clark, 1838, file no. 1416, Probate Records, St. Louis City, Missouri, http://stlcourtrecords.wustl.edu/about-clark-probate.php.
4. Deloria, *Playing Indian*; Reeve Huston, *Land and Freedom: Rural Society, Popular Protest, and Party Politics in Antebellum New York* (Oxford: Oxford University Press, 2000); William G. Robbins and James C. Foster, *Land in the American West: Private Claims and the Common Good* (Seattle: University of Washington Press, 2000); Richard Slotkin, *Regeneration through Violence: The Mythology of the American Frontier, 1600–1860* (Middletown, Conn.: Wesleyan University Press, 1973).
5. LeBeau, *Currier and Ives: America Imagined*; Miller, *Empire of the Eye*, 231–34; Sandweiss, *Print the Legend*.
6. Limerick, *The Legacy of Conquest*.
7. John Shelton Lawrence and Robert Jewett, *The Myth of the American Superhero* (Grand Rapids: W. B. Eerdmans, 2002); Smith, *Virgin Land*; Streeby, *American Sensations*.
8. For shifts in American attitudes toward the challenge of governing newly acquired territory, see Peter J. Kastor, ed., *America's Struggle with Empire: A Documentary History* (Washington: CQ Press, 2009).
9. Hietala, *Manifest Design*; LeMenager, *Manifest and Other Destinies*.
10. George Catlin, *Letters and Notes on the Manners, Customs, and Condition of the North American Indians . . .* (London: W. and A. K. Johnston, 1841); Fresonke, *West of Emerson*; Mazel, "'A Beautiful and Thrilling Specimen.'" For studies of the opposition to expansion later in the nineteenth century, see Kaplan, *The Anarchy of Empire*; John H. Schroeder, *Mr. Polk's War: American Opposition and Dissent,*

1846–1848 (Madison: University of Wisconsin Press, 1973), 107–19; Streeby, *American Sensations.*

11. O'Sullivan had used these words in various combinations before, but his articles for the *United States Magazine and Democratic Review* in the summer of 1845 provided the first cohesive argument linking Manifest Destiny to territorial conquest.

12. Yonatan Eyal, *The Young America Movement and the Transformation of the Democratic Party, 1828–61* (Cambridge: Cambridge University Press, 2007).

13. Frederick J. Turner, "Social Forces in American History," *American Historical Review* 16 (1911), 220. In recent years, Turner has received considerable examination and reexamination. For revealing analyses, see John Mack Faragher, *Rereading Frederick Jackson Turner: "The Significance of the Frontier in American History" and Other Essays* (New York: H. Holt, 1994); David J. Weber, "Turner, the Boltonians, and the Borderlands," *American Historical Review* 91 (1986), 66–80.

BIBLIOGRAPHY

ABBREVIATIONS

GMD, LOC	Geography and Map Division, Library of Congress
LOC	Library of Congress
NARA	National Archives and Records Administration
Beinecke	Beinecke Rare Book and Manuscript Library, Yale University
MoHist	Missouri History Museum
Newberry	Newberry Library

ARCHIVAL COLLECTIONS

Benjamin O'Fallon Letter-book, 1823–1829. Yale Collection of Western America, Beinecke.

Clark Family Collection. MoHist.

Edward E. Ayer Collection. Newberry.

General Daniel Bissell Papers. St. Louis Mercantile Library, University of Missouri–St. Louis.

George Washington Papers. Washington: Library of Congress Microfilm Collection.

Morse Family Papers, 1779–1868. Manuscripts and Archives, Sterling Library, Yale University.

Papers of Nicholas Biddle. Washington: Library of Congress Microfilm Collection.

Papers of Thomas Freeman, 1796–1807. Manuscripts Division, LOC.

Territorial Papers of the United States. Record Group 59, Microfilm Copy M116 (Florida), T260 (Orleans), NARA.

Thomas Jefferson Papers. Washington: Library of Congress Microfilm Collection.

PUBLISHED DOCUMENT COLLECTIONS

American State Papers: Documents, Legislative and Executive, of the Congress of the United States. Washington: Gales and Seaton, 1832–61.

Dear Brother: Letters of William Clark to Jonathan Clark. Edited by James J. Holmberg. New Haven: Yale University Press, 2002.

Debates and Proceedings of the Congress of the United States. Washington: Gales and Seaton, 1834–56.

Indian Affairs: Laws and Treaties. Stillwater, Okla.: OSU Library Digital Publications, 1999.

Jefferson Writings. Edited by Merrill D. Peterson. New York: Library of America, 1984.

Journals of the Continental Congress, 1774–1789. Washington: U.S. Government Printing Office, 1904–37.

Journal of the House of Representatives of the United States. Washington: Gales and Seaton, 1826.

The Journals of the Lewis and Clark Expedition. Edited by Gary E. Moulton et al. Lincoln: University of Nebraska Press, 1983.

The Journals of Zebulon Montgomery Pike, with Letters and Related Documents. Edited by Donald Dean Jackson. Norman: University of Oklahoma Press, 1966.

Letters of the Lewis and Clark Expedition, With Related Documents 1783–1854. Edited by Donald Dean Jackson. Urbana: University of Illinois Press, 1978.

Memoirs of John Quincy Adams, Comprising Portions of His Diary from 1795 to 1848. Edited by Charles Francis Adams. Philadelphia: J. B. Lippincott, 1874.

The Papers of Benjamin Franklin. Edited by Leonard Woods Labaree et al. New Haven: Yale University Press, 1959– . 37 vols. to date.

The Papers of George Washington: Presidential Series. Edited by W. W. Abbot et al. Charlottesville: University Press of Virginia, 1987– . 14 vols. to date.

The Papers of James Madison: Presidential Series. Edited by Robert A. Rutland et al. Charlottesville: University Press of Virginia, 1986– . 8 vols. to date.

The Papers of James Madison: Secretary of State Series. Edited by Robert J. Brugger et al. Charlottesville: University Press of Virginia, 1986– . 6 vols. to date.

The Papers of John C. Calhoun. Edited by Robert L. Meriwether et al. Columbia: University of South Carolina Press, 1959. 28 vols.

The Papers of Thomas Jefferson. Edited by Julian P. Boyd et al. Princeton: Princeton University Press, 1950– . 35 vols. to date.

The Papers of Thomas Jefferson: Retirement Series. Edited by J. Jefferson Looney. Princeton: Princeton University Press, 2004. 4 vols.

The Territorial Papers of the United States. Edited by Clarence Edward Carter. Washington: Government Printing Office, 1934–75.

Treaties and Other International Agreements of the United States of America 1776–1949. Edited by Charles E. Bevans. Washington: Government Printing Office, 1971.

MAPS

Amérique Septentrionale avec les Routes, Distances en Miles, Villages et Etablissements François et Anglois, par le Docteur Mitchel. Paris, 1777. GMD: LOC.

Arrowsmith, Aaron. *A Map Exhibiting all the New Discoveries in the Interior Parts of North America. . . .* London: A. Arrowsmith, 1802. GMD, LOC.

Arrowsmith, Aaron. *A Map of the United States of America.* New York, 1810. GMD: LOC.

Atcheson, Nathaniel. *Extract from Mitchell's map.* London, 1808. GMD: LOC.

Bowels's New one-sheet map of the United States of America with the territories belonging to Great Britain and Spain. London: Bowles and Carver, 1795. GMD, LOC.

Bradley, Abraham. *Map of the United States,* 1796. GMD, LOC.

———. *Map of the United States: exhibiting the post-roads, the situations, connexions and distances of the post-offices, stage roads, counties and principal rivers.* Philadelphia: Caldcleugh and Thomas, 1804. GMD, LOC.

———. *Map of the United States: exhibiting the post-roads, the situations, connexions and distances of the post-offices, stage roads, counties and principal rivers.* Philadelphia: Caldcleugh and Thomas, 1812. David Rumsey Map Collection, http://www.david rumsey.com.

———. *Map of the United States Intending Chiefly to Exhibit the Post Roads and Distances,* 1836. Cartographic Collection, RG 28, Library Map Collection, NARA.

Browne, Edward. *Indian land survey in Missouri,* 1822. Cartographic Collection, RG 77, Headquarters Map File, NARA.

Carte des Etats-Unis d'Amérique, et du cours du Mississippi. . . . Paris: Esnats et Railly, 1784. Edward E. Ayer Collection, Newberry.

Carte des Etatus du centre, de l'ouestet du sud des Etats-Unis, 1804. Everett D. Graff Collection.

Carte du Mississipi et de ses embranchemens. Paris, 1802. GMD, LOC.

Clark, William. *A Map of Part of the Continent of North America . . . ,* 1810. Beinecke.

———. *Plan of the N.W. Frontier,* 1813. GMD, LOC.

Commissioners, Board of. *United States, outline map showing the waters and roads of the . . . ,* 1818. Cartographic Collection, RG 77, Civil Works Map File, NARA.

A Correct Map of the United States of North America, Including the British and Spanish territories, carefully laid down agreeable to the Treaty of 1784. London, 1797.

Durnford, Elias. *Reference to the Lands Surveyed and Granted on the River Mississippi and Parts adjacent,* 1770. GMD, LOC.

Reconnaissance of the Mississippi and Ohio rivers . . . , 1821. Cartographic Collection, RG 77, Civil Works Map File, NARA.

Faden, William. *The United States of North America, with the British territories and those of Spain.* London, 1793. GMD, LOC.

Fry, Joshua, and Peter Jefferson. *A Map of the Most Inhabited Part of Virginia Containing the Whole Province of Maryland with part of Pensilvania, New Jersey and North Carolina.* London: Thos. Jefferys, 1755. GMD, LOC.

Gallatin, Albert. *Map of the Indian tribes of North America, about 1600 A.D. along the Atlantic, and about 1800 A.D. westwardly.* Washington, 1836. GMD, LOC.

Güssefeld, F. L. (Franz Ludwig). *Charte der XV Vereinigten Staaten von Nord-Ameri-can nach Murdochischer projection.* Weimar, 1800. GMD, LOC.

Hartley, David. *Hartley–Jefferson Map of the United States East of the Mississippi River,* 1784. David Harley Papers, Clements Library, University of Michigan.

Hutchins, Thomas. *A General Map of the Country on the Ohio and Muskingham show-ing the situation of the Indian-towns with respect to the Army under the command of Colonel Bouquet . . . in 1764, 1765.* GMD, LOC.

King, Nicholas. *Map of the Red River in Louisiana from the Spanish Camp where the Exploring Party of the U.S. was met by the Spanish troops to where it enters the Mis-sissippi, reduced from the protracted courses and corrected to the latitude.* Philadel-phia: F. Shallus, 1806. GMD, LOC.

Lapie, P. (Pierre). *Etats-Unis de L'Amérique Septentrionale.* Paris: Adam and Giraldon, 1810. GMD, LOC.

Lewis, Samuel, and William Harrison. *A Map of the United States: Compiled Chiefly from the State Maps and other Authentic Information.* Philadelphia: Matthew Carey, 1809. GMD, LOC.

Ludlow, Maxfield. *A Map of the State of Louisiana with part of the state of Mississippi and Alabama Territory,* 1815. Map Collection, Sterling Memorial Library, Yale Uni-versity.

———. *A Map of the State of Louisiana. With part of the State of Mississippi and Al-abama Territory. By Maxfield Ludlow. Chief Clerk, Surveyor Genls. Office, South of Tennessee.* Charles W. Warnick, J.F., 1817. GMD, LOC.

Luffman, J. *A Map of North America.* London, 1803. GMD, LOC.

Map of eastern half of the United States showing locations of military posts and bound-aries of states and territories . . . Manuscript Map, 1825. Cartographic Collection, RG 92, Post and Reservation File, NARA.

A Map of Lewis and Clark's Track, Across the Western Portion of North America from the Mississippi to the Pacific Ocean. . . . Philadelphia: Bradford and Inskeep, 1814. GMD, LOC.

[Map of the region south and west of Chicago and Fort Dearborn], ca. 1811. GMD, LOC.

Map of the United States, Canada andc. . . . London: R. Phillips, 1799. Edward E. Ayer Collection, Newberry.

Meigs, Joshua. *Survey of eastern and southeastern Missouri,* 1821. Cartographic Collec-tion, RG 77, Headquarters Map File, NARA.

Mitchell, John. *A Map of the British and French Dominions in North America . . .* Lon-don, 1755. GMD, LOC.

Osgood, Carleton. *New Map of the United States of America Including art of Louisiana Drawn from the latest authorites.* Boston, 1806. GMD, LOC.

Pownall, Thomas. *A New Map of North America.* London: Robert Sayer, 1783. GMD, LOC.

————. *A New Map of the Whole Continent of America, Divided into North and South and West Indies with a descriptive account of the European possessions, as settled by the definitive treaty of peace, concluded at Paris Feby. 10th. 1763*. London, 1777. GMD, LOC.

————. *The Provinces of New York, and New Jersey; with part of Pensilvania and the province of Quebec*. Frankfort upon the Mayn: Harry Lodowick Broenner, 1777. GMD, LOC.

Rector, William. *Sketch of the western half of the continent of North America between latitudes 35° and 52° N.; originally drawn under the inspection of William Rector, U.S. Surveyor for Missouri., and Illinois, and by him presented to the General Land office, January 21, 1818 . . .* , 1818. Cartographic Collection, RG 77, Civil Works Map File, NARA.

Robinson, Lewis. *An Improved Map of the United States of America*, 1825. GMD, LOC.

Romans, Bernard. *A General Map of the Southern British Colonies in America . . .* London: R. Sayer and J. Bennett, 1776. GMD, LOC.

————. *Maps of East and West Florida*. New York, 1781. GMD, LOC.

————. *Plan of the Harbour of Pensacola*. London: R. Sayer, 1788. GMD, LOC.

Stockdale, John. *Part of the United States of North America*. London: J. Stockdale, 1800. GMD, LOC.

Tanesse, I. *Plan of the city and suburbs of New Orleans*. New York, New Orleans: Charles Del Vecchio; P. Maspero, 1817. GMD, LOC.

Tanner, Henry Schenck. *Map of Texas with Parts of the Adjoining States*. Philadelphia: H. S. Tanner, 1837. GMD, LOC.

————. *Map of the Canals and Rail Roads of the United States reduced from the large map of the U.S.* Philadelphia: Engraved by J. Knight, 1830. GMD, LOC.

Tardieu, Pierre. *United States of Nth. America; carte des Etats-Unis de l'Amérique Septentrionale*. A Paris, 1808. GMD, LOC.

Topographical map of the city of Cincinnati, from actual survey. Doolittle and Munson, 1841. GMD, LOC.

Vance, D. H., and A. Finley. *Map of North America Including all the Recent Geographical Discoveries*, 1826. GMD, LOC.

Young, J. H., and M. Malte-Brun. *United States*. Philadelphia, 1828. GMD, LOC.

NEWSPAPERS

Berkshire [Mass.] *Reporter.*
City Gazette and Daily Advertiser. Charleston.
Connecticut Journal. New Haven.
Daily Advertiser. New York.
Daily Commercial Advertiser. St. Louis.
Eastern Argus. Portland, Mass.
Enquirer. Richmond.

The Farmers' Cabinet. Amherst, Mass.
The Green Mountain Patriot. Peacham, Vt..
Massachusetts Spy. Worcester, Mass.
Middlebury [Vt.] *Mercury.*
National Intelligencer. Washington.
New-Bedford Mercury. New Bedford, Conn.
New Hampshire Sentinel. Keene, N.H.
Newburyport Herald. Newburyport, Mass.
Northern Post. Salem, Mass.
Orleans Gazette. New Orleans.
Palladium. Frankfort.
Political Observatory. Walpole, Mass.
Providence [RI] *Phoenix.*
Republican Star. Easton, Md.
Salem [Mass.] *Gazette.*
United States Gazette. Philadelphia.
Washington Federalist.

BOOKS, ARTICLES, ESSAYS, THESES, AND PAMPHLETS

A New System of Modern Geography. Philadelphia: Mathew Carey, 1794.
Abernethy, Thomas Perkins. *Western Lands and the American Revolution.* New York: D. Appleton-Century, 1937.
Adams, Daniel. *Geography or a Description of the World.* Boston: West and Blake, 1814.
Adams, Percy G. *Travel Literature and the Evolution of the Novel.* Lexington: University Press of Kentucky, 1983.
Adelman, Jeremy, and Stephen Aron. "From Borderlands to Borders: Empires, Nation-States, and the Peoples in Between in North American History." *AHR* 104 (1999), 814–41.
Adler, Jeffrey S. *Yankee Merchants and the Making of the Urban West: The Rise and Fall of Antebellum St. Louis.* Cambridge: Cambridge University Press, 1991.
Allen, John Logan. *Lewis and Clark and the Image of the American Northwest.* New York: Dover Publications, 1991 [1975].
Ambrose, Stephen A. *Undaunted Courage: Meriwether Lewis, Thomas Jefferson, and the Opening of the American West.* New York: Simon and Schuster, 1996.
An Account of a Voyage up the Mississippi River: From St. Louis to its Source, Made Under Orders of the War Department, by Lieut. Pike, of the United States Army, in the years 1805 and 1806. Washington, 1807.
An Account of Louisiana, Being an Abstract of Documents, in the Offices of the Departments of State, and of the Treasury. Providence: Heaton and Williams, 1803.
An Account of the Red River, in Louisiana, Drawn up from the Returns of Messrs. Free-

man and Custis to the War Office of the United States, who Explored the Same, in the year of 1806. Washington, 1806.

An Historical Account of the Expedition Against the Ohio Indians, in the year 1764 . . . Philadelphia: W. Bradford, 1765.

Analysis of the Third Article of the Treaty of Cession of Louisiana. Washington, 1803.

Antelyes, Peter. *Tales of Adventurous Enterprise: Washington Irving and the Poetics of Western Expansion.* New York: Columbia University Press, 1990.

Appleby, Joyce O. *Capitalism and a New Social Order: The Republican Vision of the 1790s.* New York: New York University Press, 1984.

Aptheker, Herbert. *American Negro Slave Revolts.* New York: International Publishers, 1974.

Arenson, Adam Isaac. "City of Manifest Destiny: St. Louis and the Cultural Civil War, 1848–1877." Ph.D. diss., Yale University, 2008.

Aron, Stephen. *American Confluence: The Missouri Frontier from Borderland to Border State.* Bloomington: Indiana University Press, 2006.

———. *How the West Was Lost: The Transformation of Kentucky from Daniel Boone to Henry Clay.* Baltimore: Johns Hopkins University Press, 1996.

Bailey's Pocket Almanac, Being an American annual register, for the year of our Lord 1785. Philadelphia: Francis Bailey, 1784.

Banner, Stuart. *How the Indians Lost Their Land: Law and Power on the Frontier.* Cambridge: Belknap Press of Harvard University Press, 2005.

Barnes, Elizabeth. *States of Sympathy: Seduction and Democracy in the American Novel.* New York: Columbia University Press, 1997.

Barrow, John. *An Account of Travels into the Interior of Southern Africa.* London: T. Cadell, jun., and W. Davies, 1801.

Bartram, William. *Travels through North and South Carolina, Georgia, East and West Florida . . .* Philadelphia: James and Johnson, 1791.

Batten, Charles. *Pleasurable Instruction: Form and Convention in Eighteenth-Century Travel Literature.* Berkeley: University of California Press, 1978.

Beck, Lewis C. *A Gazetteer of the States of Illinois and Missouri . . .* Albany: C. R. and G. Webster, 1823.

Beckham, Stephen Dow, D. M. Erickson, Jeremy Skinner, and Paul Merchant. *The Literature of the Lewis and Clark Expedition: A Bibliography and Essays.* Portland, Ore.: Lewis and Clark College, 2003.

Bellesiles, Michael A. *Revolutionary Outlaws: Ethan Allen and the Struggle for Independence on the Early American Frontier.* Charlottesville: University Press of Virginia, 1993.

Bemis, Samuel Flagg. *Jay's Treaty: A Study in Commerce and Diplomacy.* New Haven: Yale University Press, 1962.

———. *Pinckney's Treaty: America's Advantage from Europe's Distress, 1783–1800.* New Haven: Yale University Press, 1960.

Benton, Thomas Hart. *Selections of Editorial Articles from the St. Louis Enquirer on the subject of Oregon and Texas, as originally published in that paper in the years 1818–19* . . . St. Louis: Missourian, 1844.

Berkhofer, Robert F. *The White Man's Indian: Images of the American Indian from Columbus to the Present.* New York: Vintage Books, 1979.

———. "The Northwest Ordinance and the Principle of Territorial Evolution." In *The American Territorial System*, ed. John Porter Bloom. Athens: Ohio University Press, 1969.

Berry, Trey, Pam Beasley, and Jeanne Clements, eds. *The Forgotten Expedition, 1804–1805: The Louisiana Purchase Journals of Dunbar and Hunter.* Baton Rouge: Louisiana State University Press, 2006.

Bettex, Albert. *The Discovery of Nature.* New York: Simon and Schuster, 1965.

Betts, Robert B. *In Search of York: The Slave Who Went to the Pacific with Lewis and Clark.* Boulder: Colorado Associated University Press, 1985.

Bieder, Robert E. *Science Encounters the Indian, 1820–1880: The Early Years of American Ethnology.* Norman: University of Oklahoma Press, 1986.

Blackhawk, Ned. *Violence Over the Land: Indians and Empires in the Early American West.* Cambridge: Harvard University Press, 2006.

Boardman, Kathleen, and Gioia Woods, eds. *Western Subjects: Autobiographical Writing in the North American West.* Salt Lake City: University of Utah Press, 2004.

Boudreau, Kristin. *Sympathy in American Literature: American Sentiments from Jefferson to the Jameses.* Gainesville: University Press of Florida, 2002.

Brackenridge, H. M. *Views of Louisiana: Together with a Journal of a Voyage up the Missouri River, in 1811.* Pittsburgh: Cramer, Spear, and Eichbaum, 1814.

Bradbury, John. *Travels in the Interior of America, in the years 1809, 1810, and 1811.* . . . Liverpool: Sherwood Neely and Jones, 1817.

Brazer, Samuel. *Address, Pronounced at Worcester, on May 12th: 1804 in commemoration of the cession of Louisiana to the United States.* Worcester: Sewall Goodridge, 1804.

Brookes, Richard. *General Gazetteer.* London: Johnson and Clarke, 1809.

———. *General Gazetteer Improved.* Philadelphia: Johnson and Warner, 1812.

Brooks, James. *Captives and Cousins: Slavery, Kinship, and Community in the Southwest Borderlands.* Chapel Hill: University of North Carolina Press, Omohundro Institute of Early American History and Culture, 2002.

Brooks, Joanna. *American Lazarus: Religion and the Rise of African-American and Native American Literatures.* Oxford: Oxford University Press, 2003.

Brown, Charles Brockden. *Monroe's Embassy, or, The Conduct of the Government, in Relation to Our Claims to the Navigation of the Mississippi.* Philadelphia: John Conrad, 1803.

Brown, Samuel R. *Western gazetteer; or emigrant's directory.* Auburn: SouthwickHC, 1817.

Brückner, Martin. "Lessons in Geography: Maps, Spellers, and Other Grammars of Nationalism in the Early Republic." *American Quarterly* 51, no. 2 (1999), 311–34.

————. *The Geographic Revolution in Early America: Maps, Literacy, and National Identity.* Chapel Hill: University of North Carolina Press, 2006.

Buckley, Jay H. *William Clark: Indian Diplomat.* Norman: University of Oklahoma Press, 2008.

Burstein, Andrew. *Sentimental Democracy: The Evolution of America's Romantic Self-image.* New York: Hill and Wang, 1999.

————. *The Inner Jefferson: Portrait of a Grieving Optimist.* Charlottesville: University Press of Virginia, 1995.

————. *The Original Knickerbocker: The Life of Washington Irving.* New York: Basic Books, 2007.

Bushman, Richard L. *The Refinement of America: Persons, Houses, Cities.* New York: Knopf: Distributed by Random House, 1992.

Cantrell, Gregg. *Stephen F. Austin, Empresario of Texas.* New Haven: Yale University Press, 1999.

Carey, Mathew. *Carey's American Atlas.* Philadelphia: Mathew Carey, 1795.

————. *Carey's American Pocket Atlas . . . With a Concise Description of Each State.* Philadelphia: Lang and Ustick, 1796.

Carstensen, Vernon. "Patterns on the American Land." *Publius* 18, no. 4 (1988), 31–39.

Cashin, Joan. *A Family Venture: Men and Women on the Southern Frontier.* Oxford: Oxford University Press, 1991.

Casper, Scott E. *Constructing American Lives: Biography and Culture in Nineteenth-Century America.* Chapel Hill: University of North Carolina Press, 1999.

Catlin, George. *Letters and Notes on the Manners, Customs, and Condition of the North American Indians . . .* London: W. and A. K. Johnston, 1841.

Cayton, Andrew R. L. *Frontier Indiana.* Bloomington: Indiana University Press, 1996.

————. *The Frontier Republic: Ideology and Politics in the Ohio Country.* Kent: Kent State University Press, 1986.

Chambers, William Nisbet. *Old Bullion Benton, Senator from the New West: Thomas Hart Benton, 1782–1858.* Boston: Little, Brown, 1956.

Chase, Philander. "A Stake in the West: George Washington as Backcountry Surveyor and Landholder." In *George Washington and the Virginia Backcountry,* ed. Warren R. Hofstra, 159–94. Madison: Madison House, 1998.

Clarkin, William. *Mathew Carey: A Bibliography of His Publications, 1785–1824.* New York: Garland, 1984.

Clokey, Richard M. *William H. Ashley: Enterprise and Politics in the Trans-Mississippi West.* Norman: University of Oklahoma Press, 1980.

Cmiel, Kenneth. *Democratic Eloquence: The Fight for Popular Speech in Nineteenth-Century America.* New York: W. Morrow, 1990.

Cohen, Peter Zachary. *The Great Red River Raft.* Niles, Ill.: A. Whitman, 1984.

Colvin, John B. *Republican Policy, or, The Superiority of the Principles of the Present Administration over those of its Enemies, who call Themselves Federalists Exemplified in the Late Cession of Louisiana.* Frederick-Town, 1802.

Combs, Jerald A. *The Jay Treaty: Political Battleground of the Founding Fathers.* Berkeley: University of California Press, 1970.

Conforti, Joseph A. *Imagining New England: Explorations of Regional Identity from the Pilgrims to the Mid-Twentieth Century.* Chapel Hill: University of North Carolina Press, 2001.

Cox, J. Wendel. "A World Together, a World Apart: The United States and the Arikaras, 1803–1851." Ph.D. diss., University of Minnesota, 1998.

Crackel, Theodore J. *Mr. Jefferson's Army: Political and Social Reform of the Military Establishment, 1801–1809.* New York: New York University Press, 1987.

Cramer, Zadok. *The Navigator: Containing Directions for Navigating the Monongahela, Allegheny, Ohio and Mississippi Rivers . . .* Pittsburgh: Z. Cramer, 1808.

———. *The Navigator: Containing Directions for Navigating the Monongahela, Allegheny, Ohio, and Mississippi Rivers, with an ample account of these much admired waters . . .* Pittsburgh: Cramer, Spear, and Eichbaum, 1811.

———. *The Navigator.* Pittsburgh, from the press of Zadok Cramer, 1806.

———. *The Ohio and Mississippi Navigator . . .* Pittsburgh: Zadok Cramer, 1802.

Crockett, Davy. *A Narrative of the Life of David Crockett.* Philadelphia, Baltimore: E. L. Carey and A. Hart; Carey, Hart, 1834.

Cronon, William. *Changes in the Land: Indians, Colonists, and the Ecology of New England.* New York: Hill and Wang, 1983.

Cumming, William Patterson. *British Maps of Colonial America.* Chicago: University of Chicago Press, 1974.

Cummings, Jacob Abbot. *School atlas to Cummings' geography.* Boston: Cummings and Hilliard, 1813.

Cutright, Paul R. "Lewis and Clark: Portraits and Portraitists." *Montana: The Magazine of Western History* 19, no. 2 (1969), 37–53.

Dana, E. *Geographical Sketches on the Western Country: Designed for Emigrants and Settlers . . .* Cincinnati: Looker, Reynolds Printers, 1819.

Dance, S. Peter. *The Art of Natural History: Animal Illustrators and Their Work.* Woodstock, N.Y.: Overlook Press, 1978.

Darby, William. *A Tour from the city of New-York, to Detroit, in the Michigan territory, made between the 2d of May and the 22d of September, 1818 . . .* New York: Kirk and Mercein, 1819.

———. *View of the United States, Historical, Geographical, and Statistical . . .* Philadelphia: H. S. Tanner, 1828.

Davidson, Cathy N. *Revolution and the Word: The Rise of the Novel in America.* New York: Oxford University Press, 1986.

Davis, Theo. *Formalism, Experience, and the Making of American Literature in the Nineteenth Century.* Cambridge: Cambridge University Press, 2007.

DeConde, Alexander. *This Affair of Louisiana.* New York: Charles Scribner's Sons, 1976.

Deloria, Philip Joseph. *Playing Indian.* New Haven: Yale University Press, 1998.

DeRogatis, Amy. *Moral Geography: Maps, Missionaries, and the American Frontier.* New York: Columbia University Press, 2003.

DeRosier, Arthur H. *William Dunbar: Scientific Pioneer of the Old Southwest.* Lexington: University Press of Kentucky, 2007.

Dewey, Frank L. *Thomas Jefferson, Lawyer.* Charlottesville: University Press of Virginia, 1986.

Diamant, Lincoln. *Bernard Romans: Forgotten Patriot of the American Revolution: Military Engineer and Cartographer of West Point and the Hudson Valley.* Harrison, N.Y.: Harbor Hill Books, 1985.

Dippie, Brian W. *Catlin and His Contemporaries: The Politics of Patronage.* Lincoln: University of Nebraska Press, 1990.

Doolittle, Amos. *A Display of the United States of America.* New Haven: Printed and Sold by A. Doolittle, 1794.

———. *A New Display of the United States.* New Haven: Amos Doolittle, 1799.

Dowd, Gregory. *A Spirited Resistance: The North American Indian Struggle for Unity.* Baltimore: Johns Hopkins University Press, 1992.

Dunbabin, J. P. D. "Red Lines on Maps: The Impact of Cartographical Errors on the Border Between the United States and British North America, 1782–1842." *Imago Mundi* 50 (1998), 105–25.

Dunbar, William, and Thomas Jefferson. "Description of a Singular Phenomenon Seen at Baton Rouge, by William Dunbar, Esq. Communicated by Thomas Jefferson, President A. P. S." *Transactions of the American Philosophical Society* 6 (1809), 25.

Dupré, E. *Atlas of the city and county of St. Louis, by congressional . . .* 1838.

Durrett, Reuben T. *John Filson, the First Historian of Kentucky.* Louisville: Printed for the Filson Club by J. P. Morton, 1884.

DuVal, Kathleen. *The Native Ground: Indians and Colonists in the Heart of the Continent.* Philadelphia: University of Pennsylvania Press, 2006.

Dyck, Reginald, and Cheli Ruetter, eds. *Crisscrossing Borders in Literature of the American West.* New York: Palgrave Macmillan, 2009.

Edney, Matthew H. *Mapping an Empire: The Geographical Construction of British India, 1765–1843.* Chicago: University of Chicago Press, 1997.

Ellicott, Andrew. *The Journal of Andrew Ellicott, Late Commissioner on Behalf of the United States During Part of the Year 1796, the Years 1797, 1798, 1799, and part of the year 1800. . . .* Philadelphia: Thomas Dobson, 1803.

———. *The Maryland, Delaware, Pennsylvania, Virginia, and North-Carolina Almanack. . . .* Baltimore: M. K. Goddard, 1780.

Ellingson, Terry Jay. *The Myth of the Noble Savage.* Berkeley: University of California Press, 2001.

Engel, Leonard, ed. *The Big Empty: Essays on Western Landscapes as Narrative.* Albuquerque: University of New Mexico Press, 1994.

Erney, Richard Alton. *The Public Life of Henry Dearborn.* New York: Arno Press, 1979.

Estes, Todd. *The Jay Treaty Debate, Public Opinion, and the Evolution of Early American Political Culture.* Amherst: University of Massachusetts Press, 2006.

Evans, Estwick. *A Pedestrious Tour, of four thousand miles through the western states and territories, during the winter and spring of 1818 interspersed with brief reflections upon a great variety of topics . . .* Concord, N.H.: Joseph C. Spear, 1819.

Everton, Michael J. "The Courtesies of Authorship: Hannah Adams and Authorial Ethics in the Early Republic." *Legacy* 20 (2003), 1–21.

Eyal, Yonatan. *The Young America Movement and the Transformation of the Democratic Party, 1828–61.* Cambridge: Cambridge University Press, 2007.

Faragher, John Mack. *Daniel Boone: The Life and Legend of an American Pioneer.* New York: Holt, 1992.

———. *Rereading Frederick Jackson Turner: "The Significance of the Frontier in American History" and Other Essays.* New York: Holt, 1994.

———. *Women and Men on the Overland Trail.* New Haven: Yale University Press, 1979.

Festa, Lynn M. *Sentimental Figures of Empire in Eighteenth-Century Britain and France.* Baltimore: Johns Hopkins University Press, 2006.

Filson, John. *A Topographical Description of the Western Territory of North America.* New York: Samuel Campbell, 1793.

———. *Adventures of Colonel Daniel Boon.* Philadelphia, 1787.

———. *The Discovery, Settlement and Present State of Kentucke.* Wilmington: James Adams, 1784.

Fischer, David Hackett. *Liberty and Freedom: A Visual History of America's Founding Ideas.* Oxford: Oxford University Press, 2005.

———, and James C. Kelly. *Bound Away: Virginia and the Westward Movement.* Charlottesville: University Press of Virginia, 2000.

Flagg, Edmund. *The Far West, or, A Tour Beyond the Mountains . . .* New York: Harper and Brothers, 1838.

Flint, Timothy. *Recollections of the Last Ten Years, passed in occasional residences and journeyings in the valley of the Mississippi, from Pittsburgh and the Missouri to the Gulf of Mexico, and from Florida to the Spanish frontier: in a series of letters to the Rev. James Flint, of Salem, Massachusetts.* Boston: Cummings, Hilliard, 1826.

Flores, Dan L. *Horizontal Yellow: Nature and History in the Near Southwest.* Albuquerque: University of New Mexico Press, 1999.

———. *Jefferson and Southwestern Exploration: The Freeman and Custis Accounts of the Red River Expedition of 1806.* Norman: University of Oklahoma Press, 1984.

Foley, William E. *The Genesis of Missouri: From Wilderness Outpost to Statehood.* Columbia: University of Missouri Press, 1989.

———. *Wilderness Journey: The Life of William Clark.* Columbia: University of Missouri Press, 2004.

———. "Lewis and Clark's American Travels: The View from Britain." *Western Historical Quarterly* 34, no. 3 (2003), 301–24.

Forbes, Robert Pierce. *The Missouri Compromise and Its Aftermath: Slavery and the Meaning of America*. Chapel Hill: University of North Carolina Press, 2007.

Franklin, Wayne. *Discoverers, Explorers, Settlers: The Diligent Writers of Early America*. Chicago: University of Chicago Press, 1979.

Freeman, Joanne B. "Dueling as Politics: Reinterpreting the Burr-Hamilton Duel." *William and Mary Quarterly*, 3d. ser., 53 (1996), 289–319.

Fresonke, Kris. *West of Emerson: The Design of Manifest Destiny*. Berkeley: University of California Press, 2003.

Furtwangler, Albert. *Acts of Discovery: Visions of America in the Lewis and Clark Journals*. Urbana: University of Illinois Press, 1993.

Gaff, Alan D. *Bayonets in the Wilderness: Anthony Wayne's Legion in the Old Northwest*. Norman: University of Oklahoma Press, 2004.

Gass, Patrick. *A Journal of the Voyages and Travels of a Corps of Discovery: Under the Command of Capt. Lewis and Capt. Clarke of the Army of the United States, from the Mouth of the River Missouri Through the Interior Parts of North America to the Pacific Ocean, during the years 1804, 1805 and 1806. . . .* Pittsburgh: Zadok Cramer, 1807.

———. *Journal of the Voyages and Travels of a Corps of Discovery Under the Command of Capt. Lewis and Capt. Clarke, of the Army of the United States, from the mouth of the river Missouri through the interior parts of North America to the Pacific Ocean, during the years 1804, 1805 and 1806*. Philadelphia: Mathew Carey, 1810 and 1812.

Gilman, Carolyn. *Lewis and Clark: Across the Divide*. Washington: Smithsonian Books, 2003.

Gitlin, Jay. *The Bourgeois Frontier: French Towns, French Traders, and American Expansion*. New Haven: Yale University Press, 2009.

Goetzmann, William H. *Army Exploration in the American West, 1803–1863*. New Haven: Yale University Press, 1959.

———. *Exploration and Empire: The Explorer and the Scientist in the Winning of the American West*. New York: Knopf, 1966.

———. *New Lands, New Men: America and the Second Great Age of Discovery*. New York: Viking, 1986.

———, and William N. Goetzmann. *The West of the Imagination*. New York: Norton, 1986.

Gough, Robert. "Officering the American Army, 1798." *William and Mary Quarterly*, 3d ser., 43 (1986), 460–71.

Govan, Thomas P. *Nicholas Biddle, Nationalist and Public Banker, 1786–1844*. Chicago: University of Chicago Press, 1959.

Greenblatt, Stephen. *Marvelous Possessions: The Wonder of the New World*. Chicago: University of Chicago Press, 1991.

Greenfield, Bruce. *Narrating Discovery: The Romantic Explorer in American Literature, 1790–1855*. New York: Columbia University Press, 1992.

Greenfeld, Liah. *Nationalism: Five Roads to Modernity*. Cambridge: Harvard University Press, 1992.

Gregg, Kate L., ed. *Westward with Dragoons: The Journal of William Clark on his Expedition to Establish Fort Osage, August 25 to September 22, 1808*. Fulton, Mo.: Ovid Bell Press, 1937.

Hallock, Thomas. *From the Fallen Tree: Frontier Narratives, Environmental Politics, and the Roots of a National Pastoral, 1749–1826*. Chapel Hill: University of North Carolina Press, 2003.

Haltman, Kenneth. *Looking Close and Seeing Far: Samuel Seymour, Titian Ramsay Peale, and the Art of the Long Expedition, 1818–1823*. University Park: Pennsylvania State University Press, 2008.

Hämäläinen, Pekka. *The Comanche Empire*. New Haven: Yale University Press, 2008.

Hanor, Jeffrey S. "The Dunbar–Hunter Expedition (1804–1805), Early Analyses of Spring Waters in the Louisiana Purchase." *Ground Water* 45, no. 6 (2007), 803–07.

Harding, Benjamin. *A Tour through the Western Country, A.D. 1818 and 1819*. New London: Samuel Green, 1819.

Harley, J. B. "Maps, Knowledge, and Power." In *The Iconography of Landscape: Essays on the Symbolic Representation, Design, and Use of Past Environments*. ed. Denis E. Cosgrove et al., 277–312. Cambridge: Cambridge University Press, 1988.

Harley, J. B., Barbara Bartz Petchenik, and Lawrence W. Towner. *Mapping the American Revolutionary War*. Chicago: University of Chicago Press, 1978.

Harrison, Lowell Hayes. *George Rogers Clark and the War in the West*. Lexington: University Press of Kentucky, 2001.

Hatzenbuehler, Ronald L., and Robert L. Ivie. *Congress Declares War: Rhetoric, Leadership, and Partisanship in the Early Republic*. Kent, Ohio: Kent State University Press, 1983.

Hendrickson, David C. *Peace Pact: The Lost World of the American Founding*. Lawrence: University Press of Kansas, 2003.

Hesford, Walter. "'Do You Know the Author?' The Question of Authorship in *Wieland*." *Early American Literature* 17 (1982), 239–48.

Hietala, Thomas R. *Manifest Design: Anxious Aggrandizement in Late Jacksonian America*. Ithaca: Cornell University Press, 1985.

Hight, Kathryn S. "'Doomed to Perish': George Catlin's Depictions of the Mandan." *Art Journal* 49, no. 2 (1990), 119–24.

History of the Expedition under the Command of Captains Lewis and Clark, to the sources of the Missouri, thence across the Rocky Mountains and down the river Columbia to the Pacific Ocean: Performed during the years 1804-5-6 by order of the government of the United States. Philadelphia: Bradford and Inskeep, 1814.

Hoffman, Ronald, Thad W. Tate, and Peter J. Albert, eds. *An Uncivil War: The Southern Backcountry During the American Revolution*. Charlottesville: University Press of Virginia, 1985.

Hood, Gary Allen. *After Lewis and Clark: The Forces of Change, 1806–1871*. Tulsa: Gilcrease Museum, 2006.

Horsman, Reginald. *Expansion and American Foreign Policy*. East Lansing: Michigan State University Press, 1967.

———. *Race and Manifest Destiny: The Origins of American Racial Anglo-Saxonism*. Cambridge: Harvard University Press, 1981.

Howe, Daniel Walker. *What Hath God Wrought: The Transformation of America, 1815–1848*. Oxford: Oxford University Press, 2007.

Hoxie, Frederick E., and Jay T. Nelson, eds. *Lewis and Clark and the Indian Country: The Native American Perspective*. Urbana: University of Illinois Press: Published for the Newberry Library, 2007.

Humboldt, Alexander von. *Atlas géographique et physique du royaume de la Nouvelle-Espagne*. Paris: F. Schoell, 1811.

———. *Geographisch- und physischer Atlas von kèonigreiche Neuspanien: gegrèundet auf astronomische, trigonometrische und barometrische Messungen*. Tèubingen: J. G. Cotta, 1810.

———, and Aimé Jacques Alexandre Goujaud Bonpland. *Voyage de Humboldt et Bonpland; voyage aux régions équinoxiales du nouveau continent*. Hildesheim, N.Y.: G. Olms, 1971.

Huston, Reeve. *Land and Freedom: Rural Society, Popular Protest, and Party Politics in Antebellum New York*. Oxford: Oxford University Press, 2000.

Hutchins, Thomas. *A Topographical Description of Virginia, Pennsylvania, Maryland and North Carolina . . .* Boston: John Norman, 1787.

———. *An Historical Narrative and Topographical Description of Louisiana and West-Florida: Comprehending the River Mississippi with its Principal Branches and Settlements . . .* Philadelphia, 1784.

———. *Proposals for Publishing by Subscription, a Map of the Coast of West-Florida. By Thomas Hutchins, late captain and engineer in the British service, and now geographer to the United States of America*. Philadelphia: Robert Aitken, 1781.

Imlay, Gilbert, and Cornelius Tiebout. *A Topographical Description of the Western Territory of North America . . .* New York: Samuel Campbell, 1793.

Isenberg, Nancy. *Fallen Founder: A Life of Aaron Burr*. New York: Viking, 2007.

Jabour, Anya. *Marriage in the Early Republic: Elizabeth and William Wirt and the Companionate Ideal*. Baltimore: Johns Hopkins University Press, 1998.

Jackson, Donald. *Thomas Jefferson and the Stony Mountains: Exploring the West from Monticello*. Urbana: University of Illinois Press, 1981.

Jackson, Leon. "Jedidiah Morse and the Transformation of Print Culture in New England, 1784–1826." *Early American Literature* 34 (1999), 2–31.

James, Edwin, ed. *Account of an Expedition from Pittsburgh to the Rocky Mountains: Performed in the Years 1819 and '20, by Order of the Hon. J. C. Calhoun, Sec'y of War, Under the Command of Major Stephen H. Long . . .* 3 vols. Philadelphia: H. C. Carey and I. Lea, 1822.

John, Richard R. *Spreading the News: The American Postal System from Franklin to Morse.* Cambridge: Harvard University Press, 1995.

Jones, Landon Y. *William Clark and the Shaping of the West.* New York: Hill and Wang, 2004.

Josephy, Alvin M., and Marc Jaffe, eds. *Lewis and Clark Through Indian Eyes.* New York: Knopf, 2006.

Kaplan, Amy. *The Anarchy of Empire in the Making of U.S. Culture.* Cambridge: Harvard University Press, 2002.

Kaplan, Catherine O'Donnell. *Men of Letters in the Early Republic: Cultivating Forums of Citizenship.* Chapel Hill: Published for the Omohundro Institute of Early American History and Culture, Williamsburg, Virginia, by the University of North Carolina Press, 2008.

Kaplan, Lawrence S. *Thomas Jefferson: Westward the Course of Empire.* Wilmington: SR Books, 1999.

Kaser, David. *Messrs. Carey and Lea of Philadelphia: A Study in the History of the Booktrade.* Philadelphia: University of Pennsylvania Press, 1957.

Kastor, Peter J. *The Nation's Crucible: The Louisiana Purchase and the Creation of America.* New Haven: Yale University Press, 2004.

———. "'What Are the Advantages of the Acquisition?': Inventing Expansion in the Early American Republic." *American Quarterly* 60, no. 4 (2008), 1003–35.

———, ed. *America's Struggle with Empire: A Documentary History.* Washington: CQ Press, 2009.

Keller, Christian B. "Philanthropy Betrayed: Thomas Jefferson, the Louisiana Purchase, and the Origins of Federal Indian Removal Policy." *Proceedings of the American Philosophical Society* 144, no. 1 (2000), 39–66.

Kennedy, Roger G. *Burr, Hamilton, and Jefferson: A Study in Character.* Oxford: Oxford University Press, 2000.

Kerber, Linda K. *Federalists in Dissent: Imagery and Ideology in Jeffersonian America.* Ithaca: Cornell University Press, 1970.

Klein, Rachel N. *Unification of a Slave State: The Rise of the Planter Class in the South Carolina Backcountry, 1760–1808.* Chapel Hill: University of North Carolina Press, 1990.

Knudson, Jerry W. "Newspaper Reaction to the Louisiana Purchase, 'This New, Immense, Unbounded World.'" *Missouri Historical Review* 43, no. 2 (1969), 182–213.

Kolk, Heidi Aronson. "The Discriminating Cicerone: Class, Cultural Identity and Social Performance in Nineteenth-Century Travel Narratives." Ph.D. diss., Washington University in St. Louis, 2003.

Kukla, John. *A Wilderness So Immense: The Louisiana Purchase and the Destiny of America.* New York: Knopf, 2003.

Lawrence, John Shelton, and Robert Jewett. *The Myth of the American Superhero.* Grand Rapids: W. B. Eerdmans, 2002.

Lawson-Peebles, Robert. *Landscape and Written Expression in Revolutionary America: The World Turned Upside Down.* Cambridge: Cambridge University Press, 1988.

LeBeau, Bryan F. *Currier and Ives: America Imagined*. Washington: Smithsonian Institution Press, 2001.

LeMenager, Stephanie. *Manifest and Other Destinies: Territorial Fictions of the Nineteenth-Century United States*. Lincoln: University of Nebraska Press, 2004.

Lemmon, Alfred E., John T. Magill, and Jason R. Wiese, eds. *Charting Louisiana: Five Hundred Years of Maps*. New Orleans: Historic New Orleans Collection, 2003.

Leonard, David A. *An Oration, Delivered at Raynham, Massachusetts, Friday, May 11th, 1804, on the Late Acquisition of Louisiana, at the Unanimous Request of the Republican Citizens of the County of Bristol*. Newport: Oliver Farnsworth, 1804.

Lepore, Jill. *A Is for American: Letters and Other Characters in the Newly United States*. New York: Alfred A. Knopf, 2002.

Letter from the Secretary of the Treasury transmitting a report prepared in obedience to a resolution of the first instant, requesting information touching any settlement contrary to law, on the public lands in the county of Madison in Mississippi territory. Washington: Roger Chew Weightman, 1809.

Lewis, G. Malcolm, ed. *Cartographic Encounters: Perspectives on Native American Mapmaking and Map Use*. Chicago: University of Chicago Press, 1998.

———. "Indicators of Unacknowledged Assimilation from Amerindian Maps on Euroamerican Maps of North America: some general principles arising from a study of La Vérendrye's composite map, 1728–29." *Imago Mundi* 38 (1986), 9–34.

Lewis, James E., Jr. *The American Union and the Problem of Neighborhood: The United States and the Collapse of the Spanish Empire, 1783–1829*. Chapel Hill: University of North Carolina Press, 1998.

Lewis, Jan. "'The Blessings of Domestic Society': Thomas Jefferson's Family and the Transformation of American Politics." In *Jeffersonian Legacies*, ed. Peter S. Onuf, 109–46. Charlottesville: University Press of Virginia, 1993.

Liebersohn, Harry. *Aristocratic Encounters: European Travelers and North American Indians*. Cambridge: Cambridge University Press, 1998.

Limerick, Patricia Nelson. *The Legacy of Conquest: The Unbroken Past of the American West*. New York: Norton, 1987.

Linklater, Andro. *Measuring America: How an Untamed Wilderness Shaped the United States and Fulfilled the Promise of Democracy*. New York: Walker, 2002.

Little, J. I. "Canadian Pastoral: Promotional Images of British Colonization in Lower Canada's Eastern Townships during the 1830s." *Journal of Historical Geography* 29, no. 2 (2003), 189–211.

Livermore, Shaw. *The Twilight of Federalism: The Disintegration of the Federalist Party, 1815–1830*. Princeton: Princeton University Press, 1962.

Ludlow, Maxfield. *To the Public*. Natchez, 1817.

Lueck, Beth Lynne. *American Writers and the Picturesque Tour: The Search for National Identity, 1790–1860*. New York: Garland Publishing, 1997.

Mackenzie, Alexander. *Voyages from Montreal, on the River St. Laurence, through the Continent of North America, to the Frozen and Pacific Oceans; in the years 1789 and 1793 . . .* London: T. Cadell Jun. and W. Davies, 1801.

Magruder, Allan Bowie. *Political, Commercial, and Moral Reflections on the Late Cession of Louisiana to the United States.* Lexington: D. Bradford, 1803.

Malone, Dumas. *Jefferson the Virginian.* Boston: Little, Brown, 1948.

Man, Felix H. *Artists' Lithographs: A World History from Senefelder to the Present Day.* New York: Putnam, 1970.

Mapp, Paul William. "European Geographic Ignorance and North American Imperial Rivalry: The Role of the Uncharted American West in International Affairs, 1713–1763." Ph.D. diss., Harvard University, 2001.

Mathews, Catharine Van Cortlandt. *Andrew Ellicott, His Life and Letters.* New York: Grafton Press, 1908.

Matson, Cathy D., and Peter S. Onuf. *A Union of Interests: Political and Economic Thought in Revolutionary America.* Lawrence: University Press of Kansas, 1990.

Matthiessen, F. O. *American Renaissance: Art and Expression in the Age of Emerson and Whitman.* London: Oxford University Press, 1941.

May, Ernest R. *The Making of the Monroe Doctrine.* Cambridge: Belknap Press of Harvard University Press, 1975.

Mazel, David. "'A Beautiful and Thrilling Specimen': George Catlin, the Death of Wilderness, and the Birth of the National Subject." In *Reading the Earth: New Directions in the Study of Literature and Environment,* ed. Michael P. Branch, 129–44. Moscow: University of Idaho Press, 1998.

McCoy, Drew R. *The Elusive Republic: Political Economy in Jeffersonian America.* New York: Norton, 1980.

———. *The Last of the Fathers: James Madison and the Republican Legacy.* Cambridge: Cambridge University Press, 1988.

———. "James Madison and Visions of American Nationality in the Confederation Period: A Regional Perspective." In *Beyond Confederation: Origins of the Constitution and American National Identity,* ed. Richard Beeman et al., 226–58. Chapel Hill: University of North Carolina Press, 1987.

McCracken, Harold. *George Catlin and the Old Frontier.* New York: Dial Press, 1959.

McGrane, R. C. "William Clark's Journal of General Wayne's Campaign." *Mississippi Valley Historical Review* 1, no. 3 (1914), 418–44.

McGuire, James. *A Literary History of the American West.* Fort Worth: Texas Christian University Press, 1987.

McKenney, Thomas Loraine. *Sketches of a Tour to the Lakes, of the character and customs of the Chippeway Indians, and of incidents connected with the Treaty of Fond du Lac.* Baltimore: F. Lucas, 1827.

M'Culloch, John. *A Concise History of the United States: From the Discovery of America, till 1807: with a correct map of the United States.* Philadelphia: John M'Culloch, 1807.

Meinig, D. W., ed. *The Interpretation of Ordinary Landscapes: Geographical Essays.* New York: Oxford University Press, 1979.

———. *The Shaping of America: A Geographical Perspective on 500 years of History.* New Haven: Yale University Press, 1986.

Melish, John. *A Description of the Roads in the United States*. Philadelphia: G. Palmer, 1814.

———. *A Military and Topographical Atlas of the United States . . .* Philadelphia: J. Melish, 1815.

———. *The Traveller's Directory through the United States. Consisting of a geographical description of the United States, with topographical tables of the counties, towns, population, etc. and a description of the roads, comp. from the most authentic materials.* Philadelphia: T. and G. Palmer, 1816.

———. *Travels in the United States of America, in the years 1806 and 1807, and 1809, 1810, and 1811 . . .* Philadelphia: T. and G. Palmer, 1812.

Merrill, Orasmus Cook. *The Happiness of America: An Oration Delivered at Shaftsbury, on the Fourth of July.* Vermont, 1804.

Message from the President of the United States, communicating discoveries made in exploring the Missouri, Red River, and Washita, by Captains Lewis and Clark, Doctor Sibley, and Mr. Dunbar; with a statistical account of the countries adjacent. February 19, 1806. Washington: A. and G. Way, 1806.

Michaels, Walter Benn, and Donald E. Pease, eds. *The American Renaissance Reconsidered.* Baltimore: Johns Hopkins University Press, 1985.

Miller, Andrew. *New States and Territories, or, The Ohio, Indiana, Illinois, Michigan, North-western, Missouri, Louisiana, Mississippi and Alabama, in their real characters, in 1818, 1819.*

Miller, Angela L. *The Empire of the Eye: Landscape Representation and American Cultural Politics, 1825–1875.* Ithaca: Cornell University Press, 1993.

Mitchell, Samuel Augustus. *Mitchell's traveller's guide through the United States, containing the principal cities, towns, andc., alphabetically arranged; together with the stage, steam-boat, canal, and railroad routes, with the distances, in miles, from place to place.* Philadelphia: Mitchell and Hinman, 1837.

Moffitt, John F., and Santiago Sebastián. *O Brave New People: The European Invention of the American Indian.* Albuquerque: University of New Mexico Press, 1996.

Monmonier, Mark S. *Drawing the Line: Tales of Maps and Cartocontroversy.* New York: H. Holt, 1995.

Moore, Glover. *The Missouri Controversy, 1819–1821.* Lexington: University of Kentucky Press, 1954.

Morse, Jedidiah. *A Report to the Secretary of War of the United States, on Indian Affairs, comprising a narrative of a tour performed in the summer of 1820.* New Haven: Converse, 1822.

———. *Geography Made Easy.* New Haven: Meigs, Bowen and Dana, 1784.

———. *Geography Made Easy: Being an Abridgment of the American Universal Geography.* Boston: J. T. Buckingham for Thomas and Andrews, 1807.

———. *The American Geography, or, A view of the present situation of the United States of America . . .* Elizabethtown: Shepard Kollock, 1789.

Moss, Richard J. *The Life of Jedidiah Morse: A Station of Peculiar Exposure.* Knoxville: University of Tennessee Press, 1995.

Nelson, W. Dale. *Interpreters with Lewis and Clark: The Story of Sacagawea and Toussaint Charbonneau*. Denton: University of North Texas Press, 2003.

Nester, William R. *From Mountain Man to Millionaire: The "Bold and Dashing Life" of Robert Campbell*. Columbia: University of Missouri Press, 1999.

Nichols, Roger L. *General Henry Atkinson, A Western Military Career*. Norman: University of Oklahoma Press, 1965.

Niles, John M. *The Life of Oliver Hazard Perry: With an appendix, comprising biographical sketches of the late General Pike, and Captain Lawrence, and a view of the present condition and future prospects of the navy of the United States*. Hartford: W. S. Marsh, 1820.

Nobles, Gregory H. *American Frontiers: Cultural Encounters and Continental Conquest*. New York: Hill and Wang, 1997.

———. "Straight Lines and Stability: Mapping the Political Order of the Anglo-American Frontier." *JAH* 80, no. 1 (1993), 9–35.

Novak, Barbara. *American Painting of the Nineteenth Century: Realism, Idealism, and the American Experience*. New York: Praeger, 1969.

———. *Nature and Culture: American Landscape and Painting, 1825–1875*. New York: Oxford University Press, 1995.

Onuf, Peter S. *Jefferson's Empire: The Language of American Nationhood*. Charlottesville: University Press of Virginia, 2000.

———. *Statehood and Union: A History of the Northwest Ordinance*. Bloomington: Indiana University Press, 1987.

———. *The Origins of the Federal Republic: Jurisdictional Controversies in the United States, 1775–1787*. Philadelphia: University of Pennsylvania Press, 1983.

———, and Nicholas G. Onuf. *Federal Union, Modern World: The Law of Nations in an Age of Revolutions, 1776–1814*. Madison: Madison House, 1993.

Owens, Robert M. *Mr. Jefferson's Hammer: William Henry Harrison and the Origins of American Indian Policy*. Norman: University of Oklahoma Press, 2007.

Owsley, Frank Lawrence, Jr., and Gene A. Smith. *Filibusters and Expansionists: Jeffersonian Manifest Destiny, 1800–1821*. Tuscaloosa: University of Alabama Press, 1997.

Padget, Martin. "Claiming, Corrupting, Contesting: Reconsidering 'The West' in Western American Literature." *American Literary History* 10, no. 2 (1998), 378–92.

Parrish, Susan Scott. *American Curiosity: Cultures of Natural History in the Colonial British Atlantic World*. Chapel Hill: University of North Carolina Press, 2006.

Parsons, Lynn H. *John Quincy Adams*. Madison: Madison House, 1998.

Pasley, Jeffrey L. *The Tyranny of Printers: Newspaper Politics in the Early American Republic*. Charlottesville: University Press of Virginia, 2001.

Pearson, Karen. "The Nineteenth-Century Colour Revolution: Maps in Geographical Journals." *Imago Mundi* 32 (1980), 9–20.

Pedley, Mary Sponberg. *The Commerce of Cartography: Making and Marketing Maps in Eighteenth-Century France and England*. Chicago: University of Chicago Press, 2005.

Perkins, Bradford. *Castlereagh and Adams: England and the United States, 1812–1823*. Berkeley: University of California Press, 1964.

———. *Prologue to War: England and the United States, 1805–1812*. Berkeley: University of California Press, 1968.

Peterson, Merrill D. *Thomas Jefferson and the New Nation: A Biography*. Oxford: Oxford University Press, 1970.

Phillips, Mark. *Society and Sentiment: Genres of Historical Writing in Britain, 1740–1820*. Princeton: Princeton University Press, 2000.

Pike, Zebulon Montgomery, and Gouverneur Kemble Warren. *An Account of Expeditions to the Sources of the Mississippi: and through the western parts of Louisiana to the sources of the Arkansaw, Kans, La Platte, and Pierre Jaun Rivers* . . . Philadelphia: C. and A. Conrad, 1810.

———. *Atlas Accompanying An Account of Expeditions to the Sources of the Mississippi and Through the western parts of Louisiana* . . . Philadelphia: C. and A. Conrad, 1810.

Preston, William. "The Accuracy of the Astronomical Observations of Lewis and Clark." *Proceedings of the American Philosophical Society* 144, no. 2 (2000), 168–91.

Price, Edward T. *Dividing the Land: Early American Beginnings of Our Private Property Mosaic*. Chicago: University of Chicago Press, 1995.

Primm, James Neal. *Lion of the Valley: St. Louis, Missouri, 1764–1980*. St. Louis: Missouri Historical Society Press; Distributed by University of Missouri Press, 1998 [1981].

Pritchard, Margaret Beck, and Henry G. Taliaferro. *Degrees of Latitude: Mapping Colonial America*. Williamsburg, Va.: Colonial Williamsburg Foundation in association with H. N. Abrams, 2002.

Prucha, Francis Paul. *The Sword of the Republic: The United States Army on the Frontier, 1783–1846*. New York: Macmillan, 1969.

Rakove, Jack N. *Original Meanings: Politics and Ideas in the Making of the Constitution*. New York: Vintage, 1997.

Ramsay, David. *An Oration on the Cession of Louisiana to the United States* . . . Charleston: W. P. Young, 1804.

Redmond, Edward J. "Mapping from Mount Vernon, 1747–1799." In *Early American Cartographies Conference*. Newberry Library, Chicago, 2006.

Reps, John William. *John Caspar Wild: Painter and Printmaker of Nineteenth-Century Urban America*. St. Louis: Missouri Historical Society Press, Distributed by University of Missouri Press, 2006.

———. *Saint Louis Illustrated: Nineteenth-Century Engravings and Lithographs of a Mississippi River Metropolis*. Columbia: University of Missouri Press, 1989.

Reynolds, Guy. "The Winning of the West: Washington Irving's 'A Tour on the Prairies.'" *Yearbook of English Studies* 34 (2004), 88–99.

Rhodes, Richard. *John James Audubon: The Making of an American*. New York: Alfred A. Knopf, 2004.

Rice, Grantland S. *The Transformation of Authorship in America*. Chicago: University of Chicago Press, 1997.

Ristow, Walter William. *Maps for an Emerging Nation: Commercial Cartography in Nineteenth-Century America.* Washington: Library of Congress, 1977.

Robbins, William G., and James C. Foster. *Land in the American West: Private Claims and the Common Good.* Seattle: University of Washington Press, 2000.

Robertson, Andrew W. "'Look on This Picture . . . And on This!' Nationalism, Localism, and Partisan Images of Otherness in the United States, 1787–1820." *AHR* 104, no. 4 (2001), 1263–80.

Robertson, Lindsay Gordon. *Conquest by Law: How the Discovery of America Dispossessed Indigenous Peoples of Their Lands.* Oxford: Oxford University Press, 2005.

Rohrbough, Malcolm J. *The Land Office Busines: The Settlement and Administration of American Public Lands, 1789–1837.* New York: Oxford University Press, 1968.

Romans, Bernard. *A Concise Natural History of East and West Florida.* . . . New York: Printed for the author, 1775.

Ronda, James P. *Astoria and Empire.* Lincoln: University of Nebraska Press, 1990.

———. *Beyond Lewis and Clark: The Army Explores the West.* Tacoma: Washington State Historical Society, 2003.

———. *Jefferson's West: A Journey with Lewis and Clark.* Charlottesville: Thomas Jefferson Foundation, 2000.

———. *Lewis and Clark Among the Indians.* Lincoln: University of Nebraska Press, 1988.

———. *The Exploration of North America.* Washington: American Historical Association, 1992.

———. *Thomas Jefferson and the Changing West: From Conquest to Conservation.* Albuquerque, St. Louis: University of New Mexico Press, Missouri Historical Society Press, 1997.

———, ed. *Revealing America: Image and Imagination in the Exploration of North America.* Lexington, Mass.: D. C. Heath, 1996.

———, ed. *Voyages of Discovery: Essays on the Lewis and Clark Expedition.* Helena: Montana Historical Society Press, 1998.

———. "Coboway's Tale: A Story of Power and Places Along the Columbia." In *Power and Place in the North American West,* ed. Richard White et al., 1–30. Seattle: University of Washington Press, 1999.

Rosowski, Susan J. *Birthing a Nation: Gender, Creativity, and the West in American Literature.* Lincoln: University of Nebraska Press, 1999.

Rothman, Adam. *Slave Country: American Expansion and the Origins of the Deep South.* Cambridge: Harvard University Press, 2005.

Rowe, John Carlos. *Literary Culture and U.S. Imperialism: From the Revolution to World War II.* Oxford: Oxford University Press, 2000.

Sachs, Aaron. *The Humboldt Current: Nineteenth-Century Exploration and the Roots of American Environmentalism.* New York: Viking, 2006.

Sandweiss, Martha A. *Print the Legend: Photography and the American West.* New Haven: Yale University Press, 2002.

Saunt, Claudio. *A New Order of Things: Property, Power, and the Transformation of the Creek Indians, 1733–1816*. Cambridge: Cambridge University Press, 1999.

Say, Thomas. *American Entomology, or Descriptions of the Insects of North America . . .* Philadelphia: S. A. Mitchell, 1824.

Sayer, Robert. *An Accurate Map of North America Describing and Distinguishing the British and French dominions on this great continent according to the definitive treaty concluded at Paris 10th February 1763*. London, 1763.

Schoolcraft, Henry Rowe. *A View of the Lead Mines of Missouri . . .* New York: Charles Wiley, 1819.

———. *Journal of a Tour into the Interior of Missouri and Arkansaw*. Londo: Sir R. Phillips, 1821.

———. *Narrative Journal of Travels through the Northwestern regions of the United States: extending from Detroit through the great chain of American lakes to the sources of the Mississippi River, performed as a member of the expedition under Governor Cass in the year 1820*. Albany: E. and E. Hosford, 1821.

———. *Narrative of an Expedition Through the Upper Mississippi to Itasca Lake: the actual source of this river: embracing an exploratory trip through the St. Croix and Burntwood (or Broule) Rivers: in 1832*. New York: Harper, 1834.

———. *The Rise of the West, or A prospect of the Mississippi Valley: A poem*. New York: W. Applegate, 1841.

———. *Travels in the Central Portions of the Mississippi Valley: comprising observations on its mineral geography, internal resources, and aboriginal population*. New York: Collins and Hannay, 1825.

Schroeder, John H. *Mr. Polk's War: American Opposition and Dissent, 1846–1848*. Madison: University of Wisconsin Press, 1973.

Schubert, Frank N. *The Nation Builders: A Sesquicentennial History of the Corps of Topographical Engineers, 1838–1863*. Washington: U.S. Army Corps of Engineers, 1988.

Schwartz, Seymour I., and Ralph E. Ehrenberg. *The Mapping of America*. Edison, N.J.: Wellfleet, 2001.

Seelye, John. "Captives, Captains, Cowboys, Indians: Frames of Reference and the American West." *American Literary History* 7, no. 2 (1995), 304–19.

Shapiro, Stephen. *The Culture and Commerce of the Early American Novel: Reading the Atlantic World-System*. University Park: Pennsylvania State University Press, 2008.

Sheehan, Bernard W. *Seeds of Extinction: Jeffersonian Philanthropy and the American Indian*. Chapel Hill: University of North Carolina Press, 1973.

Short, John R. *Representing the Republic: Mapping the United States, 1600–1900*. London: Reaktion, 2001.

Skelton, William B. *An American Profession of Arms: The Army Officer Corps, 1784–1815*. Lawrence: University Press of Kansas, 1992.

Slaughter, Thomas P. *Exploring Lewis and Clark: Reflections on Men and Wilderness*. New York: Alfred A. Knopf, 2003.

———. *The Natures of John and William Bartram.* New York: Alfred A. Knopf, 1996.

Sloan, Herbert E. *Principle and Interest: Thomas Jefferson and the Problem of Debt.* Oxford: Oxford University Press, 1995.

Slotkin, Richard. *Regeneration through Violence: The Mythology of the American Frontier, 1600–1860.* Middletown, Conn.: Wesleyan University Press, 1973.

———. *The Fatal Environment: The Myth of the Frontier in the Age of Industrialization, 1800–1890.* New York: Atheneum, 1985.

Smith, Elbert B. *Magnificent Missourian: The Life of Thomas Hart Benton.* Philadelphia: Lippincott, 1958.

Smith, Henry Nash. *Virgin Land: The American West as Symbol and Myth.* Cambridge: Harvard University Press, 1950.

Spivak, Burton. *Jefferson's English Crisis: Commerce, Embargo, and the Republican Revolution.* Charlottesville: University Press of Virginia, 1979.

Spurgeon, Sara L. *Exploding the Western: Myths of Empire on the Postmodern Frontier.* College Station: Texas A&M University Press, 2005.

Stafford, Barbara Maria. *Voyage into Substance: Art, Science, Nature, and the Illustrated Travel Account, 1760–1840.* Cambridge: MIT Press, 1984.

Stagg, J. C. A. *Mr. Madison's War: Politics, Diplomacy, and Warfare in the Early American Republic, 1783–1830.* Princeton: Princeton University Press, 1983.

———. "James Madison and the Coercion of Great Britain: Canada, the West Indies, and the War of 1812." *William and Mary Quarterly,* 3d ser., 38 (1981), 3–34.

Stahr, Walter. *John Jay: Founding Father.* New York: Palgrave Macmillan, 2005.

Stilgoe, John R. *Common Landscape of America, 1580 to 1845.* New Haven: Yale University Press, 1982.

Stoddard, Amos. *Sketches, Historical and Descriptive, of Louisiana.* Philadelphia: Mathew Carey, 1812.

Stork, William. *An Account of East-Florida, with A journal kept by John Bartram of Philadelphia, botanist to His Majesty for the Floridas; upon a journey from St. Augustine up the river St. John's.* London: W. Nicoll and G. Woodfall, 1766.

Streeby, Shelley. *American Sensations: Class, Empire, and the Production of Popular Culture.* Berkeley: University of California Press, 2002.

Sugden, John. *Blue Jacket: Warrior of the Shawnees.* Lincoln: University of Nebraska Press, 2000.

Sword, Wiley. *President Washington's Indian War: The Struggle for the Old Northwest, 1790–1795.* Norman: University of Oklahoma Press, 1985.

Tanner, Henry Schenck. *A New American Atlas, containing maps of the several States of the North American union.* Philadelphia: Henry Tanner, 1823.

———. *Memoir on the Recent Surveys, Observations, and Internal Improvements in the United States* . . . Philadelphia: Published by the author, Mifflin and Parry, 1829.

———. *The American Traveller, or, Guide through the United States* . . . Philadelphia: Henry Schenck Tanner, 1834.

Tate, Michael L. *The Frontier Army in the Settlement of the West.* Norman: University of Oklahoma Press, 1999.

Taylor, Alan. *Liberty Men and Great Proprietors: The Revolutionary Settlement on the Maine Frontier, 1760–1820.* Chapel Hill: University of North Carolina Press, 1990.

———. *William Cooper's Town: Power and Persuasion on the Frontier of the Early American Republic.* New York: Norton, 1995.

———. "Jefferson's Pacific: The Science of Distant Empire, 1768–1811." In *Across the Continent: Jefferson, Lewis and Clark, and the Making of America,* ed. Douglas Seefeldt et al., 16–44. Charlottesville: University of Virginia Press, 2005.

Terrell, John Upton. *Zebulon Pike: The Life and Times of an Adventurer.* New York: Weybright and Talley, 1968.

The Public Statutes at Large of the United States of America. Boston: Charles C. Little and James Brown, 1845.

The Travels of Capts. Lewis and Clarke: by Order of the Government of the United States, performed in the years 1804, 1805 and 1806, being upwards of three thousand miles, from St. Louis, by way of the Missouri and Columbia Rivers, to the Pacifick Ocean: containing an account of the Indian tribes, who inhabit the western part of the continent unexplored, and unknown before : with copious delineations of the manners, customs, religion, andc. of the Indians. Philadelphia: Hubbard Lester, 1809.

Thomas, John L. *A Country in the Mind: Wallace Stegner, Bernard De Voto, History, and the American Land.* New York: Routledge, 2000.

Thorne, Tanis C. *The Many Hands of My Relations: French and Indians on the Lower Missouri.* Columbia: University of Missouri Press, 1996.

Tiebout, Cornelius. *A General Atlas for the Present War. Containing six maps and one chart . . .* Philadelphia: Mathew Carey, 1794.

Tillson, Albert H., Jr. *Gentry and Common Folk: Political Culture on a Virginia Frontier, 1740–1789.* Lexington: University Press of Kentucky, 1991.

Tocqueville, Alexis de. *Democracy in America.* New York: Library of America, 2004.

Travers, Len. *Celebrating the Fourth: Independence Day and the Rites of Nationalism in the Early Republic.* Amherst: University of Massachusetts Press, 1997.

Trees, Andrew S. *The Founding Fathers and the Politics of Character.* Princeton: Princeton University Press, 2004.

———. "Private Correspondence for the Public Good: Thomas Jefferson to Elbridge Gerry, 26 January 1799." *Virginia Magazine of History and Biography* 108, no. 3 (2000), 217–55.

Tucker, Robert W., and David C. Hendrickson. *Empire of Liberty: The Statecraft of Thomas Jefferson.* New York: Oxford University Press, 1990.

Tucker, St. George. *Reflections on the Cession of Louisiana to the United States.* Washington: Samuel Harrison Smith, 1803.

Turner, Frederick J. "Social Forces in American History." *American Historical Review* 16, no. 2 (1911), 217–33.

Ulrich, Laurel Thatcher. *A Midwife's Tale: The Life of Martha Ballard, Based on Her Diary, 1785–1812*. New York: Alfred A. Knopf, 1990.

Valencius, Conevery Bolton. *The Health of the Country: How American Settlers Understood Themselves and Their land*. New York: Basic Books, 2002.

Vibert, Elizabeth. *Traders' Tales: Narratives of Cultural Encounters in the Columbia Plateau, 1807–1846*. Norman: University of Oklahoma Press, 1997.

Viola, Herman J. *Thomas L. McKenney: Architect of America's Early Indian Policy, 1816–1830*. Chicago: Sage Books, 1974.

Volney, C. F. A *View of the Soil and Climate of the United States of America . . .* Philadelphia: J. Conrad, 1804.

W.M.P. *A Poem on the Acquisition of Louisiana Respectfully Dedicated to the Committee Appointed for the Celebration of that Great Event in this City*. Charleston: Query and Evans, 1804.

Waldstreicher, David. *In the Midst of Perpetual Fetes: The Making of American Nationalism, 1776–1820*. Chapel Hill: University of North Carolina Press, 1997.

Wallace, Anthony F. C. *Jefferson and the Indians: The Tragic Fate of the First Americans*. Cambridge: Belknap Press of Harvard University Press, 1999.

———. *The Long Bitter Trail: Andrew Jackson and the Indians*. New York: Hill and Wang, 1993.

Walton, John. *John Filson of Kentucke*. Lexington: University of Kentucky Press, 1956.

Warner, Michael. *The Letters of the Republic: Publication and the Public Sphere in Eighteenth-Century America*. Cambridge: Harvard University Press, 1990.

Washington, George. *The Journal of Major George Washington sent by the Hon. Robert Dinwiddie, Esq . . .* Williamsburg: William Hunter, 1754.

Waterman, Bryan. *Republic of Intellect: The Friendly Club of New York City and the Making of American Literature*. Baltimore: Johns Hopkins University Press, 2007.

Weber, David J. *The Spanish Frontier in North America*. New Haven: Yale University Press, 1992.

———. "Turner, the Boltonians, and the Borderlands." *AHR* 91 (1986), 66–80.

Weeks, William Earl. *John Quincy Adams and American Global Empire*. Lexington: University Press of Kentucky, 1992.

Weems, Mason Locke. *A History of the Life and Death, Virtues and Exploits of General George Washington*. Philadelphia: John Bioren, 1800.

Weiss, Harry B., and Grace M. Weiss. *Thomas Say, Early American Naturalist*. Springfield, Ill.: C. C. Thomas, 1931.

Weyler, Karen Ann. *Intricate Relations: Sexual and Economic Desire in American Fiction, 1789–1814*. Iowa City: University of Iowa Press, 2004.

Whitaker, Arthur Preston. *The Mississippi Question, 1795–1803*. New York: C. Appleton-Century, 1934.

White, Richard. *The Middle Ground: Indians, Empires, and Republics in the Great Lakes Region, 1650–1815*. Cambridge: Cambridge University Press, 1991.

———. *The Roots of Dependency: Subsistence, Environment, and Social Change among the Choctaws, Pawnees, and Navajos.* Lincoln: University of Nebraska Press, 1983.

Wilson, Douglas L. "Jefferson and the Republic of Letters." In *Jeffersonian Legacies,* ed. Peter S. Onuf, 59–76. Charlottesville: University Press of Virginia, 1993.

Wilton, Andrew, and T. J. Barringer. *American Sublime: Landscape Painting in the United States, 1820–1880.* Princeton: Princeton University Press, 2002.

Winfield, Betty Houchin. "Public Perception and Public Events: The Louisiana Purchase and the American Partisan Press." In *The Louisiana Purchase: Emergence of an American Nation,* ed. Peter J. Kastor, 38–50. Washington: CQ Press, 2002.

———. "Public Perception of the Expedition." In *Lewis and Clark: Journey to Another America,* ed. Alan Taylor. St. Louis: Missouri Historical Society Press : Distributed by Booksource, 2003.

Wise, Gene. "'Paradigm Dramas' in American Studies: A Cultural and Institutional History of the Movement." *American Quarterly* 31 (1979), 293–337.

Wishart, David J. *The Fur Trade of the American West, 1807–1840: A Geographical Synthesis.* Lincoln: University of Nebraska Press, 1992.

Wood, Gordon S. *The Creation of the American Republic, 1776–1787.* New York: Norton, 1969.

———. *The Radicalism of the American Revolution.* New York: Knopf, 1992.

———. "Interests and Disinterestedness in the Making of the Constitution." In *Beyond Confederation: Origins of the Constitution and American National Identity,* ed. Richard R. Beeman et al., 69–112. Chapel Hill: University of North Carolina Press, 1987.

Wright, N. Hill. *Monody, on the Death of Brigadier General Zebulon Montgomery Pike: and other poems.* Middlebury, Vt.: Slade and Ferguson, 1814.

Wunder, John. "American Law and Order Comes to the Mississippi Territory: The Making of Sargent's Code, 1798–1800." *Journal of Mississippi History* 38 (1976), 131–55.

Young, J. H. *Mitchell's Travellers guide through the United States.* Philadelphia: S. Augustus Mitchell, 1832.

———. *The Tourist's Pocket Map of the State of Illinois, exhibiting its internal improvements, roads, distances, and c.,.* Philadelphia: S. A. Mitchell, 1838.

ACKNOWLEDGMENTS

More than anything else I have written, this book benefited from the support of institutions. That is the case only in part because my research materials were located in institutional collections or because this project benefited from institutional financial assistance. Rather, the expertise of staff and scholars at those institutions as well as recent digital initiatives at various institutions proved invaluable for conceptualizing, researching, organizing, and, in the end, writing this book. As a result, I want to acknowledge the tremendous debt I owe to those institutions and, more important, the individuals associated with them.

The first of those institutions is my home institution, Washington University in St. Louis. This book emerged from questions I found myself asking while teaching a course on the Lewis and Clark Expedition in Wash. U.'s American Culture Studies Program (AmCS). The course began when I was a postdoctoral student, and the team that taught the course—Wayne Fields, David Konig, and Barbara Schaal—first got me wondering about the representational challenges posed by the North American West. Teaching in AmCS in the years that followed further revealed the potential of cross-disciplinary approaches. In addition to Wayne Fields, the long-serving director of AmCS, and his successor, Randy Calvert, I remain grateful to the program's staff: Carolyn Gerber, Deborah Jaegers, Heidi Kolk, Tina Marti, and Sarah Smith-Frigerio. It was also one of my colleagues in AmCS, Angela Miller, whose expertise proved so helpful as I struggled to make sense of visual culture.

Meanwhile, my colleagues in the History Department provided thoughtful and thought-provoking ideas on this project. David Konig and Christine Johnson helped me think through the intersection of representation and political culture, while Iver Bernstein has been invaluable as I struggled to make

sense of antebellum political culture. The junior faculty reading group—
consisting primarily of colleagues who do *not* study the United States—gave
me excellent feedback on the earliest incarnations of the manuscript. Three
different department chairs (Derek Hirst, Hillel Kieval, and, most recently,
Jean Allman) and the department's staff (Sheryl Peltz and Margaret Williams)
helped create the environment within the department that supported this
project.

The preliminary work on this book occurred during a fellowship at the
Washington University Center for the Humanities, and I want to thank the
center's director, Gerald Early; the associate director, Jian Leng; and the center's staff. The Center for the Humanities is a new institution at Washington
University, and yet it has already established itself as a vital catalyst for promoting scholarship within the humanities and connections across disciplines.
Erin McGlothlin and Harriet Stone, my fellow fellows (a tongue-twister if
ever there was one) at the center in the spring of 2006, provided a great sound-
ing board as I began this project.

Moving outside Wash. U., I want to thank the institutional repositories
where I conducted most of the archival research for this book: the Missouri
History Museum, the St. Louis Mercantile Library, the Geography and Map
Division at the Library of Congress, the Beinecke Rare Book and Manuscript
Library at Yale University, and the Newberry Library in Chicago. Grants from
the Beinecke and the Newberry provided the financial support I needed to
conduct these research trips. I especially want to thank James Ackerman,
Gregg Ames, Robert Archibald, John Aubrey, Charles Brown, Debbie Cribbs,
Laura Diel, Julie Dunn-Morton, John Hebert, John Hoover, Robert Karrow,
George Miles, and Edward Redmond.

Some of those same institutions also provided the opportunity to present
early versions of this material. I am grateful to the Early American Cartographies Conference at the Newberry, the Howard R. Lamar Center for the
Study of Frontiers and Borders at Yale, the Missouri History Museum, the
St. Louis Mercantile Library, the Freeman and Custis Bicentennial Conference at LSU-Shreveport, the Bill Lane Center for the American West at Stan-
ford University, and the Historic New Orleans Collection for the chance to
speak on themes emerging from this book. I also want to thank Antigoni and
Everett Ladd for inviting me to give a series of talks at training workshops for
the National Geospatial-Intelligence Agency. Those talks provided an ideal
opportunity to talk about landscape description with people who practice it
for a living. Finally, I want to thank Megan Sanders's 2008–09 second grade

class at New City School for the pleasure of speaking with them about map-making in the age of Lewis and Clark.

In addition to the assistance I received from these institutions on site, I was able to finish this book much faster thanks to a series of important institutional digital initiatives. The American Memory Collection at the Library of Congress, the digital image collection at the Yale University Library, and the Website created by David Rumsey (who possesses one of world's great cartographic collections) were of immeasurable help. I emphasize the importance of those collections because they have been costly and time-consuming to create. Working on this book confirmed in my own mind how digital initiatives have democratized historical research. These online collections provided an important supplement to my work in archival collections, but they would be absolutely essential to researchers who do not have the benefit of research accounts or travel fellowships.

Combining everything into a book occurred with help from Yale University Press. I want to thank my editor, Chris Rogers, as well as his assistant, Laura Davulis, for supporting this project. The anonymous readers for the early versions of my manuscript gave enormously helpful suggestions for how to produce a better book. I thank Lawrence Kenney for his excellent work editing the manuscript. Finally, I want to thank Ann-Marie Imbornoni, who supervised the production process.

Material from this book first appeared in the following publications: "'What Are the Advantages of the Acquisition?': Inventing Expansion in the Early American Republic," *American Quarterly* 60 (2008), 1003–35; and "Writing a History for Exploration: What Became of Thomas Freeman and Peter Custis?" in *Freeman and Custis Red River Expedition of 1806: Two Hundred Years Later*, ed. Laurence M. Hardy, 325–44, *Bulletin of the Museum of Life Sciences* 14, Louisiana State University in Shreveport, 2008.

Shifting from institutions to individuals, I want to thank John Logan Allen, John Mack Faragher, and Landon Jones for their advice throughout this project. I am particularly grateful to Bill Foley, Carolyn Gilman, and Jim Ronda, all of whom are terrific historians who shared their expertise on Lewis and Clark with the generosity they have displayed in so many circumstances. I remain grateful to Nancy Hoskins in New Haven and Mette Shayne and David Harrison in Chicago for making me feel at home in unfamiliar cities. Jay Gitlin not only helped me feel welcome while conducting research in New Haven, but also gave me, in organizing the Frontier Cities conference in 2007–08, an ideal opportunity to think through some major themes of this book.

I owe a special note of thanks to my family: my wife, Shannon Lopata Kastor, and our sons, Sam and Tommy.

Finally, this book is dedicated to my Grandpa Ged. The first humanities scholar I ever knew, he reveled in the study of early modern British literature, but always with a historical awareness and deep research in historical archives. He was the first person to tell me how textual materials help explain culture. Although I didn't know it at the time, it was from him that I also learned that scholarship could be fun.

INDEX